The Aims of Argument
A Brief Guide

SEVENTH EDITION

The Aims of Argument
A Brief Guide

Timothy W. Crusius
Southern Methodist University

Carolyn E. Channell
Southern Methodist University

McGraw Hill *Connect Learn Succeed*™

The McGraw-Hill Companies

Mc Graw Hill

Connect
Learn
Succeed™

Published by McGraw-Hill, a business unit of The McGraw-Hill Companies, Inc., 1221 Avenue of the Americas, New York, NY 10020. Copyright © 2011, 2009, 2006, 2003, 2000, 1998, 1995 by The McGraw-Hill Companies, Inc. All rights reserved. No part of this publication may be reproduced or distributed in any form or by any means, or stored in a database or retrieval system, without the prior written consent of The McGraw-Hill Companies, Inc., including, but not limited to, any network or other electronic storage or transmission, or broadcast for distance learning. Some ancillaries, including electronic and print components, may not be available to customers outside the United States.

This book is printed on acid-free paper.

2 3 4 5 6 7 8 9 0 DOC/DOC 1 0 9 8 7 6 5 4 3 2

ISBN: 978-0-07-338384-2
MHID: 0-07-338384-8

Vice President, Editorial: *Michael Ryan*
Director, Editorial: *Beth Mejia*
Publisher: *David S. Patterson*
Sponsoring Editor: *Christopher Bennem*
Development Editor: *Janice Wiggins-Clarke*
Managing Editor: *Marley Magaziner*
Marketing Director: *Allison Jones*
Marketing Manager: *Tierra Morgan*
Media Project Manager: *Bethuel Jabez*
Production Editor: *Ruth Sakata Corley*
Cover Designer: *Andrei Pasternak*
Photo Researcher: *LouAnn Wilson*
Senior Buyer: *Laura Fuller*
Production Service: *Matrix Productions, Inc.*
Composition: *10/12 Sabon by Laserwords Private Limited*
Printing: *45# New Era Matte by R.R. Donnelley & Sons*

Cover image: © *2009 Corey Holms/Flickr/Getty Images*

Credits: *The credits section for this book begins on page 346–347 and is considered an extension of the copyright page.*

Library of Congress Cataloging-in-Publication Data

Crusius, Timothy W., 1950-
    The aims of argument: a brief guide/Timothy W. Crusius,
Carolyn E. Channell.—7th ed.
        p. cm.
    ISBN 978-0-07-338384-2
    1. English language—Rhetoric—Handbooks, manuals, etc.   2. Persuasion (Rhetoric)—
Handbooks, manuals, etc.   3. Report writing—Handbooks, manuals, etc.
    I. Channell, Carolyn E. II. Title.

PE1431.C778 2010
808'.042—dc22

                                                                            2010040475

The Internet addresses listed in the text were accurate at the time of publication. The inclusion of a website does not indicate an endorsement by the authors or McGraw-Hill, and McGraw-Hill does not guarantee the accuracy of the information presented at these sites.

www.mhhe.com

For W. Ross Winterowd

As its first six editions were, the seventh edition of *The Aims of Argument* is different from other argumentation texts because it remains the only one that focuses on the aims, or purposes, of argument. That this book's popularity increases from edition to edition tells us that our approach does in fact satisfy the previously unmet need that moved us to become textbook authors.

NOTES ON THIS TEXT'S ORIGINS

With more than sixty years of teaching experience between us, we had tried most argument books. Many of them were good, and we learned from them. However, we found ourselves adopting a text not so much out of genuine enthusiasm but because it had fewer liabilities. We wondered why we were so lukewarm about even the best argumentation textbooks. We boiled our dissatisfaction down to a few major criticisms:

- Most treatments were too formalistic and prescriptive.
- Most failed to integrate class discussion and individual inquiry with written argumentation.
- Apart from moving from simple concepts and assignments to more complicated ones, no book offered a learning sequence.
- Despite the fact that argument, like narrative, is clearly a mode or means of discourse, not a purpose for writing, no book offered a well-developed view of the aims or purposes of argument.

We thought that these shortcomings had undesirable consequences in the classroom, including the following:

- The overemphasis on form confused students with too much terminology, made them doubt their instincts, and drained away energy from inventing and discovering good arguments. Informal argumentation is not formal logic but open-ended and creative.

- The separation of class discussion from composing created a hiatus between oral and written argument. Students had difficulty seeing the relation between the two and using insights from each to improve the other.

- The lack of a learning sequence—of assignments that build on each other—meant that courses in argumentation were less coherent and meaningful than they could be. Students did not understand why they were doing what they were doing and could not envision what might come next.

- Finally, inattention to what people actually use argument to accomplish resulted in too narrow a view of argument and in unclear purposes for writing. Because instruction was mainly limited to what we call arguing to convince, students took argument only as monologues of advocacy. They ignored inquiry.

We set out to solve these problems. The result is a book different from any other argument text because it focuses on four aims of argument:

Arguing to inquire, questioning opinions

Arguing to convince, making cases

Arguing to persuade, appealing to the whole person

Arguing to mediate, finding common ground between conflicting positions

COMMON QUESTIONS ABOUT THE AIMS OF ARGUMENT

Instructors have certain questions about these aims, especially how they relate to one another. Here are some of the most frequently asked questions:

1. *What is the relative value of the four aims? Because mediation comes last, is it the best or most valued?* No aim is "better" than any other aim. Given needs for writing and certain audiences, one aim is more appropriate than another for the task at hand. Mediation comes last because it integrates inquiry, convincing, and persuading.

2. *Must inquiry be taught as a separate aim?* No. It *may* be taught as a separate aim, but we do not intend this "may" as a "must." Teaching inquiry as a distinct aim has certain advantages. Students need to learn how to engage in constructive dialogue, which is more disciplined and more focused than most class discussion. Once they see how it is done, students enjoy dialogue with one another and with texts. Dialogue helps students think through their arguments and imagine reader reaction to what they say, both of which are crucial to convincing and

persuading. Finally, as with mediation, inquiry offers avenues for assignments other than the standard argumentative essay.

3. *Should inquiry come first?* For a number of reasons, inquiry has priority over the other aims. Most teachers are likely to approach inquiry as prewriting, preparatory to convincing or persuading. And commonly, we return to inquiry when we find something wrong with a case we are trying to construct, so the relationship between inquiry and the other aims is also recursive.

   Moreover, inquiry has psychological, moral, and practical claims to priority. When we are unfamiliar with an issue, inquiry comes first psychologically, as a felt need to explore existing opinion. Regardless of what happens in the "real world," convincing or persuading without an open, honest, and earnest search for the truth is, in our view, immoral. Finally, inquiry goes hand in hand with research, which requires questioning the opinions encountered.

4. *Isn't the difference between convincing and persuading more a matter of degree than kind?* Sharp distinctions can be drawn between inquiry and mediation and between both of these aims and the monologues of advocacy, convincing, and persuading. But convincing and persuading do shade into one another so that the difference is clearest at the extremes, with carefully chosen examples. Furthermore, the "purest" appeal to reason—a legal brief, a philosophical or scientific argument—appeals in ways beyond the sheer cogency of the case. Persuasive techniques are submerged but not absent in arguing to convince.

   Our motivation for separating convincing from persuading is not theoretical but pedagogical. Case-making is complex enough that attention to logical appeal by itself is justified. Making students conscious of the appeals to character, emotion, and style while they are learning to cope with case-making can overburden them to the point of paralysis.

   Regardless, then, of how sound the traditional distinction between convincing and persuading may be, we think it best to take up convincing first and then persuasion, especially because what students learn in the former can be carried over intact into the latter. And because one cannot make a case without unconscious appeal to character, emotional commitments (such as values), and style, teaching persuasion is a matter of exposing and developing what is already there in arguing to convince.

Here are the central tenets of an approach based on aims of argument:

- *Argumentation is a mode or means of discourse, not an aim or purpose for writing;* consequently, we need to teach the aims of argument.
- *The aims of argument are linked in a learning sequence so that convincing builds on inquiry, persuasion on convincing, and all three*

contribute to mediation; consequently, we offer a learning sequence for conceiving a course or courses in argumentation.

We believe in the sequence as much as the aims. We think that many will come to prefer it over any other approach.

Of course, textbooks are used selectively, as teachers and programs need them in achieving their own goals. As with any other text, this one can be used selectively, ignoring some parts, playing up others, designing other sequences, and so on. If you want to work with our learning sequence, it's there for creative adaptation. If not, the text is flexible enough for almost any course structure or teaching method.

A NOTE ABOUT THE READINGS

We have avoided the "great authors, classic essays" approach. We tried instead to find bright, contemporary people arguing well from diverse viewpoints—articles and chapters similar to those that can be found in our better journals and trade books, the sort of publications students should read most in doing research. We have not presented any issue in simple pro-and-con fashion, as if there were only two sides.

Included in the range of perspectives are arguments made with both words and images. We include a full instructional chapter examining visual arguments such as editorial cartoons, advertisements, public sculpture, and photographs.

A FINAL WORD ABOUT THE APPROACH

Our approach is innovative. But is it better? Will students learn more? Will instructors find the book more satisfying and more helpful than what they currently use? Our experience—both in using the book ourselves and in listening to the responses of those who have read it or tested it in the classroom or used it for years—is that they will. Students complain less about having to read this book than about having to read others used in our program. They do seem to learn more. Teachers claim to find the text stimulating, something to work with rather than around. We hope your experience is as positive as ours has been. We invite your comments and will use them in the perpetual revision that constitutes the life of a text and our lives as writing teachers.

NEW TO THE SEVENTH EDITION

The writing assignments in the book have been thoroughly revised, and we did so through a lengthy process of writing, rewriting, and revision, aided by extensive input from reviewers and classroom testing. Here are the results:

1. **A new assignment chapter, Chapter 4, "Writing a Critique"** Following Chapter 2, "Reading an Argument," and Chapter 3, "Analyzing an

Argument," this chapter offers a fully developed pedagogy for responding critically to arguments. It can be used to guide a distinct assignment or to help students assess arguments they encounter in research.

2. **A new version of "Arguing to Inquire," Chapter 8** Inquiry in argument amounts to "joining the conversation," comparing existing arguments on controversial issues. Our new chapter takes students through understanding and assessment of conflicting positions, with the goal of discovering the good reasons and evidence in each and reaching a position of their own. Cultivating rational inquiry has always been an important goal for this book, but we think this new chapter does it better than before.

3. **A new version of "Arguing to Convince," Chapter 9** The familiar emphasis on case-making remains central, but we think the process offered is easier for students to understand and more efficient to teach.

4. **A new version of "Arguing to Persuade," Chapter 10** "Motivating action" remains our focus, which means, as it always has for us, appealing to the whole person, integrating argument with ethical, emotional, and stylistic inducement. We believe, however, that the instruction offered makes the challenge of persuading more accessible to students, with advice and guidance they can more readily implement in their own writing.

5. **New readings and student examples in all four of the new assignment chapters** Nothing enlivens teaching composition quite like some fresh material. Besides new readings to work with, we offer more of them on topics we think your students will find especially engaging. The new student examples were gathered not only to provide better models but also for the following key innovation.

6. **Greater emphasis on revision** In most books, student examples are finished products, models only, which reveal little of what went on to make the examples successful. We now have excerpts from early drafts, motivations for revising them are addressed, followed by revised drafts so that students can see the concrete improvements only genuine revision can achieve. As all writing teachers know, better writing cannot result so long as students think of writing as "cleaning up" a first draft. They must learn to revise. We think our new way of presenting student examples will help.

Besides these major additions and changes, those familiar with the Sixth Edition will detect many more: other new readings and visual examples, for instance, and an updating of "Writing Research-Based Arguments." We have enlarged the Glossary and developed the entries to help your students understand the terminology of argument better. We think the work that went into this new edition of *Aims* was well worth the effort and hope you will too.

Revised Online Learning Center

In addition to the many changes the seventh edition offers in the text itself, this edition of *Aims* is accompanied by a newly revised Online Learning Center, accessible at www.mhhe.com/crusius. The site features all the tools of Catalyst 2.0, McGraw-Hill's award-winning writing and research Web site. You will find integrated references throughout the text, pointing you to additional online coverage of the topic at hand.

The instructor's manual has been significantly revised by the authors and is available on the instructors' side of the Online Learning Center. Contact your McGraw-Hill sales representative for access.

Online Course Delivery and Distance Learning

In addition to the Web site, McGraw-Hill offers the following technology products for composition classes. The online content of *The Aims of Argument* is supported by WebCT, Blackboard, eCollege.com, and most other course systems.

ACKNOWLEDGMENTS

We have learned a great deal from the comments of both teachers and students who have used this book, so please continue to share your thoughts with us.

We wish to acknowledge the work of the following reviewers who guided our work on the seventh edition: Cora Agatucci, Central Oregon Community College; Allan Johnston, DePaul University & Columbia College; Ann Krooth, Diablo Valley College; Michael Lee, Columbia Basin College; Dorothy Leman, Central Oregon Community College; Judy M. Lloyd, Southside Virginia Community College; Jim McKeown, McLennan Community College; Anne M. Reid, Colorado State University, Ft. Collins; and Daniel Asher Wolkow, Eastern New Mexico University-Roswell.

Aaron Downey of Matrix Productions, our production editor, and Kay Mikel, our copyeditor, went far beyond the call of duty. Christopher Bennem and Janice Wiggins-Clarke, our editors, showed their usual brilliance and lent their unflagging energy throughout the process that led to this new edition of *Aims*.

A special thanks to Marcella Stark, research librarian at SMU, for all her help with updating the research chapter.

Timothy Crusius
Carolyn Channell
Dallas, Texas

Our goal in this book is not just to show you how to construct an argument but also to make you more aware of why people argue and what purposes argument serves. Consequently, Part Two of this book introduces four specific aims that people have in mind when they argue: to inquire, to convince, to persuade, and to mediate. Part One precedes the aims of argument and focuses on understanding argumentation in general, reading and analyzing arguments, writing a critique, doing research, and working with such forms of visual persuasion as advertising.

The selections in Parts One and Two offer something to emulate. All writers learn from studying the strategies of other writers. The object is not to imitate what a more experienced writer does but to understand the range of strategies you can use in your own way for your own purposes.

Included are arguments made with words and images. We have examples of editorial cartoons, advertisements, and photographs.

This book concludes with two appendixes. The first is on editing, the art of polishing and refining prose, and finding common errors. The second deals with fallacies and critical thinking. Consult these resources often as you work through the text's assignments.

Arguing well is difficult for anyone. We have tried to write a text no more complicated than it has to be. We welcome your comments to improve future editions. Write us at

The Rhetoric Program
Dallas Hall
Southern Methodist University
Dallas, Texas 75275

or e-mail your comments to

cchannel@mail.smu.edu
tcrusius@mail.smu.edu

Timothy W. Crusius is professor of English at Southern Methodist University, where he teaches beginning and advanced composition. He's the author of books on discourse theory, philosophical hermeneutics, and Kenneth Burke. He resides in Dallas with his wife, Elizabeth, and their children, Micah and Rachel.

Carolyn E. Channell taught high school and community college students before coming to Southern Methodist University, where she is now a senior lecturer and specialist in first-year writing courses. She resides in Richardson, Texas, with her husband, David, and "child," a boxer named Gretel.

BRIEF CONTENTS

CONTENTS

CHAPTER 7

Ethical Writing and Plagiarism   167

PART TWO

THE AIMS OF ARGUMENT   177

CHAPTER 8

Joining the Conversation: Arguing to Inquire   179

CHAPTER 9

Making Your Case: Arguing to Convince   207

CHAPTER 10

Motivating Action: Arguing to Persuade   241

CHAPTER 11

Resolving Conflict: Arguing to Mediate 271

Concept Close-Up Boxes

Best Practices Boxes

The Aims of Argument
A Brief Guide

Resources for
Reading and Writing
Arguments

RESOURCES FOR READING AND WRITING ARGUMENTS

Understanding Argument

The Aims of Argument is based on two key concepts: argument and rhetoric. These days, unfortunately, the terms *argument* and *rhetoric* have acquired bad reputations. The popular meaning of *argument* is *disagreement;* we think of raised voices, hurt feelings, winners and losers. Most people think of *rhetoric,* too, in a negative sense—as language that sounds good but evades or hides the truth. In this sense, rhetoric is the language we hear from the politician who says anything to win votes, the public relations person who puts "positive spin" on dishonest business practices, the buck-passing bureaucrat who blames the foul-up on someone else, the clever lawyer who counterfeits passion to plead for the acquittal of a guilty client.

The words *argument* and *rhetoric,* then, are commonly applied to the darker side of human acts and motives. This darker side is real—arguments are often pointless and silly, ugly and destructive; all too often, rhetoric is empty words contrived to mislead or to disguise the desire to exert power. But this book is not about that kind of argument or that kind of rhetoric. Here we develop the meanings of *argument* and *rhetoric* in an older, fuller, and far more positive sense—as the language and art of mature reasoning.

WHAT IS ARGUMENT?

In this book, **argument** means *mature reasoning*. By *mature,* we mean an attitude and approach to argument, not an age group. Some older adults are incapable of mature reasoning, whereas some young people reason very well. And all of us, regardless of age, sometimes fall short of mature reasoning. What is "mature" about the kind of argument we have in mind? One meaning of *mature* is "worked out fully by the mind" or "considered" (*American Heritage Dictionary*). Mature decisions, for example, are thoughtful ones, reached slowly after full consideration of all the consequences. And this is true also of mature reasoning.

The second term in this definition of argument also needs comment: *reasoning.* If we study logic in depth, we find many definitions of reasoning, but *reasoning* here means *an opinion plus a reason (or reasons) for holding that opinion.* As we will see shortly, good arguments require more than this; to be convincing, reasons must be developed with evidence like specific facts and examples. However, understanding the basic form of "opinion-plus-a-reason" is the place to begin when considering your own and other people's arguments.

WHAT IS RHETORIC?

Over time, the meanings of most words in most languages change—sometimes only a little, sometimes a lot. The word *rhetoric* is a good example of a big change. As indicated already, the popular meaning of *rhetoric* is empty verbiage—the art of sounding impressive while saying little—or the art of verbal deception. This meaning of *rhetoric* confers a judgment, and not a positive one.

In contrast, in ancient Greece, where rhetoric was invented about 2,500 years ago, *rhetoric* referred to the art of public speaking. The Greeks recognized that rhetoric could be abused, but, for their culture in general, it was not a negative term. They had a goddess of persuasion (see Figure 1.1), and they respected the power of the spoken word to move people. It dominated their law courts, their governments, and their public ceremonies and events. As an art, the spoken word was an object of study. People enrolled in schools of rhetoric to become effective public speakers. Further, the ancient rhetoricians put a high value on good character. Not just sounding ethical but being ethical contributed to a speaker's persuasive power.

This old, highly valued meaning of rhetoric as oratory survived well into the nineteenth century. In Abraham Lincoln's day, Americans assembled by the thousands to hear speeches that went on for hours. For them, a good speech held the same level of interest as a big sporting event does for people today.

In this book, we are interested primarily in various ways of using *written* argument, but the rhetorical tradition informs our understanding of mature reasoning.

If argument is mature reasoning, then rhetoric is its *art*—that is, how we go about arguing with some degree of success. Just as there is an art of

Defining Mature Reasoning

Argument as mature reasoning means

- Defending *not the first position* you might take on an issue *but the best position*, determined through open-minded inquiry
- Providing reasons for holding that position that can earn the respect of an audience

painting or sculpture, so is there an art of mature reasoning. Since the time of Aristotle, teachers of rhetoric have taught their students *self-conscious* ways of reasoning well and arguing successfully. The study of rhetoric, therefore, includes both what we have already defined as reasoning *and* ways of appealing to an audience. These include efforts to project oneself as a good and intelligent person as well as efforts to connect with the audience through humor, passion, and image.

Figure 1.1

Peitho, the goddess of persuasion, was often involved in seductions and love affairs. On this piece (a detail from a terra-cotta kylix, c. 410 BCE), Peitho, the figure on the left, gives advice to a dejected-looking woman, identified as Demonassa. To the right, Eros, the god of love, stands with his hand on Demonassa's shoulder, suggesting the nature of this advice.

CONCEPT

Defining Rhetoric

Rhetoric is the art of argument as mature reasoning. The study of rhetoric develops self-conscious awareness of the principles and practices of mature reasoning and effective arguing.

AN EXAMPLE OF ARGUMENT

So far, we have been talking about argument in the abstract—definitions and explanations. We need a concrete example of mature reasoning. One thing mature reasoning does is challenge unexamined belief, the stances people take without much thought. The following argument by a syndicated columnist would have us reassess a word that often has negative associations.

The Other F Word

LEONARD PITTS

1   Women must stop recoiling from the very word that stands for their liberation. Brace yourself. I'm going to use a word that offends folks. I'm talking the "F" word. Feminist.

2   This woman sent me an e-mail Monday and it got me thinking. See, in describing herself, she assured me she was not a "women's libber"—the late 1960s equivalent of feminist. She also said she was retired from the U.S. Navy. There was, it seemed to me, a disconnect there: She doesn't believe in women's liberation, yet she is retired from a position that liberation made possible.

3   Intrigued, I asked my 17-year-old daughter if she considers herself a feminist. She responded with a mildly horrified no. This, by the way, is the daughter with the 3.75 GPA who is presently pondering possible college majors including political science, psychology and . . . women's studies. I asked her to define "feminist." There began a halting explanation that seemed to suggest shrillness wrapped around obnoxiousness. Abruptly, she stopped. "It's hard to explain," she said.

4   Actually, it's not. Jessica Valenti, author of *Full Frontal Feminism: A Young Woman's Guide to Why Feminism Matters,* calls it the I'm-Not-A-Feminist-But syndrome. As in the woman who says, "I'm not a feminist, but . . ." and then "goes on to espouse completely feminist values. I think most women believe in access to birth control, they want equal pay for equal work, they want to fight against rape and violence against women."

5   "Feminist," it seems, has ended up in the same syntactical purgatory as another once-useful, now-reviled term: liberal. Most people endorse what that word has historically stood for—integration, child labor laws, product safety—yet they treat the word itself like anthrax. Similarly, while it's hard to imagine that any young woman really wants to return to the days of barefoot, pregnant and making meatloaf, many

now disdain the banner under which their gender fought for freedom. They scorn feminism even as they feast at a table feminism prepared.

6   Says Ms. Valenti, "The word has been so effectively misused and so effectively mischaracterized by conservatives for so long that women are afraid to identify with it. They'll say everything under the sun that's feminist, but they won't identify with it because they've been taught feminists are anti-men, feminists are ugly."

7   Dr. Deborah Tannen agrees. She is a professor of linguistics at Georgetown University and author of a number of books on gender and communication, including: *You're Wearing That? Understanding Mothers and Daughters in Conversation.* "The reason, I believe, is that meanings of words come from how they're used. And since the word 'feminist' is used as a negative term rather than a positive one, people don't want to be associated with it."

8   With apologies to Malcolm X, they've been had, they've been hoodwinked, they've been bamboozled. And it's sad. I've lost track of how many times, visiting high schools or teaching college classes, I have met bright girls juggling options and freedoms that would've been unthinkable a generation ago, smart young women preparing for lives and careers their foremothers could not have dreamt, yet if you use the "F" word, they recoil.

9   We have, I think, lost collective memory of how things were before the F-word. Of the casual beatings. Of casual rape. Of words like "old maid" and "spinster." Of abortion by coat hanger. Of going to school to find a man. Of getting an allowance and needing a husband's permission. Of taking all your spirit, all your dreams, all your ambition, aspiration, creativity, and pounding them down until they fit a space no larger than a casserole dish.

10   "I'm not a feminist, but . . . ?" That's a fraud. It's intellectually dishonest. And it's a slap to the feminists who prepared the table at which today's young women sup.

11   So for the record, I am a feminist. My daughter is, too.

12   She doesn't know it yet.

Leonard Pitts, "The Other F Word," *Miami Herald*, February 14, 2008, p.19A. Reprinted by permission of McClatchey Interactive West.

Discussion of "The Other F Word"

Leonard Pitts's argument is an example of a type or *genre* of written persuasion, the opinion column. Let's examine his argument and what makes it mature.

The first question we should ask of any argument we are analyzing is, What is Pitts's *claim* or position? *All claims are answers to questions.* In this case, the question is, How should we assess the statement "I'm not a feminist, but . . ."? His answer: "That's a fraud. It's intellectually dishonest. And it's a slap to the feminists who prepared the table at which today's young women sup" (paragraph 10). His claim is that "women must stop recoiling from the very word that stands for their liberation" (paragraph 1).

What reasoning does he use to justify his claim? He points to a fundamental contradiction. Women reject the label "feminist" but support most or all of what feminism achieved for women. In essence, they are denying what they are. He goes on to support this reasoning with evidence drawn from expert opinion, from Jessica Valenti and Deborah Tannen.

What makes Pitts's argument mature, an example of the kind of reasoning worth learning how to do? His position is obviously more mature than his daughter's, who thinks that a feminist is always "shrillness wrapped around obnoxiousness." However, the difference here is not age but rather *awareness*. The retired Navy woman has the same problem as the much younger daughter: recoiling from the very word that stands for her liberation. Neither seem aware of what feminism has accomplished for women or the history of oppression that Pitts summarizes so well in paragraph 9. Pitts's greater awareness contributes greatly to the maturity of his reasoning.

However, another sign of maturity may be equally important. *Pitts's opinion is consistent with his actual beliefs.* Too often we are reluctant to claim what we actually think, usually because we are overly concerned about the reactions of other people. Of course, nothing is gained by offending others needlessly. Tact matters. But we need to be honest, and we need to be consistent—more than that, we must have the courage to say what we think. We also gain nothing by being evasive.

In recognizing the maturity of Pitts's argument, we should not be too respectful of it. Mature reasoning should be challenged by mature criticism. For instance, is it always the case that "I am not a feminist, but . . ." amounts to intellectual fraud? Perhaps the retired Navy woman did not know that her opportunities resulted from feminist agitation. You cannot commit fraud—tell a lie about what you know the truth is—if you do not know the truth. Nor is it necessarily fraudulent to know the truth but also wish to avoid a label that puts you at a disadvantage. Perhaps some women know they are feminists but wish to be called something else because the word has negative connotations. If so, being a good strategist is not the same thing as committing fraud.

FOLLOWING THROUGH

Any good piece of writing can give you ideas for your own writing. The Pitts editorial calls labeling into question, and you can probably recall when someone applied a label with negative connotations to you or to some group to which you belong. Choose an instance and either accept the label and defend it as something positive or reject it and show why it should not be applied to you or your group.   •

FOUR CRITERIA OF MATURE REASONING

Students often ask, "What does my professor want?" Although you will be writing many different kinds of papers in response to the assignments in this textbook, your professor will most likely look for evidence of mature reasoning. When we evaluate student work, we use four criteria.

Mature Reasoners Are Well Informed

Your opinions must develop from knowledge and be supported by reliable and current evidence. If the reader feels that the writer "doesn't know his or her stuff," the argument loses all weight and force.

You may have noticed that people have opinions about all sorts of things, including subjects they know little or nothing about. The general human tendency is to have the strongest opinions on matters about which we know the least. Ignorance and inflexibility go together because it is easy to form an opinion when few or none of the facts get in the way and we can just assert our prejudices. Conversely, the more we know about most topics, the harder it is to be dogmatic. We find ourselves changing or at least refining our opinions more or less continuously as we gain more knowledge.

Mature Reasoners Are Self-Critical and Open to Constructive Criticism from Others

We have opinions about all sorts of things that do not matter much to us, casual opinions we have picked up somehow and may not even bother to defend if challenged. But we also have opinions in which we are heavily invested, sometimes to the point that our whole sense of reality, right and wrong, good and bad—our very sense of ourselves—is tied up in them. These opinions we defend passionately.

On this count, popular argumentation and mature reasoning are alike. Mature reasoners are often passionate about their convictions, as committed to them as the fanatic on the street corner is to his or her cause. A crucial difference, however, separates the fanatic from the mature reasoner. The fanatic is all passion; the mature reasoner is able and willing to step back and examine even deeply held convictions. "I may have believed this for as long as I can remember," the mature reasoner says, "but is this conviction really justified? Do the facts support it? When I think it through, does it really make sense? Can I make a coherent and consistent argument for it?" These are questions that do not concern the fanatic and are seldom posed in the popular argumentation we hear on talk radio or TV.

In practical terms, being self-critical and open to well-intended criticism boils down to this: Mature reasoners can and do change their minds when they have good reasons to do so. In popular argumentation, changing one's mind can be taken as a weakness, as "wishy-washy," and so people tend to go on advocating what they believe, regardless of what anyone else says. But there is nothing wishy-washy about, for example, confronting the facts, about realizing that what we thought is not supported by the available evidence. In such a case, changing one's mind is a sign of intelligence and the very maturity mature reason values.

Mature Reasoners Argue with Their Audiences or Readers in Mind

Nothing drains energy from argument more than the feeling that it will accomplish nothing. As one student put it, "Why bother? People just go on thinking what they want to." This attitude is understandable. Popular, undisciplined argument often does seem futile: minds are not changed; no progress is made; it is doubtful that anyone learned anything. Sometimes the opposing positions only harden, and the people involved are more at odds than before.

Why does this happen so often? One reason is that nobody is listening to anyone else. We tend to hear only our own voices and see only from our own points of view. But there is another reason: The people making the arguments have made no effort to reach their audience. This is the other side of the coin of not listening—when we do not take other points of view seriously, we cannot make our points of view appealing to those who do not already share them.

To have a chance of working, arguments must be *other-directed*, attuned to the people they want to reach. This may seem obvious, but it is also commonly ignored and not easy to do. We have to imagine the other guy. We have to care about other points of view, not just see them as obstacles to our own. We have to present and develop our arguments in ways that will not turn off the very people for whom we are writing. In many ways, *adapting to the audience* is the biggest challenge of argument.

Mature Reasoners Know Their Arguments' Contexts

All arguments are part of an ongoing conversation. We think of arguments as something individuals make. We think of our opinions as *ours*, almost like private property. But arguments and opinions have pasts: Other people argued about more or less the same issues and problems before—often long before—we came on the scene. They have a present: Who's arguing what now, the current state of the argument. And they have a future: What people will be arguing about tomorrow, in different circumstances, with knowledge we lack now.

So most arguments are not the isolated events they seem to be. Part of being well informed is knowing something about the history of an argument. By understanding an argument's past, we learn about patterns that will help us develop our own position. To some extent, we must know what is going on now and what other people are saying to make our own reasoning relevant. And although we cannot know the future, we can imagine the drift of the argument, where it might be heading. In other words, there is a larger context we need to join—a big conversation of many voices to which our few belong.

WHAT ARE THE AIMS OF ARGUMENT?

The heart of this book is Part Two, the section titled "The Aims of Argument." In conceiving this book, we worked from one basic premise: Mature reasoners do not argue just to argue; rather, they use argument to accomplish something: *to inquire* into a question, problem, or issue (commonly part of the research process); *to convince* their readers to assent to an opinion, or

Four Criteria of Mature Reasoning

MATURE REASONERS ARE WELL INFORMED

Their opinions develop out of knowledge and are supported by reliable and current evidence.

MATURE REASONERS ARE SELF-CRITICAL AND OPEN TO CONSTRUCTIVE CRITICISM FROM OTHERS

They balance their passionate attachment to their opinions with willingness to evaluate and test them against differing opinions, acknowledge when good points are made against their opinions, and even, when presented with good reasons for doing so, change their minds.

MATURE REASONERS ARGUE WITH THEIR AUDIENCES OR READERS IN MIND

They make a sincere effort to understand and connect with other people and other points of view because they do not see differences of opinion as obstacles to their own points of view.

MATURE REASONERS KNOW THEIR ARGUMENTS' CONTEXTS

They recognize that what we argue about now was argued about in the past and will be argued about in the future, that our contributions to these ongoing conversations are influenced by who we are, what made us who we are, where we are, what's going on around us.

---

claim; *to persuade* readers to take action, such as buying a product or voting for a candidate; and *to mediate* conflict, as in labor disputes, divorce proceedings, and so on.

Let's look at each of these aims in more detail.

Arguing to Inquire

Arguing to **inquire** is using reasoning to determine the best position on an issue. We open the "Aims" section with inquiry because mature reasoning is not a matter of defending what we already believe but of questioning it. Arguing to inquire helps us form opinions, question opinions we already have, and reason our way through conflicts or contradictions in other people's arguments on a topic. Inquiry is open-minded, and it requires that we make an effort to find out what people who disagree think and why.

The ancient Greeks called argument as inquiry *dialectic;* today we might think of it as **dialogue** or serious conversation. There is nothing confrontational about such conversations. We have them with friends, family, and colleagues, even with ourselves. We have these conversations in writing too, as we make notations in the margins of the arguments we read.

Inquiry centers on questions and involves some legwork to answer them—finding the facts, doing research. This is true whether you are inquiring into what car to buy, what major to choose in college, what candidate to vote for, or what policy our government should pursue on any given issue.

Arguing to Convince

The goal of inquiry is to reach some kind of conclusion on an issue. Let's call this conclusion a **conviction** and define it as "an earned opinion, achieved through careful thought, research, and discussion." Once we arrive at a conviction, we usually want others to share it. The aim of further argument is to secure the assent of people who do not share our conviction (or who do not share it fully).

Argument to **convince** centers on making a case, which means offering reasons and evidence in support of our opinion. Arguments to convince are all around us. In college, we find them in scholarly and professional writing. In everyday life, we find arguments to convince in editorials, courtrooms, and political speeches. Whenever we encounter an opinion supported by reasons and asking us to agree, we are dealing with arguing to convince.

Arguing to Persuade

Like convincing, persuasion attempts to earn agreement, but it wants more. **Persuasion** attempts to influence not just thinking but also behavior. An advertisement for Mercedes-Benz aims to convince us not only that the company makes a high-quality car but also that we should go out and buy one. A Sunday sermon asks for more than agreement with some interpretation of a biblical passage; the minister wants the congregation to live according to its message. Persuasion asks us to do something—spend money, give money, join a demonstration, recycle, vote, enlist, acquit. Because we do not always act on our convictions, persuasion cannot rely on reasoning alone. It must appeal in broader, deeper ways.

Persuasion appeals to readers' emotions. It tells stories about individual cases of hardship that move us to pity. It often uses photographs, as when charities confront us with pictures of poverty or suffering. Persuasion uses many of the devices of poetry, such as patterns of sound, repetitions, metaphors, and similes to arouse a desired emotion in the audience.

Persuasion also relies on the personality of the writer to an even greater degree than does convincing. The persuasive writer attempts to represent something higher or larger than him- or herself—some ideal with which the reader would like to be associated. For example, a war veteran and hero like Senator John McCain naturally brings patriotism to the table when he makes a speech.

Arguing to Mediate

By the time we find ourselves in a situation where our aim is to **mediate**, we will have already attempted to convince an opponent to settle a conflict or

Comparing the Aims of Argument

The aims of argument have much in common. For example, besides sharing argument, they all tend to draw on sources of knowledge (research) and to deal with controversial issues. But the aims also differ from one another, mainly in terms of purpose, audience, situation, and method, as summarized here and on the inside back cover.

	Purpose	Audience	Situation	Method
Inquiry	Seeks truth	Oneself, friends, and colleagues	Informal; a dialogue	Questions
Convincing	Seeks assent to a thesis	Less intimate; wants careful reasoning	More formal; a monologue	Case-making
Persuading	Seeks action	More broadly public, less academic	Pressing need for a decision	Appeals to reason and emotions
Mediating	Seeks consensus	Polarized by differences	Need to cooperate, preserve relations	"Give-and-take"

We offer this chart as a general guide to the aims of argument. Think of it as the big picture you can always return to as you work your way through Part Two, which deals with each of the aims in detail.

dispute our way. Our opponent will have done the same. Yet neither side has secured the assent of the other, and "agreeing to disagree" is not a practical solution because the participants must decide what to do.

In most instances of mediation, the parties involved try to work out the conflict themselves because they have some relationship they wish to preserve—as employer and employee, business partners, family members, neighbors, even coauthors of an argument textbook. Common differences requiring mediation include the amount of a raise or the terms of a contract. In private life, mediation helps roommates live together and families decide on everything from budgets to vacation destinations.

Just like other aims of argument, arguing to mediate requires sound logic and the clear presentation of positions and reasons. However, mediation challenges our interpersonal skills more than do the other aims. Each side must listen closely to understand not just the other's case but also the emotional commitments and underlying values. When mediation works, the opposing sides begin to converge. Exchanging viewpoints and information and building empathy enable all parties to make concessions, to loosen their hold on their original positions, and finally to reach consensus—or at least a resolution that all participants find satisfactory.

Reading an Argument

In a course in argumentation, you will read many arguments. Our book contains a wide range of argumentative essays, some by students, some by established professionals. In addition, you may find arguments on your own in books, newspapers, and magazines, or on the Internet. You will read them to develop your understanding of argument. That means you will analyze and evaluate these texts—known as **critical reading.** Critical reading involves special skills and habits that are not essential when you read a book for information or entertainment. This chapter discusses those skills and habits.

By the time most students get to high school, reading is no longer taught. While there is plenty to read, any advice on *how to read* is usually about increasing vocabulary or reading speed, not reading critically. This is too bad because in college you are called on to read more critically than ever.

Have patience with yourself and with the texts you work with in this book. Reading will involve going through a text more than once, no matter how careful that single reading may be. You will go back to a text several times, asking new questions with each reading. That takes time, but it is time well spent. Just as when you see a film a second time, you notice new details, so each reading increases your knowledge of a text.

Before we start, a bit of advice: Attempt critical reading only when your mind is fresh. Find a place conducive to concentration—such as a table in the library. Critical reading requires an alert, active response.

THE FIRST ENCOUNTER: SEEING THE TEXT IN CONTEXT

Critical reading begins not with a line-by-line reading but with a fast overview of the whole text, followed by some thinking about how the text fits into a bigger picture, or *context*, which we describe shortly.

We first **sample** a text rather than read it through. Look at the headings and subdivisions. They will give a sense of how the text is organized. Note what parts look interesting and/or hard to understand. Note any information about the author provided before or after the text itself, as well as any publication information (where and when the piece was originally published). Look at the opening and closing paragraphs to discern the author's main point or view.

Reading comprehension depends less on a large vocabulary than on the ability to see how the text fits into contexts. Sampling will help you consider the text in two contexts that are particularly important:

1. *The general climate of opinion* surrounding the topic of the text. This includes debate on the topic both before and since the text's publication.

2. *The rhetorical context* of the text. This includes facts about the author, the intended audience, and the setting in which the argument took place.

Considering the Climate of Opinion

Familiarity with the climate of opinion will help you view any argument critically, recognize a writer's biases and assumptions, and spot gaps or errors in the information. Your own perspective, too, will affect your interpretation of the text. So think about what you know, how you know it, what your opinion is, and what might have led to its formation. You can then interact with a text, rather than just read it passively.

◎◎ FOLLOWING THROUGH

An argument on the topic of body decoration (tattoos and piercing) appears later in this chapter. "On Teenagers and Tattoos" is about motives for decorating the body. As practice in identifying the climate of opinion surrounding a topic, think about what people say about tattooing. Have you heard people argue that it is "low-class"? a rebellion against middle-class conformity? immoral? an artistic expression? a fad? an affront to school or parental authority? an expression of individuality? If you would not want a tattoo, why not? If you have a tattoo, why did you get it? In your writer's notebook, jot down some positions you have heard debated, and state your own viewpoint.   •

Considering the Rhetorical Context

Critical readers also are aware of the **rhetorical context** of an argument. They do not see the text merely as words on a page but as a contribution to some debate among interested people. Rhetorical context includes the author, the intended audience, and the date and place of publication. The reader who knows something about the author's politics or affiliations will have an advantage over the reader who does not. Also, knowing if a periodical is liberal, like *The Nation,* or conservative, like *National Review,* helps.

An understanding of rhetorical context comes from both external and internal clues—information outside the text and information you gather as you read and reread it. You can glean information about rhetorical context from external evidence such as publishers' notes about the author or about a magazine's editorial board or sponsoring foundation. You can find this information in any issue of a periodical or by following an information link on the home page of an online publication.

You also may have prior knowledge of rhetorical context—for example, you may have heard of the author. Or you can look in a database (see pages 111, 112–115) to see what else the author has written. Later, when you read the argument more thoroughly, you will enlarge your understanding of rhetorical context as you discover what the text itself reveals about the author's bias, character, and purpose for writing.

In sum, the first encounter with a text is preliminary to a careful, close reading. It prepares you to get the most out of the second encounter. If you are researching a topic and looking for good sources of information and viewpoints about it, the first encounter with any text will help you decide whether you want to read it at all. A first encounter can be a time-saving last encounter if the text does not seem appropriate or credible.

◎◎ FOLLOWING THROUGH

Note the following information about "On Teenagers and Tattoos."

> *When* published: In 1997, reprinted fall 2000.
>
> *Where* published: In the *Journal of the American Academy of Child & Adolescent Psychiatry,* published by the American Academy of Child and Adolescent Psychiatry, then reprinted in *Reclaiming Children and Youth.*
>
> Written by *whom:* Andrés Martin, MD. Martin is an associate professor of child psychiatry at the Yale Child Study Center in New Haven, CT.

Then do a fast sampling of the text itself. In your writer's notebook, make some notes about what you expect to find in this argument. What do you think the author's perspective will be, and why? How might it differ from that of a teen, a parent, a teacher? Do the subheadings give you any idea of the main point? Do you notice at the opening or closing any repeated ideas that might give a clue to the author's claim? To whom do you imagine the author was writing, and what might be the purpose of an essay in a journal such as the one that published his argument?   •

Guidelines for Determining Rhetorical Context

To determine an argument's rhetorical context, answer the following questions:

Who wrote this argument, and what are his or her occupation, personal background, and political leanings?

To whom do you think the author is writing? Arguments are rarely aimed at "the general public" but rather at a definite target audience, such as "entertainment industry moguls," "drivers in Dallas," or "parents of teenagers."

Where does the article appear? If it is reprinted, where did it appear originally? What do you know about the publication?

When was the argument written? If not recently, what do you know about the time during which it appeared?

Why was the article written? What prompted its creation, and what purpose does the author have for writing?

AN ARGUMENT FOR CRITICAL READING

On Teenagers and Tattoos

ANDRÉS MARTIN

The skeleton dimensions I shall now proceed to set down are copied verbatim from my right arm, where I had them tattooed: as in my wild wanderings at that period, there was no other secure way of preserving such valuable statistics.

—Herman Melville, *Moby Dick*

1   Tattoos and piercing have become a part of our everyday landscape. They are ubiquitous, having entered the circles of glamour and the mainstream of fashion, and they have even become an increasingly common feature of our urban youth. Legislation in most states restricts professional tattooing to adults older than 18 years of age, so "high end" tattooing is rare in children and adolescents, but such tattoos are occasionally seen in older teenagers. Piercings, by comparison, as well as self-made or "jailhouse" type tattoos, are not at all rare among adolescents or even among school-age children. Like hairdo, makeup, or baggy jeans, tattoos and piercings can be subject to fad influence or peer pressure in an effort toward group affiliation. As with any other fashion statement, they can be construed as bodily aids in the inner struggle toward identity consolidation, serving as adjuncts to the defining and sculpting of the self by means of external manipulations. But unlike most other body decorations, tattoos and piercings are set apart by their irreversible and permanent nature, a quality at the core of their magnetic appeal to adolescents.

2   Adolescents and their parents are often at odds over the acquisition of bodily decorations. For the adolescent, piercing or tattoos may be seen as personal and beautifying statements, while parents may construe them as oppositional

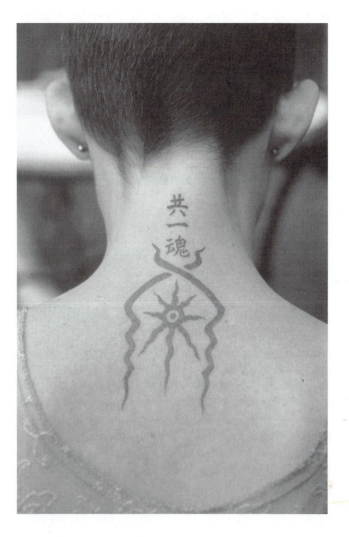

and enraging affronts to their authority. Distinguishing bodily adornment from self-mutilation may indeed prove challenging, particularly when a family is in disagreement over a teenager's motivations and a clinician is summoned as the final arbiter. At such times it may be most important to realize jointly that the skin can all too readily become but another battleground for the tensions of the age, arguments having less to do with tattoos and piercings than with core issues such as separation from the family matrix. Exploring the motivations and significance underlying tattoos (Grumet, 1983) and piercings can go a long way toward resolving such differences and can become a novel and additional way of getting to know teenagers. An interested and nonjudgmental appreciation of teenagers' surface presentations may become a way of making contact not only in their terms but on their turfs: quite literally on the territory of their skins.

3   The following three sections exemplify some of the complex psychological underpinnings of youth tattooing.

IDENTITY AND THE ADOLESCENT'S BODY

4   Tattoos and piercing can offer a concrete and readily available solution for many of the identity crises and conflicts normative to adolescent development. In using such decorations, and by marking out their bodily territories, adolescents can support their efforts at autonomy, privacy, and insulation. Seeking individuation, tattooed adolescents can become unambiguously demarcated from others and singled out as unique. The intense and often disturbing reactions that are mobilized in viewers can help to effectively keep them at bay, becoming tantamount to the proverbial "Keep Out" sign hanging from a teenager's door.

5   Alternatively, feeling prey to a rapidly evolving body over which they have no say, self-made and openly visible decorations may restore adolescents' sense of normalcy and control, a way of turning a passive experience into an active identity. By indelibly marking their bodies, adolescents can strive to reclaim their bearings within an environment experienced as alien, estranged, or suffocating or to lay claim over their evolving and increasingly unrecognizable bodies. In either case, the net outcome can be a resolution to unwelcome impositions: external, familial, or societal in one case; internal and hormonal in the other. In the words of a 16-year-old girl with several facial piercings, and who could have been referring to her body just as well as to the position within her family: "If I don't fit in, it is because I say so."

INCORPORATION AND OWNERSHIP

6   Imagery of a religious, deathly, or skeletal nature, the likenesses of fierce animals or imagined creatures, and the simple inscription of names are some of the time-tested favorite contents for tattoos. In all instances, marks become not only memorials or recipients for dearly held persons or concepts: they strive for incorporation, with images and abstract symbols gaining substance on becoming a permanent part of the individual's skin. Thickly embedded in personally meaningful representations and object relations, tattoos can become not only the ongoing memento of a relationship, but at times even the only evidence that there ever was such a bond. They can quite literally become the relationship itself. The turbulence and impulsivity of early attachments and infatuations may become grounded, effectively bridging oblivion through the visible reality to tattoos.

7   Case Vignette: "A," a 13-year-old boy, proudly showed me his tattooed deltoid. The coarsely depicted roll of the dice marked the day and month of his birth. Rather disappointed, he then uncovered an immaculate back, going on to draw for me the great "piece" he envisioned for it. A menacing figure held a hand of cards: two aces, two eights, and a card with two sets of dates. "A's" father had belonged to Dead Man's Hand, a motorcycle gang named after the set of cards (aces and eights) that the legendary Wild Bill Hickock had held in the 1890s when shot dead over a poker table in Deadwood, South Dakota. "A" had only the vaguest memory of and sketchiest information about his father, but he knew he had died in a motorcycle accident: The fifth card marked the dates of his birth and death.

8   The case vignette also serves to illustrate how tattoos are often the culmination of a long process of imagination, fantasy, and planning that can start at an early age. Limited markings, or relatively reversible ones such as piercings, can at a later time scaffold toward the more radical commitment of a permanent tattoo.

THE QUEST OF PERMANENCE

9   The popularity of the anchor as a tattoo motif may historically have had to do less with guild identification among sailors than with an intense longing for rootedness and stability. In a similar vein, the recent increase in the popularity and acceptance of tattoos may be understood as an antidote or counterpoint to our urban and nomadic lifestyles. Within an increasingly mobile society, in which relationships are so often transient—as attested by the frequencies of divorce, abandonment, foster placement, and repeated moves, for example—tattoos can be a readily available source of grounding. Tattoos, unlike many relationships, can promise permanence and stability. A sense of constancy can be derived from unchanging marks that can be carried along no matter what the physical, temporal, or geographical vicissitudes at hand. Tattoos stay, while all else may change.

10   Case Vignette: A proud father at 17, "B" had had the smiling face of his 4-month-old baby girl tattooed on his chest. As we talked at a tattoo convention, he proudly introduced her to me, explaining how he would "always know how beautiful she is today" when years from then he saw her semblance etched on himself.

11   The quest for permanence may at other times prove misleading and offer premature closure to unresolved conflicts. At a time of normative uncertainties, adolescents may maladaptively and all too readily commit to a tattoo and its indefinite presence. A wish to hold on to a current certainty may lead the adolescent to lay down in ink what is valued and cherished one day but may not necessarily be in the future. The frequency of self-made tattoos among hospitalized, incarcerated, or gang-affiliated youths suggests such motivations: A sense of stability may be a particularly dire need under temporary, turbulent, or volatile conditions. In addition, through their designs teenagers may assert a sense of bonding and allegiance to a group larger than themselves. Tattoos may attest to powerful experiences, such as adolescence itself, lived and even survived together. As with Moby Dick's protagonist, Ishmael, they may bear witness to the "valuable statistics" of one's "wild wandering(s)": those of adolescent exhilaration and excitement on the one hand; of growing pains, shared misfortune, or even incarceration on the other.

12   Adolescents' bodily decorations, at times radical and dramatic in their presentation, can be seen in terms of figuration rather than disfigurement, of the natural body being through them transformed into a personalized body (Brain, 1979). They can often be understood as self-constructive and adorning efforts, rather than prematurely subsumed as mutilatory and destructive acts. If we bear all of this in mind, we may not only arrive at a position to pass more reasoned clinical judgment, but become sensitized through our patients' skins to another level of their internal reality.

REFERENCES

Brain, R. (1979). *The decorated body.* New York: Harper & Row.
Grumet, G. W. (1983). Psychodynamic implications of tattoos. *American Journal of Orthopsychiatry, 53,* 482–92.

Andrés Martin, "On Teenagers and Tattoos," *Journal of the American Academy of Child & Adolescent Psychiatry,* vol. 36, no. 6 (June 1997), pp. 860–861. Reprinted by permission of Lippincott Williams & Wilkins.

THE SECOND ENCOUNTER: READING AND ANALYZING THE TEXT

We turn now to suggestions for reading and analyzing. These are our own "best practices," what we do when we prepare to discuss or write about a written text. Remember, when you read critically, your purpose goes beyond merely finding out what an argument says. The critical reader is different from the target audience. As a critical reader, you are more like the food critic who dines not merely to eat but to evaluate the chef's efforts.

To see the difference, consider the different perspectives that an ant and a bird would have when looking at the same suburban lawn. The ant is down among the blades of grass, climbing one and then the next. It's a close look, but the view is limited. The bird in the sky above looks down, noticing the size and shape of the yard, the brown patches, the difference between the grass in this yard and the grass in the surrounding yards. The bird has the big picture, the ant the close-up. Critical readers move back and forth between the perspective of the ant and the perspective of the bird, each perspective enriching the other. The big picture helps one notice the patterns, even as the details offer clues to the big picture.

Because critical reading means interacting with the text, be ready with pencil or pen to mark up the text. Highlighting or underlining is not enough. Write comments in the margin.

Wrestling with Difficult Passages

Because one goal of the second encounter is to understand the argument fully, you will need to determine the meanings of unfamiliar words and difficult passages. In college reading, you may encounter new words. You may find allusions or references to other books or authors that you have not read. You may encounter metaphors and irony. The author may speak ironically or for another person. The author may assume that readers have lived through all that he or she has or share the same political viewpoint. All of this can make reading harder. Following are common features that often make reading difficult.

Unfamiliar Contexts

If the author and his or her intended audience are removed from your own experience, you will find the text difficult. Texts from a distant culture or time will include concepts familiar to the writer and original readers but not to you. This is true also of contemporary writing intended for specialists. College increases your store of specialized knowledge and introduces you to new (and old) perspectives. Accepting the challenge of difficult texts is part of college. Look up concepts you don't know. Your instructors can also help you to bridge the gap between your world and the text's.

Contrasting Voices and Views

Authors may state viewpoints that contradict their own. They may concede that part of an opposing argument is true, or they may put in an opposing view to refute it. These voices and viewpoints may come as direct quotations or paraphrases. To avoid misreading these views as the author's, be alert to words that signal contrast. The most common are *but* and *however.*

Allusions

Allusions are brief references to things outside the text—to people, works of art, songs, events in the news—anything in the culture that the author assumes he or she shares knowledge of with readers. Allusions are one way for an author to form a bond with readers—provided the readers' and authors' opinions are the same about what is alluded to. Allusions influence readers. They are persuasive devices that can provide positive associations with the author's viewpoint.

In "On Teenagers and Tattoos," the epigraph (the quotation that appears under the title of the essay) is an allusion to the classic novel *Moby Dick.* Martin alludes to the novel again in paragraph 11. He assumes that his readers know the work—not just its title but also its characters, in particular, the narrator, Ishmael. And he assumes his readers would know that the "skeleton dimensions" of a great whale were important and that readers would therefore understand the value of preserving these statistics. The allusion predisposes readers to see that there are valid reasons for permanently marking the body.

Specialized Vocabulary

If an argument is aimed at an audience of specialists, it will undoubtedly contain vocabulary peculiar to that group or profession. Martin's essay contains social science terminology: "family matrix" and "surface presentations" (paragraph 2), "individuation" (paragraph 4), "grounded" (paragraph 6), "sense of constancy" (paragraph 9), and "normative uncertainties" (paragraph 11).

The text surrounding these terms provides enough help for most readers to get a fair understanding. For example, the text surrounding *individuation* suggests that the person would stand out as a separate physical presence; this is not quite the same as *individuality,* which refers more to one's character. Likewise, the text around *family matrix* points to something the single word *family* does not: it emphasizes the family as the surroundings in which one develops.

If you need to look up a term and a dictionary does not seem to offer an appropriate definition, go to one of the specialized dictionaries available on the library reference shelves. (See pages 102–112 for more on these.)

If you encounter an argument with more jargon than you can handle, you may have to accept that you are not an appropriate reader for it. Some readings are aimed at people with highly specialized graduate degrees or training. Without advanced courses, no one could read these articles with full comprehension, much less critique their arguments.

◎◎ FOLLOWING THROUGH

Find other words in Martin's essay that sound specific to the field of psychology. Use the surrounding text to come up with laypersons' terms for these concepts.   •

Missing Persons

A common difficulty with scientific writing is that it can sound disembodied and abstract. You won't find a lot of people doing things in it. Sentences are easiest to read when they take a "who-does-what" form. However, these can be rare in scientific writing. Many of Martin's sentences have abstract subjects and nonaction verbs like *be* and *become*:

> *An interested and nonjudgmental appreciation of teenagers' surface presentations* may become a way of making contact not only in their terms but on their turfs. . . .

In at least one other sentence, Martin goes so far in leaving people out that his sentence is grammatically incorrect. Note the dangling modifier:

> Alternatively, *feeling prey to a rapidly evolving body over which they have no say,* self-made and openly visible decorations may restore adolescents' sense of normalcy and control, a way of turning a passive experience into an active identity.

The italicized phrase describes adolescents, not decorations. If you have trouble reading passages like this, take comfort in the fact that the difficulty is not your fault. Recasting the idea into who-does-what can clear things up:

> Teens may feel like helpless victims of the changes taking place in their bodies. They may mark themselves with highly visible tattoos and piercings to regain a sense of control over their lives.

Passive Voice

Passive voice is another common form of the missing-person problem. In an active-voice sentence, we see our predictable who-does-what pattern:

Active voice: The rat ate the cheese.

In passive-voice sentences, the subject of the verb is not an agent; it does not act.

Passive voice: The cheese was eaten by the rat.

At least in this sentence, we know who the agent is. But scientists often leave out any mention of agents. Thus, in Martin's essay we have sentences like this one:

Adolescents' bodily decorations . . . *can be seen* in terms of figuration rather than disfigurement. . . .

Who can see them? Martin means that *psychiatrists should see tattoos* as figuration rather than disfigurement. But that would sound too committed, not scientific. Passive-voice sentences are common in the sciences, part of an effort to sound objective.

If you learn to recognize passive voice, you can often mentally convert the troublesome passage into active voice, making it clearer. Passive voice takes this pattern:

A helping verb in some form of the verb *to be: Is, was, were, has been, will be, will have been, could have been,* and so forth.

Followed by a main verb, a past participle: Past participles end in *ed, en, g, k,* or *t.*

Some examples:

The car *was being driven* by my roommate when we had the wreck.

Infections *are spread* by bacteria.

The refrain *is sung* three times.

◎◎ FOLLOWING THROUGH

Convert the following sentences into active voice. We have put the passive-voice verbs in bold type, but you may need to look at the surrounding text to figure out who the agents are.

A sense of constancy **can be derived** from unchanging marks that **can be carried** along no matter what the physical, temporal, or geographical vicissitudes at hand. (paragraph 9)

To edit this one, ask *who* can derive what and *who* can carry what.

The intense and often disturbing reactions that **are mobilized** in viewers can help to effectively keep them at bay, becoming tantamount to the proverbial "Keep Out" sign hanging from a teenager's door. (paragraph 4)

To edit, ask *what* mobilizes the reactions in other people.   •

Using Paraphrase to Aid Comprehension

As we all know, explaining something to someone else is the best way to make it clear to ourselves. Putting an author's ideas into your own words, **paraphrasing** them, is like explaining the author to yourself. For more on paraphrasing, see Chapter 6, pages 127–129.

Paraphrase is often longer than the original because it loosens up what is dense. In paraphrasing, try to make both the language and the syntax (word order) simpler. Paraphrase may require two sentences where there was one. It looks for plainer, more everyday language, converts passive voice to active voice, and makes the subjects concrete.

Analyzing the Reasoning of an Argument

As part of your second encounter with the text, pick out its reasoning. The reasoning is the author's case, which consists of the *claim* (what the author wants the readers to believe or do) and the *reasons* and *evidence* offered in support of it. State the case in your own words and describe what else is going on in the argument, such as the inclusion of opposing views or background information.

If a text is an argument, we can state what the author wants the readers to believe or do, and just as important, *why*. We should look for evidence presented to make the reasons seem believable. Note claims, reasons, and evidence in the margins as you read.

Reading Martin's Essay

Complex arguments require critical reading. Two critical-reading skills will help you: subdividing the text and considering contexts.

Finding Parts

Critical readers break texts down into parts. By *parts*, we mean groups of paragraphs that work together to perform some role in the essay. Examples of such roles are to introduce, to provide background, to give an opposing view, to conclude, and so on.

Discovering the parts of a text can be simple. Authors often make them obvious with subheadings and blank space. Even without these, transitional expressions and clear statements of intention make subdividing a text almost as easy as breaking a Hershey bar into its already well-defined segments. However, some arguments are more loosely constructed, their subdivisions less readily discernible. Even so, close inspection will usually reveal subdivisions, and you should be able to see the roles played by the various chunks.

We have placed numbers next to each paragraph in the essays reprinted in our text. Numbering makes it easier to refer to specific passages and to discuss parts.

Martin helps us see the parts of his essay by announcing early on, in paragraph 3, that it will have three sections, each "exemplify[ing] some of the complex psychological underpinnings of youth tattooing." Martin's essay can thus be subdivided as follows:

1. Epigraph
2. Paragraphs 1, 2, and 3: the introduction

Guidelines for Paraphrasing

- Use your own words, but do not strain to find a different word for every single one in the original. Some of the author's plain words are fine.
- If you take a phrase from the original, enclose it in quotation marks.
- Use a simpler sentence pattern than the original, even if it means making several short sentences. Aim for clarity.
- Check the surrounding sentences to make sure you understand the passage in context. You may want to add an idea from the context.
- Try for who-does-what sentences.

3. Paragraphs 4 and 5: an example
4. Paragaphs 6, 7, and 8: another example
5. Paragraphs 9, 10, and 11: a third example
6. Paragraph 12: the conclusion

Using Context

Taking the larger view again, we can use context to help pick out the reasoning. Although a quick reading might suggest that Martin is arguing that teens have good reasons for decorating their bodies, we need to recall that the essay appeared in a journal for psychiatrists—doctors, not parents or teachers. Martin is writing to other psychiatrists and psychologists, clinicians who work with families. Reading carefully, we learn that his audience is an even smaller portion of this group: clinicians who have been "summoned as the final arbiter" in family disputes involving tattoos and other body decoration (paragraph 2). Because journals such as the *Journal of the American Academy of Child & Adolescent Psychiatry* are aimed at improving the practice of medicine, we want to note sentences that tell these readers what they ought to do and how it will make them better doctors.

Identifying the Claim and Reasons

The claim: Martin is very clear about his claim, repeating it three times, using just slightly different wording:

> His readers should "[explore] **the motivations and significance [underlying]** **tattoos and piercings. . . ."** (paragraph 2)
>
> His readers should have "[a]**n interested and nonjudgmental appreciation** **of teenagers' surface presentations. . . ."** (paragraph 2)
>
> His readers should see "[a]**dolescents' bodily decorations . . . in terms of** **figuration rather than disfigurement. . . ."** (paragraph 12)

Asked to identify Martin's claim, you could choose any one of these statements.

The reason: The reason is the "because" part of the argument. Why should the readers believe or do as Martin suggests? We can find the answer in paragraph 2, in the same sentences with his claim:

Because doing so **"can go a long way toward resolving . . . differences and can become a novel and additional way of getting to know teenagers."**

Because doing so **"may become a way of making contact not only in their terms but on their turfs. . . ."**

And the final sentence of Martin's essay offers a third version of the same reason:

Because **"we may not only arrive at a position to pass more reasoned clinical judgment, but become sensitized through our patients' skins to another level of their internal reality."**

Again, we could choose any one of these sentences as the stated reason, or paraphrase his reason. Using paraphrase, we can begin to outline the case structure of Martin's argument:

Claim: Rather than dismissing tattoos as disfigurement, mental health professionals should take a serious interest in the meaning of and motivation behind the tattoos.

Reason: Exploring their patients' body decorations can help them gain insight and make contact with teenagers on teenagers' own terms.

Where is Martin's evidence? Martin tells us that the three subsections will "exemplify some of the complex psychological underpinnings of youth tattooing." In each, he offers a case, or vignette, as evidence.

Example and evidence (paragraphs 4 and 5): Tattoos are a way of working out identity problems when teens need either to mark themselves off from others or to regain a sense of control of a changing body or an imposing environment. The sixteen-year-old-girl who chose not to fit in.

Example and evidence (paragraphs 6, 7, and 8): Tattoos can be an attempt to make the intangible a tangible part of one's body. The thirteen-year-old boy remembering his father.

Example and evidence (paragraphs 9, 10, and 11): Tattoos are an "antidote" to a society that is on the run. The seventeen-year-old father.

THE THIRD ENCOUNTER: RESPONDING CRITICALLY TO AN ARGUMENT

Once you feel confident that you have the argument figured out, you are ready to respond to it, which means evaluating and comparing it with other perspectives, including your own. Only by *writing words* can you respond critically. As the reading expert Mortimer Adler says in *How to Read a Book,*

Reading, if it is active, is thinking, and thinking tends to express itself in words, spoken or written. The person who says he knows what he thinks but cannot express it in words usually does not know what he thinks. (49)

Ways to Annotate

- Paraphrase the claim and reasons next to where you find them stated.

- Consider: Does the author support his or her reasons with evidence? Is the evidence sufficient in terms of both quantity and quality?

- Circle the key terms. Note how the author defines or fails to define them.

- Ask: What does the author assume? Behind every argument, there are assumptions. For example, a baseball fan wrote to our local paper arguing that the policy of fouls after the second strike needs to be changed. His reason was that the fans would not be subjected to such a long game. The author assumed that a fast game of hits and outs is more interesting than a slow game of strategy between batters and pitchers. Not every baseball fan shares that assumption.

- Note any contradictions you see, either within the text itself or with anything else you've read or learned.

- Consider the implications of the argument. If we believe or do what the author argues, what is likely to happen?

- Think of someone who would disagree with this argument, and say what that person might object to.

- If you see any opposing views in the argument, question the author's fairness in presenting them. Consider whether the author has represented opposing views fairly or has set them up to be easily knocked down.

- Ask: What is the author overlooking or leaving out?

- Consider: Where does the argument connect with anything else you have read?

- Consider: Does the argument exemplify mature reasoning as explained in Chapter 1, "Understanding Argument"?

- Ask: What aim does the argument seem to pursue? One of the four in the box on page 13, or some combination of them?

- Ask: What kind of person does the author sound like? Mark places where you hear the author's voice. Describe the tone. How does the author establish credibility—or fail to?

- Note the author's values and biases, places where the author sounds liberal or conservative, religious or materialistic, and so on.

- Note places where you see clues about the intended audience of the argument, such as appeals to their interests, values, tastes, and so on.

Annotation Is Key

We suggest that you annotate heavily. **Annotation** simply means making a note. Use the margins, and/or writer's notebook, for these notes of critical response. Many writers keep reading journals to practice active interaction with what they read and to preserve the experience of reading a text they want to remember.

What should you write about? Think of questions you would ask the author if he or she were in the room with you. Think of your own experience with the subject. Note similarities and contrasts with other arguments you have read or experiences of your own that confirm or contradict what the author is saying. Write about anything you notice that seems interesting, unusual, brilliant, or wrong. *Comment, question*—the more you actually write on the page, the more the text becomes your own. And you will write more confidently about a text you own than one you are just borrowing.

The list in the Best Practices box on page 29 will give you more ideas for annotations.

A concluding comment about responses: Even if you agree with an argument, think about who might oppose it and what their objections might be. Challenge the views you find most sympathetic.

Following is an example of annotation for part of Martin's argument.

Sample Annotations

How is he defining "solution"? Do tattoos solve a problem or just indicate one?

It seems like there are more mature ways to do this.

Or would it cause parents to pay attention to them rather than leave them alone?

Is he implying that the indelible mark is one they will not outgrow? What if they do?

Tattoos and piercing can offer a concrete and readily available <u>solution</u> for many of the identity crises and conflicts normative to adolescent development. In using such decorations, and by marking out their bodily territories, adolescents can support their efforts at autonomy, privacy, and insulation. Seeking individuation, tattooed adolescents can become unambiguously demarcated from others and singled out as unique. The intense and often disturbing reactions that are mobilized in viewers can help to effectively <u>keep them at bay,</u> becoming tantamount to the proverbial "Keep Out" sign hanging from a teenager's door.

Alternatively, feeling prey to a rapidly evolving body over which they have no say, self-made and openly visible decorations may restore adolescents' sense of <u>normalcy</u> and control, a way of turning a passive experience into an active identity. By indelibly marking their bodies, adolescents can strive to reclaim their bearings within an environment experienced as alien, estranged, or suffocating or to lay claim over their evolving and increasingly unrecognizable bodies. In either case, the net outcome <u>can be a resolution to</u> unwelcome impositions: external, familial, or societal in one case, internal and hormonal in the other. In the words of a 16-year-old girl with several facial piercings, and who could have been referring to her body just as well as to the position within her family: "If I don't fit in, it is because I say so."

What is normal?

Would he say the same about anorexia?

5

Does he assume this family needs counseling—or will not need it? He says the problem is "resolved."

CHAPTER 3

Analyzing an Argument:
The Toulmin Method

In Chapter 2, we discussed the importance of reading arguments critically: breaking them down into their parts to see how they are put together, noting in the margins key terms that are not defined, and raising questions about the writer's claims or evidence. Although these general techniques are sufficient for analyzing many arguments, sometimes—especially with intricate arguments and with arguments we sense are faulty but whose weaknesses we are unable to specify—we need a more systematic technique.

In this chapter, we explain and illustrate such a technique based on the work of Stephen Toulmin, a contemporary philosopher who has contributed a great deal to our understanding of argumentation. This method will allow you to analyze the logic of any argument; you will also find it useful in examining the logic of your own arguments as you draft and revise them.

A PRELIMINARY CRITICAL READING

Before we consider Toulmin, let's first explore the following argument carefully. Use the general process for critical reading we described in Chapter 2.

Rising to the Occasion of Our Death

WILLIAM F. MAY

William F. May (b. 1927) is a distinguished professor of ethics at Southern Methodist University. The following essay appeared originally in *The Christian Century* (1990).

1   For many parents, a Volkswagen van is associated with putting children to sleep on a camping trip. Jack Kevorkian, a Detroit pathologist, has now linked the van with the veterinarian's meaning of "putting to sleep." Kevorkian conducted a dinner interview with Janet Elaine Adkins, a 54-year-old Alzheimer's patient, and her husband and then agreed to help her commit suicide in his VW van. Kevorkian pressed beyond the more generally accepted practice of passive euthanasia (allowing a patient to die by withholding or withdrawing treatment) to active euthanasia (killing for mercy).

2   Kevorkian, moreover, did not comply with the strict regulations that govern active euthanasia in, for example, the Netherlands. Holland requires that death be imminent (Adkins had beaten her son in tennis just a few days earlier); it demands a more professional review of the medical evidence and the patient's resolution than a dinner interview with a physician (who is a stranger and who does not treat patients) permits; and it calls for the final, endorsing signatures of two doctors.

3   So Kevorkian-bashing is easy. But the question remains: Should we develop a judicious, regulated social policy permitting voluntary euthanasia for the terminally ill? Some moralists argue that the distinction between allowing to die and killing for mercy is petty quibbling over technique. Since the patient in any event dies—whether by acts of omission or commission—the route to death doesn't really matter. The way modern procedures have made dying at the hands of the experts and their machines such a prolonged and painful business has further fueled the euthanasia movement, which asserts not simply the right to die but the right to be killed.

4   But other moralists believe that there is an important moral distinction between allowing to die and mercy killing. The euthanasia movement, these critics contend, wants to engineer death rather than face dying. Euthanasia would bypass dying to make one dead as quickly as possible. It aims to relieve suffering by knocking out the interval between life and death. It solves the problem of suffering by eliminating the sufferer.

5   The impulse behind the euthanasia movement is understandable in an age when dying has become such an inhumanly endless business. But the movement may fail to appreciate our human capacity to rise to the occasion of our death. The best death is not always the sudden death. Those forewarned of death and given time to prepare for it have time to engage in acts of reconciliation. Also, advanced grieving by those about to be bereaved may ease some of their pain. Psychiatrists

have observed that those who lose a loved one accidentally have a more difficult time recovering from the loss than those who have suffered through an extended period of illness before the death. Those who have lost a close relative by accident are more likely to experience what Geoffrey Gorer has called limitless grief. The community, moreover, may need its aged and dependent, its sick and its dying, and the virtues which they sometimes evince—the virtues of humility, courage, and patience—just as much as the community needs the virtues of justice and love manifest in the agents of care.

6   On the whole, our social policy should allow terminal patients to die, but it should not regularize killing for mercy. Such a policy would recognize and respect that moment in illness when it no longer makes sense to bend every effort to cure or to prolong life and when one must allow patients to do their own dying. This policy seems most consonant with the obligations of the community to care and of the patient to finish his or her course.

7   Advocates of active euthanasia appeal to the principle of patient autonomy—as the use of the phrase "voluntary euthanasia" indicates. But emphasis on the patient's right to determine his or her destiny often harbors an extremely naïve view of the uncoerced nature of the decision. Patients who plead to be put to death hardly make unforced decisions if the terms and conditions under which they receive care already nudge them in the direction of the exit. If the elderly have stumbled around in their apartments, alone and frightened for years, or if they have spent years warehoused in geriatrics barracks, then the decision to be killed for mercy hardly reflects an uncoerced decision. The alternative may be so wretched as to push patients toward this escape. It is a huge irony and, in some cases, hypocrisy to talk suddenly about a compassionate killing when the aging and dying may have been starved for compassion for many years. To put it bluntly, a country has not earned the moral right to kill for mercy unless it has already sustained and supported life mercifully. Otherwise we kill for compassion only to reduce the demands on our compassion. This statement does not charge a given doctor or family member with impure motives. I am concerned here not with the individual case but with the cumulative impact of a social policy.

8   I can, to be sure, imagine rare circumstances in which I hope I would have the courage to kill for mercy—when the patient is utterly beyond human care, terminal, and in excruciating pain. A neurosurgeon once showed a group of physicians and an ethicist the picture of a Vietnam casualty who had lost all four limbs in a landmine explosion. The catastrophe had reduced the soldier to a trunk with his face transfixed in horror. On the battlefield I would hope that I would have the courage to kill the sufferer with mercy.

9   But hard cases do not always make good laws or wise social policies. Regularized mercy killings would too quickly relieve the community of its obligation to provide good care. Further, we should not always expect the law to provide us with full protection and coverage for what, in rare circumstances, we may morally need to do. Sometimes the moral life calls us out into a no-man's-land where we cannot expect total security and protection under the law. But no one said that the moral life is easy.

A STEP-BY-STEP DEMONSTRATION OF THE TOULMIN METHOD

The Toulmin method requires an analysis of the claim, the reasons offered to support the claim, and the evidence offered to support the reasons, along with an analysis of any refutations offered.

Analyzing the Claim

Logical analysis begins with identifying the *claim,* the thesis or central contention, along with any specific qualifications or exceptions.

Identify the Claim

First, ask yourself, *What statement is the author defending?* In "Rising to the Occasion of Our Death," William F. May spells out his claim in paragraph 6:

> [O]ur social policy should allow terminal patients to die, but it should not regularize killing for mercy.

In his claim, May supports passive euthanasia (letting someone die by withholding or discontinuing treatment) but opposes "regularizing" (making legal or customary) active euthanasia (administering, say, an overdose of morphine to cause a patient's death).

Much popular argumentation is sometimes careless about what exactly is being claimed: Untrained arguers too often content themselves with merely taking sides ("Euthanasia is wrong"). Note that May, a student of ethics trained in philosophical argumentation, makes a claim that is specific. Whenever an argument does not include an explicit statement of its claim, you should begin your analysis by stating the writer's claim yourself.

Look for Qualifiers

Next, ask, *How is the claim qualified?* Is it absolute, or does it include words or phrases to indicate that it may not hold true in every situation or set of circumstances?

May qualifies his claim in paragraph 6 with the phrase "On the whole," indicating that he recognizes possible exceptions. Other qualifiers include "typically," "usually," and "most of the time." Careful arguers are wary of making absolute claims. Qualifying words or phrases are used to restrict a claim and improve its defensibility.

Find the Exceptions

Finally, ask, *In what cases or circumstances would the writer not press his or her claim?* Look for any explicit exceptions the writer offers.

May is quite clear in paragraph 8 about when he would not press his claim:

> I hope I would have the courage to kill for mercy—when the patient is utterly beyond human care, terminal, and in excruciating pain.

Once he has specified these abstract conditions, he offers a chilling example of a case in which mercy killing would be appropriate. Nevertheless, he insists that such exceptions are rare and thus do not justify making active euthanasia legal or allowing it to become common policy.

Summarize the Claim

At this point it is a good idea to write out the claim, its qualifiers, and its exceptions so that you can see all of them clearly:

> (qualifier) "On the whole"
>
> (claim) "our social policy should allow terminal patients to die, but it should not regularize killing for mercy"
>
> (exception) "when the patient is utterly beyond human care, terminal, and in excruciating pain"

Analyzing the Reasons

Once you have analyzed the claim, you should next identify and evaluate the reasons offered for the claim.

List the Reasons

Begin by asking yourself, *Why is the writer advancing this claim?* Look for any statement or statements that are used to justify the thesis. May groups all of his reasons in paragraph 5:

> The dying should have time to prepare for death and to reconcile with relatives and friends.
>
> Those close to the dying should have time to come to terms with the impending loss of a loved one.
>
> The community needs examples of dependent but patient and courageous people who sometimes do die with dignity.
>
> The community needs the virtues ("justice and love") of those who care for the sick and dying.

When you list reasons, you need not preserve the exact words of the arguer; often, doing so is impossible because reasons are not always spelled out. Be very careful, however, to adhere as closely as possible to the writer's language. Otherwise, your analysis can easily go astray, imposing a reason of your own that the writer did not have in mind.

Note that reasons, like claims, can be qualified. May does not say, for instance, that "the aged and dependent" *always* show "the virtues of humility, courage, and patience." He implicitly admits that they can be ornery and cowardly as well. But for May's purposes it is enough that they sometimes manifest the virtues he admires.

List the reasons following your summary of the claim, qualifiers, and exceptions. One possibility is to list them beneath the summary of the claim in the form of a tree diagram (see the model diagram in the Concept Close-up box on page 38).

Examine the Reasons

There are two questions to ask as you examine the reasons. First, *Are they really good reasons?* A reason is only as good as the values it invokes or implies. A value is something we think is good—that is, worth pursuing for its own sake or because it leads to attaining other goods. For each reason, specify the values involved and then determine whether you accept those values as generally binding.

Second, *Is the reason relevant to the thesis?* In other words, does the relationship between the claim and the reason hold up to examination? For example, the claim "You should buy a new car from Fred Freed" cannot be supported by the reason "Fred is a family man with three cute kids."

Be careful as you examine whether reasons are good and whether they are relevant. No other step is as important in assessing the logic of an argument.

To illustrate, consider May's first reason: Those who know they are about to die should have time to prepare for death and to seek reconciliation with people from whom they have become estranged. Is this a good reason? Yes, because we value the chance to prepare for death and to reconcile with estranged friends or family members.

But is the reason relevant? May seems to rule out the possibility that a dying person seeking active euthanasia would be able to prepare for death and reconcile with others. However, terminally ill people who decide to arrange for their own deaths may make any number of preparations beforehand, so the connection between this reason and May's claim is weak. To accept a connection, we would have to assume that active euthanasia necessarily amounts to a sudden death without adequate preparation. We are entitled to question the relevance of the reason, no matter how good it might be in itself.

◎◎ FOLLOWING THROUGH

Examine May's second, third, and fourth reasons on your own. Make notes about each reason, evaluating how good each is in itself and how relevant it is to the thesis. Create your own diagram based on the model on page 38. •

Analyzing the Evidence

Once you have finished your analysis of the reasons, the next step is to consider the evidence offered to support any of those reasons.

List the Evidence

Ask, *What kinds of evidence (data, anecdotes, case studies, citations from authority, and so forth) are offered as support for each reason?* Some arguments advance little in the way of evidence. May's is a good example of a moral argument about principles; such an argument does not require much evidence. Lack of evidence, then, is not always a fault. For one of his reasons, however, May does offer some evidence: After stating his second reason in paragraph 5—the chance to grieve before a loved one dies—he invokes authorities who agree with him about the value of advanced grieving.

Examine the Evidence

Two questions apply. First, *Is the evidence good?* That is, is it sufficient, accurate, and credible? Second, *Is it relevant to the reason it supports?* The evidence May offers in paragraph 5 is sufficient. We assume his citations are accurate and credible as well. We would also accept them as relevant because, apart from our own experience with grieving, we have to rely on expert opinion. (See Chapter 6 for a fuller discussion of estimating the adequacy and relevance of evidence.)

Noting Refutations

A final step is to assess an arguer's refutations. In a refutation, a writer anticipates potential objections to his or her position and tries to show why they do not undermine the basic argument. A skilled arguer uses them to deal with any obvious objections a reader is likely to have.

First, ask, *What refutations does the writer offer?* Summarize them. Then ask, *How does the writer approach each objection?* May's refutation occupies paragraph 7. He recognizes that the value of free choice lends weight to the proeuthanasia position, and so he relates this value to the question of "voluntary euthanasia." Because in our culture individual freedom is so strong a value, May does not question the value itself; rather, he leads us to question whether voluntary euthanasia is actually a matter of free choice. He suggests that unwanted people may be coerced into "choosing" death or may be so isolated and neglected that death becomes preferable. Thus, he responds to the objection that dying people should have freedom of choice where death is concerned.

Summarizing Your Analysis

Once you have completed your analysis, it is a good idea to summarize the results in a paragraph or two. Be sure to set aside your own position on the issue, confining your summary to the argument the writer makes.

Although May's logic is strong, it is not fully compelling. He qualifies his argument and uses exceptions effectively, and his single use of refutation is skillful. However, he fails to acknowledge that active euthanasia need not be a sudden decision leading to sudden death. Consequently, his reasons for supporting passive euthanasia can be used to support at least some cases of active euthanasia as well. It is here—in the linkage between reasons and claim—that May's argument falls short. Furthermore, we may question whether the circumstances under which May would permit active euthanasia are in fact as rare as he suggests. Many people are beyond human care, terminal, and in pain, and many others suffer acute anguish for which they might legitimately seek the relief of death.

Model Toulmin Diagram for Analyzing Arguments

The Case
Claim: _____ { Qualifier?

Exceptions?

Reason:	Reason:	Reason:	Reason:
What makes this reason relevant?	What makes this reason relevant?	What makes this reason relevant?	What makes this reason relevant?
What makes this reason good?	What makes this reason good?	What makes this reason good?	What makes this reason good?
What evidence supports this reason?	What evidence supports this reason?	What evidence supports this reason?	What evidence supports this reason?

The Refutation

Objection:	Objection:	Objection:	Objection:
Rebuttal:	Rebuttal:	Rebuttal:	Rebuttal:

A FINAL NOTE ABOUT LOGICAL ANALYSIS

No method for analyzing arguments is perfect, and no method can guarantee that everyone using it will assess an argument the same way. Uniform results are not especially desirable anyway. What would be left to talk about? The point of argumentative analysis is to step back and examine an argument carefully, to detect how it is structured, to assess the cogency and power of its logic. The Toulmin method helps us move beyond a hit-or-miss approach to logical analysis, but it cannot yield a conclusion as compelling as mathematical proof.

Toulmin Analysis

A. ANALYZE THE CLAIM

1. **Find the claim.** In many arguments, the claim is never explicitly stated. When it isn't, try to make the implied claim explicit by stating it in your own words. (Note: If, after careful analysis, you aren't sure *exactly* what the writer is claiming, you've found a serious fault in the argument.)

2. **Look for qualifiers.** Is the claim absolute? Or is it qualified by some word or phrase like *usually* or *all things being equal*? If the claim is absolute, can you think of circumstances in which it might not apply? If the claim is qualified, why is it not absolute? That is, is there any real thought or content in the qualifier—good reasons for qualifying the claim?

3. **Look for explicit exceptions to the claim.** If the writer has pointed out conditions in which he or she would not assert the claim, note them carefully.

Summarize steps 1–3. See the diagram on page 38.

B. ANALYZE THE REASONS

1. **Find the reason or reasons advanced to justify the claim.** All statements of reason will answer the question "Why are you claiming what you've claimed?" They can be linked to the claim with *because*. As with claims, reasons may be implied. Dig them out and state them in your own words. (Note: If, after careful analysis, you discover that the reasons aren't clear or relevant to the claim, you should conclude that the argument is either defective and in need of revision or invalid and therefore unacceptable.)

2. **Ponder each reason advanced.** Is the reason good in itself? Is the reason relevant to the thesis? Note any problems.

List the reasons underneath the claim. See the diagram on page 38.

C. ANALYZE THE EVIDENCE

1. **For each reason, locate all evidence offered to back it up.** Evidence is not limited to hard data. Anecdotes, case studies, and citations from authorities also count as evidence. (Note: Not all reasons require extensive evidence. But we should be suspicious of reasons without evidence, especially when it seems that evidence ought to be available. Unsupported reasons are often a sign of bad reasoning.)

2. **Ponder each piece of evidence.** Is it good? That is, is it accurate and believable? Is it relevant to the reason it supports? Note any problems.

List the evidence underneath the claim. See the diagram on page 38.

D. EXAMINE THE REFUTATIONS

If there are refutations—efforts to refute objections to the case—examine them. If not, consider what objections you think the writer should have addressed.

Convincing and persuading always involve more than logic, and, therefore, logical analysis alone is never enough to assess the strength of an argument. For example, William May's argument attempts to discredit those like Dr. Jack Kevorkian who assist patients wishing to take their own lives. May depicts Kevorkian as offering assistance without sufficient consultation with the patient. Is his depiction accurate? Clearly, we can answer this question only by finding out more about how Kevorkian and others like him work. Because such questions are not a part of logical analysis, they have not been of concern to us in this chapter. But any adequate and thorough analysis of an argument must also address questions of fact and the interpretation of data.

CHAPTER 4

Writing a Critique

In Chapter 2 you learned how to read an argument critically, in Chapter 3 how to analyze one. This chapter pulls those lessons together around the genre of critique, a written assessment of an argument.

WHAT IS A CRITIQUE?

When you evaluate someone else's argument, you offer a **critique,** "a written estimate of the merits of a performance" (*New Grolier's Webster International Dictionary*). We encounter them in "Letters to the Editor" in newspapers, in magazines that include reader responses to articles in previous issues, and in blogs devoted to some controversial issue or cause. The basic situation is always the same: Someone writes an argument urging readers to believe or do something; a reader responds by "estimat[ing] the merits" of the argument, agreeing or disagreeing (or some of both), and explaining why.

A critique, then, is part of a public conversation conducted in writing. It is not a put-down, an attack on someone's argument, but rather rational assessment, part of a search for truth.

Context and Critique

Most written arguments are "stand-alone" texts—an opinion column in a newspaper or online, an article in a magazine or on a Web site, and so on. However, they are not as isolated as they seem. Authors create **context**, a background against which they want you to see their argument—current events, an ongoing debate about the topic, and so on.

Context *always* matters for the following reasons:

- *Context is the key to understanding an argument.* For example, increasing the availability of loans for college students makes sense within the rapid increase of higher education costs.

- *Context is the key to understanding why people disagree.* Those who favor increasing loans often see the issue in the context of opportunity, making college possible for modest-income students. Those who oppose it often see loans in the context of too much personal debt.

- *Context is the key to understanding your response.* If you or your family cannot afford college and you have taken full advantage of other forms of aid, loans may be very appealing.

We'll return to context often in this chapter.

WHY CRITIQUE AN ARGUMENT?

See Chapter 9, "Making Your Case: Arguing to Convince" for convincing, concerned with influencing what people think. See Chapter 10, "Motivating Action: Arguing to Persuade" for persuasion, concerned with motivating people to act.

On occasion you will make arguments designed to change someone's mind or to move others to action. Every day, however, you will hear or read the arguments of other people, in conversation, in books and magazines, on television, radio, and the Net, in business meetings and community gatherings. Short of becoming a hermit, there is no way to avoid arguments designed to influence what you think and do. Professors assign critiques because they know how often you will need to assess arguments.

Good arguments must be distinguished from bad ones. That is the stake that you and all thoughtful people have in evaluating arguments.

HOW DOES CRITIQUING AN ARGUMENT WORK?

You may have noticed that most people only react to arguments. They just agree or disagree, sometimes with much heat and noise. A good example is talk radio: Listeners call in to voice all kinds of opinions about political issues or the performance of their local sports team. Many people avoid such exchanges because they feel nothing is accomplished. "It's just a shouting match," they say.

Why does public discussion often seem pointless? The problem is not in exchanging opinions. Saying what we think gets things off our chest. Hearing what other people think is stimulating. The problem is that public discussion tends to *stop* at exchanging opinions and reacting to them.

The crucial next step is critique, evaluating arguments, the move from stating opinions to questioning them. How does it work?

The Art of Questioning: Probing an Opinion

Opinions take the form of claims or statements. For example,

> The United States should promote the spread of democracy as part of its foreign policy in the Middle East.

Because democracy has a high value for us, this opinion can easily go unchallenged. To open it up for assessment, what questions could you ask?

- You could ask about *key terms*. What does "promote" mean? For the Bush administration after the 9/11 terrorist attack, it meant using our military to remove totalitarian governments in both Afghanistan and Iraq. Should we go that far in promoting democracy?

- You could ask about *context*. What is the potential for democracy in the Middle East? Muslim countries typically do not separate religion from government; without such a separation, can we promote democracy as we understand it?

- You could ask about what the *data* indicate. How many Middle Eastern countries were democratic ten years ago? How many are now? What's the trend? How stable are the democracies in the Middle East?

- You could ask about various ways to *interpret the data*. Is democracy an advantage for the United States in the Middle East? Have the outcomes of elections favored our interests? How many of the friendly governments in the region are not democracies?

◎◎ FOLLOWING THROUGH

Bring the op-ed pages from two or three days of your local newspaper to class. Examine the opinions expressed by the editorial staff, letters to the editor, and opinion columnists. Select two or three of the most interesting ones and probe them in class using the four assessment questions.

Evaluating arguments includes more than assessing claims and many more questions than the four discussed so far. Nevertheless, *the basic move for evaluating arguments is posing questions*. Without it discussion stalls at merely reacting to opinions.

READING

The following reading will help you see in detail how critiques work and what to do in a situation that calls for evaluating an argument.

Responses to Arguments Against the Minimum Legal Drinking Age

DAVID J. HANSON

David J. Hanson is Professor Emeritus of Sociology at SUNY, Potsdam, and an expert on issues related to alcohol use. This piece came from his Web site, funded by the Distilled Spirits Council of the United States.

Hanson responds to arguments advanced by a government agency, the National Institute on Alcohol Abuse and Alcoholism (NIAAA), against lowering the drinking age to eighteen. As you read, consider how important *point of view* is in critiquing arguments. Being clear about what you think is one of the keys to a good critique.

Context: The first two sentences identify the source of the argument critiqued and what it's about.

The federal government is spending taxpayer money in a questionable political campaign to defend the minimum drinking age against attempts in some states to lower it. In "Responses to Arguments against the Minimum Drinking Age," the National Institute on Alcohol Abuse and Alcoholism (NIAAA) identifies arguments against the minimum legal drinking age and then suggests counter-arguments. But in doing so, it plays fast and loose with the facts, a common tactic in politics.

Preview: Summarizes major point.

Argument: "If I'm old enough to go to war, I should be old enough to drink."

The long list of what people can do legally at age eighteen makes prohibition of alcohol seem much more arbitrary than the usual point about fighting in a war.

Actually the argument is much stronger than the NIAAA acknowledges. The fact is that citizens are legally adults at the age of 18. They can marry, vote, adopt children, own and drive automobiles, have abortions, enter into legally binding contracts, operate businesses, purchase or even perform in pornography, give legal consent for sexual intercourse, fly airplanes, hold public office, serve on juries that convict others of murder, hunt wildlife with deadly weapons, be imprisoned, be executed, be an employer, sue and be sued in court, and otherwise conduct themselves as the adults they are. And, of course, they can serve in the United States armed services and give their lives defending their country. One of the very few things they can't legally do is consume an alcohol beverage. They can't even have a celebratory sip of champagne at their own weddings.

Part of what makes this critique so powerful is that Hanson responds not only to the NIAAA's arguments but also to their counter-arguments, what they say in response to challenges from the other side.

Counter-Argument: Federal agents suggest pointing out that people can obtain a hunting license at age 12 and a driver's license at age 16.

Ironically, this actually strengthens the argument against treating legal adults as children with regard to alcohol beverages. People can hunt wildlife with a deadly weapon at age 12 but can't be trusted with a beer at age 20?

The government also suggests pointing out that people must be 25 to serve in the U.S. House of Representatives, 30 to serve in the Senate, and 35 to serve as President. But these unusual restrictions were imposed well over two hundred years ago in a new country that was still largely reluctant to grant rights and in which neither women nor African Americans were trusted to vote. We're now in the 21st century enjoying widespread rights and also a time when young people are infinitely more sophisticated. Clearly, the agency's arguments are extremely weak and unconvincing.

6   **Argument:** "Europeans let their teens drink from an early age, yet they don't have the alcohol-related problems we do."

7 | **Counter-Argument:** The NIAAA responds that "the idea that Europeans do not have alcohol-related problems is a myth." But no one suggests that Europeans have no drinking-related problems. Here the agency is guilty of using the straw person tactic—create a very weak argument and then shoot it down.

8 | In reality, research for decades has demonstrated that those countries and groups in Europe and elsewhere in which most people regularly drink but have few drinking-related problems all share three common characteristics:

1. Alcohol is seen as a rather neutral substance in and of itself. It's neither a poison nor a magic elixir. It's how it's used that's important.

2. People have two equally acceptable choices:

   • Abstain or

   • Drink in moderation.

   What's never acceptable is the abuse of alcohol by anyone of any age. Period.

3. People learn about drinking alcohol in moderation from an early age in the safe and supportive environment of the home, and they do so by good parental example. All of these groups would agree that it's better to learn about drinking in the parents' house than in the fraternity house.

These three points show how research information can be used for critique and how to summarize what it says effectively.

9 | Age 21 is actually the highest minimum legal drinking age in the entire world and is a radical social experiment both internationally and in terms of our own national history. Those who call for all adults to be able to drink are traditionalists, whereas those who insist on age 21 are radicals.

Good use of historical and current knowledge about the drinking age to show that the current law is out of step.

10 | **Argument:** Lower rates of alcohol-related crashes among 19- to 20-year-olds aren't related to the age 21 policy, but rather they're related to increased drinking-driver educational efforts, tougher enforcement, and tougher drunk-driving penalties."

11 | **Counter-Argument:** The agency wants us to argue that "Careful research has shown the decline was not due to DUI enforcement and tougher penalties, but is a direct result of the legal drinking age" and that "Achieving long-term reductions in youth drinking problems requires an environmental change so that alcohol is less accessible to teens."

12 | However, there are a number of weaknesses in what the bureaucrats want us to say. It's true that lower rates of alcohol-related traffic accidents now occur among drivers under the age of 21. But they've also been declining among those age 21 and older, with one notable exception.

13 | Raising the minimum legal drinking age has resulted in an apparent displacement of large numbers of alcohol-related traffic fatalities from those under the age of 21 to those age 21 to 24. In short, raising the drinking age simply changed the ages of those killed.

Arguments often cite only those facts that support their position. Critique should cite evidence damaging to the argument that has been omitted.

14 | The argument that we need to make alcohol less accessible to adults under the age of 21 fails to recognize the fact, well established by governmental surveys, that it's easier for young people to obtain marijuana than alcohol.

When you can show a past policy has failed, one like the present one advocated or defended, you have a strong point for critique.

It's also foolish to think that effective prohibition can be imposed on young adults. The U.S. already tried that with the entire population during National Prohibition (1920–1933). The result was less frequent drinking but more heavy, episodic drinking. The effort to impose prohibition on young adults has driven drinking underground and promoted so-called binge drinking. This is a natural and totally predictable consequence of prohibition.

Argument: "We drank when we were young and we grew out of it. It's just a phase that all students go through."

Exposes what may be the hidden agenda: a desire to discourage alcohol use altogether. Shows that the NIAAA's argument is at odds with the 21 age position defended.

Counter-Argument: Interestingly, NIAAA wants us to argue that "Unfortunately, many teens will not 'grow out of it.'" Implicit is the belief that adults should not consume alcohol even when legally able to do so. The agency apparently envisions a society in which abstention from alcohol is the norm, a vision that it shares with temperance and prohibition advocates.

While not all students will try alcohol, virtually all normal young people will do so and they will do so without ill effects. But NIAAA wants us to promote the discredited and simplistic "stepping stone" hypothesis that suggests that drinking leads to smoking, which leads to marijuana, which leads to crack, which leads to cocaine, which leads to degradation and illness, which leads to death.

19   **Argument:** "Making it illegal to drink until 21 increases the desire for the 'forbidden fruit.' Then, when students turn 21, they'll drink even more."

20   **Counter-Argument:** NIAAA wants us to assert incorrectly that "Actually the opposite is true. Early legal access to alcohol is associated with higher rates of drinking as an adult."

Critique ends with the author's strongest point: that the 21 age has an effect opposite to its intention.

In reality, research has clearly demonstrated the "forbidden fruit" phenomenon among adults under the age of 21. On the other hand, there is no evidence that the increased desire to drink continues after students turn 21. In fact, upon turning age 21, many adults find that it's no longer so much fun to get into bars and drink precisely because it is legal for them to do so.

QUESTIONS FOR DISCUSSION

1. There is no question that alcohol abuse is connected with many problems: highway deaths and serious injuries, date rape, spousal abuse, and ruined careers. Are any of these problems connected to the current legal drinking age?

2. Critiques can be critiqued. For example, Hanson points to the ambiguous results of National Prohibition (paragraph 15). But if we set the legal drinking age at eighteen, we will still be prohibiting alcohol consumption below eighteen. The issue, then, is not prohibition, but where we draw the line. Isn't what happened between 1920 and 1933 irrelevant to the argument?

Strategies for Critiquing Arguments

It is one thing to know that you do not agree with an argument you hear or read, quite another to respond to it with more than just "I'm not convinced." Hanson shows us some of the many ways we can say something about arguments, both those we support and those we do not.

In paragraph 3, for instance, Hanson expands on the assertion that people old enough to fight in a war should be old enough to drink. As he points out, eighteen-year-olds have many freedoms and responsibilities. One way to respond to a point you agree with is to *offer more examples* that illustrate the validity of the point.

In paragraphs 7 and 8, Hanson responds to the NIAAA argument that Europeans do have alcohol-related problems. You can use his strategies:

1. *Resist allowing an argument to "shift ground."* The NIAAA claims something no one denies: there are problems with alcohol in Europe. The issue is whether the lower drinking age in Europe is relevant to the problems.

2. *Supply counter-evidence.* Hanson goes on to specify the social conditions in regions such as Europe where alcohol is consumed from an early age with few negative consequences.

3. *Put the issue in a wider context.* Hanson points out that twenty-one is the "highest legal drinking age in the entire world" and deviates from the usual practice in our own history.

◎◎ FOLLOWING THROUGH

In class discussion, characterize the strategies Hanson uses in paragraphs 10–21. Which seem most convincing to you? Why do they work so well?   •

CLAIMING VOICE IN EVALUATING AN ARGUMENT

The voice of critique or analysis shares much in common with the voice of case-making: the emphasis is on stating your position clearly, directly, and forcefully, favoring a middle style more formal than conversation, but less formal than a public speech. Also like making a case, critique's voice should be the calm voice of reason, of opinions stated precisely and defended well. (See Chapter 9, pages 214–215, for claiming voice in making a case.)

Here is a good example of the analytical voice in paragraph 1 of Hanson's critique:

> The federal government is spending taxpayer money in a questionable political campaign to defend the minimum drinking age against attempts in some states to lower it. In "Responses to Arguments against the Minimum Drinking Age," the National Institute on Alcohol Abuse and Alcoholism (NIAAA) identifies arguments against the minimum legal drinking age and then suggests counter-arguments. But in doing so, it plays fast and loose with the facts, a common tactic in politics.

Notice that you can say that an argument "plays fast and loose with the facts" or that it is illogical or inconsistent, providing you can back it up and make your accusations stick, as Hanson does in the rest of his article.

Your voice in critique, therefore, depends largely on *how you assess the quality of the argument you are critiquing.* Hanson clearly thinks the NIAAA's argument is politically motivated, not supported by available data, and poorly reasoned as well. He therefore does not give it the respect he might extend to an argument with only minor flaws, an argument that needs revision rather than rejection.

THE ASSIGNMENT

If your instructor does not assign one, locate any short (750–1,000 words) argument on a controversial topic and write a paper of about the same length critiquing it.

Topic and Focus

Obviously, you need to respond to what the article says. However, you can relate the argument's topic to matters the author does not mention. For example, an article advocating laws prohibiting handheld cell phone use by drivers may focus entirely on this particular device. You might respond by pointing to other driver distractions that also contribute to accidents, such as putting CDs in audio equipment. Perhaps the real problem is driver distraction in general, not cell phone use in particular?

Audience

Usually you will write to the same readership your argument addresses. However, when an argument you are responding to targets only one of several readerships with a stake in the topic, it is legitimate to respond by addressing your critique to one of the other audiences. For example, an argument addressed only to parents about a public school issue, such as classes that are too large, might well address the students affected by too large classes instead.

Voice and Ethos

Be sincere, project confidence, have command of the facts and what they mean, and show respect for the argument you are evaluating.

Writing Assignment Suggestions

This assignment could be written in many genres, the most common being a letter to the editor of a newspaper or magazine; as an op-ed piece; as a response to a blog; as a short article for a newspaper or magazine or newsletter; as an assessment of a classroom discussion, debate, chat room exchange; public speech; or some other oral argument.

We suggest that you pick an argument you disagree with or an argument you partly agree with and partly disagree with in almost equal measure. It makes little sense to critique an argument you find wholly convincing.

CHOOSING AN ARGUMENT

When you have a choice, opt for the provocative or extreme argument. They almost beg for critique, and evaluating them is more fruitful than the predictable position defended in predictable ways.

You can locate suitable arguments by recalling something you read in a newspaper, magazine, or on a Web site, by doing subject searches on LexisNexis (see page 111 for how to use this resource), and by Googling a topic in the news. Consider also the following possibilities.

- *Class readings.* Class readings can provide arguments for critique, especially if the readings themselves are arguments.
- *Local news or observation.* Read your local and campus newspapers for arguments relating to your community. Sometimes these can be more interesting than overworked topics like abortion or gun control.
- *Internet discussions.* Blogs are often good sources for arguments. Visit blogs on issues of public concern, such as National Public Radio's blog at www.npr.org/blogs/talk/.

EXPLORING YOUR TOPIC

So that you can see how to explore the argument you have selected or been assigned, we need to work with an example argument. Here's one on an issue of some concern on most college campuses. Read it once or twice, just to understand what it says and to form a first reaction to it.

Open Your Ears to Biased Professors

DAVID FRYMAN

> David Fryman was a senior at Brandeis University when he wrote this opinion column for the school's newspaper, *The Justice.* He's offering advice to younger college students who often encounter professors with political opinions different from those endorsed at home or in their local communities. Fryman's question is, How should they respond?

1   One of the most important lessons I've learned in three years of higher education is the value of creativity and critical thinking, particularly when confronted with a professor whose ideology, political leanings or religious viewpoint fly in the face of what I believe. In fact, with a good professor, this should happen often. It is part of a professor's job to challenge you, force you to reconsider, encourage you to entertain new ideas and the like.

2   My first year here, it bothered me. Some professors subtly endorsed certain ways of thinking over others without always justifying their biases. They offered opinions on issues beyond their academic expertise. Many showed partiality to the political left or right.

3   How should we react when a professor with a captive audience advances a perspective we find offensive, insulting or just ridiculous? Perhaps we would benefit from treating our professors, who often double as mentors and advisers, the same way that we're taught to approach great works of literature: With critical respect.

4   The truth is many faculty members are at the top of their fields. They read, write and teach for a living. We're generally talking about the most well-educated and well-read members of society. So when a professor has something to say about politics, religion, war or which movie should win the Academy Award, I think it's a good idea to take him seriously.

5   It certainly doesn't follow, though, that there's a direct relationship between what a professor says and what's true. In fact, there may be no relationship at all. While our professors generally are leading scholars, some are also biased and fallible. I don't mean this as an insult. Professors are human beings and, as such, carry with them a wide array of hang-ups and prejudices.

6   Interestingly enough—if not ironically—our professors often teach us how to deal with biased and opinionated scholars like themselves. When we read novels, journal articles, essays and textbooks for class, we're taught—or at least this has been my experience—to be critical. We're expected to sift through material and distinguish between what holds water and what doesn't, what is based on reasoned analysis and what is mere speculation.

7   If we treat our professors similarly it should no longer bother us when they use the classroom as their soapbox. They have important things to say and we're here to learn from them. I've come to appreciate professors' opinions on a variety of issues not directly related to the subject at hand, and I think it helps us build relationships with them. While it's unfair for a professor to assign high grades only to students who echo their view or to make others feel uncomfortable to disagree, I prefer that professors be honest about what they think.

8   While it's a disservice to our own education to be intimidated or too easily persuaded by academic clout, it's just as problematic, and frankly silly, to categorically reject what a professor has to say because we take issue with his ideology, political leanings, religious views or cultural biases.

9   It's become popular, particularly among conservatives responding to what they perceive as a liberal bias in academia, to criticize professors for espousing personal views in the classroom. The ideal, they argue, is to leave students ignorant to their instructors' beliefs.

10   First of all, I think there's a practical problem with this strategy. It's more difficult to be critical if we're unsure where our professors stand. For the same reason that it's often helpful to have background information about an author before analyzing his work, it's useful to see our professors' ideological cards on the table. For instance, if I know my professor loves hunting and believes everybody should have firearms in his basement then when I hear his interpretation of the Second Amendment, I'm better equipped to evaluate his thoughts.

11   Secondly, if we proscribe what views may or may not be expressed in the classroom, we limit our own access to potentially useful information. Even if most

of the extraneous digressions aren't worthy, every once in a while we might hear something that goes to the heart of an important issue. To limit this because we don't trust our own critical abilities is cowardly.

12   To return to the question I posed above: How should we respond to politically charged, opinionated, biased professors? I think we should listen.

Forming a First Impression

It is impossible to read an argument without having some kind of response to it. Let's not imagine that objectivity or neutrality is either possible or desirable. Start by being honest with yourself about what your first impression is.

◎◎ FOLLOWING THROUGH

After reading your argument, state your reaction simply and directly. Write it down in your notebook or a computer file reserved for this assignment. Read the selection again. Is your reaction changing? How? Why?

The first response of most of our students to Fryman was favorable. He offered practical advice, and more appealing yet, *safe* advice. You may have had an entirely different reaction. First reactions cannot be right or wrong, good or bad. They just are what they are. The important thing is that *you* know what your reaction is.

Stepping Back: Analyzing the Argument

Critiques require **critical distance** from first responses. "Critical distance" does not mean "forget your first response." On the contrary, first impressions often turn out to be sound. Critical distance does mean setting your first response aside for a while so that you can think the argument through carefully.

Use the questions in the Best Practices box to guide your analysis. It deals with parts of an argument that can be challenged. In contrast, there is nothing to be gained by challenging the following items:

- *Values everyone in our culture accepts.* For example, Fryman appeals to "creativity and critical thinking" (paragraph 1). Who can argue against these two values?

- *Statements of personal feelings.* For example, Fryman states that he was bothered at first by opinionated professors (paragraph 2). We can't say, "No you weren't."—or "You shouldn't have been." What would be the point?

- *Information only the author would know.* For example, if Fryman had mentioned something he read or heard that caused him to be more tolerant of bias in the classroom, we would just have to accept what he says.

- *Incidental facts whose accuracy is not important for the argument.* For example, if Fryman had referred to a particular class and professor, we

Concepts and Questions for Analyzing an Argument

1. *The claim or thesis.* Find the main point the writer wants you to believe and/or be persuaded to do. Sometimes the claim will be stated, sometimes implied. Ask, Is the claim clear and consistent? Is it absolute, no exceptions allowed? Assess the claim: Is it reasonable, desirable, practical?

2. *The reasons.* Find answers to the question, Why? That is, given the claim, what explains or justifies it? Like the claim, reasons will be stated or implied. Ask, Does each reason actually explain or justify the thesis? How convincing is the reason?

3. *The evidence.* Reasons will be supported or developed with something: more reasoning, examples, data, or expert opinion. Look at the evidence offered for each reason and ask, Does the evidence actually support the reason? How convincing is each piece of evidence, and how convincing is the evidence for each reason taken together?

4. *Key terms.* Often without defining them, writers use words that should be carefully pondered. When a claim is justified, for instance, as the right or moral thing to do, we need to ask what "right" or "moral" means in this case.

5. *Assumptions.* It is impossible to argue without assuming many things— and "assume" means "often not stated." Ask, What must I believe to accept that claim, or reason, or piece of evidence? Is the assumption "safe," something that any reasonable person would also assume?

6. *Implications.* Like assumptions, implications are usually not stated. To uncover them, ask, If I accept this statement, what follows from it? Are its implications acceptable or not?

7. *Analogies.* Many arguments use comparisons and some depend on them—on reasoning based on something being like something else. Look for analogies. Ask, Are the items compared close enough to permit reasoning by similarity? How important are the differences between the items compared?

would have to accept the information as factual. Even if his memory was faulty, it does not matter so far as assessing the argument is concerned.

Here are some illustrations of how the analytical concepts and questions apply to Fryman's argument:

1. *Thesis*

   Fryman: College students should listen to biased and opinionated professors with critical respect.

   Comment: Note that you have to piece together the thesis from several statements he makes. We can respond by saying, "What sort of opinions *merit* critical respect?"

2. *Reasons*

   Fryman: "Many faculty members are at the top of their fields."

   Comment: Clearly, this statement is a reason—it explains why the author thinks students should accord professors respect. We can respond by saying, "Yes, some professors are quite accomplished *in their fields*. But when they venture outside them, do their opinions count for more than any other relatively well-informed person's?"

3. *Evidence*

   Fryman: "Many [professors] showed partiality to the political left or right."

   Comment: In backing up one of his statements—that it bothered him at first when professors offered their opinions—he points to political bias as one of the irritating factors. We can respond by saying, "*Under what circumstances* would expression of political opinions be appropriate?"

4. *Key terms*

   Fryman: "hang-ups and prejudices"

   Comment: Fryman admits that professors have such things when he talks about the relationship between opinions and truth (paragraph 5). We can respond by saying, "What exactly is a 'hang-up,' and how do we distinguish it from a legitimate concern with something?" Or, "We *all* have 'prejudices.' When are they justified and therefore worth taking seriously?"

5. *Assumptions*

   Fryman: He assumes that there are no ethical constraints on what professors should talk about in class.

   Comment: We can respond by asking, "Shouldn't there be professional ethics at work here? What moral or ethical principles should govern what's discussed and under what conditions?"

6. *Implications*

   Fryman: He implies that students should tolerate whatever the professor dishes out.

   Comment: We can respond by saying, "How much student toleration is too much toleration? Suppose that a professor is openly sexist, for instance? Shouldn't we not only reject the opinions but also report the behavior to university authorities?"

7. *Analogies*

   Fryman: He compares the approach students should take to opinionated professors with the critical respect accorded great works of literature (paragraph 3).

   Comment: We can respond by saying, "Great works of literature have typically survived for years. We call them classics. Does it make sense to meet the casual opinions of professors the same way that we approach Shakespeare?"

FOLLOWING THROUGH

If you are working alone on an argument, use the seven questions in the Best Practices box. Record the results in your notebook, your computer file for this assignment, or online as a blog that presents the argument and your analysis of it.

If your class is working on the same argument, divide into small groups of about three or four people and do an analysis. Share what your group found with the class as a whole in discussion. •

Doing Research

Logical analysis focuses on *what an argument says*. The challenge of analysis is to discover what you can say back.

As important as analysis is, there is another way to explore an argument. Test what it says *against reality,* your experience with life and the world, what you know about the topic, and what you can find out from research.

The Art of Questioning: Inquiry into the Fit of Argument and Reality

The following questions should help you test the argument against reality:

1. What is my own experience with the topic or issue or problem the argument takes up?

   In the case of Fryman's argument, when have the comments of "biased teachers" been illuminating or helpful to you? When have they been boring, irritating, or useless? What's the difference between the two?

2. What relevant information do I have from reading or from some other source?

   Perhaps you have heard other students complain about professors pushing their political convictions on their students. What did they say? Did their complaints seem justified? Why or why not?

3. What could I find out from research that might be relevant to assessing the argument?

   Most arguments suggest opportunities for at least checking up on information relevant to the argument. For instance, you might investigate the idea of academic freedom. How does it apply to professors? How does it apply to students? (For detailed guidance on ways to research any topic, see Chapter 6, pages 97–115.)

4. If the argument reasons from data, in what other ways might the data be interpreted?

   Research will often lead you to other arguments that interpret the same or similar data differently or that supply additional data the argument you are critiquing did not know or ignored. For example, arguments for stronger border patrol enforcement sometimes fail to mention that about 40% of illegal immigrants got here legally and simply stayed. Enhanced border control obviously will have no effect on that group.

5. In what other contexts might the argument be placed?

All arguments state or assume a context within which what they say is valid or true. What other contexts might be relevant? For instance, using the Constitution as context, the Supreme Court has ruled that public flag-burning qualifies as free speech. You could reason based on some other context, such as the wisdom of burning a flag as a gesture of protest. Does it make a point or just make people mad?

◎◎ FOLLOWING THROUGH

In your notebook or computer file, sum up the results of applying the above questions. Highlight the best insight you gained. It could be a major point in your critique, perhaps even the central point around which you structure it. •

Preparing to Write

Thoughtful exploration of an argument—responding to what it says and pondering its fit with reality—results in much you *could* say. However, a critique is not a collection of comments or a list of criticisms. Rather it's *a coherent evaluation from a particular point of view,* your view. Consequently, in preparing to write, formulating your stance matters most.

Formulating Your Stance

Stances toward an argument range from total acceptance to total rejection, with many possibilities in between. You can reject an argument in general, but see value in a part of it. You can accept an argument in general, but with major reservations. The key question is, *What do you really think?*

Here are a few of the stances our students took on "Opening Your Ears to Biased Professors."

1. He focuses entirely on what *students* should do. He's one-sided. The key question is, What should professors do to deserve the critical respect Fryman says students should have?

2. He says students should listen with critical respect. Fine, but shouldn't we do more than that? If professors are free to give their opinions on just about anything in class, shouldn't students have at least the freedom to question the opinions offered?

3. Professors should limit their opinions to the subject matter of the course and topics they have special knowledge about. They shouldn't offer opinions on "politics, religion, war, or which movie should win the Academy Award" if these topics do not arise from the course's subject matter.

⊙⊙ FOLLOWING THROUGH

Using the examples above as models, write down your stance. If you are having difficulty, consider the following possibilities:

- *Return to your first impression.* Perhaps a revised version can be your stance.
- *Review the statements in the argument that you found open to question.* Is there a pattern in your criticisms? Or perhaps one statement stands out from the rest and seems central? Your stance may be implied in your most important criticism.
- *Do you detect one place where the reasoning breaks down?* Try fashioning your stance around the reasoning you think the author should have used to reach conclusions you favor.
- *Look for places where the author's view of reality or what is needed or desirable part company with yours.* Your stance may be implied in it.
- *Talk through possible stances with another student or your instructor.* Just talking helps, and sometimes a comment from someone else can help your stance emerge.

Sometimes you will discover your best stance only through writing a first draft. For now, try out the stance that appeals to you most. You can always revise and rewrite. •

Consider Your Reader, Purpose, and Tone

As you approach the first draft, review the key variables discussed earlier (page 47). In sum,

Reader. Most critiques address the same audience as the argument.

Purpose. A critique contributes to a conversation seeking the truth about a controversial issue or question. Connect your criticisms with the truth as you see it.

Tone. You want to sound engaged, fair, balanced, and respectful. Assert your criticisms firmly and forcefully.

⊙⊙ FOLLOWING THROUGH

Add notes about the key variables to your stance statement. Answer these questions: Do you intend to address the same readers that the argument does? Why or why not? How *exactly* does your version of the truth differ from the author's and how great is the difference? How friendly to the author do you want to sound? •

DRAFTING YOUR PAPER

As you write your paper, focus on organization and development. The following guidance should help.

Organization

Whether you write first drafts in chunks and then fit them together or write from a plan more or less in sequence, beginning to end, have the following organizational principles in mind:

Introduction

Begin by identifying the argument you are critiquing: who wrote it and for what group of readers, when and where it appeared, what it is about, and the position the author takes. Make your own stance clear and give it an emphatic position, near the end of your introduction.

Body

From everything you found questionable in the argument, select *only* what is relevant to your stance. No one expects a critique to deal with everything an argument says or everything that can be said about it.

Do not let the order of the argument determine the order of your critique. Order in relation to your stance and for maximum impact on your readers.

If you can say positive things, deal with these points first. Readers listen to the negative more willingly after hearing the positive.

Conclusion

Short critiques of short arguments do not need summarizing conclusions. Strive instead for a clincher, the memorable "parting shot" expressing the gist or main thrust of your response.

Development

For each part of your critique, you have many options for development. Here are some of them.

Introduction

Besides identifying the argument and taking your stance, you can also include material about context, background information, and a preview of your critique. A critique of Fryman, for instance, might deal with his argument in the context of efforts to restrict academic freedom; research about the author might reveal relevant background information, such as what was happening at Brandeis University when he wrote the article. Previews summarize the points you are going to make in the order in which you are going to discuss them.

Body

Take up one point at a time. Each point will challenge either the reasoning of the argument or its fit with reality. If the former, be sure to explain inconsistencies or contradictions fully, so that your reader understands exactly where and why the reasoning went wrong. See Hanson's critique (pages 44–46) for examples. If the latter, provide counter-evidence from personal experience, general knowledge, or research.

Conclusion

To clinch your critique, consider the following possibilities: a memorable quotation with a comment on it from you; a return to a key statement or piece of information in your introduction that you can now develop more fully; remind the reader of your strongest point with additional support or commentary.

REVISING YOUR DRAFT

Whenever time permits, it is best to get away from your draft for a day or two, come back to it fresh, assess it first yourself, and then seek input from others. The Best Practices checklist should help both you and the persons you consult in assessing the first draft.

Excerpts from a Sample Discovery Draft

The following excerpts come from student D. D. Solomon's draft in response to the Fryman argument.

Excerpt 1: Introduction

"Open Your Ears to Biased Professors," by David Fryman, deals with a common complaint among students: teachers who express their political or religious views in class. The article was published in *The Justice,* Brandeis University's student newspaper. In the article Fryman discusses how students should deal with a professor's opinion that differs from a student's own. By examining the situation from a student perspective, Fryman illuminates the implications and ramifications of professor bias. The author concludes that bias should be avoided, but if it isn't, students should deal with the situation by following several basic guidelines.

Excerpt 2: D. D.'s Critique

Although Fryman is right about how students should respond, he left out the obligations professors have. Fryman dealt with how teachers sometimes deviate from the topic at hand, and begin to speak of their own personal opinions on a topic. In my ethics class last year, my teacher told us she was a lesbian. In one of our discussions we spoke about gay rights, and whether or not marriage should be legal for homosexuals. She believed strongly in the right of homosexuals to marry. Some of the students, including myself, did not agree with her. Yet, when we tried to discuss our side of the issue, she cut us off. Fryman neglected to discuss such instances when a teacher's opinions infringe on the students' right to open debate.

Critique Revision Checklist

1. Look at all places where you have summarized or paraphrased the argument. Compare them against the text. Are they accurate? Do they capture the author's apparent intent as well as what she or he says?

2. Locate the argument's context—the existing view or views the author addressed. If the critique does not mention context, would it improve if it did? If so, where might a discussion of context work best?

3. Critiques are written either to the same readers the author attempted to reach or for readers with a stake in the argument the author left out. Where in the critique can you detect the writer appealing to readers? Compare the opening paragraphs with the ending ones. Is the reader conception consistent?

4. Critiques seek the truth about some controversial issue or question. What is the issue or question the argument addresses? Is it stated in the critique? Does the difference between the author's view of the truth and the view in the critique emerge clearly? If not, what could be done to make the difference sharper?

5. Underline the critique's stance. Is it stated explicitly and early in the essay? Examine each critical point. How does it develop, explain, or defend the stance? Consider cutting anything not related to the stance.

6. Check the flow of the critical points. Does each connect to the one before it and the one after? If not, consider rearranging the sequence. How might one point set up or lead to another better?

7. How does the critique sound? The tone should be thoughtfully engaged, fair, balanced, and respectful, but also confident and forceful. Look for places where the tone might make the wrong impression. Consider ways to improve it.

Fryman believed that professors should express their stands on controversial issues. When expressing his or her opinion, professors should not neglect to introduce all aspects of the issue at hand. Sometimes professors get caught up in their own view too much and fall into preaching, rather than sharing what they know with the class. Students should hear about other viewpoints so they can view many sides of the issue. The professor should offer his own position as an opinion, not as fact, and should encourage students to form their own opinions.

Fryman fails to deal with the negative impact when teachers stray from the subject matter of the course. His point that teachers should express their opinions is relevant only when related to the topic at hand. In my ethics class, the teacher was always returning to the issue of gay rights, even when the topic of discussion didn't relate to it. She wanted to convert students to her point of view more than teach us ethics.

Example Assessment: Sizing Up D. D.'s First Draft

D. D. felt that his first draft lacked punch and that the body of his critique did not unfold the way he wanted it to. Questions 4 and 5 in the revision checklist helped him see why he felt his paper lacked punch. Fryman sees biased professors as a fact that students must cope with as constructively as they can. For D. D. the professor–student relationship should be a two-way street. He did not bring out this fundamental difference well.

A student collaborator helped him see why his critical points did not flow as well as he wished. "What should come first," D. D.'s partner asked, "staying on topic or not ignoring student opinions?"

Finally, D. D.'s instructor helped him detect another problem, a place where he did not represent Fryman's position accurately. "The author concludes that bias should be avoided," D. D. claimed. "Does he?" his teacher asked, adding, "Where?" D. D. could not find it in the argument because Fryman does not say it.

D. D. had much to consider and a number of decisions to make. The revised draft appears below and on page 61.

Develop a Revision Strategy

Make a list of both your assessments of the draft and those of anyone who responded helpfully to it. Which criticisms seem valid or sound? Take these and plan your second draft. It can be a sentence or two, "I'll cut this, rearrange that, and add a point here," a full-blown outline, or something in between. *The important thing is to have a clear idea of what you plan to do and in what order.*

Before attempting your revision, read D. D.'s revised draft. It is a good example of what cutting, adding, and rearranging can do.

REVISED DRAFT: D. D. SOLOMON'S EVALUATION OF FRYMAN'S ARGUMENT

"How Professors Should Deal with Their Biases"

D. D. SOLOMON

1   "Open Your Ears to Biased Professors," by David Fryman, deals with a common complaint among students: teachers who express their political or religious views in class. Fryman believes that students should treat the personal opinions of professors with critical respect. I agree, but think that his view is one-sided and therefore not fully persuasive.

2   Because he is writing only to students, he has very little to say about how professors should conduct themselves. Fryman deals with the problem of bias as if only what students should do matters. Actually, professors have more responsibility.

They're older, more knowledgeable, and more experienced. I think if professors are going to express their political and religious views in class, they should do so in certain ways or not do it at all.

3   Fryman fails to consider professors who try to convert students to their own ideology. Because professors know so much, they can appear very appealing to students who have not encountered an issue before. By leaving out other interpretations, the professor assures that students hear only the teacher's side, which does not allow students to form their own conclusions. I saw this happen in a government class which discussed the 2008 Presidential election. Most of the class did not know much about politics, and therefore accepted the professor's view completely. They didn't have the critical capacity Fryman assumes all college students have. Certainly professors should challenge students, but what my government professor did was convert.

4   Sometimes professors get caught up in their own view too much and fall into preaching, rather than sharing all they know with the class. Students should hear about other viewpoints so they can view all sides of the issue. Furthermore, the professor should offer his own opinion as an opinion, not as a fact, and encourage students to form their own opinions.

5   Unfortunately, professors who want to convert students don't want students to form their own opinions but rather believe what the professor thinks. In my ethics class last year, my teacher told us she was a lesbian. In one of our discussions we spoke about gay rights, and whether or not marriage should be legal for homosexuals. She believed strongly in the right of homosexuals to marry. Some of the students, including me, did not agree with her. Yet, when we tried to discuss our side of the issue, she cut us off. Fryman neglects to discuss such instances when a teacher's opinions infringe on the students' right to open debate. I believe that if teachers can express their opinions openly in class, the students should be able to express theirs.

6   Finally, Fryman fails to deal with the negative impact when teachers stray from the subject matter of the course. In my ethics class, the teacher was always returning to the issue of gay rights, even when the topic of discussion didn't relate to it. She wanted to convert students to her point of view more than teach us ethics. Because she lacked restraint, the class spent too much class time on one issue.

7   I agree that professors should share their opinions with the class and students should listen and learn from them. But opinions must be distinguished from facts. Students should hear about other opinions besides the professor's. There should be open discussion, and students who have opinions different from the professor's should feel free to express them. Professors should stay on topic and not allow themselves to talk about just whatever happens to be on their mind. Most of all, education shouldn't be conversion. A professor is not a preacher and shouldn't take that role.

Responding to D. D.'s Revision Draft

It is remarkable how much a paper can improve if genuine effort goes into revising. Note especially in D. D.'s revised draft that

- He got his own view stated "up front," in the introduction, and sharply distinguished from Fryman's.

- He completely reorganized his key point, that education should not be a process of conversion.
- He pulled his whole view together well at the end.

Edit Your Paper

Edit your own draft to eliminate errors.

It is easy to overlook small-scale editing problems. Someone else's eyes and ears can be a big help. Exchange your edited paper with another student. Help each other find and correct any remaining errors.

Make a list of the editing problems. List words you misspelled. If you did not punctuate a sentence correctly, write the sentence down and circle or underline the correct mark of punctuation. Add to this list when you get the marked paper back from your instructor.

Always check your next paper for the problems listed first. In this way you can gradually reduce error. Continue this practice with everything you write. It will improve your grades and make you a better writer.

CHAPTER SUMMARY

For nearly everything people do, there is a natural way to go about it and an educated way. The natural way to approach disagreement is to "have at it" in a free-for-all kind of way. People want to be heard, but too often they do not want to listen; hardly anything receives careful thought or discussion. The natural way is open, democratic, often exciting, and even therapeutic. But too often the point of it all—finding the truth insofar as we can hope to discover it—gets lost.

The educated way of critique works by listening, taking in what other people say, and probing it through questions, testing it thoughtfully for both logical cogency and for its adequacy in coping with reality. It enables thought and discussion rather than merely an exchange of opinion.

CHAPTER 5

Reading and Writing about Visual Arguments

We live in a world awash in pictures. We turn on the TV and see not just performers, advertisers, and talking heads but also dramatic footage of events from around the world, commercials as visually creative as works of art, and video images to accompany popular music. We boot up our computers and surf the Net; many of the waves we ride are visual swells, enticing images created or enhanced by the very machines that take us out to sea. We drive our cars through a gallery of street art—on billboards and buildings and on the sides of buses and trucks. We go to malls and window-shop, entertained by the images of fantasy fulfillment each retailer offers. Print media are full of images; in our newspapers, for instance, photos, drawings, and computer graphics vie with print for space. Even college textbooks, once mostly blocks of uninterrupted prose with an occasional black-and-white drawing or photo, now often have colorful graphics and elaborate transparency overlays.

Like language, visual images are rhetorical. They persuade us in obvious and not-so-obvious ways. And so we need some perspective on visual rhetoric; we need to understand its power and how to use it effectively and responsibly.

UNDERSTANDING VISUAL ARGUMENTS

Visual rhetoric is *the use of images, sometimes coupled with sound or appeals to the other senses, to make an argument or persuade us to act as the image-maker would have us act.* Probably the clearest examples are advertisements and political cartoons, a few of which we will examine shortly. But visual rhetoric is everywhere. We do not ordinarily think, say, of a car's body style as "rhetoric," but clearly it is, because people are persuaded to pay tens of thousands of dollars for the sleekest new body style when they could spend a few thousand for an older car that would get them from home to work or school just as well.

"READING" IMAGES

Rhetorical analysis of visual rhetoric involves examining images to see how they attempt to convince or persuade an audience. Pictures are symbols that must be read, just as language is read. To read an argument made through images, a critic must be able to recognize allusions to popular culture. For example, Americans know that the white mustaches on the celebrities in the milk commercials refer to the way children drink milk; more recently, the milk mustache symbolizes the ad campaign itself, now part of our culture.

As with inquiry into any argument, we ought to begin with questions about rhetorical context: When was the visual argument created and by whom? To what audience was it originally aimed and with what purpose? Then we can ask what claim a visual argument makes and what reasons it offers in support of that claim. Finally, as with verbal texts that make a case, we can examine visual arguments for evidence, assumptions, and bias, and we can ask what values they favor and what the implications of accepting their argument are.

However, many visuals do not even attempt reasoning; they rely instead on emotional appeals. Such appeals are most obvious in advertising, where the aim is to move a target audience to buy a service or product. In many advertisements, especially for products like beer, cigarettes, and perfume, where the differences are subjective, emotional appeal is all there is. Most emotional appeals work by promising to reward our desires for love, status, peace of mind, or escape from everyday responsibilities.

Advertisements also use ethical appeals, associating their claim with values the audience approves of and wants to identify with—such as images that show nature being preserved, races living in harmony, families staying in touch, and people attaining the American dream of upward mobility.

In evaluating the ethics of visual rhetoric, we need to consider whether the argument is at least reasonable: Does the image demonstrate reasoning, or does it oversimplify and mislead? We will want to look at the emotional and ethical appeals to decide if they pander to audience weaknesses and prejudices or manipulate fantasies and fears.

Figure C-1

Figure C-6

Figure C-7

Figure C-8

ANALYSIS: FIVE COMMON TYPES OF VISUAL ARGUMENT

In this section, we analyze some visual arguments in various genres: advertisements, editorial cartoons, public sculpture, news photographs, and graphics. We show how "reading" visual texts requires interpretive skills and how interpretive skills, in turn, depend on cultural knowledge.

Advertisements

We begin with a classic ad for Charlie perfume from 1988 that created quite a stir when it first appeared (see Figure C-1 in the color section). As James B. Twitchell noted in his *Twenty Ads That Shook the World,* the shot of a woman giving a man an encouraging fanny pat "subverted sexism, turned it on its head, [and] used it against itself." At first the editors at the *New York Times* "refused to run the ad, saying it was in 'poor taste.'" But the ad proved irresistibly appealing when it appeared in women's magazines. Why did it work so well?

Twitchell argues that "Charlie is not just in charge, she is clearly enjoying dominance."

> She is taller than her partner. . . . Not only does he have part of his anatomy removed from the picture so that the Charlie bottle can be foregrounded, and not only does she have the jaunty scarf and the cascading hair of a free spirit, but she is delivering that most masculine of signifiers, the booty pat. . . . In football especially, the pat signifies comradeship . . . and is applied dominant to submissive. . . . The coach delivers it to a hulking [player] returning to the field of battle. . . . When Charlie bestows it on her gentleman friend . . . , she is harvesting a rich crop of meaning. The tide has turned, and now men are getting their butts slapped, by of all people, women. (170)

It is possible, of course, to read the pat in other ways—for example, as the kind of thing a dominant man might do to a subordinate woman at the office, inappropriate behavior now widely understood as sexual harassment. But no matter how you read it, there is no doubt that the ad tapped into the woman's movement at a time when women routinely endured sexism at work. No wonder that the ad was hugely popular.

The other ads in our color section work in different ways. Try your hand at analyzing their persuasive power.

QUESTIONS FOR DISCUSSION

1. Figure C-2 may look like a poster but it is actually a "semi-postal" stamp, so called because a percentage of its cost goes to the cause it advocates. This stamp has raised over $22 million for breast cancer research since it was issued in 1998. What are the sources of its appeal?

2. Figure C-3, from the Southampton Anti-Bias Task Force, depends for full impact on remembering a crayon labeled *flesh* that was the color of the

center crayon in the photo. People in their forties and fifties or older remember that crayon. What, then, is the ad's appeal for them? What does it say about skin color to younger people who do not remember the crayon?

3. Figure C-4 is a striking example of the power of photography and probably digital and other ways of enhancing photographs. How might women respond to it? How might men?

4. If Figure C-4 features the art of photography in selling a product through making it glamorous, C-5 is deliberately unglamorous, depicting women more as they are. How does it work to promote Dove products?

5. Figure C-6, the Adidas ad, ingeniously exploits how the eye can be fooled by what it *expects* to see rather than what is actually there. Did you see the shadow at first simply as the runner's shadow? What made you reevaluate what you were seeing? What's the impact of playing with perception in this case?

6. As a class project, find ads for the same product in magazines that appeal to different market segments, as defined by age, income, sex, ethnicity, and so on. Compare and contrast the ads to see how they are designed to appeal to their target audiences.

Editorial Cartoons

Editorial cartoons comment on events and issues in the news. They are funny but offer concise arguments too. Most political cartoons rely on captions and dialogue to make their argument, combining the visual and verbal. Consider the one by Mike Keefe (Figure 5.1) that comments on the impact of computers.

Figure 5.1

Mike Keefe, dePIXion Studios. Reprinted with permission.

The cartoon illustrates well how "reading" a visual argument depends on shared cultural knowledge. The image of a thirsty man crawling on hands and knees through a desert stands for anything important that humans lack. The cartoon depicts our common metaphor for the Internet, the "information superhighway," literally. The man has too much information and not enough wisdom. To read the argument of the cartoon and appreciate its humor, the viewer has to know about the overwhelming glut of information on the Internet, suggested by the size of the letters on the road. The cartoon "argues" that relying on the Internet will deprive a civilization of the wisdom to sustain a good life.

QUESTIONS FOR DISCUSSION

1. Cartoons probably are most persuasive when they satirize a familiar problem, as in the information superhighway example in Figure 5.1. A similar cartoon is Stuart Carlson's in Figure 5.3 (page 69). However, although most Americans struggle with the Net's information glut, fewer, but still a large percentage, drive gas-guzzling vehicles. If you do not, how do you react to Carlson's cartoon? Why do you react the way you do? If you drive a gas guzzler or would like to, is the cartoon still amusing? Why or why not?

2. Some cartoons are "factional," created by one side in a controversy to ridicule the position of the other side. Contrasting examples appear in Figure 5.2. Clearly, neither cartoon will persuade anyone whose position is held up to ridicule. Yet, factional cartoons are common. They must serve some purpose. How do you think they work?

3. Find a recent editorial cartoon on an issue prominent in the news. Bring it to class and be prepared to explain its persuasive tactics. Consider also the fairness of the cartoon. Does the cartoon minimize the complexity of the issue it addresses?

Public Sculpture

Public sculptures, such as war memorials, aim to teach an audience about a nation's past and to honor its values. An example that can be read as an argument is the Marine Corps Memorial, erected in 1954 on the Mall in Washington, D.C. (see Figure 5.4). It honors all Marines who have given their lives by depicting one specific act of bravery, the planting of the American flag on Iwo Jima, a Pacific island captured from the Japanese in 1945. The claim the sculpture makes is clear: Honor your country. The image of the soldiers straining every muscle gives the reason: These men made extreme sacrifices to preserve the values symbolized by this flag. The sculpture also communicates through details like the wind-whipped flag.

The Iwo Jima sculpture is traditional, glorifying victory on enemy soil. Compare it with the Vietnam War Memorial, dedicated in Washington, D.C., in November 1982. Maya Lin designed what we now call "the Wall" while

Figure 5.2

Jim McCloskey, *The News Leader*, Staunton, Virginia. Reprinted by permission.

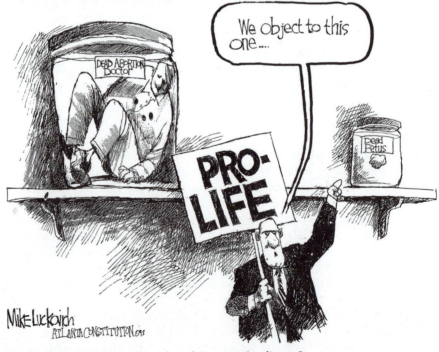

By permission of Mike Luckovich and Creators Syndicate, Inc.

Figure 5.3

Figure 5.4

Figure 5.5

Figure 5.6

an undergraduate student at Yale. Her design was controversial because it was so unconventional (see Figures 5.5 and 5.6, page 70) and antiwar. Its black granite slates are etched with the names of war dead; it honors individuals who died in a war that tore the nation apart.

QUESTIONS FOR DISCUSSION

1. Because it does not portray a realistic scene as the Iwo Jima Memorial does, the Wall invites interpretation and analysis. If you have visited it, try to recall your reaction. What details led to your interpretation? Could you characterize the Wall as having logical, ethical, and emotional appeals?

2. Find public sculpture or monuments to visit and analyze. Alone or with some classmates, take notes and photographs. Then develop your interpretation of the sculpture's argument, specifying how visual details contribute to the case, and present your analysis to the class. Compare your interpretation with those of your classmates.

News Photographs

While some news photographs may seem merely to record an event, the camera is not objective. The photographer makes many decisions—whether to snap a picture, when to snap it, what to include and exclude from the image—and decisions about light, depth of field, and so on. Figure 5.7 (page 72), a photograph that appeared in the *New York Times,* shows a scene photographer Bruce Young encountered while covering a snowstorm that hit Washington, D.C. in January 1994. The storm was severe enough to shut down the city and most government offices. Without the caption supplied by the *New York Times,* readers might not recognize the objects in the foreground as human beings, homeless people huddled on benches, covered by undisturbed snow.

The picture depicts homelessness in America as a national disgrace. The White House in the background is our nation's "home," a grand and lavishly decorated residence symbolic of national wealth. In the foreground, the homeless people look like bags of garbage, marring the picture of the snow-covered landscape. No blame attaches to the homeless for their condition; they are too pathetic under their blankets of snow. The picture shows the homeless as a fact of life in our cities, challenging the idealized image of our nation.

QUESTIONS FOR DISCUSSION

1. Figure C-7 in the color section depicts the family of Sgt. Jose M. Velez standing over his casket. Sgt. Velez was killed in Iraq. Any thoughtful response to such a photo has to be complex. How would you describe your response? To what extent is your view of the war in Iraq relevant?

Figure 5.7

2. Figure C-8 is a shot of the Tour de France, the annual bicycling race that Lance Armstrong made almost as big an event in the United States as it is in Europe. What impression does the photo convey? What details in the photo convey the impression?

3. The news photos in Figure 5.8 show events of humanitarian concern: U.S. Army personnel helping earthquake victims in Haiti, and refugees in Chad fleeing from Arab militias as a result of civil war in that African country. What details make the photographs effective in arousing viewers' interest and sympathy for the victims of such events? What do such photos add to news stories?

4. In a recent newspaper or news magazine, look for photos you think are effective when combined with a story about a controversial issue. What perspective or point of view do the pictures represent? How do you read their composition, including camera angle, light conditions, foreground and background, and so on?

www.mhhe.com/**crusius** To find more photographs to analyze, check out:

Writing > Visual Rhetoric Tutorial > Catalyst Image Bank

Figure 5.8

Graphics

Visual supplements to a longer text such as an essay, article, or manual are known as **graphics.** Most graphics fall into one of the following categories:

Tables and charts (typically an arrangement of data in columns and rows that summarizes the results of research)

www.mhhe.com/**crusius**

If you want information on using PowerPoint to create graphics, go to

Writing > PowerPoint Tutorial

Graphs (including bar, line, and pie graphs)

Photographs

Drawings (including maps and cartoons)

Although charts and tables are not images, they present data in visual form. Tables display information economically in one place so that readers can assess it as they read and find it easily afterward if they want to refer to it again. Consider Figure 5.9, which combines a table with bar graphs. It comes from a study of poverty in the United States. Note how much information is packed into this single visual and how easy it is to read, moving top to bottom and left to right through the categories. Consider how many long and boring paragraphs it would take to say the same thing in prose.

Graphs are usually no more than tables transformed into visuals we can interpret more easily. Bar graphs are best at showing comparisons at some single point in time. In contrast, line graphs reveal trends—for example, the performance of the stock market. Pie graphs highlight relative proportions well. When newspapers want to show us how the federal budget is spent, for example, they typically use pie graphs with the pieces labeled in some way to represent categories such as national defense, welfare, and entitlement programs. What gets the biggest pieces of the pie becomes *instantly clear* and *easy to remember*—the two major purposes of all graphs. Graphs do not make arguments, but they deliver evidence powerfully.

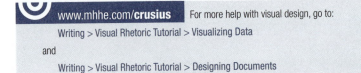

www.mhhe.com/**crusius**   For more help with visual design, go to:

Writing > Visual Rhetoric Tutorial > Visualizing Data

and

Writing > Visual Rhetoric Tutorial > Designing Documents

As graphics, photographs represent people, objects, and scenes realistically. For instance, owner's manuals for cars often have a shot of the engine compartment that shows where fluid reservoirs are located. Clearly, such photos serve highly practical purposes, such as helping us locate the dipstick. But they're also used, for example, in biographies; we get a better sense of, say, Abraham Lincoln's life and times when pictures of him, his family, his home, and so on are included. But photographs can do much more than inform. They can be highly dramatic and powerfully emotional in ways that only the best writers can manage with prose. Photos are often potent persuaders.

Photographs, however, are not analytical—by their nature, they give us the surface, only what the camera can "see." A different type of graphic, the drawing, is preferable when we want to depict how something is put together or structured. For instance, instructions for assembling and installing a ceiling

Figure 5.9

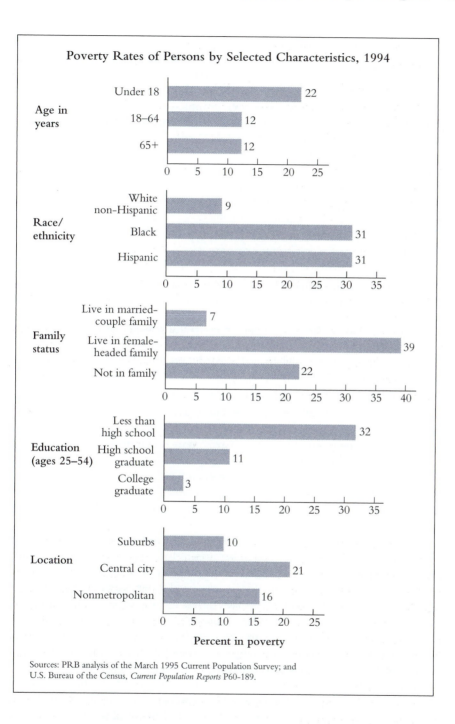

Poverty Rates of Persons by Selected Characteristics, 1994

Sources: PRB analysis of the March 1995 Current Population Survey; and U.S. Bureau of the Census, *Current Population Reports* P60-189.

fan or a light fixture usually have many diagrams—a large one showing how all the parts fit together and smaller ones that depict steps in the process in more detail. Corporate publications often include diagrams of the company's organizational hierarchy. Scientific articles and textbooks are full of drawings or illustrations created with computer graphics; science writers want us to understand structures, particularly internal structures, impossible to capture on film. For example, our sense of DNA's double-helical structure comes entirely from diagrams.

The following article illustrates how a variety of graphics can contribute to the effectiveness of a written text.

The Rise of Renewable Energy

DANIEL M. KAMMEN

This article appeared in the September 2006 issue of *Scientific American*. Daniel Kammen is Distinguished Professor of Energy at the University of California, Berkeley, where he founded and directs the Renewable and Appropriate Energy Laboratory.

Renewable energy refers to any source of power that does not depend on the limited supply of fossil fuels, such as oil or coal, and produces relatively little or none of the greenhouse gases that contribute significantly to global warming. There are many renewable energy sources. Kammen discusses the potential of solar power, wind power, and biofuels such as ethanol.

1   No plan to substantially reduce greenhouse gas emissions can succeed through increases in energy efficiency alone. Because economic growth continues to boost the demand for energy—more coal for powering new factories, more oil for fueling new cars, more natural gas for heating new homes—carbon emissions will keep climbing despite the introduction of more energy-efficient vehicles, buildings and appliances. To counter the alarming trend of global warming, the U.S. and other countries must make a major commitment to developing renewable energy sources that generate little or no carbon.

2   Renewable energy technologies were suddenly and briefly fashionable three decades ago in response to the oil embargoes of the 1970s, but the interest and support were not sustained. In recent years, however, dramatic improvements in the performance and affordability of solar cells, wind turbines and biofuels—ethanol and other fuels derived from plants—have paved the way for mass commercialization. In addition to their environmental benefits, renewable sources promise to enhance America's energy security by reducing the country's reliance on fossil fuels from other nations. What is more, high and wildly fluctuating prices for oil and natural gas have made renewable alternatives more appealing.

3   We are now in an era where the opportunities for renewable energy are unprecedented, making this the ideal time to advance clean power for decades to come. But the endeavor will require a long-term investment of scientific, economic and political resources. Policymakers and ordinary citizens must demand action and challenge one another to hasten the transition.

LET THE SUN SHINE

4   Solar cells, also known as photovoltaics, use semiconductor materials to convert sunlight into electric current. They now provide just a tiny slice of the world's electricity: their global generating capacity of 5,000 megawatts (MW) is only 0.15 percent of the total generating capacity from all sources. Yet sunlight could potentially supply 5,000 times as much energy as the world currently consumes. And thanks to technology improvements, cost declines and favorable policies in many states and nations, the annual production of photovoltaics has increased by more than 25 percent a year for the past decade and by a remarkable 45 percent in 2005. The cells manufactured last year added 1,727 MW to worldwide generating capacity, with 833 MW made in Japan, 353 MW in Germany and 153 MW in the U.S.

5   Solar cells can now be made from a range of materials, from the traditional multicrystalline silicon wafers that still dominate the market to thin-film silicon cells and devices composed of plastic or organic semiconductors. Thin-film photovoltaics are cheaper to produce than crystalline silicon cells but are also less efficient at turning light into power. In laboratory tests, crystalline cells have achieved efficiencies of 30 percent or more; current commercial cells of this type range from 15 to 20 percent. Both laboratory and commercial efficiencies for all kinds of solar cells have risen steadily in recent years, indicating that an expansion of research efforts would further enhance the performance of solar cells on the market.

6   Solar photovoltaics are particularly easy to use because they can be installed in so many places—on the roofs or walls of homes and office buildings, in vast arrays in the desert, even sewn into clothing to power portable electronic devices. The state of California has joined Japan and Germany in leading a global push for solar installations; the "Million Solar Roof" commitment is intended to create 3,000 MW of new generating capacity in the state by 2018. Studies done by my research group, the Renewable and Appropriate Energy Laboratory at the University of California, Berkeley, show that annual production of solar photovoltaics in the U.S. alone could grow to 10,000 MW in just 20 years if current trends continue.

7   The biggest challenge will be lowering the price of the photovoltaics, which are now relatively expensive to manufacture. Electricity produced by crystalline cells has a total cost of 20 to 25 cents per kilowatt-hour, compared with four to six cents for coal-fired electricity, five to seven cents for power produced by burning natural gas, and six to nine cents for biomass power plants. (The cost of nuclear power is harder to pin down because experts disagree on which expenses to include in the analysis; the estimated range is two to 12 cents per kilowatt-hour.) Fortunately, the prices of solar cells have fallen consistently over the past decade, largely because of improvements in manufacturing processes. In Japan, where 290 MW of solar generating capacity were added in 2005 and an even larger amount was exported, the cost of photovoltaics has declined 8 percent a year; in California, where 50 MW of solar power were installed in 2005, costs have dropped 5 percent annually.

8   Surprisingly, Kenya is the global leader in the number of solar power systems installed per capita (but not the number of watts added). More than 30,000 very small solar panels, each producing only 12 to 30 watts, are sold in that country

A world of clean energy could rely on wind turbines and solar cells to generate its electricity and biofuels derived from switchgrass and other plants to power its vehicles.

KENN BROWN

annually. For an investment of as little as $100 for the panel and wiring, the system can be used to charge a car battery, which can then provide enough power to run a fluorescent lamp or a small black-and-white television for a few hours a day. More Kenyans adopt solar power every year than make connections to the country's electric grid. The panels typically use solar cells made of amorphous silicon; although these photovoltaics are only half as efficient as crystalline cells, their cost is so much lower (by a factor of at least four) that they are more affordable and useful for the two billion people worldwide who currently have no access to electricity. Sales of small solar power systems are booming in other African nations as well, and advances in low-cost photovoltaic manufacturing could accelerate this trend.

9   Furthermore, photovoltaics are not the only fast-growing form of solar power. Solar-thermal systems, which collect sunlight to generate heat, are also undergoing a resurgence. These systems have long been used to provide hot water for homes or factories, but they can also produce electricity without the need for expensive

solar cells. In one design, for example, mirrors focus light on a Stirling engine, a high-efficiency device containing a working fluid that circulates between hot and cold chambers. The fluid expands as the sunlight heats it, pushing a piston that, in turn, drives a turbine.

10   In the fall of 2005 a Phoenix company called Stirling Energy Systems announced that it was planning to build two large solar-thermal power plants in southern California. The company signed a 20-year power purchase agreement with Southern California Edison, which will buy the electricity from a 500-MW solar plant to be constructed in the Mojave Desert. Stretching across 4,500 acres, the facility will include 20,000 curved dish mirrors, each concentrating light on a Stirling engine about the size of an oil barrel. The plant is expected to begin operating in 2009 and could later be expanded to 850 MW. Stirling Energy Systems also signed a 20-year contract with San Diego Gas & Electric to build a 300-MW, 12,000-dish plant in the Imperial Valley. This facility could eventually be upgraded to 900 MW.

GROWING FAST, BUT STILL A SLIVER

Solar cells, wind power and biofuels are rapidly gaining traction in the energy markets, but they remain marginal providers compared with fossil-fuel sources such as coal, natural gas and oil.

THE RENEWABLE BOOM

Since 2000 the commercialization of renewable energy sources has accelerated dramatically. The annual global production of solar cells, also known as photovoltaics, jumped 45 percent in 2005. The construction of new wind farms, particularly in Europe, has boosted the worldwide generating capacity of wind power 10-fold over the past decade. And the production of ethanol, the most common biofuel, soared to 36.5 billion liters last year, with the lion's share distilled from American-grown corn.

Photovoltaic Production

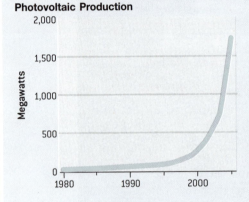

Wind Energy Generating Capacity

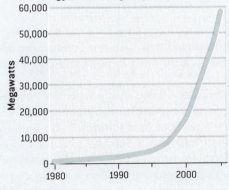

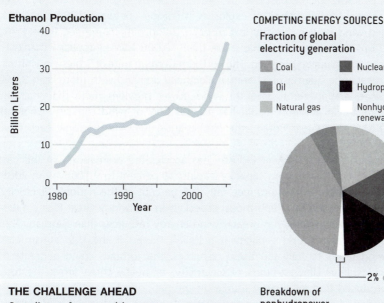

THE CHALLENGE AHEAD

Suppliers of renewable energy must overcome several technological, economic and political hurdles to rival the market share of the fossil-fuel providers. To compete with coal-fired power plants, for example, the prices of solar cells must continue to fall. The developers of wind farms must tackle environmental concerns and local opposition. Other promising renewable sources include generators driven by steam from geothermal vents and biomass power plants fueled by wood and agricultural wastes.

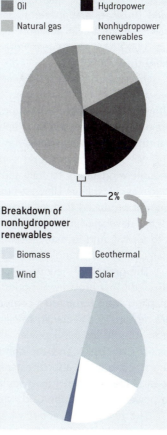

11   The financial details of the two California projects have not been made public, but electricity produced by present solar-thermal technologies costs between five and 13 cents per kilowatt-hour, with dish-mirror systems at the upper end of that range. Because the projects involve highly reliable technologies and mass production, however, the generation expenses are expected to ultimately drop closer to four to six cents per kilowatt-hour—that is, competitive with the current price of coal-fired power.

BLOWING IN THE WIND

12   Wind power has been growing at a pace rivaling that of the solar industry. The worldwide generating capacity of wind turbines has increased more than 25 percent

a year, on average, for the past decade, reaching nearly 60,000 MW in 2005. The growth has been nothing short of explosive in Europe—between 1994 and 2005, the installed wind power capacity in European Union nations jumped from 1,700 to 40,000 MW. Germany alone has more than 18,000 MW of capacity thanks to an aggressive construction program. The northern German state of Schleswig-Holstein currently meets one quarter of its annual electricity demand with more than 2,400 wind turbines, and in certain months wind power provides more than half the state's electricity. In addition, Spain has 10,000 MW of wind capacity, Denmark has 3,000 MW, and Great Britain, the Netherlands, Italy and Portugal each have more than 1,000 MW.

13   In the U.S. the wind power industry has accelerated dramatically in the past five years, with total generating capacity leaping 36 percent to 9,100 MW in 2005. Although wind turbines now produce only 0.5 percent of the nation's electricity, the potential for expansion is enormous, especially in the windy Great Plains states. (North Dakota, for example, has greater wind energy resources than Germany, but only 98 MW of generating capacity is installed there.) If the U.S. constructed enough wind farms to fully tap these resources, the turbines could generate as much as 11 trillion kilowatt-hours of electricity, or nearly three times the total amount produced from all energy sources in the nation last year. The wind industry has developed increasingly large and efficient turbines, each capable of yielding 4 to 6 MW. And in many locations, wind power is the cheapest form of new electricity, with costs ranging from four to seven cents per kilowatt-hour.

14   The growth of new wind farms in the U.S. has been spurred by a production tax credit that provides a modest subsidy equivalent to 1.9 cents per kilowatt-hour, enabling wind turbines to compete with coal-fired plants. Unfortunately, Congress has repeatedly threatened to eliminate the tax credit. Instead of instituting a long-term subsidy for wind power, the lawmakers have extended the tax credit on a year-to-year basis, and the continual uncertainty has slowed investment in wind farms. Congress is also threatening to derail a proposed 130-turbine farm off the coast of Massachusetts that would provide 468 MW of generating capacity, enough to power most of Cape Cod, Martha's Vineyard and Nantucket.

15   The reservations about wind power come partly from utility companies that are reluctant to embrace the new technology and partly from so-called NIMBY-ism. ("NIMBY" is an acronym for Not in My Backyard.) Although local concerns over how wind turbines will affect landscape views may have some merit, they must be balanced against the social costs of the alternatives. Because society's energy needs are growing relentlessly, rejecting wind farms often means requiring the construction or expansion of fossil fuel–burning power plants that will have far more devastating environmental effects.

GREEN FUELS

16   Researchers are also pressing ahead with the development of biofuels that could replace at least a portion of the oil currently consumed by motor vehicles. The most common biofuel by far in the U.S. is ethanol, which is typically made from corn and blended with gasoline. The manufacturers of ethanol benefit from a

substantial tax credit: with the help of the $2-billion annual subsidy, they sold more than 16 billion liters of ethanol in 2005 (almost 3 percent of all automobile fuel by volume), and production is expected to rise 50 percent by 2007. Some policy-makers have questioned the wisdom of the subsidy, pointing to studies showing that it takes more energy to harvest the corn and refine the ethanol than the fuel can deliver to combustion engines. In a recent analysis, though, my colleagues and I discovered that some of these studies did not properly account for the energy content of the by-products manufactured along with the ethanol. When all the inputs and outputs were correctly factored in, we found that ethanol has a positive net energy of almost five megajoules per liter.

17   We also found, however, that ethanol's impact on greenhouse gas emissions is more ambiguous. Our best estimates indicate that substituting corn-based etha-nol for gasoline reduces greenhouse gas emissions by 18 percent, but the analysis is hampered by large uncertainties regarding certain agricultural practices, particu-larly the environmental costs of fertilizers. If we use different assumptions about these practices, the results of switching to ethanol range from a 36 percent drop in emissions to a 29 percent increase. Although corn-based ethanol may help the U.S. reduce its reliance on foreign oil, it will probably not do much to slow global warming unless the production of the biofuel becomes cleaner.

18   But the calculations change substantially when the ethanol is made from cel-lulosic sources: woody plants such as switchgrass or poplar. Whereas most makers of corn-based ethanol burn fossil fuels to provide the heat for fermentation, the

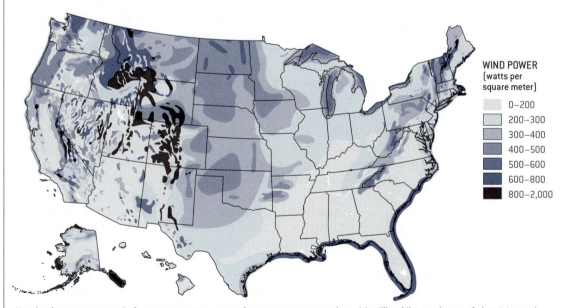

America has enormous wind energy resources, enough to generate as much as 11 trillion kilowatt-hours of electricity each year. Some of the best locations for wind turbines are the Great Plains states, the Great Lakes and the mountain ridges of the Rockies and the Appalachians.

producers of cellulosic ethanol burn lignin—an unfermentable part of the organic material—to heat the plant sugars. Burning lignin does not add any greenhouse gases to the atmosphere, because the emissions are offset by the carbon dioxide absorbed during the growth of the plants used to make the ethanol. As a result, substituting cellulosic ethanol for gasoline can slash greenhouse gas emissions by 90 percent or more.

19   Another promising biofuel is so-called green diesel. Researchers have produced this fuel by first gasifying biomass—heating organic materials enough that they release hydrogen and carbon monoxide—and then converting these compounds into long-chain hydrocarbons using the Fischer-Tropsch process. (During World War II, German engineers employed these chemical reactions to make synthetic motor fuels out of coal.) The result would be an economically competitive liquid fuel for motor vehicles that would add virtually no greenhouse gases to the atmosphere. Oil giant Royal Dutch/Shell is currently investigating the technology.

THE NEED FOR R&D

20   Each of these renewable sources is now at or near a tipping point, the crucial stage when investment and innovation, as well as market access, could enable these attractive but generally marginal providers to become major contributors to regional and global energy supplies. At the same time, aggressive policies designed to open markets for renewables are taking hold at city, state and federal levels around the world. Governments have adopted these policies for a wide variety of reasons: to promote market diversity or energy security, to bolster industries and jobs, and to protect the environment on both the local and global scales. In the U.S. more than 20 states have adopted standards setting a minimum for the fraction of electricity that must be supplied with renewable sources. Germany plans to generate 20 percent of its electricity from renewables by 2020, and Sweden intends to give up fossil fuels entirely.

21   Even President George W. Bush said, in his now famous State of the Union address this past January, that the U.S. is "addicted to oil." And although Bush did not make the link to global warming, nearly all scientists agree that humanity's addiction to fossil fuels is disrupting the earth's climate. The time for action is now, and at last the tools exist to alter energy production and consumption in ways that simultaneously benefit the economy and the environment. Over the past 25 years, however, the public and private funding of research and development in the energy sector has withered. Between 1980 and 2005 the fraction of all U.S. R&D spending devoted to energy declined from 10 to 2 percent. Annual public R&D funding for energy sank from $8 billion to $3 billion (in 2002 dollars); private R&D plummeted from $4 billion to $1 billion (see box, "R&D Is key").

22   To put these declines in perspective, consider that in the early 1980s energy companies were investing more in R&D than were drug companies, whereas today investment by energy firms is an order of magnitude lower. Total private R&D funding for the entire energy sector is less than that of a single large biotech company. (Amgen, for example, had R&D expenses of $2.3 billion in 2005.) And as R&D spending dwindles, so does innovation. For instance, as R&D funding for photovoltaics and wind

power has slipped over the past quarter of a century, the number of successful patent applications in these fields has fallen accordingly. The lack of attention to long-term research and planning has significantly weakened our nation's ability to respond to the challenges of climate change and disruptions in energy supplies.

23   Calls for major new commitments to energy R&D have become common. A 1997 study by the President's Committee of Advisors on Science and Technology and a 2004 report by the bipartisan National Commission on Energy Policy both recommended that the federal government double its R&D spending on energy. But would such an expansion be enough? Probably not. Based on assessments of the cost to stabilize the amount of carbon dioxide in the atmosphere and other studies that estimate the success of energy R&D programs and the resulting savings from the technologies that would emerge, my research group has calculated that public funding of $15 billion to $30 billion a year would be required—a fivefold to 10-fold increase over current levels.

24   Greg F. Nemet, a doctoral student in my laboratory, and I found that an increase of this magnitude would be roughly comparable to those that occurred during previous federal R&D initiatives such as the Manhattan Project and the Apollo program, each of which produced demonstrable economic benefits in addition to meeting its objectives. American energy companies could also boost their R&D spending by a factor of 10, and it would still be below the average for U.S. industry overall. Although government funding is essential to supporting early-stage technologies, private-sector R&D is the key to winnowing the best ideas and reducing the barriers to commercialization.

25   Raising R&D spending, though, is not the only way to make clean energy a national priority. Educators at all grade levels, from kindergarten to college, can stimulate public interest and activism by teaching how energy use and production affect the social and natural environment. Nonprofit organizations can establish a series of contests that would reward the first company or private group to achieve a challenging and worthwhile energy goal, such as constructing a building or appliance that can generate its own power or developing a commercial vehicle that can go 200 miles on a single gallon of fuel. The contests could be modeled after the Ashoka awards for pioneers in public policy and the Ansari X Prize for the developers of space vehicles. Scientists and entrepreneurs should also focus on finding clean, affordable ways to meet the energy needs of people in the developing world. My colleagues and I, for instance, recently detailed the environmental benefits of improving cooking stoves in Africa.

26   But perhaps the most important step toward creating a sustainable energy economy is to institute market-based schemes to make the prices of carbon fuels reflect their social cost. The use of coal, oil and natural gas imposes a huge collective toll on society, in the form of health care expenditures for ailments caused by air pollution, military spending to secure oil supplies, environmental damage from mining operations, and the potentially devastating economic impacts of global warming. A fee on carbon emissions would provide a simple, logical and transparent method to reward renewable, clean energy sources over those that harm the economy and the environment. The tax revenues could pay for some of the social

R&D IS KEY

Spending on research and development in the U.S. energy sector has fallen steadily since its peak in 1980. Studies of patent activity suggest that the drop in funding has slowed the development of renewable energy technologies. For example, the number of successful patent applications in photovoltaics and wind power has plummeted as R&D spending in these fields has declined.

U.S. R&D SPENDING IN THE ENERGY SECTOR

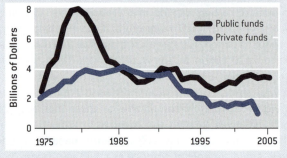

LAGGING INNOVATION IN PHOTOVOLTAICS . . .

. . . AND IN WIND POWER

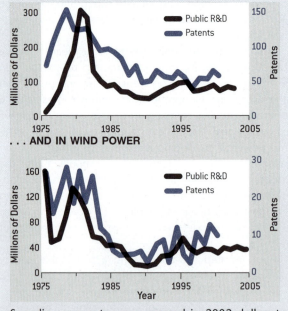

Spending amounts are expressed in 2002 dollars to adjust for inflation.

costs of carbon emissions, and a portion could be designated to compensate low-income families who spend a larger share of their income on energy. Furthermore, the carbon fee could be combined with a cap-and-trade program that would set limits on carbon emissions but also allow the cleanest energy suppliers to sell permits to their dirtier competitors. The federal government has used such programs with great success to curb other pollutants, and several northeastern states are already experimenting with greenhouse gas emissions trading.

27   Best of all, these steps would give energy companies an enormous financial incentive to advance the development and commercialization of renewable energy sources. In essence, the U.S. has the opportunity to foster an entirely new industry. The threat of climate change can be a rallying cry for a clean-technology revolution that would strengthen the country's manufacturing base, create thousands of jobs and alleviate our international trade deficits—instead of importing foreign oil, we can export high-efficiency vehicles, appliances, wind turbines and photovoltaics. This transformation can turn the nation's energy sector into something that was once deemed impossible: a vibrant, environmentally sustainable engine of growth.

Understanding Kammen's Graphics

The article certainly informs, and the graphics present information economically, clearly, and memorably. However, Kammen's central purpose is to convince us that renewable energy has enormous potential and needs significantly more public attention, research investment, and commercial development than it is currently getting. "Let's commit ourselves to renewable energy" is its central message, and so this apparently informative article is actually an argument. The graphics, therefore, function mainly as evidence to back up Kammen's main contentions. Let's examine the first two and reserve the others for your own analysis.

The opening drawing, an example of what's called an "artist's conception," depicts a green world, powered entirely by renewables, where agriculture and city exist side by side. The combine in the field runs on electricity generated by huge solar panels, perhaps using biofuels on days without sun, while wind (note the turbines in the background) and sun (note the solar panels on the roof of the houses in the right foreground) work together to provide all the power needed by the city. In the original color drawing, the sky is deep blue merging into purple, suggesting lack of pollution, and the fields are various shades of green and gold, with obvious implications.

"Why an artist's conception?" you might ask. The obvious answer, of course, is no such communities exist today to photograph. The article needs a way to stimulate our imagination, to help us envision a world that could be, where energy is cheap, abundant, inexhaustible, and, most of all, clean. Caught as we are in a world that burns oil, natural gas, and coal to supply nearly all energy, we have trouble conceiving a world powered by renewables. Anything we cannot conceive, we cannot aspire to—hence the importance of establishing this vision of the future.

The drawing, then, is persuasive: "Just imagine the possibilities" is the message. The box titled "Growing Fast . . ." (pages 80–81), in contrast, gives us the facts. Solar, wind, and ethanol production are all sharply up worldwide, as the three line graphs show, but the top pie graph puts the upswing in perspective—only a tiny sliver, 2%, of the world's power comes currently from renewables. The pie graph on the bottom depicts the relative proportions of green energy in use, showing us, among other things, that the enormous potential of wind and solar power has yet to be aggressively exploited. Finally, the prose combined with the visuals summarizes knowledge that the graphs and photos could not supply, making the box a fine example of combining visuals with words.

The "Growing Fast . . ." box packs a lot of information into an attractive space; it would take many pages to describe it in prose, boring pages of data that would not have half the impact of the graphics. That is part of why it is persuasive—we can see the big picture without trudging through many pages of text. But to appreciate its full persuasive power, the implications of the box and the opening drawing must be combined. The drawing seems almost futuristic, as if we will wait a long time to see anything like it, whereas the box shows us that it is all tantalizingly within reach. We just have to do more with what we have. And so, in sum, the message is simple and upbeat: "We can do it."

QUESTIONS FOR DISCUSSION

1. Graphics, we must always remember, *supplement* texts. Reread the section "Blowing in the Wind," an allusion to a famous song by Bob Dylan, and then examine the map of the United States (page 83), which depicts the 11 trillion kilowatt-hours of wind energy that could be generated in the United States each year. What do text and graphic working together "say"?

2. We see what could happen in the map—wind power harnessed to full potential. And so we ask, Why not? The box "R&D Is Key" (page 86) tells us what the main problem is—not nearly enough R&D. The problem is not putting enough money in research and scientific innovation. We are not going to get there if we don't. Work backwards from this box: How do all the graphics link to one another to answer closely related questions? How much of Kammen's case for renewables is made in the graphics? If we had only the text without the graphics, how much persuasive power would be lost?

3. To see the potential for adding graphics in your own writing, bring a recent paper you wrote to class. If you did not use graphics, consider whether the paper can be improved with graphic support. If so, given your audience and purposes, what graphic types would you use and why? If you did use graphics, be prepared to discuss them—what you did and why, and how you went about securing or creating the visuals. If you now see ways to improve them, discuss what you would do as well.

WRITING ASSIGNMENTS

Assignment 1: Analyzing an Advertisement or Editorial Cartoon

Choose an ad or cartoon from a current magazine or newspaper. First, inquire into its rhetorical context: What situation prompted its creation? What purpose does it aim to achieve? Where did it originally appear? Who is its intended audience? What would they know or believe about the product or issue? Then inquire into the argument being made. Consider the following points: What visual metaphors or allusions appear? What prior cultural knowledge and experiences would the audience need to "read" the image? Consider how the visual argument might limit the scope of the issue or how it might play to the audience's biases, stereotypes, or fears. After thorough inquiry, reach some conclusion about the effectiveness and ethics of your ad or cartoon. Write your conclusion as a thesis or claim. Use your analysis to convince, supporting it with evidence gathered during inquiry.

STUDENT SAMPLE   Analysis Of Visual Rhetoric

The following student essay is an example of Assignment 1. Before you begin your own essay, read it and discuss the conclusions reached about an advertisement for Eagle Brand condensed milk. We were unable to obtain permission to reprint the advertisement under discussion, but the descriptions of it should make the analysis easy to follow.

A Mother's Treat
Kelly Williams

1   Advertisements are effective only if they connect with their audiences. Advertisers study the group of people they hope to reach and know what the group values and what images they have of themselves. Often these images come from social expectations that tell businessmen, mothers, fathers, teens that they should look or act a certain way. Most people adhere to the norms because they give social status. Advertisers tend to look to these norms as a way to sell their products. For example, an ad depicts a man in an

expensive suit driving a luxury car, and readers assume he is a lawyer, physician, or business executive. Such people will buy this car because they associate it with the status they want to project. Likewise, some advertisements manipulate women with children by associating a product with the ideal maternal image.

2   An advertisement for Eagle Brand condensed milk typifies this effort. The advertisement appeared in magazines aimed at homemakers and in *People* magazine's "Best and Worst Dressed" issue of September 1998. The readers are predominantly young women; those with children may be second-income producers or single mothers. They are struggling to raise a family and have many demands on their time. They feel enormous pressure to fulfill ideal work and domestic roles.

3   The advertisement creates a strong connection with a maternal audience. The black-and-white photograph depicts a young girl about kindergarten age. The little girl's facial expression connotes hesitation and sadness. In the background is a school yard. Other children are walking toward the school, their heads facing down, creating a feeling of gloom. All readers will recognize the situation. The little girl is about to attend her first day of school. One could easily guess that she is looking back at her mother with a sense of abandonment, pleading for support.

4   The wording of the text adds some comic relief. The ad is not intended to make the readers sad. The words seem to come from the mind of the child's mother. "For not insisting on bunny slippers for shoes, for leaving Blankie behind, for actually getting out of the car. . . ." These words show that the mother is a good mother, very empathetic. Even the print type is part of the marketing strategy. It mimics a "proper" mother's handwriting. There are no sharp edges, implying softness and gentleness.

5   The intent is to persuade mothers that if they buy Eagle Brand milk and make the chocolate bar treat, they will be good mothers like the speaker in the ad. It tells women that cooking such treats helps alleviate stressful situations in everyday family life. The little girl reminds mothers of their duty to comfort their kids. She evokes the "feminine" qualities of compassion, empathy, and protectiveness.

6   The ad also suggests that good mothers reward good behavior. As the ad says, "It's time for a treat." But good mothers would also know that "Welcome Home Chocolate Bars" are rich, so this mother has to say, "I'll risk spoiling your dinner." The invisible mother in the ad is ideal because she does care about her child's nutrition, but more about the emotional state of her child.

7   In many ways this ad is unethical. While the ad looks harmless and cute, it actually reinforces social pressures on women to be "perfect" mothers. If you don't bake a treat to welcome your child back home after school, you are failing as a mother. The recipe includes preparation time, showing that the treat can be made with minimal effort. It gives mothers no excuse for not making it. Moreover, the advertisement obviously exploits children to sell their product.

8   Desserts do not have much nutritional value. It would be hard to make a logical case for Welcome Home Bars, so Eagle Brand appeals to emotion. There's nothing wrong with a treat once in a while, but it is wrong to use guilt and social pressure to persuade mothers to buy a product.

Assignment 2: Analyzing and Creating Posters or Flyers

As a class project, collect copies of posters or flyers you find around your campus. It is true that information in our culture is plentiful and cheap, but attention is at a premium. Creators of posters and flyers must compete not only with each other but with all other visual sources of information to catch and keep our attention. How well do the posters and flyers your class found work? Why do some catch and hold attention better than others?

Create a poster or flyer to publicize an event, an organization, a student government election, or anything else relevant to your campus life. Use the best posters and flyers you found as a model, but do not be reluctant to use color, type sizes, images, and so on in your own way.

Assignment 3: Using Visual Rhetoric to Promote Your School

Colleges and universities compete fiercely for students and are therefore as concerned about their image as any corporation or politician. As a class project, collect images your school uses to promote itself, including brochures for prospective students, catalogs, class lists, and Web home pages. Choose three or four of the best ones, and in class discussions analyze them. Then, working in groups of three or four students or individually, do one or all of the following:

1. Find an aspect of your college or university overlooked in the publications that you believe is a strong selling point. Employing photographs, drawings, paintings, or some other visual medium, create an image

appropriate for one of the school publications. Compose an appealing text to go with it. Then, in a page or two, explain why you think your promotional image would work well.

2. If someone in the class has the computer knowledge, create an alternative to your school's home page, or make changes that would make it more appealing to prospective students and their parents.

3. Imagine that for purposes of parody or protest you wanted to call attention to aspects of your school that the official images deliberately omit. Proceed as in item 1. In a short statement, explain why you chose the image you did and what purpose(s) you want it to serve.

4. Select a school organization (a fraternity or sorority, a club, etc.) whose image you think could be improved. Create a promotional image for it either for the Web or for some other existing publication.

5. As in item 3, create a visual parody of the official image of a school organization, perhaps as an inside joke intended for other members of the organization.

Assignment 4: Analyzing Your Own Visual Rhetoric

Study all the images your class created as argument and/or persuasion in the previous assignment. Select an image to analyze in depth. Write an essay that addresses these questions:

What audience does the image intend to reach?

What goal did the creator of the image seek to accomplish?

If something is being argued, ask:

What thesis is advanced by the image or accompanying text?

Do aspects of the image or text function as reasons for holding the thesis?

If an image persuades more than it argues, attempt to discover and understand its major source of appeal. Persuasion appeals to the whole person in an effort to create **identification,** a strong linking of the reader's interests and values with the image that represents something desired. Hence, we can ask

How do the images your class created appeal to the audience's interests and values?

Do the images embody emotional appeals? If so, how?

Assignment 5: Using Graphics to Supplement Your Own Writing or Other Texts

Select an essay that could be improved either by adding graphics or by revising the graphics used. Working alone or collaboratively with a writing group, revise it. For help with using graphics effectively in your writing, see the

Guidelines for Using Visuals

Graphics come in a variety of useful forms: as tables to display numerical data economically, as graphs to depict data in a way that permits easy comparison of proportions or trends, as photographs to convey realism and drama, and as drawings to depict structures. Whatever graphics you use, be sure to do the following:

- Make sure every graphic has a definite function. Graphics are not decorative and should never be "thrown" into an essay.

- Choose the kind or form of visual best suited to convey the point you are trying to make.

- Design graphics so that they are easy to interpret. That is, keep them simple, make them large enough to be read without strain, and use clear labeling.

- Place graphics as close as possible to the text they explain or illustrate. Remember, graphics should be easier to understand than the text they supplement.

- Refer to all your graphics in the text. Readers usually need both the graphic and a text discussion for full understanding.

- Acknowledge the creator or source of each graphic next to the graphic itself. As long as you acknowledge the source or creator, you can borrow freely, just as you can with quotations from texts. Of course, if you wish to publish an essay that includes borrowed graphics, you must obtain written permission.

Best Practices box "Guidelines for Using Visuals." You have many revision options: Besides adding visuals, you can cut unneeded ones, redesign existing ones, change media (for example, from a photo to a drawing), change image types (for example, from a table to a graph), and so on. Revising graphics always means reworking the text as well. Expect changes in one to require changes in the other.

Assignment 6: Presenting Information Using PowerPoint

Revise and present the written text in Assignment 6 as an oral presentation using PowerPoint. If you do not know how to use PowerPoint, have another student who does show you how, or use the tutorial that comes with the program.

PowerPoint is a powerful tool for presenting visuals in a talk. *But it is more often used poorly, as a crutch for nervous speakers, than it is used well, to supplement a talk.* Inexperienced speakers want the audience's eyes on anything else but them, so they pack everything they have to say into the PowerPoint slides and have the audience looking at the projections all through

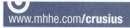

www.mhhe.com/**crusius**

For further help on using Power-Point, visit the online tutorial at:

Writing > PowerPoint Tutorial

the speech. Do not do this. Use PowerPoint to present your graphics to the audience and to summarize major points. Otherwise, keep the audience looking at and listening to you, not staring at a projection screen. Show them a graphic, for instance, and then discuss it, but do not leave it on screen to distract attention from you. Do not read from your text or memorize it, but talk from a few notes to remind yourself of what you need to say. Remember: PowerPoint complements a speech in much the same way graphics complement a written text. Do not let it take over or allow anxiety to cause you to lean on it too hard.

CHAPTER 6

Writing Research-Based Arguments

Most arguments are researched writing. You need to read sources to inform yourself about your topic, and then you need to cite sources in order to convince your readers that you have a good case. An argument with no research behind it is generally weak. Many published arguments may not appear to have research behind them. In journalism, sources may not be documented, but the authors have had to dig to learn the facts, and when they use someone else's views, they introduce that person as an authority because naming authorities' credentials strengthens a case.

Nevertheless, a researched argument must be your own case, with your own angle on the topic, not a case borrowed from your sources. The trick to writing well with sources is to keep them from taking over. You must be in charge, using your sources as supporting characters in what must remain your own show. This chapter will cover finding sources, evaluating them, using them in your own writing, and citing them correctly. To help you stay in charge through this whole process, we will emphasize the role of writing "behind the scenes" *before* you begin drafting your paper. The more you use writing to interact with your sources, to know them well, and to see what supporting parts they might play, the more you will be ready to write as the author—the authority—of an argument of your own: an argument with your own claim, your own voice, your own design.

Using your sources with this kind of confidence helps reduce the possibility of misusing a source. Misuse of a source includes

- Taking material out of context and misrepresenting the viewpoint of the author. Most texts include "multiple voices"—that is, writers may describe opposing views, or they may speak ironically, so a casual reader may misunderstand their viewpoint. Applying the critical reading skills described in Chapter 2 will keep you from misusing a source.

- Using material without giving credit to the source. If you use someone else's words, you must put quotation marks around them. If you use someone else's ideas, even in your own words, you must give that other person credit. Failure to do so is plagiarism. Because plagiarism is a growing problem, partly owing to the ease with which material can be cut and pasted from online sources, we have devoted Chapter 7 to ethical writing and plagiarism. Because some plagiarism is not intentional—students may not understand what constitutes fair use of a source or may not realize how to paraphrase adequately and accurately—we recommend that you read this brief chapter before you start working with the sources you find.

www.mhhe.com/**crusius**

For more information on plagiarism, go to:

Research > Plagiarism

Research takes time and patience; it takes initiative; it takes genuine curiosity. You have to recognize what you do not know and be willing to accept good evidence even if it contradicts what you previously believed. The first step in research is finding an issue that is appropriate.

FINDING AN ISSUE

Let's say you have been assigned to write an argument on an issue of current public concern. If you have no idea what to write about, what should you do?

Understand the Difference between a Topic and an Issue

People argue about issues, not about topics. For example, global warming is a topic. It is the warming of the earth's atmosphere, a scientific observation. However, people argue about many issues related to the topic of global warming, such as whether human activity has contributed to the temperature increase. This was the argument made by the film *An Inconvenient Truth*. The conversation on that issue is subsiding because even the oil companies have come to accept the evidence about the effects of manmade greenhouse gases. But other issues remain, such as what sources of energy are the best alternatives to the fuels that produce greenhouse gases and how individuals might change their lifestyles to make less of an impact on global climate. The point here: To write a good argument, you must explore genuine questions at issue, not just topics. Furthermore, you should explore a question that really interests you. You also must care about your issue.

Find Issues in the News

Pay attention to the news and to the opinions of newsmakers, leaders, and commentators. College students are busy, but there are some easy ways to keep abreast of issues in the news. Here are hints for various news sources.

The Internet

Set one of the major news organizations or newspapers as your home page so that when you turn on your computer, the news will be the first thing you see. Some options are

Cable News Network	<http://www.cnn.com>
Microsoft NBC News	<http://www.msnbc.com>
National Public Radio News	<http://www.npr.org/>
The *New York Times*	<http://www.nytimes.com>
The *Wall Street Journal*	<http://www.wsj.com>

If you moved away to go to college, choose the online version of your hometown paper as a way of keeping in touch with events back home as well as around the world.

Library Online Databases and Resources

Your college library likely subscribes to many online databases and resources that you can search to find issues of current interest. See pages 107–112 for more about online library resources. A good place to look for issues is CQ Researcher. See Figure 6.1 for a look at this Web site. This division of Congressional Quarterly (CQ Press) allows you to search for issues and browse reports and pro–con statements from professional researchers. Although the reports offer only a general overview, they are a good starting point for further research, as each report concludes with a bibliography listing books, articles, and Web sites about the issue.

Magazines and Newspapers

Browse your campus bookstore or library for magazines devoted to news and current affairs. In the library, ask for directions to the "recent periodicals" area. In addition to the obvious choices such as *Time* and *Newsweek*, look for the more opinionated magazines such as *Utne Reader, New Republic,* and *National Review.* For more coverage of issues, look for *Atlantic Monthly, Harper's, Science,* and *National Geographic.*

Lectures, Panel Discussions, Class Discussions, Conversations

Hearing in person what others have to say on an issue will help expose the important points and raise questions for research. Seek out discussion of issues you are considering for research.

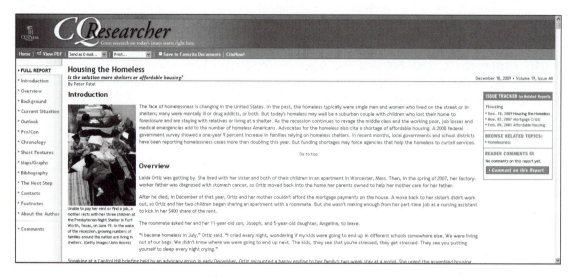

Figure 6.1

CQ *Researcher* home page. *The menu on the left allows you to browse through a list of issues and find articles for researching them.*

Personal Observations

The best way to find an engaging issue is to look around you. Your instructor may not give you total freedom to choose an issue, but many current events and social concerns touch our daily lives. For example, the student whose paper we use as an example of researched writing found her issue when she realized the connection between something close to home that had been bothering her and the general topic area her instructor had specified for the class: global warming.

Finding an Issue on the Topic of Global Warming: A Student Example

Student Julie Ross was in a class that had been assigned the topic of global warming. To find an issue, Julie attended an on-campus screening of *An Inconvenient Truth,* followed by a panel discussion featuring representatives of government agencies, environmentalists, and professors of earth science. Julie asked the panelists what individual citizens could do to reduce their contributions to greenhouse gases. One panelist suggested that consuming "less stuff" would make a difference because the production of consumer goods contributes to carbon dioxide and other greenhouse gases. Because Julie was already fuming about old houses on her street being torn down and replaced with supersized McMansions, she decided to research the question of how destructive this kind of development is, not just to the immediate neighborhood, but also to the planet. She began wondering about its contribution to global warming and how much more energy it demands, because the new houses use much more energy than the ones they replace. She decided to write her paper to an audience of home buyers. If she could discourage them from buying these huge new houses, the developers would have to stop building them. To make a convincing case, Julie needed to find good arguments for preserving the older homes and evidence about how much more energy the large new homes use than the older, smaller ones. Julie's paper appears on pages 157–166.

---

www.mhhe.com/**crusius**   You'll find more tools to help you find an issue at:
Learning > Links Across the Curriculum > Refdesk.com

FINDING SOURCES

The prospect of doing research can be overwhelming, given the many possible avenues to explore: the Internet, newspapers, magazines and journals, and all kinds of books. You need a strategy to guide you most efficiently to the best sources on your topic. The quality of your paper depends on its ingredients; you want to find not just *any* sources but the most credible, appropriate, and—if you are writing about current events—the most recent.

As you begin your research, two tips will make the journey much more efficient and orderly—and less stressful.

1. Keep a research log. Keep a record of your research by writing informally about what you do in each session of searching. Some things to record are:

   - search terms you used, noting which ones were good and which were less productive
   - ideas and questions that occur to you while browsing and reading
   - notes about catalogs and indexes you searched on any particular day
   - complete bibliographical information about each source you plan to use and notes about what the source contains and how you might use it
   - personal responses to sources you read and notes about how different sources compare or contrast on the same topic or issue

   Your research log could be handwritten in a notebook or typed into a computer file or an electronic source management tool like Zotero or EndNote, available through many schools' library Web sites. You may have folders for different kinds of notes (such as search terms or responses to sources). You may organize all or part of your log like a diary with daily notes on the progress of your research. In whatever form or forms you choose, a research log helps you keep track of sources so you do not have to retrace steps, and it positions you to have your own views and voice when writing your argument.

2. Make and store complete copies of sources that you may use. Depending on the source, you may make photocopies or printouts or download documents (such as PDFs) of sources you think you will use. You will want to annotate all your sources and mark them up, and your instructor might require that you submit them with your paper. When copying, be sure to get all the information; avoid cutting off page numbers. With a book, capture the title page and the copyright page on the flip side; you will need this information when citing the source. With online sources, when given the option, choose to print out PDF files because these have page numbers, which makes citing much easier. Also copy any information about the author. Clip, clamp, and label these copies. Keep them in a file folder or binder.

Field Research

Consider beginning your research with what you can observe. That means going out into the "field," as researchers call it, and recording what you see, either in written notes or with photographs or drawings. Field research also can include recording what you hear, in audiotapes and in notes of interviews and conversations. An interview can take place online, through e-mails or a chat, if you can preserve it. Following are some suggestions for field research.

Observations

Do not discount the value of your own personal experiences as evidence in making a case. You will notice that many writers of arguments offer as evidence what they themselves have seen, heard, and done.

Alternatively, you may seek out a specific personal experience as you inquire into your topic. For example, one student writing about homelessness in Dallas decided to visit a shelter. She called ahead to get permission and schedule the visit. Her paper was memorable because she was able to include the stories and physical descriptions of several homeless women, with details of their conversations.

Julie Ross began her research by walking the streets of her neighborhood, photographing the stark contrasts of size and style between the older homes and the new ones built on the sites of torn-down houses. Her photographs provided evidence for her case against supersized homes in historic communities.

Questionnaires and Surveys

You may be able to get information on some topics, especially if they are campus related, by doing surveys or questionnaires. This can be done very efficiently in electronic versions (Web-based or e-mail). Be forewarned, however, that it is very difficult to conduct a reliable survey.

First, there is the problem of designing a clear and unbiased survey instrument. If you have ever filled out an evaluation form for an instructor or a course, you will know what we mean about the problem of clarity. For example, one evaluation might ask whether an instructor returns papers "in a reasonable length of time"; what is "reasonable" to some students may be too long for others. As for bias, consider the question "Have you ever had trouble getting assistance from the library's reference desk?" To get a fair response, this questionnaire had better also ask how many requests for help were handled promptly and well. If you do decide to draft a questionnaire, we suggest you do it as a class project so that students on all sides of the issue can contribute and troubleshoot for ambiguity.

Second, there is the problem of getting a representative response. For the same reasons we doubt the results of certain magazine-sponsored surveys of people's sex lives, we should be skeptical about the statistical accuracy of surveys targeting a group that may not be representative of the whole. For example, it would be impossible to generalize about all first-year college students in the United States based on a survey of only your English class— or even the entire first-year class at your college.

Surveys can be useful, but design, administer, and interpret them carefully.

Interviews

You can get a great deal of current information by talking to experts. As with any kind of research, the first step in conducting an interview is to decide exactly what you want to find out. Write down your questions.

The next step is to find the right person to interview. As you read about an issue, note the names (and possible biases) of any organizations mentioned; these may have local offices, the telephone numbers of which you could easily find. In addition, institutions such as hospitals, universities, and large corporations have public relations offices whose staffs provide information. Also, do not overlook the expertise available from faculty members at your own school.

Once you have determined possible sources for interviews, you must begin a patient and courteous round of telephone calls, continuing until you connect with the right person; this can take many calls. If you have a subject's e-mail address, you might write to introduce yourself and request an appointment for a telephone interview.

Whether your interview is face to face or over the telephone, begin by acknowledging that the interviewee's time is valuable. Tell the person something about the project you are working on, but withhold your own position on any controversial matters. Sound neutral and be specific about what you want to know. Take notes, and include the title and background of the person being interviewed and the date of the interview, which you will need to cite this source. If you want to tape the interview, ask permission first. Finally, if you have the individual's mailing address, send a thank-you note after the interview.

If everyone in your class is researching the same topic and more than one person wants to contact the same expert, avoid flooding that person with requests. One or two students could do the interview and report to the class, or the expert could visit the class.

Library and Internet Research

Since much of what is now published in print is also available online, the distinction between library and Internet research has blurred. You will be able to find many magazines, scholarly journals, and newspapers through the Internet, and many Internet sites through your library's online directories. Because so many documents are now electronic—even if they appeared first in print—librarians have coined the term "born digital" to distinguish purely cyberspace documents from documents that were born in print but have been made available online.

With the daily additions to information, articles, images, and even books available online, the resources for searching it are constantly being upgraded. The advice in this chapter should get you started, but it's always a good idea to consult your library's reference librarians for help with finding sources on your topic. They know what is in your school's library, what is online, and what the latest tools are for finding any kind of source. You will find these librarians at the reference desk; every library has one.

www.mhhe.com/**crusius**   To find online guidance for using the library, check out:
Research > Using the Library

Kinds of Sources

The various kinds of sources available in print and online include books and periodicals as well as electronic media.

Books   Nonfiction books generally fall into three categories:

Monographs: Monographs are sustained arguments on a single topic. To use them responsibly, you should know the complete argument; that means reading the entire book, which time may not allow. Possibly, reading the introduction to a book will acquaint you with the author's argument well enough that you can selectively read sections of the book. Decide if you have time to use a book responsibly. Sometimes you can find a magazine or journal article by the author that covers some of the same ground as the book but in a condensed way.

Anthologies: These are collections of essays and articles, usually by many different writers, selected by an editor, who writes an introductory essay. Anthologies are good sources for short papers because they offer multiple voices, and each argument can be read in one sitting. Pay attention to whether a book is an anthology because you will cite these anthology selections differently from a regular book. Look near the back of the book for information about the author of any selection you choose to use.

Reference books: These are good for gathering background information and specific facts on your topic. You can find these online and on the library shelves; they cannot be checked out. Reference books include specialized encyclopedias on almost any subject, such as *The Encyclopedia of Politics and Religion* (CQ Press, 2007). We will tell you below how to search for encyclopedias and other reference books. Many reference books are now available electronically.

A note of caution about Wikipedia: *Wikipedia* is not a scholarly publication. In fact, it encourages a democratic notion of knowledge in which anyone can contribute, add to, alter, or delete material that has been posted on a topic. Although the editors scan it regularly for misinformation, errors, and deliberate lies, there is no guarantee that what you find there is credible. We suggest you use it for background information and for links to other, more authoritative sources whose authors' credentials you can confirm. Check any facts you plan to use in your papers against other, more scholarly sources.

A note of caution about general encyclopedias: Multivolume online and print encyclopedias such as *Britannica* and *Microsoft Encarta* are good for background knowledge as you begin research on a topic or for fact-checking while you are writing. However, college students should not use general encyclopedias as primary sources. The entries do not cover topics in depth and are not usually products of original research. It is better to use specialized encyclopedias and reference works or books and articles by specialists in your topic.

Periodicals Periodicals are published periodically—daily, weekly, monthly, quarterly. They include the following types:

Articles in scholarly journals: These journals are usually published by university presses and aimed at readers in a particular scholarly discipline: Both the authors and intended readers are professors and graduate students. Scholarly articles are contributions to ongoing debates within a discipline. Therefore, they are credible sources, but scan them for accessibility. If you are not familiar with the debate they are joining, you may not find them accessible enough to use responsibly. Seek your instructor's help if you find a source hard to comprehend. Scholarly journals are usually born in print and put online, but some are born digital.

Articles in magazines: Magazines—print, online, and the born digital "e-zines"—are good sources for short papers. Magazine articles vary greatly, depending on their intended readership. Some magazines, such as *Atlantic Monthly, Harper's, National Review, New Republic,* the *New Yorker,* and even *Rolling Stone,* offer articles by scholars and serious journalists. They give arguments on current public issues by the same people who write for scholarly journals, but the articles are aimed at an educated public readership, not other scholars. These are perfect for familiarizing yourself with viewpoints on an issue. You can find even more accessible articles and arguments in weekly newsmagazines, including columns by nationally syndicated writers. Trade magazines are good for business-related topics; Julie Ross found several online magazines published for the building industry. Many advocacy groups also publish magazines in print and online. Julie found ecological advocacy groups' magazines, such as *E: The Environmental Magazine,* helpful in her research.

Newspapers: Newspapers are ideal sources for arguments and information on current as well as historical issues. Feature articles, which are long and in-depth, usually present the reporter's angle on the topic; opinion columns are arguments and therefore good for getting perspectives on your topic. Major national newspapers such as the *Washington Post, Wall Street Journal,* and *New York Times* should be available online through your library's catalog, as will the local newspaper for your college's city or town. Below, we tell more about how to search for newspaper articles.

Audiovisual Materials   You should be aware of the many resources for finding visuals to use in your paper and also to view as sources of information. You can find images by searching the Internet. Also, your library's online resources page may have a link to digital resources, as does the Library of Congress's Digital Collections and Services, which is a free resource available online. See Figure 6.2, for a look at this Web site.

Web Sites   Web sites include nearly every kind of source described above and more. You have to evaluate everything you find in the wild and open world of cyberspace, but nearly all research institutes and centers associated with universities, advocacy groups, government bureaus, and political organizations are excellent sources for your arguments. Also, most writers these days have their own page on the Web, where you can go to find more about their lives, views, and other writing, so the Web is a great resource for learning more about your sources. The only problem is searching the Web efficiently, and we offer advice later in this chapter on how to zero in on the best sites for your topic.

Blogs, Listservs, Usenet Groups, Message Boards   The Web has become an exciting place for dialogue, where scholars within an area of interest can argue with each other and ask each other for help with their research. Although a first-year student may not feel ready to enter these discussions,

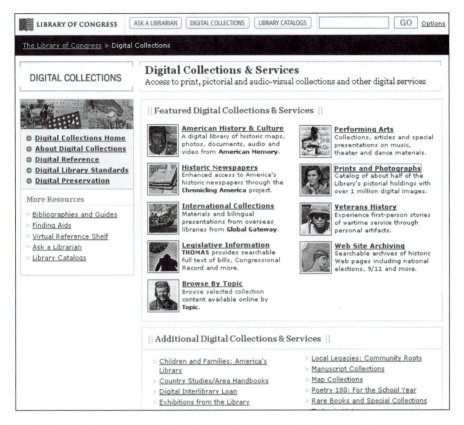

Figure 6.2

This page from the Library of Congress Web site gives you an idea of the range of audiovisual material available to you.

"lurking"—reading a discussion without contributing to it—is a great way to learn about the debates firsthand. And an intelligent question will find people ready to share their knowledge and opinions. We'll tell you later in this chapter about directories that will take you to the most relevant resources for your topic.

Choose the Best Search Terms

The success of your search depends on what terms you use. Before beginning, write down, in your notebook or research log, possible terms that you might use in searching for sources on your topic. Do this by examining your research question to find its key terms. As you begin doing your research, you will discover which of these terms are most productive and which you can cross out. Adapt your search terms as you discover which ones are most productive.

We'll use Julie's search to illustrate how to find the best search terms. Julie's research question was, What are the negative effects of tearing down older homes and replacing them with bigger new ones? Julie wanted to know more about the environmental effects of large homes, both on climate change globally and on the local neighborhoods.

Use Keyword Searching   Keyword searches use as search terms the words that most often are used to refer to your topic. Julie's topic, the construction of large new houses replacing old ones, is often referred to as the teardown trend, so she used "teardowns" in a keyword search.

Use Phrase Searching   You can combine words to create a search term. When you do this, your search engine may want you to put quotation marks or parentheses around the combined terms so it recognizes them as one idea. For example, Julie also used the phrase "neighborhood preservation" to find sources on her topic.

Use Boolean Searching   Boolean searching (named after nineteenth-century English logician George Boole) allows you to narrow or broaden your search by joining words with AND OR NOT

AND: "home size" AND "energy consumption"

Using AND narrowed Julie's search. However, she found nothing by combining "home size" AND "global warming." She needed to think more specifically about the connection between home size and global warming: Energy consumption is the link. (Note: Google and most other search engines automatically put AND in when you type words in succession.)

OR: "green houses" OR "sustainable homes"

Using OR broadened the search, yielding more hits. Using OR is helpful if you know your subject has many synonyms, such as *youth, teenagers, students.*

NOT: "green house" NOT agriculture

Using NOT limited the search by eliminating references to hothouses in agriculture.

Use Subject Words   Keyword searches may not work well in some indexes and databases that have been compiled under strict subject headings. Different search engines and databases will have different official subject headings. For example, the Library of Congress uses "electric automobiles" as a subject heading, whereas the online library subscription database Academic OneFile uses the subject heading "electric cars."

Most university libraries use the Library of Congress subject words for books in their online catalogs. You can go to the Library of Congress Subject

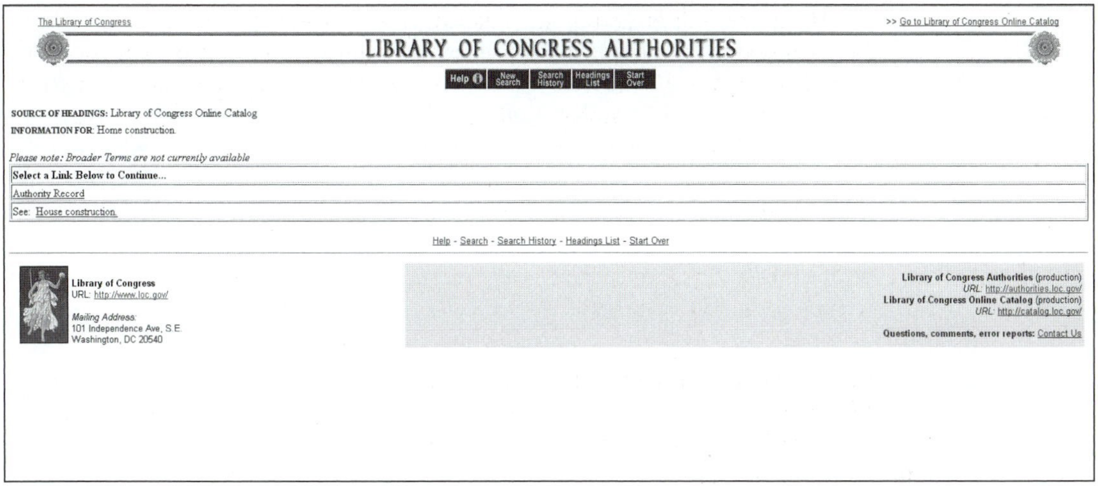

Figure 6.3

The Library of Congress Authorities Web site will tell you the correct search term for finding books on your topic.

Authorities site to find the correct subject headings. When Julie went to the Library of Congress Subject Authorities site, she found that "house construction" was the correct search term, not "home construction."

The Library of Congress helps you find correct subject headings at its Library of Congress Authorities Web site: <http://authorities.loc.gov/>. Figure 6.3 shows the results of a search for correct subject headings. Or you can go directly to your library's catalog and type what you think might a good search term. The catalog should then direct you to the correct subject heading for that topic. For example, if you type in "electric cars" in your library catalog, you will be told to "See 'electric automobiles'."

Searching Your Library

Because much of the research material on the Internet is available for free through your school's library, it makes sense to start with your library's resources. Why pay for something that you already have free access to through your college or university? Also, unlike much of what you find on the Internet, the materials available through your library have been selected by scholars, editors, and librarians, so you can be more confident about the credibility of what you find.

Don't assume that searching the library means using bound books and periodicals only, or even going there in person. Libraries are going electronic, giving you online access to more high quality, full-text sources than you will find on the Web. Libraries subscribe to online indexes and

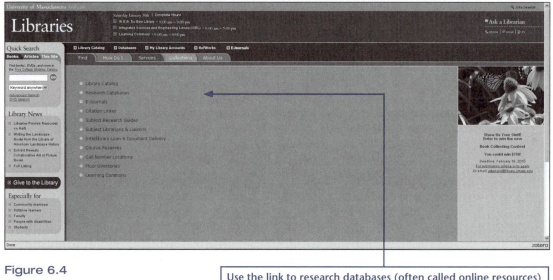

Figure 6.4
A library home page

Use the link to research databases (often called online resources) to find articles in magazines, newspapers, and scholarly journals.

journals that cannot be found through search engines like Google and Yahoo!. Your enrollment at school gives you access to these resources, which are described later in this chapter. Your library's online home page is the gateway to all the library's resources. Figure 6.4 is an example of a library home page. Many librarians create research guides to the resources their library offers in various subject areas, including first-year writing, as shown in Figure 6.5.

Your Library's Online Catalog

Your library's online catalog is the gateway to a wealth of sources: books, both printed and online in the form of e-books that you can "check out" and download; full-text online newspapers, including the complete archives of these papers; indexes to individual articles in magazines, newspapers, and scholarly journals, including links to the full text of most of them online; audiovisual materials; maps; and reference books of all kinds. Visit the home page of your library's online catalog and explore the places it will take you. In the library catalog, you can search for books by title, author, subject, and keyword, as well as their Library of Congress call numbers. Here are some tips:

In a title search: If you know a title you are looking for, do a title search with as much of the title needed to distinguish it from other titles. Omit initial articles (*a, the, an*).

In a subject search: You will need to know what "subject heading" the Library of Congress has given your topic. Julie, for example, found

Figure 6.5

A research guide to college writing

no books in her library catalog when she typed in "home construction" but found twenty-five books when she typed in "house
construction." See pages 105–107 for more about subject headings.
Or just try a keyword search, described below.

In a keyword search: This kind of search is more forgiving than a
subject search and can be helpful if you don't know the exact right
word. Put quotation marks around phrases: "global warming." You
can use AND or OR to combine terms: "teardowns" AND "neighborhood preservation."

The library's online catalog will also tell you if your library subscribes to a
particular newspaper or magazine. The catalog will not tell you about individual articles or stories in these periodicals, but you can find them by searching the publication's own online index or the online databases in your library,
described on the next page. Most university libraries now subscribe to major
U.S. newspapers and have full-text archives online. Do a title search to find
out if your library has a particular newspaper.

To locate reference books, combine your keyword search with words like
encyclopedia, dictionary, or *almanac,* and you will find both online and

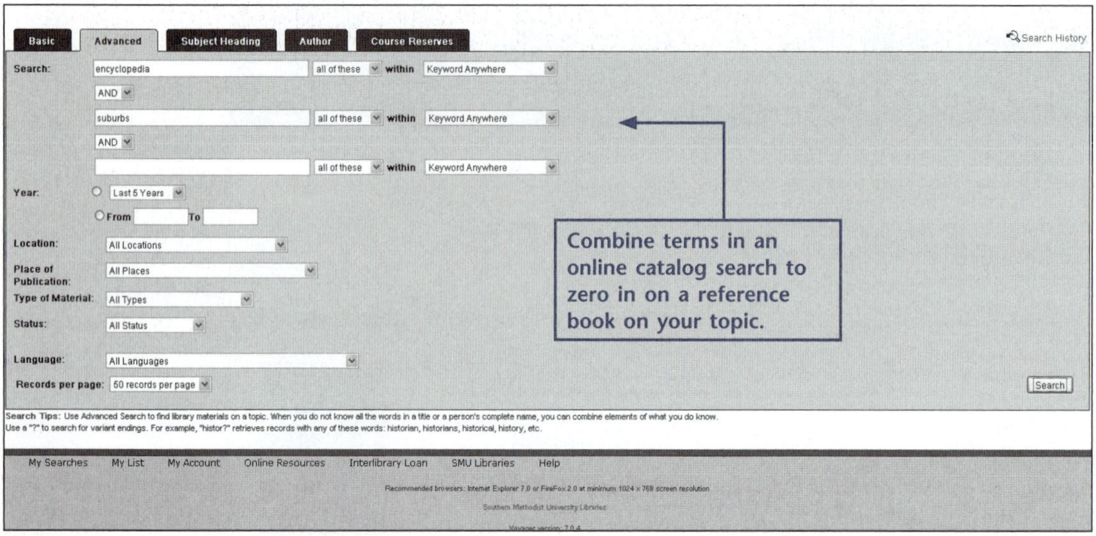

Figure 6.6

A search in an online catalog for specialized encyclopedias about suburbs

on-the-shelf reference books. For an example of such a search and an example of a result, see Figures 6.6 and 6.7.

Your Library's Online Resources

Your school library's purchased online resources are available only to students, faculty, and staff. Students can access them on campus or off campus by using a password. The main Web page of most university libraries offers a link to a page listing the online resources available to you. These usually include reference resources: dictionaries such as the Oxford English Dictionary; electronic encyclopedias, journals, and magazines; and most important, licensed databases to help you search for a wide variety of sources on any topic, both on and off the Web.

These databases are indexes to articles in periodicals: magazines, scholarly journals, and newspapers. You search them by typing in a subject, keyword, author, or title. In most cases the search will produce a list of articles, an abstract of the article, and often, a link to full text of the article, which you can then save or print out.

If the full text is not available online, the database will tell you if the periodical is in your library's holdings. You may be able to access it electronically through the online catalog. This is why it is good to know which magazines, journals, and newspapers are cataloged along with the books in your library's online catalog.

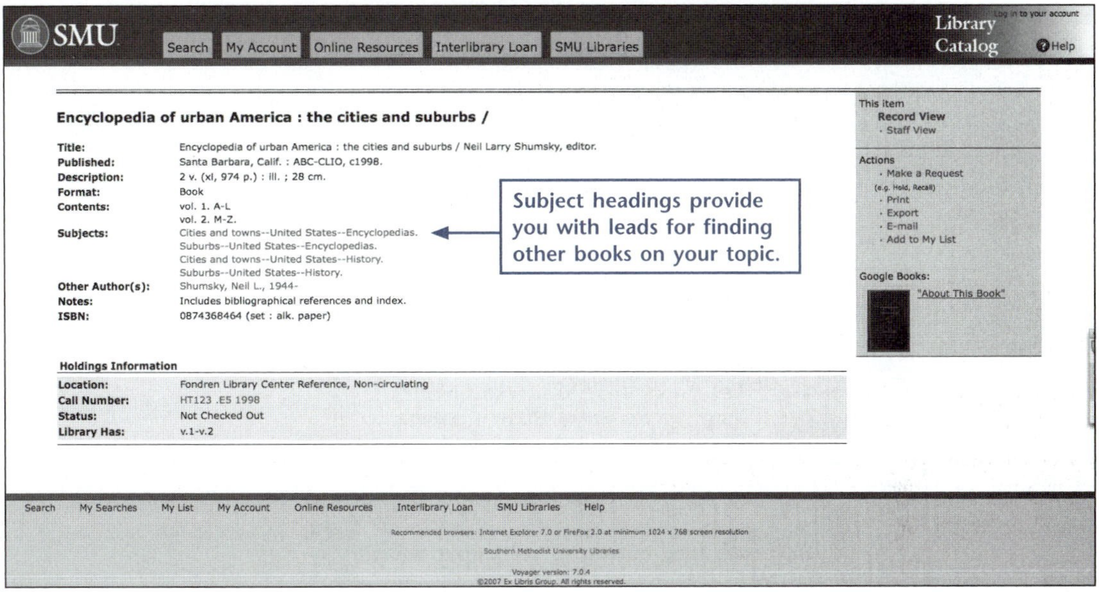

Figure 6.7

The result of an online search for encyclopedias about suburbs

Never use the abstract of an article as a source. Abstracts may not be written by the source's author; they may not be accurate. Most important, you cannot get the in-depth understanding of a source that would allow you to use it accurately.

The following are some common databases subscribed to by college libraries:

Academic Search Complete

Academic OneFile

LEXIS-NEXIS Academic

Business Source Complete

Communication and Mass Media Complete

Film and Television Literature Index

TOPICsearch (good for social, political, and other topics popular in classroom discussions)

Using the "advanced search" in databases like Academic OneFile and Academic Search Complete (illustrated in Figure 6.8) allows you to combine terms to narrow your search. Julie Ross eliminated all hits not related to housing by including "houses" as a second term in her search. Note that both

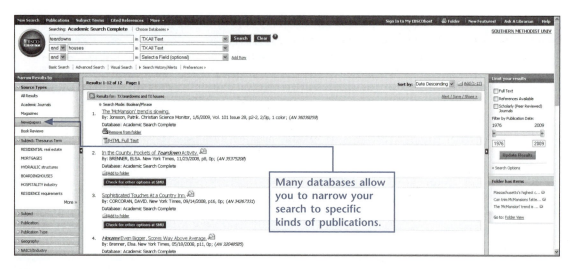

Figure 6.8

Results of an advanced search for newspaper articles in a database

databases allow you to select from academic journals, popular magazines, newspapers, or all three. The search in Figure 6.8 targeted newspapers only.

Internet Research

www.mhhe.com/**crusius**

For further advice on using the Internet to conduct research, go to:

Research > Using the Internet

Because the Internet is so large—estimated to contain over 11.5 billion Web pages—we want to caution you about the potential for wasting time if you start browsing with one of the common search engines such as Yahoo! or Google. However, there are some ways to use search engine features to narrow your search. One of those ways is to limit your search to certain domains.

Domains

Every Internet address or URL (Uniform Resource Locator) has certain components; it helps to know a little about them. What is known as the "top level domain name" tells you something about who put the site on the Web. For Web sites from the United States, the following are the four most common top level domain names. Web sites from other nations typically have instead an abbreviation of the country's name.

Commercial (.com) "Dot com" sites include businesses and their publications—such as the real estate newsletter at <http://www.teardowns.com>—other commercial publications, such as magazines; and personal Web pages and blogs, such as those created on Blogger.com. The example, www.teardowns.com, is a site assisting builders who want to construct on the sites of torn-down houses. Although you will find magazine and newspaper articles through search engines like Yahoo! and Google, a better way to ensure that you get them in full text for free is to find them through your library's licensed databases, as described on page 110. Because so much of the Web is commercial sites, you will probably want to use the advanced search options explained in the next section to filter "dot com" sites from your search.

Nonprofit Organizations (.org) "Dot org" sites include organizations and advocacy groups, such as the National Trust for Historic Preservation at <http://www.nationaltrust.org/teardowns/>. Their purpose is to raise awareness of, participation in, and donations to their causes.

Educational Institutions (.edu) "Dot edu" sites contain research and course materials of public and private schools, colleges, and universities. The URL <http://sciencepolicy.colorado.edu/> is a site for a center at University of Colorado at Boulder doing research on science, technology, and public policy. Although mostly what you find at these sites is the work of professors, some of the material may be by graduate and undergraduate students, so as always, check out the author's credentials.

Government Agencies (.gov) "Dot gov" sites are useful for getting the latest information about any aspect of American government or about government agencies and policies. The URL <http://www.census.gov/> leads to articles published by the U.S. Census Bureau.

Advanced Features for Searching the Web

Search engines provide a variety of ways to focus your search, and Google has some that are especially useful for students.

Advanced Searches Search engines will let you customize your search, allowing you to limit your search to just one or two of the domains listed above, or to exclude one. Filtering out the "dot com" sites is like turning on a spam blocker, so you will get fewer hits by writers with no academic or professional credentials. Figure 6.9 shows how to filter Web searches.

Google Specialized Searches Google offers an ever-increasing number of specific kinds of searches, such as News Archives, Books, Images, and Earth. Many link you to materials that you will have to pay for. However, you can probably find many of these for free through your school library, which

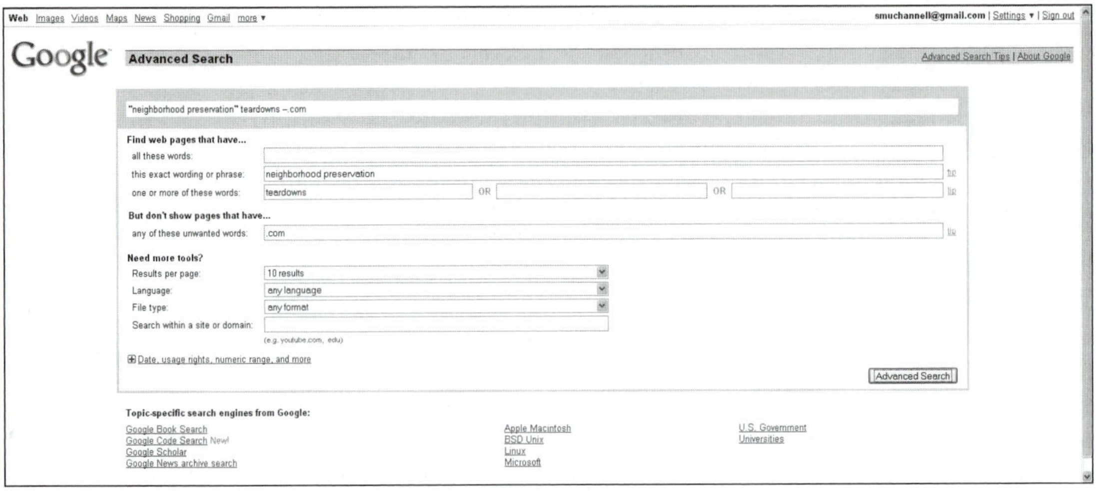

Figure 6.9

Narrow your Google searches by using the advanced search window to combine terms and exclude Web sites in specific domains, like .com.

subscribes to the archives of many magazines and newspapers. See the earlier section, "Your Library's Online Resources," on page 110.

Google Scholar   Google Scholar is where your library and the Internet intersect. Google Scholar is an index to scholarly articles and book reviews, many of them available at your university library. If you open Google Scholar from a computer on campus or if your home computer connects to your school's network (or if you have a password that will grant you off-campus access to your school's network), you will be able to access full texts of materials available from your school's library.

Subject Directories to the Web

You can narrow your search for Web sites by going first to a subject directory that organizes Web sites by topic (Figure 6.10). Some examples are

Google

Yahoo!

Exalead

Infomine (assembled by librarians, not machines)

About.com

Other Web Resources: Blogs, Listservs, Message Boards, and Chat Groups

Don't overlook the potential of interactive sites on the Internet. Many authors of your sources have blogs and personal Web pages where they try

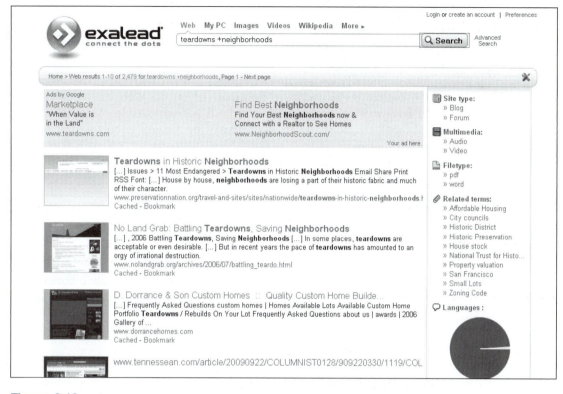

Figure 6.10

Exalead is a new competitor to Google that you may want to try.

out new ideas and get feedback from others interested in their topics. As a student, you may not feel ready to join these conversations, but you can learn a lot by lurking—that is, just reading them. You can find them by using "blogs," "listservs," "message board," or "chat room" as a search term in your browser.

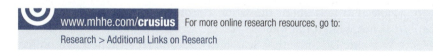

www.mhhe.com/**crusius** For more online research resources, go to:

Research > Additional Links on Research

EVALUATING SOURCES

Before beginning to read and evaluate your sources, you may need to reevaluate your issue. If you have been unable to find many sources that address the question you are raising, consider changing the focus of your argument.

Once you are sure that sources are available on your topic, use the following method to record and evaluate them.

www.mhhe.com/**crusius**

For a tutorial on evaluating sources, go to:

Research > Source Evaluation Tutor: CARS

Eliminate Inappropriate Sources

You may find that some books and articles are intended for audiences with more specialized knowledge than you have. If you have trouble using a source, put it aside, at least temporarily.

Also, carefully review any electronic sources you are using. Although search engines make it easy to find material on the Web, online documents often have met no professional standards for scholarship. Material can be "published" electronically without review by experts, scholars, and editors that must occur in traditional publishing. Nevertheless, you will find legitimate scholarship on the Internet—news reports, encyclopedias, government documents, and even scholarly journals appear online. The freedom of electronic publishing creates an exciting and democratic arena, but it also puts a much heavier burden on students and researchers to ensure that the sources they use are worthy of readers' respect.

Carefully Record Complete Bibliographic Information

For every source you consider using, be sure to record full bibliographic information (Figure 6.11). Take this information from the source itself, not from an index, which may be incomplete or inaccurate. If you make a record of this information immediately, you will not have to go back later to fill in omissions.

Read the Source Critically

As discussed in Chapter 2, critical reading depends on having some prior knowledge of the subject and the ability to see a text in context. As you research a topic, your knowledge naturally becomes deeper with each article you read. But your sources are not simply windows, giving you a clear view; whether argumentative or informative, they have bias. Before looking through them, you must look *at* your sources. Know the answers to the following questions.

Who Is the Writer, and What Is His or Her Bias?

Is there a note that tells about the writer's professional title or institutional affiliation? If not, search the Internet for the writer's personal home page or university Web site. Do an author search in your library's catalog and online databases to find other books and articles by the writer.

How Reliable Is the Source?

Again, checking for credibility is particularly important when you are working with electronic sources. For example, one student found two sites on the Web, both through a keyword search on "euthanasia." One, entitled "Stop

Print Sources	Electronic Sources
Book • Author's full name (or authors' names) • Title of book, including subtitle • City where published • Publisher • Year published	**Document found on the Internet:** • Author's full name (or authors' names) • Title of the work • Original print date, if applicable • Title of the database or Web site • URL • Date you accessed the document
Article or essay in a collection • Author's full name (or authors' names) • Title of article or essay • Title of book • Editor's name (or editors' names) • City where published • Publisher • Year published • Inclusive page numbers of the article.	**Web site, listserv, or blog:** • Author's full name (or authors' names) • Title of post or subject line • Title of Web site or blog • Date of the posting • URL • Date you accessed the site
Article in a periodical • Author's full name (or authors' names) • Title of the article • Title of the periodical • Date of the issue • Volume number, if given • Library database if retrieved online (example, Academic OneFile) and date you retrieved it • Page numbers on which article appears	

Figure 6.11

Working bibliography entries

the Epidemic of Assisted Suicide," was posted by a person identified only by name, the letters MD, and the affiliation "Association for Control of Assisted Suicide." There was no biographical information, and the "snail mail" address was a post office box. The other Web site, "Ethics Update: Euthanasia," was posted by a professor of philosophy at the University of San Diego whose home page included a complete professional biography detailing his education, titles, and the publishers of his many books and articles. The author gave his address at USD in the Department of Philosophy. The student decided that, although the first source had some interesting information—including examples of individual patients who were living with pain rather than choosing suicide—it was not a source that skeptical readers would find credible. Search engines often land you deep within a Web site, and you have to visit the site's home page to get any background information about the source and its author. Be suspicious of sites that do not contain adequate source information; they probably aren't reliable.

*"I just feel fortunate to live in a world with so
much disinformation at my fingertips."*

When Was This Source Written?

If you are researching a current issue, decide what sources are too old. Arguments on current issues often benefit from earlier perspectives.

Where Did This Source Appear?

If you are using an article from a periodical, be aware of the periodical's readership and editorial bias. For example, *National Review* is conservative, *The Nation* liberal. An article in the *Journal of the American Medical Association* will usually defend the medical profession. Looking at the table of contents and scanning editorial statements will give you a feel for the periodical's politics. Also look at the page that lists the publisher and editorial board. You will find, for example, that *New American* is published by the ultra-right-wing John Birch Society. If you need help determining bias, ask a librarian. A reference book that lists periodicals by subject matter and explains their bias is *Magazines for Libraries*.

Additional Guidelines for Evaluating Internet Sources

1. Look at the last segment of the domain name, which will tell you who developed the site. The most reliable ones are developed by colleges and universities (.edu) or by the government (.gov). Of course, commercial sites (.com, .biz) are profit-minded.

2. Does the site have a link to information about the person or organization that put it on the Internet? What can you find out about the education and professional credentials of the author or sponsor?

3. If the site is run by an organization, how is it funded? On the site or elsewhere, look for information about funding and donations. Look for conflict of interest or bias in, for example, a site that publishes about the environment but whose corporate donors have been charged with violating environmental protection laws.

4. Check whether the source includes a bibliography, a sign of scholarly work.

5. A tilde (~) indicates a personal page; these pages must be evaluated with special care.

What Is the Author's Aim?

First, determine whether the source informs or argues. Both are useful and both will have some bias. When your source is an argument, note whether it aims primarily to inquire, to convince, to persuade, or to mediate.

How Is the Source Organized?

If the writer doesn't use subheadings or chapter titles, break the text into parts yourself and note what function each part plays in the whole.

Special Help with Evaluating Web Sites

The Internet is a dangerous place for researchers in a hurry. If you are not careful to look closely at what you find on the Web, you could embarrass yourself badly. For example, why would a college student want to cite a paper written for a high school class? Many high school teachers put their best student papers on class sites—good papers, but nevertheless, not exactly the kind of authority a college student should be citing. So before choosing to use something from the Web, go through the following checklist:

1. **Know the site's domain.** See pages 112–113 for how to read a Web address and what the various domain suffixes tell you about the site. Note if the site is commercial, educational, governmental, or some

kind of advocacy group. Advocacy groups are usually indicated by *.org* in the domain name. Commercial sites may be advertising something—they are not disinterested sources.

2. **Find the home page.** A search engine or online directory may take you to a page deep within the site; always look for links back to the home page because that is where you can find out more about the bias of the site and the credentials of the people behind it.

3. **Read about the bias and mission of the site.** At the home page, you should see a link to more information about the site—often the link is called "About Us" or "Mission Statement." Follow it and learn about the ideology of the site and how it compares with your own bias and that of other sources you are using.

4. **Read about the credentials of the site's creators.** The creators' degrees and professional affiliations should be easy to find. Regard any site as bogus if the only link to finding more about the authors is an e-mail address. Also, note whether the credentials of its board of directors or trustees are in the fields of specialization for your topic. For example, many writers for some Web sites on global warming dispute scientific findings, but are not scientists. They may be economists or historians.

5. **Note if the site reports on its funding and donors.** The rule of "follow the money" becomes important when you are using sources outside of the academic world. Think tanks and advocacy groups receive money from large corporations. Consider how the funding might influence their research and reported findings. There should be a link to material about funding, corporate sponsors, and the group's annual tax reports.

6. **Note how current the site is.** Near the beginning or the end of any Web site or part of a Web site, you should be able to find a note about when the site was last updated. You will need this information in order to cite the site—a site that has not been updated in years is not a good choice.

The Web site for the National Trust for Historic Preservation (Figure 6.12), where Julie found a speech about the effects of teardowns on neighborhoods, checks out as a credible site. From the home page, Julie was able to link to a page titled "About the National Trust" (Figure 6.13), where she learned that it is a private, nonprofit organization founded in 1949 and dedicated to saving historical places. It advocates for legislation to protect communities and places of cultural heritage. The home page also provides a link titled "Funding," with information about donations, corporate sponsors, and tax returns. A link to the organization's "Management" gave the credentials of its trustees and its executive staff, including Richard Moe, the author of the speech. Julie learned that Moe graduated from

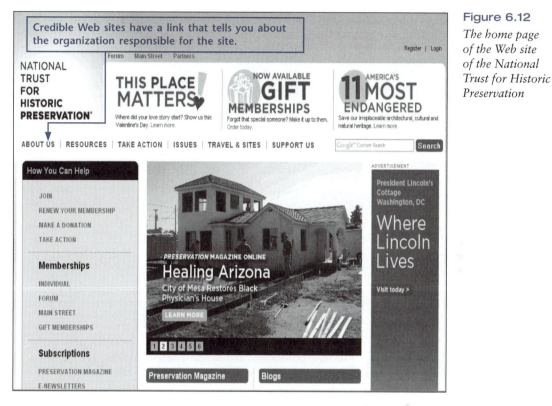

Figure 6.12

*The home page
of the Web site
of the National
Trust for Historic
Preservation*

Williams College in 1959 and from the University of Minnesota Law
School in 1966. He has been president of the National Trust since 1993.
He is an honorary member of The American Institute of Architects and
coauthor of a book titled *Changing Places: Rebuilding Community in the
Age of Sprawl,* published in 1997. Clearly, this source from a Web site
passed the test.

USING SOURCES

The first way to use your sources is to familiarize yourself with viewpoints
on your topic. Your thesis will grow out of your research; you do not do
research to find information to support a position you have not investigated.
In high school, you may have grabbed quotations or facts from a source; in
college you must know the source itself, including something about the
author and the author's argument, unless your source is an encyclopedia or

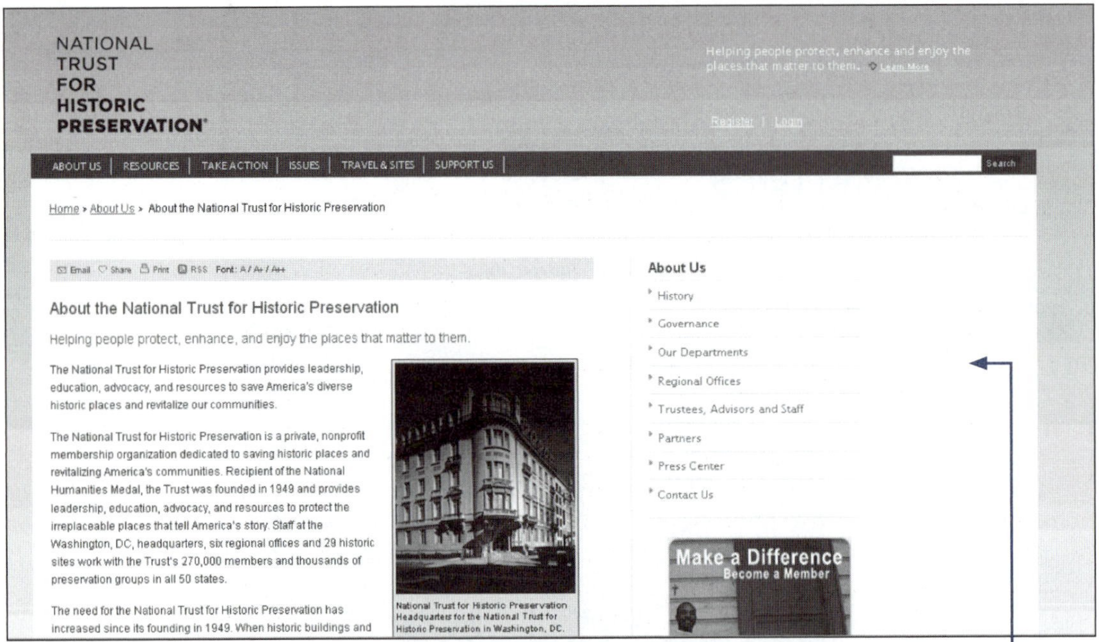

Figure 6.13
"About Us" page on Web site

The organization should provide information about its purpose, history, governance and annual financial reports, and leaders. Reject Web sites that do not provide such information.

almanac or other reference work. For more on getting to know sources, read Chapter 2, "Reading an Argument," and the preceding section in this chapter, "Evaluating Sources," pages 116–121.

When you have gathered and evaluated some sources, you should next spend some time with each one, reading it, marking it up, and writing about it in your notebook or on a notepad. This essential step will help you use your sources confidently and accurately in a paper with your own angle and voice. One teacher calls this step "writing in the middle" because it bridges the gap between the sources you have found and the paper you will turn in. If you skip this step, you risk misrepresenting your source, taking material out of context, plagiarizing (see Chapter 7, "Ethical Writing and Plagiarism"), or, more commonly, letting your sources take over with too much of their voice and wording, resulting in a paper that sounds patched together.

Because you should not use a source that you have not read in its entirety, we reproduce below one of Julie Ross's sources for her argument on neighborhood preservation. We will demonstrate various kinds of informal writing about this source.

Note that we have annotated this reading, an important step you should perform for every source you plan to use.

Battling Teardowns, Saving Neighborhoods

RICHARD MOE, president of the National Trust for Historic Preservation

Speech given to the Commonwealth Club, San Francisco, CA; June 28, 2006.

Note author's credentials

A growing disaster is tearing apart many of America's older neighborhoods. They're being devoured, one house at a time, here in the Bay Area, across California, and in scores of communities from coast to coast.

I'm talking about teardowns—the practice of purchasing and demolishing an existing house to make way for a new, much bigger house on the same site. Teardowns wreck neighborhoods. They spread through a community like a cancer, destroying the character and livability that are a neighborhood's lifeblood. I believe teardowns represent the biggest threat to America's older neighborhoods since the heyday of urban renewal and interstate highway construction during the 1950s and 60s.

Quotable passage here

Claim

Here's how it works: Developers and home-buyers look through desirable neighborhoods for a building lot that can lawfully accommodate a much bigger house than that which currently stands on it. The property is acquired, the existing house is torn down and a bigger house is constructed in its place. There are variations: Sometimes a large estate is leveled and subdivided to accommodate several new houses; in others, several smaller houses are cleared to make way for a single, massive new one.

Extent of the problem

It's a simple process, but it can totally transform the streetscape of a neighborhood and destroy its character. It's especially destructive in older and historic communities.

Teardowns are occurring all over America—from fashionable resorts such as Palm Beach and Palm Springs to the inner-ring suburbs around Washington and Chicago and the Richmond District here in San Francisco. The trend has become so alarming that the National Trust included "Teardowns in Historic Neighborhoods" on our list of America's 11 Most Endangered Historic Places in 2002. Back then, we identified 100 communities in 20 states that were having major problems with teardowns. That statistic was troubling in 2002—but four years later, the news is much worse: Today we can document the impact of teardowns in more than 300 communities in 33 states. The National Association of Home Builders says that 75,000 houses are razed and replaced with larger homes each year. . . .

Background information

This disaster goes by many names. In New Jersey, the practice is often called "bash-and-build." In Colorado, teardowns are known as "scrape-offs." In Oregon, the new houses are sometimes called "snout houses" because of the big, protruding garages that dominate their facades. In other places they're known simply—and aptly—as "bigfoots" or "monster homes."

Extent of the problem

Whatever you call it, one teardown usually sparks others. A New Jersey builder says, "It's a trend that keeps on rolling. Builders used to be afraid to be the first person in a neighborhood to tear a house down. Now they're looking around and saying they don't mind taking the risk."

Why is this happening?

Three factors are at work in the spread of teardowns.

10

More background

The first is the rise in real-estate prices. In some areas, home values have doubled or tripled over the past decade, and this leads developers to look for "undervalued" properties—many of which exist in older neighborhoods.

One reason for teardowns

The second factor is the trend toward bigger houses. In 1950, the average American home incorporated less than 1,000 sq. ft. By 2005, the average new home had more than doubled in size, to 2,412 sq. ft. According to the National Association of Home Builders, almost 40% of new homes have four or more bedrooms; that's more than twice as many as in the early 1970s—despite the fact that the average family size decreased during that same period. Subdivisions of luxury homes of 5,000 sq. ft. and more are becoming commonplace. Clearly, burgers and french fries aren't the only things in America being "super-sized."

Other reasons for teardowns

The final factor is that many people are looking for an alternative to long commutes or are simply fed up with the soulless character of sprawling new subdivisions. For these people, older in-town neighborhoods and inner-ring suburbs are enormously appealing because of their attractive architecture, mature landscaping, pedestrian orientation, easy access to public transportation and amenities such as local shopping districts, libraries and schools.

The problem is that too many people try to impose their preference for suburban-style mini-mansions on smaller-scale neighborhoods where they just don't fit. And since most of these older areas offer few vacant lots for new construction, the pressure to demolish existing houses can be intense. A modest cottage gets torn down and hauled off to the landfill, and what goes up in its place is "Tara" on a quarter-acre lot.

Reason against tearing down: effect on neighborhood

Neighborhood livability is diminished as trees are removed, backyards are eliminated, and sunlight is blocked by bulky new structures built right up to the property lines. Economic and social diversity are reduced as costly new "faux chateaux" replace more affordable houses—including the modest "starter homes" that our parents knew and that first-time homebuyers still search for today. . . .

15

While the destruction of historic houses is wasteful, environmentally unsound and unnecessary, it's often just the beginning of the problems caused by teardowns.

It's not uncommon for a demolished older home to be replaced with a new one that is three times as big as any other house on the block. These structures loom over their neighbors and break the established building patterns of the area. Front yards are often given over to driveways, and three- or four-car garages are the dominant elements in the façade. Floor plans are often oriented to private interior spaces, making the new houses look like fortresses that stand totally aloof from their surroundings. . . .

Another reason against teardowns

Apart from their visual impact, teardowns can profoundly alter a neighborhood's economic and social environment. A rash of teardowns can cause property taxes to rise—and while this may be a good thing for communities in search of revenue, it can drive out moderate-income or fixed-income residents. Those who remain start to feel they've lost control of their neighborhood to developers and speculators. A house that once might have been praised as "charming and historic" now gets marketed as "older home on expansive lot"—which is realtor language for "teardown." Once that happens—once the value of an older house is perceived to be less than that of the land it's built on—the house's days are probably numbered. And sadly, the neighborhood's days as a viable historic enclave may be numbered too.

It doesn't have to be this way. There are alternatives to teardowns.

Alternatives to tearing down

First of all, prospective builders should realize that most older, established neighborhoods simply can't accommodate the kind of sprawling new mini-mansion that is appropriate on a suburban cul-de-sac. People who want to move into the city can often find development opportunities in underused historic buildings and vacant land in older areas. Even in areas where vacant land is scarce, existing older houses can be enlarged in sensitive ways: A new zoning ordinance in Coronado, California, for example, gives homebuilders "bonus" square footage if they incorporate design elements that maintain the historic character of the community.

20   No one is saying that homebuyers shouldn't be able to alter or expand their home to meet their needs, just as no one is saying that older neighborhoods should be frozen in time like museum exhibits. A neighborhood is a living thing, and change is both inevitable and desirable. The challenge is to manage change so that it respects the character and distinctiveness that made these neighborhoods so appealing in the first place.

Qualification of his argument

Let me mention a few things that people and communities can do.

First and most important, communities must realize that they aren't helpless in the face of teardowns. They have choices: They can simply take the kind of community they get, or they can go to work to get the kind of community they want. They have to decide what they like about the community and don't want to lose. They must develop a vision for the future of their community, including where and how to accommodate growth and change. Then they must put in place mechanisms to ensure that their vision is not compromised.

Solutions to the problem

Ideally, this consensus-building should take place as part of a comprehensive planning process—but that can take time, and sometimes the pressure of teardowns calls for immediate action. In those situations, some communities have provided a "cooling-off" period by imposing a temporary moratorium on demolition. This moratorium prevents the loss of significant structures while allowing time for residents and city officials to develop effective means of preserving neighborhood character.

One of those means is local historic district designation. Notice that I said "local historic district." Many people believe that listing a property in the National Register of Historic Places is enough to protect it, but that isn't true. The only real protection comes through the enactment of a local ordinance that regulates demolition, new construction and alteration in a designated historic area. More than 2,500 communities across the country have enacted these ordinances. Most of them require that an owner get permission before demolishing or altering a historic building; many also offer design guidelines to ensure that new buildings will harmonize with their older neighbors.

More solutions

25   If historic district designation isn't feasible or appropriate, other forms of regulation may work. Conservation districts or design-review districts can address issues such as demolition and new construction with less administrative burden than

historic districts. Floor-area ratios or lot-coverage formulas can remove the economic incentive for teardowns by limiting the size of new buildings. In the same way, setback requirements, height limits and open-space standards can help maintain traditional neighborhood building patterns. At least two communities in San Mateo County have recently adopted regulations of this sort to limit the height and floor area of newly built homes.

Not all approaches require government involvement. Local preservation organizations or neighborhood groups can offer programs to educate realtors and new residents about the history of older neighborhoods and provide guidance in rehabbing or expanding older houses. They can acquire easements to ensure that the architectural character of historic buildings is permanently protected. They can provide low-interest loans to help encourage sensitive rehabilitation. Incentives such as these are particularly effective when combined with technical assistance and some form of tax abatement from state or local government.

Opposing view and rebuttal

Some people go so far as to claim that teardowns actually support smart growth by directing new-home construction to already-developed areas, thereby increasing density and offering an alternative to suburban sprawl. Again, I disagree.

Tearing down a smaller house to build a bigger one simply adds square footage, not population density. In addition, teardowns affect neighborhood livability, reduce affordability, consume energy, and send thousands of tons of demolition debris to landfills. That doesn't sound like smart growth to me.

Equally important, teardowns exact too high a price in the wasteful destruction of our nation's heritage. Of course we need to encourage investment in existing communities as an alternative to sprawl—but not at the expense of the historic character that makes older neighborhoods unique, attractive and livable. Some say that change is simply the price of progress—but this kind of change isn't progress at all; it's chaos.

30   The National Trust is committed to helping local residents put the brakes on teardowns. It will be a huge job—but it's eminently worthy of our best efforts.

America's older neighborhoods are important chapters in the story of who we are as a nation and a people. Working together, we can keep that story alive. Working together, we can keep America's older and historic communities intact so that generations to come can live in them, learn from them, be sheltered and inspired by them—just as we are today.

Writing Informally to Gain Mastery over Your Sources

The more you engage your sources with informal "talk-back" such as annotations, notebook responses to the ideas in the sources, notebook entries that make connections between and among ideas in sources, and paraphrases and summaries that make you really think about the key points and passages, the easier it will be for you to assume the voice of authority when it is time to start drafting your paper. Here are some suggestions for writing in the middle zone between researching and drafting.

1. Annotate the Source

Use the advice in Chapter 2, "Reading an Argument," which suggests things to look for in sources that are arguments. If a source is not an argument, annotate to comment on the author's angle, bias, and main points.

2. Respond to the Source in Your Notebook

After annotating, write more in your notebook about how you might use the source. If you have roughed out a case, note which reason or reasons of your own case this source could help you develop. If you find a new reason for your case, note it and think how you could develop it with your own observations and other sources you have found.

If you think the source will be mainly useful for facts, make a note about what kind of facts it has and the page numbers, so that when you start drafting, you can find them quickly.

If the author is an expert or authority, note the credentials or at least where you can go to find these as you start drafting—perhaps the author's Web page or a biographical note at the end of the book or article.

If this will be a major source for your paper, you should be sure you grasp the most important concepts in it. Look for the passages that pose a challenge; to use the source with authority, you need to own, not borrow, these ideas. That means instead of just dropping them in as quotations, you will have to work them in, explaining them in your own words. Try out *paraphrases* (see more on paraphrases in item 3 in this list) to make these points completely clear to you and then respond to the major ideas with what you think about them: If it's a good idea, why do you think so? What in your own experiences (field research) confirms it? What can you add of your own as you discuss this idea in your paper?

Look for memorable passages that are worth *direct quotations* (see more on direct quotations in this chapter's section on incorporating source material). The best quotes are strongly worded opinions and writing that cannot be paraphrased without losing its punch.

Think about how additional research might help you develop an idea given to you by this source.

The box on page 128 shows some notes Julie put in her notebook after deciding to use the National Trust source.

3. Paraphrase Important Ideas from the Source

Although you will use paraphrases as you incorporate material from your sources into your essay, consider paraphrase as a study skill that helps you understand key ideas by putting them into your own words. It helps you to "own" the key ideas rather than simply borrowing the author's words to insert into your paper. Here are some suggestions for paraphrasing:

- Read the entire source or section in which the passage appears. You cannot write a good paraphrase of a passage you have taken out of

Notes on Moe, Richard. "Battling Teardowns."

- *Perfect source for my paper. I need to mention the National Trust for Historic Preservation. This source supports my "preserve the neighborhood character" reason. Good description of the garages—"snout houses." Also mention the way these new houses block the sunlight. Good on the economic impact on the older people in my neighborhood. Many can't afford to stay. This source helps explain why.*

- *I also hadn't thought about how these homebuyers are destroying the very thing that makes them want to live here. Old charm won't last if everybody does what they are doing. This could appeal to their interest—restore, not tear down.*

- *I like the part about allowing for change. I'll use this quote: "A neighborhood is a living thing. Change is both inevitable and desirable." What kinds of changes would I consider OK? Could a new house of different architectural style actually add character to the neighborhood? Maybe look for a source that describes some kind of acceptable change.*

- *He mentions the other part of my case, the environment, but not enough to use this source for that part.*

context. Surrounding sentences will provide information essential for understanding the material you are paraphrasing, and to make the idea clear to yourself, you may need to add some of that information to your paraphrase. Later, if you use the paraphrase in your paper, you will need to provide enough context so that your readers will understand the idea as well.

- Read the passage several times through, including surrounding text, until you think you understand it. Annotate it. Look up any words that are even slightly unfamiliar to you.

- Put the text away so that you will not be tempted to look at it. Then think of the main ideas and try to put each one into your own words and your own wording. A paraphrase must not be an echo of the original's sentence patterns with synonyms plugged in. That is really a form of plagiarism because it involves "stealing" the author's sentence pattern. You may want to break up complex sentences into shorter, more simple ones that make the idea easier to comprehend.

- Do not feel that you must find a substitute word for every ordinary word in the passage. For example, if a passage has the word *children*, don't feel you have to say *kids*.

- Go back and check your paraphrase against the original to see if you have accurately represented the full content of the original passage. Make adjustments as needed.

Examples of Adequate and Inadequate Paraphrasing

Original Passage:

> Some people go so far as to claim that teardowns actually support smart growth by directing new-home construction to already-developed areas, thereby increasing density and offering an alternative to suburban sprawl. Again, I disagree. Tearing down a smaller house to build a bigger one simply adds square footage, not population density.

Inadequate Paraphrase: This example borrows too much of the wording and sentence patterns (underlined) from the original text by Moe.

> <u>Some people</u> even <u>claim</u> that tearing down old houses <u>supports smart growth</u> by increasing <u>new-home construction</u> and density in <u>already developed areas.</u> Therefore, teardowns are <u>an alternative to suburban sprawl.</u> Moe disagrees because tearing down small houses and building bigger ones only <u>adds</u> more <u>square footage,</u> not more people.

Inadequate Paraphrase: The paraphrase below doesn't do justice to the idea: It does not include the concept of smart growth; it does not mention the problem of new development in suburban areas versus rebuilding in existing neighborhoods; and it does not give Moe credit for the opinion.

> It's not smart to tear down old houses and replace them with bigger ones because you don't get more population density.

Good Paraphrase: This explains "smart growth," gives Moe credit, and represents all the points in original sentence patterns. It even offers an interpretation at the end.

> Smart growth is an attempt to develop cities while minimizing suburban sprawl. According to Moe, tearing down older, small homes in close-in neighborhoods and replacing them with bigger ones is not really "smart growth" because bigger houses do not necessarily increase population density; they just offer more square footage for the same size household. So they are really a kind of urban sprawl.

4. Write Summaries of Portions of a Source

As a way to help get your own handle on important sections of a source, write a summary of it in your notebook. That means putting just the most important parts of the text into your own words (paraphrase) and joining them into a smooth paragraph. To write a summary, follow these steps.

1. Read and reread the portion of a text you want to summarize, looking up unfamiliar words.
2. Choose the main points.
3. Paraphrase them, using the advice on paraphrasing above.
4. Combine sentences to make the new version as concise as possible.

Guidelines for Summarizing

1. Read and reread the original text until you have identified the claim and the main supporting points. You ought to be able to write an outline of the case, using your own words. Depending on your purpose for summarizing and the amount of space you can devote to the summary, decide how much, if any, of the evidence to include.

2. Make it clear at the start whose ideas you are summarizing.

3. If you are summarizing a long passage, break it down into subsections and work on summarizing one at a time.

4. As with paraphrasing, work from memory. Go back to the text to check your version for accuracy.

5. Maintain the original order of points, with this exception: If the author delayed presenting the thesis, refer to it earlier in your summary.

6. Use your own words.

7. Avoid quoting entire sentences. If you want to quote keywords and phrases, incorporate them into sentences of your own, using quotation marks around the borrowed words.

Here is an example of a portion of Richard Moe's speech that Julie used in her paper by shortening it and presenting it in her own words. The underlined sections are the ones she deemed important enough to go into the summary.

Original Passage:

> Three factors are at work in the spread of teardowns.
> The first is the rise in real-estate prices. In some areas, home values have doubled or tripled over the past decade, and this leads developers to look for "undervalued" properties—many of which exist in older neighborhoods.
> The second factor is the trend toward bigger houses. In 1950, the average American home incorporated less than 1,000 sq. ft. By 2005, the average new home had more than doubled in size, to 2,412 sq. ft. According to the National Association of Home Builders, almost 40% of new homes have four or more bedrooms; that's more than twice as many as in the early 1970s—despite the fact that the average family size decreased during that same period. Subdivisions of luxury homes of 5,000 sq. ft. and more are becoming commonplace. Clearly, burgers and french fries aren't the only things in America being "super-sized."
> The final factor is that many people are looking for an alternative to long commutes or are simply fed up with the soulless character of sprawling new subdivisions. For these people, older in-town neighborhoods and inner-ring suburbs are enormously appealing because of their attractive

Guidelines for Writing with Sources

Avoid plagiarism by *distinguishing sharply* between quoting and paraphrasing. Anytime you take exact words from a source, even if it is only a phrase or a significant word, you are quoting. You must use quotation marks and documentation. If you make any change at all in the wording of a quotation, you must indicate the change with square brackets. If you remove any words from a direct quotation, use ellipses (three spaced dots) to indicate the deletion. If you use your own words to summarize or paraphrase portions of a source, name that source in your text and document it. Be careful to use your own words when paraphrasing and summarizing.

1. Use an attributive tag such as "According to . . ." to introduce quotations both direct and indirect. Don't just drop them in.

2. Name the person whose words or idea you are using. Provide the full name on first mention.

3. Identify the author(s) of your source by profession or affiliation so that readers will understand the significance of what he or she has to say. Omit this if the speaker is someone readers are familiar with.

4. Use transitions into quotations to link the ideas they express to whatever point you are making.

5. If your lead-in to a quotation is a phrase, follow it with a comma. But if your lead-in can stand alone as a sentence, follow it with a colon.

6. Place the period at the end of a quotation or paraphrase, after the parenthetical citation, except with block quotations. (See page 136 for treatment of block quotations.)

architecture, mature landscaping, pedestrian orientation, easy access to public transportation and amenities such as local shopping districts, libraries and schools.

Julie's Summary:

Moe sees three reasons for the increase in teardowns:

*   In the past decade, the value of houses has doubled or tripled, except in some older neighborhoods. Developers look for these "'undervalued' properties" to build on.

*   Homebuyers want more space, with the average home size going from 1,000 square feet in 1950 to 2,412 square feet in 2005.

*   Some homebuyers desire to move from the "soulless . . . sprawling subdivisions" to close-in neighborhoods that have more character and more amenities, such as public transportation and local shopping.

5. Write Capsule Summaries of Entire Sources

Writers frequently have to summarize the content of an entire source in just a brief paragraph. Such summaries appear in the introduction to a volume of

Sample Entry in an Annotated Bibliography

Here is an annotated bibliography entry for Julie's National Trust source.

Moe, Richard. "Battling Teardowns, Saving Neighborhoods." *The National Trust for Historic Preservation.* June 28, 2006. Web. Jan. 21, 2007.

In this transcript of a speech given to a San Francisco civic organization, Moe, who is president of the National Trust for Historic Preservation, argues that builders should respect the integrity of older neighborhoods and that local residents should join the Trust's efforts to block the teardown trend, which is fueled by rising real estate values, homebuyers' desire for bigger houses, and fatigue with life in the distant suburbs. Teardowns "wreck neighborhoods" by removing trees and backyards, blocking the sun, ruining historic character, raising taxes so that poorer residents are forced out, and generating environmental waste. Communities can organize to fight teardowns by applying for historical designation or other kinds of government regulations on building as well as offering incentives for realtors and new buyers to respect neighborhood quality.

collected essays, in an opening section of scholarly articles in which the author reviews previously published literature on the topic, and at the end of books or articles in annotated bibliographies or works cited lists. The purpose of these is to let other scholars know about sources they might also want to consult.

If your class is working on a common topic, your instructor may ask the class to assemble a working bibliography of sources all of you have found, including a brief summary of each one to let other students know what the source contains. This is called an "annotated bibliography." Following is some advice on creating capsule summaries and annotated bibliographies.

1. As explained in Chapter 2, "Reading an Argument," read and annotate the entire source, noting claims, reasons, the subdivisions into which the text breaks down, and definitions of words you looked up.

2. Working with one subdivision at a time, write paraphrases of the main ideas in each. Decide how much specific evidence would be appropriate to include, depending on the purpose of your summary. As with any paraphrase, work from memory and recheck the original later for accuracy.

3. You may include brief direct quotations, but avoid quoting whole sentences. That is not efficient.

4. Join your paraphrases into a coherent and smooth paragraph.

5. Edit your summary to reduce repetitions and to combine points into single sentences where possible.

Note that a good capsule summary restates the main points; it doesn't just describe them.

> *Not:* Moe gives three reasons for the rise of the teardown trend.

> *But:* Moe argues that the teardown trend is fueled by rising real estate values, homebuyers' desire for bigger houses, and fatigue with life in the distant suburbs.

6. Dialogue about Sources

Inside or outside of class, any conversations you can have about your research with others researching the same topic will help you get an angle and an understanding of your sources. This is the reason many scholars keep blogs— a blog is a place to converse about ideas. Your instructor may set up an electronic bulletin board for students to chat about their research, or you might make your own blog with friends and start chatting.

INCORPORATING AND DOCUMENTING SOURCE MATERIAL

We turn now to the more technical matter of how to incorporate source material in your own writing and how to document it. You incorporate material through direct quotation or through summary or paraphrase; you document material by naming the writer and providing full publication details of the source—a two-step process. In academic writing, documenting sources is essential, with one exception: You do not need to document sources of factual information that can easily be found in common references, such as an encyclopedia or atlas, or of common knowledge. See page 168 in Chapter 7, "Ethical Writing and Plagiarism," for more explanation of common knowledge.

Different Styles of Documentation

Different disciplines have specific conventions for documentation. In the humanities, the most common style is the Modern Language Association (MLA). In the physical, natural, and social sciences, the American Psychological Association (APA) style is most often used. We will illustrate both in the examples that follow. Both MLA and APA use parenthetical citations in the text and simple, alphabetical bibliographies at the end, making revision and typing much easier. (For a detailed explanation of these two styles, visit the Web sites for the MLA and the APA.)

In both MLA and APA formats, you provide some information in the body of your paper and the rest of the information under the heading "Works Cited" (MLA) or "References" (APA) at the end of your paper. The following summarizes the essentials of both systems.

www.mhhe.com/**crusius**

For Web sites with information on documentation styles, go to:

Research > Annotated Links to Documentation Sites

www.mhhe.com/**crusius**

You can find more documentation information at:

Research > Links to Documentation Sites

www.mhhe.com/**crusius**

For a student sample of a paper
in MLA format, go to:

Research > Sample Paper
in MLA Style

MLA Style

In parentheses at the end of both direct and indirect quotations, supply the last name of the author of the source and the exact page number(s) where the quoted or paraphrased words appear. Online sources often have no page numbers. If an online source is a PDF file, it should have page numbers. You need to use them. If the name of the author appears in your sentence that leads into the quotation, omit it in the parentheses.

Direct quotation with source identified in the lead-in:

> According to Jessie Sackett, a member of the U.S. Green Building Council, home ownership is "the cornerstone of the American dream. Recently, however, we've realized that keeping that dream alive for future genera-tions means making some changes to how we live today" (36).

Indirect quotation with source cited in parenthetical citation:

> A spokesperson for the U.S. Green Building Council reminds us that home ownership is fundamental to the American dream; however, in order to preserve that dream for the generations to come, we need to develop more energy efficient houses and lifestyles today (Sackett 36).

APA Style

www.mhhe.com/**crusius**

For a student sample of a paper
in APA format, go to:

Research > Sample Paper
in APA Style

In parentheses at the end of direct or indirect quotations, place the author's last name, the date published, and the page number(s) where the cited mate-rial appears. If the author's name appears in the sentence, the date of publi-cation should follow it in parentheses; the page number still comes at the end of the sentence. Unlike MLA, the APA style uses commas between the parts of the citation and "p." or "pp." before the page numbers.

Direct quotation with source cited in the lead-in:

> Jessie Sackett (2006), a member of the U.S. Green Building Council, writes, "Owning a home is the cornerstone of the American dream. Recently, however, we've realized that keeping that dream alive for future generations means making some changes to how we live today" (p. 36).

Indirect quotation with source cited in parenthetical citation:

> A spokesperson for the U.S. Green Building Council reminds us that home ownership is fundamental to the American dream; however, in order to preserve that dream for the generations to come, we need to develop more energy efficient houses and lifestyles today (Sackett, 2006, p. 36).

Direct Quotations

Direct quotations are exact words taken from a source. The simplest direct quotations are whole sentences worked into your text, as illustrated in the following excerpt. Any citations in the text of your paper must match up with an entry on the works cited or reference list.

MLA Style

> Richard Moe of the National Trust for Historic Preservation explains, "The problem is that too many people try to impose their preference for suburban-style mini-mansions on smaller scale neighborhoods where they just don't fit."

This source will be listed in the MLA Works Cited list as follows:

> Moe, Richard. "Battling Teardowns, Saving Neighborhoods." *The National Trust for Historic Preservation.* 28 June 2006. Web. 15 Jan. 2007.

APA Style

> Richard Moe (2006) of the National Trust for Historic Preservation explains, "The problem is that too many people try to impose their preference for suburban-style mini-mansions on smaller scale neighborhoods where they just don't fit."

This source will be listed in the APA reference list as follows:

> Moe, R. (2006, June 28). Battling teardowns, saving neighborhoods. Retrieved Jan. 15, 2007, from *The National Trust for Historic Preservation* Web site: http://www.nationaltrust.org/news/ 2006/20060628_speech_sf.html

Altering Direct Quotations with Ellipses and Square Brackets

Although there is nothing wrong with quoting whole sentences, it is often more economical to quote some words or parts of sentences from the original in your own sentences. When you do this, use *ellipses* (three evenly spaced periods) to signify the omission of words from the original; use square *brackets* to substitute words, to add words for purposes of clarification, and to change the wording of a quotation so that it fits gracefully into your own sentence. (If ellipses already appear in the material you are quoting and you are omitting additional material, place your ellipses in square brackets to distinguish them.)

The following passages illustrate quoted words integrated into the sentence, using ellipses and square brackets. The citation is in MLA style.

Square Brackets Use square brackets to indicate any substitutions or alterations to a direct quotation.

Original passage:

> Teardowns wreck neighborhoods. They spread through a community like a cancer, destroying the character and livability that are a neighborhood's lifeblood.

Passage worked into the paper: Part of the quotation has been turned into paraphrase.

> Moe compares the teardown trend to a cancer on the community: "Teardowns wreck neighborhoods. They [destroy] the character and livability that are a neighborhood's lifeblood."

Ellipses Use three spaced periods to indicate where words have been removed from a direct quotation.

Original passage:

> Almost every one of these new, large homes is made out of wood—roughly three-quarters of an acre of forest. Much of the destructive logging around the world is fueled by our demand for housing. But homebuilding doesn't have to translate into forest destruction. By using smart design and forest-friendly products, builders can create new homes that save trees and money.
>
> Many houses today are still built using outdated, inefficient construction methods. About one-sixth of the wood delivered to a construction site is never used, but simply hauled away as waste.

Passage worked into the paper: Two entire sentences have been removed, replaced with ellipses, because they were not relevant to the point Julie was making. There are no quotation marks because this will be a blocked quotation in the paper.

> Almost every one of these new, large homes is made out of wood—roughly three-quarters of an acre of forest. Much of the destructive logging around the world is fueled by our demand for housing. . . . Many houses today are still built using outdated, inefficient construction methods. About one-sixth of the wood delivered to a construction site is never used, but simply hauled away as waste.

Using Block Quotations

In MLA style, if a quoted passage runs to more than four lines of text in your essay, indent it one inch (ten spaces of type) from the left margin, double-space it as with the rest of your text, and omit quotation marks. In block quotations, a period is placed at the end of the final sentence, followed by one space and the parenthetical citation.

> In a consumer society, when people see their neighbors driving a new car, they think they need to buy a new one too. This is called "keeping up with the Joneses." Gregg Easterbrook has coined a new phrase, "call and raise the Joneses." He explains his new term this way:
>
> > In call-and-raise-the-Joneses, Americans feel compelled not just to match the material possessions of others, but to stay ahead. Bloated

> houses, for one, arise from a desire to call-and-raise-the-Joneses—
> surely not from a belief that a seven-thousand-square-foot house that
> comes right up against the property setback line would be an ideal
> place in which to dwell. (140)

In APA style, use the block form for quotations of more than forty words.
Indent the block five spaces from the left margin. Double-space all blocked
quotations.

Indirect Quotations

Indirect quotations are paraphrases or summaries of a source. Here is how
this quotation might be incorporated in a paper as an indirect quotation.

MLA Style

> A spokesperson for the U.S. Green Building Council reminds us that home
> ownership is fundamental to the American dream; however, in order to
> preserve that dream for the generations to come, we need to develop
> more energy efficient houses and lifestyles today (Sackett 36).

The entry in the Works Cited list would appear as follows:

> Sackett, Jessie. "The Green American Dream: LEED for Homes Is Cur-
> rently Being Piloted." *The LEED Guide: Environmental Design & Con-
> struction*. 9.6 (2006): 36+. *Academic OneFile*. Web. 18 Oct. 2006.

APA Style

> A spokesperson for the U.S. Green Building Council reminds us that home
> ownership is fundamental to the American dream; however, in order to
> preserve that dream for the generations to come, we need to develop
> more energy efficient houses and lifestyles today (Sackett, 2006, p. 36).

The entry in the References list would appear as follows:

> Sackett, J. (2006). The green American dream: LEED for homes is cur-
> rently being piloted. *The LEED Guide: Environmental Design & Con-
> struction*. 9.6 (2006): 36+. Retrieved from Academic OneFile.

In-Text References to Electronic Sources

The conventions just described apply to print sources. Adapt the examples
to Internet and other electronic sources. Because you must include the electronic sources in your works-cited or reference list, your in-text citations
should connect the material quoted or paraphrased in your text to the match-
ing work or posting on the list. Therefore, your in-text citation should begin
with the author's name or, lacking that, the title of the work or posting. The
APA format requires that you also include the posting date.

Leading into Direct Quotations

Direct quotations need to be set up, not dropped into your paper. Setting up a quotation means leading into it with words of your own. A lead-in may be a short introductory tag such as "According to Smith," if you have already introduced Smith, but lead-ins usually need more thought. You need to connect the quotation to the ideas surrounding it in the original source.

Provide enough of the original context to fit the quotation coherently into your paragraph. You may need to paraphrase some of the surrounding sentences from the original source from which the quotation was taken. If you have not done so already, you may need to introduce the speaker of the words, along with his or her credentials if the speaker is an important writer or authority.

Here is an example of a quotation that does not fit coherently into the student's paper.

Quotation dropped in:

Affluent Americans are buying new super-sized homes in older, urban residential areas. These lots were once occupied by historic and humble homes. "Teardowns wreck neighborhoods. They [destroy] the character and livability that are a neighborhood's lifeblood" (Moe).

Here is how Julie Ross led into the same quotation so that her readers would know more about the speaker and his point.

Quotation worked in:

Affluent Americans are buying new super-sized homes in older, urban residential areas. These lots were once occupied by historic and humble houses. The older houses are now known as "teardowns." In their place, towering "McMansions" dominate the street. Richard Moe, President of the National Trust for Historic Preservation, reports that teardowns affect over 300 U.S. cities, with a total of 75,000 older houses razed each year. Moe compares the teardown trend to a cancer on the community: "Teardowns wreck neighborhoods. They [destroy] the character and livability that are a neighborhood's lifeblood."

Introduces the speaker.

Provides context for the quotation.

Parenthetical citation of author's name not needed because author is cited in text.

CREATING WORKS CITED AND REFERENCE LISTS

At the end of your paper, include a bibliography of all sources that you quoted, paraphrased, or summarized. If you are using MLA style, your heading for this list will be *Works Cited*; if you are using APA style, it will be *References*. In either case, the list is in alphabetical order based on either the author's (or editor's) last name or—in the case of unidentified authors—the first word of the title, not counting the articles *a, an, the*. The entire list is double-spaced both within and between entries. See the Works Cited page of the sample student paper at the end of this chapter for the correct indentation and spacing.

www.mhhe.com/**crusius**

For an electronic tool that helps create properly formatted works-cited pages, go to:

Research > Bibliomaker

Note that MLA format requires that the first line of each entry be typed flush with the left margin; subsequent lines of each entry are indented half an inch (five spaces on a keyboard). The APA recommends the same indentation.

The following examples illustrate the correct MLA and APA style for the types of sources you will most commonly use.

MLA Style for Entries in the Works Cited List

The following pages show examples of how to cite the most commonly used kinds of sources in papers for first-year writing assignments. When putting entries into the Works Cited list,

- Put all entries, regardless of their genres and media, in alphabetical order according to the first word in each entry. This will usually be the lead author's or editor's last name or—if no author is named—the first word in the title that is not an article (*a, an, the*). See page 140 for an example.
- Do not number the entries.
- Double-space within and between entries; the list should look like the spacing in the rest of the paper.
- Begin each entry at the left margin and indent all subsequent lines by five spaces (one-half inch).
- Italicize titles of books, periodicals like magazines and journals, films, and other major works like Web sites and blogs.
- Put quotation marks around titles of articles and essays contained in periodicals or books of collected works, and around pages or posts found on a Web site.
- Capitalize all words in titles and subtitles except for articles (*a, an, the*), coordinating conjunctions (*and, or, but*) and prepositions. Always capitalize the first and last word of a title, regardless of its part of speech.
- Include subtitles of works; separate them from the title with a colon.

Books

The first word in each entry on the Works Cited list must match the in-text citation. The essential items are the

1. author's or editor's name, followed by a period (unless no author or editor is listed);
2. title of the work, followed by a period;
3. place of publication, followed by a colon;
4. publisher, followed by a comma; and
5. date of publication.

Do not cite page numbers for chapters or portions of entire books. Do cite page numbers for items in an anthology or collected set of works.

Book by a Single Author

> Urrea, Luis Alberto. *The Devil's Highway: A True Story.* New York: Little, 2004. Print.

Two or More Books by the Same Author   Instead of repeating the author's name in your Works Cited list, give the name in the first entry only. For subsequent works, use three hyphens in place of the name, followed by a period. Arrange the works in alphabetical order according to the first word in the title of the work, excluding articles (*a, an, the*).

> Obama, Barack. *The Audacity of Hope: Thoughts on Reclaiming the American Dream.* New York: Crown, 2006. Print.
>
> ———. *Dreams from My Father: A Story of Race and Inheritance.* 1995. New York: Three Rivers, 2004. Print.

Note: For republished works, include the original date of publication immediately after the book's title.

Book by Two or Three Authors   Put the name of the principal author (first author) first, beginning with his or her last name. Place a comma after the first author's name. Put the names of second and third authors in the regular order from first name to last name.

> Small, Gary, and Gigi Vorgan. *iBrain: Surviving the Technological Alteration of the Modern Mind.* New York: HarperCollins, 2008. Print.
>
> Booth, Wayne, Gregory G. Colomb, and Joseph Williams. *The Craft of Research.* 2nd ed. Chicago: U of Chicago P, 2003. Print.

Book by Four or More Authors   You can use only the first author's name and the Latin abbreviation et al., meaning "and others." It is also correct to list all the authors in order, as with two or three authors.

> Bellah, Robert N., et al. *Habits of the Heart: Individualism and Commitment in American Life.* New York: Harper, 1958. Print.

Book with No Author or Editor   Begin the citation with the title. In the Works Cited list, ignore articles *a, an,* and *the* when placing in alphabetical order.

> *The New York Times Guide to Essential Knowledge: A Desk Reference for the Curious Mind.* New York: St. Martin's, 2004. Print.

Book by a Corporate Author or Government Agency   Treat the corporation or agency as an author.

> Modern Language Association. *MLA Handbook for Writers of Research Papers.* 7th ed. New York: Modern Language Association of America. 2009. Print.

Anthology or Edited Compilation Place a comma after the editor's name and add the abbreviation for editor.

> Shreve, Susan Richards, ed. *Dream Me Home Safely: Writers on Growing Up in America*. Boston: Houghton, 2003. Print.

Work in an Anthology For works in collections of essays, poetry, and short stories, put the author of the individual work first, followed by its title in quotation marks, then the title of the collection in italics. The editor's name follows in normal order. Note that entries for works in anthologies do include the inclusive page numbers of the selection.

> Nguyen, Bich Minh. "Toadstools." *Dream Me Home Safely: Writers on Growing Up in America*. Ed. Susan Richards Shreve. Boston: Houghton, 2003. 129–132. Print.

Two or More Works from the Same Anthology If you are using more than one selection from an anthology, you will need three entries in your Works Cited list, one for the entire work, opening with the name of its editor, and one for each of the items, opening with the name of its author. Following the title of the work, you simply put the last name of the editor to refer your readers to the entire book, followed by the inclusive page numbers of each selection. Place each entry in its alphabetically determined spot on the Works Cited list, as illustrated below.

> Griffith, Patricia. "The Spiral Staircase." Shreve 73–81.
>
> MacDonald, Michael Patrick. "Spitting Image." Shreve 112–122.
>
> Shreve, Susan Richards, ed. *Dream Me Home Safely: Writers on Growing Up in America*. Boston: Houghton Mifflin, 2003. Print.

Translation

> Eco, Umberto. *The Name of the Rose*. Trans. William Weaver. San Diego: Harcourt, 1983. Print.

Later Edition of a Book Directly after the title, abbreviate the edition number without italics.

> Williams, Joseph M. *Style: Ten Lessons in Clarity and Grace*. 9th ed. New York: Pearson, 2007. Print.

Preface, Introduction, Foreword or Afterword Not by the Book's Author or Editor Open the entry with the name of the author of the part of the book; then provide the name of the section, followed by title of the book. If the book is a reprint, follow the title with the original date of publication. Use the word *by* before the author of the book. Indicate the inclusive page numbers for the part of the book you used as your source.

> Brogan, D. W., Introduction. *The Education of Henry Adams: An Autobiography.* 1918. By Henry Adams. Boston: Houghton, 1961. v–xviii. Print.

Reprinted Book   Directly after the title, include the original date of publication.

> Adams, Henry. *The Education of Henry Adams: An Autobiography.* 1918. Boston: Houghton, 1961. Print.

One Volume of a Multivolume Work   Directly after the title of the work, indicate the volume number you used.

> Churchill, Winston. *A History of the English-speaking Peoples.* Vol. 3. London: Cassell, 1956–58. Print.

More than One Volume of a Multivolume Work   After the title, indicate the total number of volumes in the work.

> Churchill, Winston. *A History of the English-speaking Peoples.* 4 vols. London: Cassell, 1956–58. Print.

Book That Is Part of a Series   After the medium (print) put the name of the series and a series number for the work if available. Do not italicize the series title.

> Horning, Alice, and Anne Becker, eds. *Revision: History, Theory, and Practice.* Lafayette, IN: Parlor Press, 2006. Print. Reference Guides to Rhetoric and Composition.

Signed Article in a Reference Book   Cite the name of the author, the title of the entry, the title of the reference work, name of the editor, and publication information. Do not include page numbers if entries appear in alphabetical order.

> Zangwill, O. L. "Hypnotism, History of." *The Oxford Companion to the Mind.* Ed. Richard L. Gregory. New York: Oxford UP, 1987. Print.

Unsigned Article in a Reference Book   Open with the title of the entry. Include page numbers if entries do not appear in alphabetical order.

> "A Technical History of Photography." *The New York Times Guide to Essential Knowledge: A Desk Reference for the Curious Mind.* New York: St. Martin's, 2004. 104–112. Print.

Religious Text Italicize the title and provide names of editors and/or translators and the publication information.

> *The Holy Bible.* Revised Standard Version. Cleveland: World, 1962. Print.

> *The Bhagavad Gita: According to Paramhansa Yogananda.* Ed. Swami
>   Kriyananda. Nevada City, CA: Crystal Clarity, 2008. Print.

Articles in Periodicals

The essential items in entries for articles in periodicals are the

1. author's name, followed by a period;
2. title of the article, followed by a period, all in quotation marks;
3. title of the publication, italicized;
4. volume number (if given);
5. date (if given), followed by a colon;
6. inclusive page numbers followed by a period; and
7. medium (print).

Article in a Weekly Magazine In the following example, the magazine was dated both July 6 and July 13. In such a case, use a comma between the two dates.

> Levy, Ariel. "Nora Knows What to Do." *The New Yorker* 6, 13 July 2009:
>   60–69. Print.

Article in a Monthly Magazine Abbreviate all months except May, June, and July.

> Mooney, Chris. "Climate Repair Made Simple." *Wired* July 2008: 128–133.
>   Print.

Article in a Print Newspaper Give the day, month, year, and edition, if specified; use abbreviations. Give section and page number. If pages are not consecutive, put a plus sign after the first page number.

> Yoon, Carol Kaesuk. "Reviving the Lost Art of Naming the World."
>   *New York Times* 11 Aug. 2009, natl. ed.: D1+. Print.

Review Open with name of reviewer and title of review, if there is one. Add abbreviation for "review of," not italicized, followed by the title of the work being reviewed, and its author or performer.

> Hofferth, Sandra. "Buying So Children Belong." Rev. of *Longing and
>   Belonging: Parents, Children, and Consumer Culture,* by Allison J.
>   Pugh. *Science* 324 (26 June 2009): 1674. Print.

Editorial in a Newspaper—No Named Author

"Disfigured Democracy: Health Care Extremism Exposes Our Uglier Side." Editorial. *Dallas Morning News* 13 Aug. 2009: A14. Print.

Letter to the Editor of a Newspaper or Magazine

Reed, Glenn. "Not Enough Fish in the Sea." Letter. *Harper's* Aug. 2009: 5. Print.

Article in a Journal with Volume Numbers   Put the volume number, a period, and the issue number after the title of the article. Put the month (if given) and the year in parentheses.

Bracher, Mark. "How to Teach for Social Justice: Lessons from *Uncle Tom's Cabin* and Cognitive Science." *College English* 71.4 (March 2009): 363–388. Print.

Other Genres as Sources

Advertisement in Print Medium   Open with the name of the item or service being advertised.

Daedalus Books. Advertisement. *Harper's* Aug. 2009: 6. Print.

Art Reproduction   Treat art found in books in the same way you treat essays found in edited collections. Open the entry with the artist's name, followed by the title of the work and the date it was created, if available. Before the publication information, include where the original work of art may be found.

O'Keefe, Georgia. *Light/17: Evening Star, No. V.* 1917. The Marion Koogler McNay Art Museum. *O'Keefe and Texas.* By Sharyn R. Udall. San Antonio: The Marion Koogler McNay Art Museum, 1998. Print.

Personal Interview   Give the name of the person interviewed, the kind of interview (personal, telephone), and the date it took place.

Coman, Carolyn. Telephone interview. 15 Aug. 2009.

Sources on the Internet

The essential items in entries for electronic sources are as follows (as available):

1. Name of author, editor (ed.), performer (perf.), or translator (trans.)
2. Title of work
3. Version or edition
4. Publisher or sponsor of the site
5. Date last updated (or n.d.)
6. Medium (Web)
7. Date you accessed the site

Web Site or Independent Online Work

It is not necessary to include the URL of a Web site unless your reader would have difficulty finding the site through a search engine.

Pew Hispanic Center
A PewResearchCenter Project

Chronicling Latinos' diverse experiences in a changing America

Search site...   Search   RSS

| Home | About the Center ▾ | Publications ▾ | Data and Resources ▾ | Download Datasets ⬇ | Sign Up for Updates ✉ |

Publications

Latest Pew Hispanic Center Publications

7.22.2009
Mexican Immigrants: How Many Come? How Many Leave?
The flow of immigrants from Mexico to the United States has declined sharply since mid-decade, but there is no evidence of an increase in Mexican-born migrants returning home from the U.S.

Survey data from the U.S. and Mexico reveal a large flow of migrants back to Mexico, but the size of the return flow appears to be stable since 2006. As for immigration to the U.S. from Mexico, surveys from both countries attest to recent substantial decreases in the number of new arrivals, reinforced by U.S. Border Patrol data showing markedly reduced apprehensions of Mexicans trying to cross into the United States illegally.

7.13.2009
Puerto Ricans in the United States, 2007

5.28.2009
Latino Children: A Majority Are U.S.-Born Offspring of Immigrants
The number of Hispanic children has nearly tripled since 1980 and their demographic profile has changed. More than half of the nation's 16 million Hispanic children are now "second generation," meaning they are the U.S.-born sons or daughters of at least one foreign-born parent. In 1980, a majority of Hispanic children were third or higher generation -- the U.S.-born sons or daughters of U.S.-born parents. This report also looks at the differences in the socio-economic profile and legal status of Hispanic children by generation.

5.28.2009
Who's Hispanic?
Is Judge Sonia Sotomayor the first Hispanic ever nominated to the U.S. Supreme Court, or does that distinction belong to Justice Benjamin Cardozo, who served on the court from 1932-38 and whose family tree apparently had some roots in Portugal? The question of who's Hispanic -- and who isn't -- turns out to be pretty complicated.

5.12.2009

Publications
Latest Publications
Complete Publication Archive

Publications by Topic
Demography
Immigration
Economics
Labor
Education
Politics
Identity
Remittances
Election '08

Publications by Year
2009
2008
2007
2006
2005
2004
2003
2002

Title of the Web site.

Find the person responsible for the site by clicking on the links that tell more about the Web site. Clicking on "About the Center" tells that Paul Taylor is the Director of the Pew Hispanic Center. If there is no author, editor, director, compiler, or corporate author, begin your works cited entry with the title of the Web site.

Date of most recent update of the site.

Medium (Web)

Date you accessed the Web site

Find the publisher or sponsor by also clicking on links that tell more "about" the Web site. Most home pages will provide the sponsor's name, as in our example. Clicking on "About the Center" tells that the Web site is a project of the Pew Research Center.

Example Entry for Entire Web Site

> Taylor, Paul, dir. *Pew Hispanic Center.* Pew Research Center, 22 July 2009. Web. 20 Aug. 2009.

Title of overall Web site

Publisher of the Web site

Date of the publication

Author of article

Title of article

Medium (Web)

Date you accessed the document

Example Entry for Document Found on a Web Site

> Fry, Richard. "The Changing Pathways of Hispanic Youths into Adulthood." *Pew Hispanic Center.* Pew Research Center, 7 Oct. 2009. Web. 15 Oct. 2009.

Personal Web Site   If the site has no title, use "home page" or other descriptive title. If there is no sponsoring organization, use N.p. to indicate no publisher.

> Langer, Ellen. Home page. N.p. 2009. Web. 28 July 2009.

Article in an Online Newspaper   Put the Web site in italics; follow with the name of the sponsor or publisher, not italicized.

> Hotz, Robert L. "Creative Destruction on a Cosmic Scale: Scientists Say Asteroid Blasts, Once Thought Apocalyptic, Fostered Life on Earth by Carrying Water and Protective Greenhouse Gas." *Wall Street Journal*. Wall Street Journal, 14 Aug. 2009. Web. 15 Aug. 2009.

Article in an Online Magazine

> MacFarquhar, Larissa. "Who Cares If Johnny Can't Read? The Value of Books Is Overstated." *Slate*. 17 April 1997. Web. 12 April 2009.

Article in an Online Scholarly Journal   After the author and article title, include the volume and issue number (if given) and the inclusive page numbers (if given.) The following periodical is published annually, so it has a volume number only.

> O'Dwyer, Kathleen. "Nietzsche's Reflections on Love." *Minerva—An Internet Journal of Philosophy* 12 (Nov. 2008): 37–77. Web. 12 Oct. 2009.

Article Accessed through a Library Subscription Database   Italicize the name of the subscription database as well as the title of the publication containing the article.

> Wolf, Maryanne, and Mirit Barzillai. "The Importance of Deep Reading." *Educational Leadership*. 66: 6 March 2009: 32–37. *Academic Search Complete*. Web. 6 March 2009.

Government Document on the Web

> United States. National Endowment for the Arts. *To Read or Not to Read: A Question of National Consequence*. Nov. 2007. Web. 8 April 2009.

Article in an Online Reference Work   If unsigned, open with the title of the article. When alphabetizing, ignore opening article (*a, an, the*).

> "The Biological Notion of Individual." *Stanford Encyclopedia of Philosophy*. 9 Aug. 2007. The Metaphysics Research Lab, Stanford U. Web. 26 Mar. 2009.

Blog Entry   Put the title of the post in quotation marks and the blog title in italics.

> Postrel, Virginia. "Naomi Wolf and the Phenomenology of Angelina Jolie."
>   *Dynamist.* 19 June 2009. Web. 8 July 2009.

Broadcast or Published Interview   Open with the names of the interviewee or interviewees; then provide the interviewer's name and the title of the interview, followed by the publisher, a comma, and the date it was published or put on the Web.

> Ganguly, Sumit, and Minxin Pei. Interview by Jayshree Bajoria.
>   "Balancing India and China." Council on Foreign Relations, 6 Aug.
>   2009. Web. 13 Aug. 2009.

Student Sample of a Research Paper in MLA Style

See pages 157–166 for a student's paper using MLA documentation.

Using APA Documentation Style

The American Psychological Association style of documentation is used not only in the field of psychology but also in education, anthropology, social work, business, and other behavioral and social sciences. The conventions of APA style aim to achieve an objective and impersonal tone. In the text, authors are usually referred to by last name only, and direct quotations are rare.

Like MLA, the APA system requires that a writer acknowledge the source of all direct quotations, paraphrased and summarized ideas from sources, and information that is not common knowledge. Citing is a two-step process: a brief in-text reference to the author and date of publication, and a longer entry with complete bibliographical information in the References list at the end of the article or book. Citing page numbers is required for direct quotations and highly specific data but not for summarizing or paraphrasing ideas found throughout a text.

In-text Citations

For both direct and indirect quotations, including paraphrased information that is not common knowledge, the basic in-text citation provides the last name of the author of the source, directly followed by the year the source was published. The following examples show options for citing in-text.

Paraphrased Reference to Source by One Author Named in the Sentence

> The playground is a space where gender identities are constructed.
> Paechter (2007) argues that boys who are physically passive on the
> playground move into the marginal spaces occupied by girls and younger
> children, and thus become stigmatized by other boys as effeminate.

Paraphrased Reference to Source by One Author Cited Only in Parenthetical Citation

> The playground is a space where gender identities are constructed. Boys who are physically passive on the playground move into the marginal spaces occupied by girls and younger children, and thus become stigmatized by other boys as effeminate (Paechter, 2007).

Direct Quotation with Author Named in the Sentence

> According to Yoon (2009) anthropologists have found that people around the world create remarkably similar categories when labeling plants and animals, a phenomenon known as folk taxonomy. Yoon finds consensus about such categories as trees, vines, and bushes especially interesting "since there is no way to define a tree versus a bush" (p. D4). In naming the world around them, people appear "unconsciously to follow a set of unwritten rules" (p. D1).

Direct Quotation with Author Named in Parenthetical Citation

> Anthropologists have found that people around the world create remarkably similar categories when labeling plants and animals, a phenomenon known as folk taxonomy (Yoon, 2009). Consensus about such categories as trees, vines, and bushes is especially interesting "since there is no way to define a tree versus a bush" (p. D4). In naming the world around them, people appear "unconsciously to follow a set of unwritten rules" (p. D1).

Source with Two Authors Give both authors' last names each time you refer to the source. If you name them as part of your sentence, use *and* to join them: Wolf and Barzillai (2009). If you name them in parentheses, use an ampersand as shown in the example below.

> Reading is far from our other natural human functions of seeing, moving, speaking, and thinking. Reading is an invented cognitive function, and understanding how it works illustrates the amazing plasticity of the brain (Wolf & Barzillai, 2009).

Source with Three or More Authors In your in-text citation, give all authors' last names in your first reference to the work. Write out *and* when the list is part of your sentence. Subsequent references should give only the first author's name followed by et al. (not in italics).
First reference:

> Radeloff, Hammer, and Stewart (2005) studied the impact of housing density on forests in the Midwestern United States.

Later references:

> Radeloff et al. (2005) argue that rural sprawl has more impact on forests than urban sprawl because even though rural sprawl is less dense, its effects are spread over larger areas that once were forests.

Two Authors with the Same Last Name   Include identifying initials before each last name.

> S. Young (2007) complains that scientists study earth-eating, or geophagia, only from the standpoint of their own disciplinary interests. Thus, there is no "global perspective of all the possible benefits and all the possible negative consequences of geopaghia" (p. 67).

Citations within Quotations   You will often find that your source cites other sources. Do not put these sources on your References list unless you also read them and used them in your paper. When quoting, include the citations as they appear in the passage you are quoting.

> Cantarero (2007) notes that moral, political, and economic factors enter in to what people think is good to eat. He offers the example of advertising:
>
> > By associating values with products, producers seek to increase their sales. According to the principle of incorporation (Rozin and Nemeroff, 1989; Fischler, 1992) subjects acquire the symbolic qualities of ingested food. Thus, ingestion goes beyond the satisfaction of hunger, deep into the sphere of mentalities and internalizes an ideological language which is "artificially" built. (p. 207)

If you have more than one source for the same point or information, you put both in the parenthetical citation.

With blocked quotations, place final period before the parenthetical citation.

Long Quotations   For direct quotations of forty or more words, omit quotation marks and display the quotation as a block of text set in from the left margin by about one-half inch (in the same place as a new paragraph's opening). Double-space the entire quotation. See the example above on Citations within Quotations.

Work with No Author or Editor   If no author or editor is named, you will use the title of the work in both in-text citations and Reference entries. If the title is long, you should abbreviate it. Use double quotation marks around the title of an article, a chapter, or a Web page. Italicize the title of a periodical, book, or report. The example below shows a Web site.

> The Law School Aptitude Test (LSAT) measures ability to read and comprehend in-depth texts with insight, to draw "reasonable inferences" from readings, and to analyze and evaluate the reasoning of others' arguments ("About the LSAT," 2009).

Personal Communications Personal communications such as letters and interviews are cited in text only, as in the following example.

> Carolyn Coman described her use of storyboarding to focus on the emotional impact of significant scenes in her fiction (C. Coman, personal communication, August 15, 2009).

Reference List Examples

Below are examples of how to cite the most commonly used kinds of sources in papers using the APA style of documentation. First, some general advice:

- Begin the list on a new page and center the word "References" at the top. (Do not enclose it in quotation marks.)
- Put all entries, regardless of their genres and media, in alphabetical order according to the author's (or editor's) last name, followed by the initials of the author's given name or names.
- If no author is named, use the first word in the title that is not an article (*a, an, the*). See page 183 for an example.
- Put the year, month, and date of publication immediately after the author's (or editor's) name, in parentheses.
- Do not number the entries.
- Double-space within and between entries; the list should look like the spacing in the rest of the paper.
- Begin each entry at the left margin and indent all subsequent lines by five spaces (one-half inch).
- Italicize titles of books and periodicals like magazines and journals.
- Do not enclose titles of articles in quotation marks.
- Capitalize only the first words of titles and subtitles, unless they are proper nouns (names).
- Capitalize the full names of periodicals, journals, and newspapers.

See the following list of examples for more help with citing specific kinds of sources.

Books

Book by a Single Author

> Paechter, C. F. (2007). *Being boys, being girls: Learning masculinities and femininities.* New York: McGraw-Hill.

Two or More Books by the Same Author List the works in order of publication, with the earliest first.

> Obama, B. (2004). *Dreams from my father: A story of race and inheritance.* New York: Three Rivers. (Original work published 1995)

Obama, B. (2006). *The audacity of hope: Thoughts on reclaiming the American dream.* New York: Crown.

Book by Two or More Authors   List all authors by last name and initials. Put commas between items in this list. Use an ampersand (&) before the final name.

Small, G., & Vorgan, G. (2008). *iBrain: Surviving the technological alteration of the modern mind.* New York: HarperCollins.

Booth, W., Colomb, G., & Williams, J. (2003). *The craft of research* (2nd ed.). Chicago: U of Chicago Press.

Book by a Corporate Author or Government Agency   Treat the corporation or agency as an author. If the author and publisher are the same, put "author" after the place of publication.

American Psychological Association. (2010). *Publication manual of the American Psychological Association* (6th ed.). Washington DC: Author.

Edited Compilation   Between the editor's name and the date, put the abbreviation for editor(s).

MacClancy, J., Henry, J., & Macbeth, H. (Eds.). (2007). *Consuming the inedible: Neglected dimensions of food choice.* New York: Berghahn Books.

Selection in an Edited Compilation   For articles in edited works, put the author of the individual work first, followed by the year of publication, and then the title of the article, followed by the word "In" and the editor or editors' names and the title of the collected work. The inclusive pages of the selection follow the title of the book, in parentheses. End the citation with place and name of publisher.

Young, S. (2007). A vile habit? The potential biological consequences of geophagia, with special attention to iron. In J. MacClancy, J. Henry, & H. Macbeth (Eds.), *Consuming the inedible: Neglected dimensions of food choice* (pp. 67–79). New York: Berghahn Books.

Edition Other than the First   Put the edition number in parentheses after the title.

Williams, J. M. (2007). *Style: Ten lessons in clarity and grace* (9th ed.). New York: Pearson Longman.

Translation   Put the translator's initials and last name, followed by the abbreviation for translator in parentheses, after the book's title.

Durkheim, E. (1984). *The division of labor in society.* (W. D. Halls, Trans.). New York: Free Press. (Original work published 1933)

Preface, Introduction, Foreword or Afterword Not by the Book's Author or Editor Open the entry with the name of the author of the part of the book; then put the date in parentheses and write out the name of the section written by this author. Follow with publication information for the rest of the book. Do not give page numbers in the References list.

> Coser, L. A. (1984). Introduction. In E. Durkheim, *The division of labor in society.* (W. D. Halls, Trans.). New York: Free Press. (Original work published 1933)

Reprinted Book Indicate original date of publication in parentheses.

> Obama, B. (2004). *Dreams from my father: A story of race and inheritance.* New York: Three Rivers. (Original work published 1995)

Note: The in-text citation should include both dates. (2004/1995).

One Volume of a Multivolume Work Directly after the author, indicate the inclusive dates of the volumes. After the title of the work, indicate in parentheses the volume number you used.

> Churchill, W. (1956–58). *A history of the English-speaking peoples* (Vol. 3). London: Cassell.

Article in a Reference Book Include inclusive page numbers for the entry after the title of the book. Put parentheses around page number or numbers.

> Zangwill, O. L. (1987). "Hypnotism, history of." In R. L. Gergory (Ed.), *The Oxford companion to the mind* (pp. 330–334.) New York: Oxford University Press.

Unsigned Article in a Reference Book Open with the title of the entry. Put parentheses around page numbers.

> A technical history of photography. (2004). *The New York Times guide to essential knowledge: A desk reference for the curious mind* (pp. 104–112). New York: St. Martin's.

Articles in Periodicals

For newspaper articles, use p. and pp. before page number. For magazine and journal articles, do not use p. or pp. Instead, put volume # in italics followed by the page numbers, separated with a comma.

Article in a Newspaper Give the day, month, year, and edition if specified. List all page numbers if the article appeared on discontinuous pages.

Yoon, C. K. (2009, August 11). Reviving the lost art of naming the world. *The New York Times,* pp. D1, D4.

Article in a Monthly Magazine

Mooney, C. (2008, July). Climate repair made simple. *Wired,* 128–133.

Article in a Weekly Magazine Include the day as well as the month and year.

Gladwell, M. (2009, October 19). "Offensive play: How different are dogfighting and football?" *The New Yorker,* 50–59.

Article in a Journal Paginated by Volume Put the volume number, a period, and the issue number after the title of the article. Put the month (if given) and the year in parentheses. Include inclusive page numbers for the article.

Bracher, M. (2009, March). How to teach for social justice: Lessons from *Uncle Tom's Cabin* and cognitive science. *College English* 71(4), 363–388.

Article in a Journal Paginated by Issue Put the issue number in parentheses after the volume. The volume number is italicized. The issue number is not.

Wolf, M., & Barzillai M. (2009, March). The importance of deep reading. *Educational Leadership, 66*(6), 32–37.

Newspaper Article with an Anonymous Author Open citation with title of the article. When alphabetizing, ignore opening articles (*a, an, the*).

Moon travel uncertain. (2009, August 14). *Dallas Morning News,* p. 12A.

Review Open with name of reviewer and title of review, if there is one. Put "Review of," followed by the item being reviewed, all in square brackets. Note that the volume number of the magazine is in italics, followed by a comma and the page number, not italicized.

Hofferth, S. (2009, June 26). Buying so children belong. [Review of the book *Longing and belonging: Parents, children, and consumer culture].* Science, *324,* 1674.

Editorial in a Newspaper—No Author Given Put the genre (editorial) in square brackets.

Disfigured democracy: Health care extremism exposes our uglier side. (2009, August 13). [Editorial]. *Dallas Morning News,* p. A14.

Letter to the Editor of a Newspaper or Magazine Put the genre (letter to the editor) in square brackets.

> Meibers, R. (2009, July). Thou shall kill. [Letter to the editor]. *Harper's,* 4.

Advertisement in Print Medium

> Daedalus Books. (2009, August). [Advertisement]. *Harper's,* 6.

Sources on the Internet

Article in an Online Newspaper Put the title of the newspaper in italics, followed by the URL of the paper's Web site.

> Hotz, R. L. (2009, August 14). Creative destruction on a cosmic scale: Scientists say asteroid blasts, once thought apocalyptic, fostered life on earth by carrying water and protective greenhouse gas. *Wall Street Journal.* Retrieved from http://online.wsj.com/home-page

Article in a Journal Accessed through Library Subscription Database Include the name of the database only if you think it unlikely that multiple databases would carry the article or that the article would be difficult to find.

Online Journal Article with Digital Object Identifier (DOI) Because uniform resource locators (URLs) often change, a new method of locating online materials has been developed. Increasingly, you will find that articles have an alphanumeric identification string, usually located near the copyright date in the article. You can also find it in the bibliographic information in the library's full record display. Use the DOI, if available, instead of the URL from which you retrieved the online article. Include the issue number in italics after the journal title. Conclude the entry with inclusive page numbers and the DOI.

> McGrevey, M., & Kehre, D. (2009). Stewards of the public trust: Federal laws that serve servicemembers and student veterans. *New Directions for Student Services, 126,* 89–94. doi: 10.1002/ss.320

Article in an Online Magazine without a DOI If there is no DOI, conclude the entry with "retrieved from" and the URL.

> MacFarquhar, L. (1997, April 17). Who cares if Johnny can't read? The value of books is overstated. *Slate.* Retrieved from http://www.slate.com/id/3128/

Article in an Online Scholarly Journal without DOI Volume number follows the journal title. If there is an issue number, it goes in parentheses after the volume number. In this case, there is no issue number because the journal is published annually.

> O'Dwyer, K. (2008). Nietzsche's reflections on love. *Minerva—An Internet Journal of Philosophy, 12,* 37–77. Retrieved from http://www.mic .ul.ie/stephen/vol12/Nietzsche.pdf

Article in an Online Encyclopedia or Reference Work   If the entry is unsigned, open with its title, as in the second example below.

> Botstein, L. (2005). Robert Maynard Hutchins and the University of Chicago. In J. Reiff, A. D. Keating, & J. R. Grossman (Eds.), *Encyclopedia of Chicago.* Retrieved from http://www.encyclopedia .chicagohistory.org
>
> The biological notion of individual. (2007, August 9). In E. N. Zalta (Ed.), *Stanford Encyclopedia of Philosophy.* Retrieved from http://plato.stanford.edu/

Blog Post   Give the URL but not the title of the blog.

> Postrel, V. (2009, June 19). Naomi Wolf and the phenomenology of Angelina Jolie. [Web log message]. Retrieved from http://www.dynamist.com/weblog/

Other Genres as Sources

Published or Broadcast Interview   Include the medium in which the interview was published.

> Ganguly, S., & Pei, M. (2009, August 6). Interview by J. Bajoria. Balancing India and China [Audio podcast.] Council on Foreign Relations. Retrieved from http://www.cfr.org/

Personal Interviews   Personal communication such as interviews and letters are not included in the list of references in APA style. However, you need to cite them in the text as described on page 151.

Student Sample of a Research Paper in APA Style

See pages 181–184 for an article using APA documentation.

STUDENT SAMPLE: A RESEARCH PAPER (MLA STYLE)

Ross 1

Standard heading

Julie Ross
ENGL 1301, Section 009
April 20, 2007
Professor Channell

Title centered

Why Residential Construction Needs to Get a Conscience

Entire essay is double-spaced

Introduction announces topic

Poses issue the argument will address

No word breaks at end of lines

Author's last name and page number in MLA style

Full name and credentials of authors who have expertise

Home ownership is a significant part of the American dream. Americans take great pride in putting down roots and raising a family in a good neighborhood. And, if a recent boom in residential construction is any indication, more Americans are realizing that dream. In addition to the number of new homes being built, the average home size has also grown significantly, almost twice as large as in the 1960s ("How to Build"). The question is: what is the impact of super-sized houses on our neighborhoods and our environment?

In big cities like Dallas, huge new houses are springing up in the outer-ring suburbs like Frisco and Flower Mound. The National Association of Homebuilders reports that the average size of a single-family home has grown from 983 square feet in 1950 to 2,434 square feet in 2005, "even as the average household shrunk from 3.4 to 2.6 people" (Brown 23). This desire for more living space keeps cities sprawling outward as developers look for open land. However, urban residential areas are also now impacted by new building. Affluent Americans are buying new super-sized homes in older, urban residential areas. These lots were once occupied by historic and humble houses. The older houses are now known as "teardowns." In their place, towering "McMansions" dominate the street. Richard Moe, President of the National Trust for Historic Preservation, reports that

www.mhhe.com/**crusius**

For another model essay in MLA format, go to:

Research > Sample Paper in MLA Style

Ross 2

teardowns affect over 300 U.S. cities, with a total of 75,000 older houses razed each year.

Moe compares the teardown trend to a cancer on the community: "Teardowns wreck neighborhoods. They [destroy] the character and livability that are a neighborhood's lifeblood." He sees three reasons for the rise in teardowns:

- In the past decade, the value of houses has doubled or tripled, except in some older neighborhoods. Developers look for these "'undervalued' properties" to build on.

- Homebuyers demand more space.

- Some homebuyers want to move from the "soulless . . . sprawling subdivisions" to close-in neighborhoods that have more character and more amenities, such as public transportation and local shopping.

Moe explains, "The problem is that too many people try to impose their preference for suburban-style mini-mansions on smaller scale neighborhoods where they just don't fit."

My neighborhood in Dallas, known as Lakewood Heights, has been plagued by more than its share of tearing down and building up. Once famous for its 1920s Craftsman and Tudor architecture, my quiet residential street is now marred by rows of McMansions, bustling traffic, and noisy, new construction. These colossal residences vary little in outward appearance from one to the next. "Starter mansions" as they are often called, have no particular architectural style and only remotely resemble Tudor or Craftsman styles. No matter where you look, these giants tower over their single-story neighbors, blocking the sunlight and peering into once-private backyards from their tall, garish peaks.

Paraphrases for information from source, quotations for opinions

Colon after full-sentence as introductory tag

Reasons against teardowns begin

Personal observation as support for this reason

Another reason against tearing down

Ross 3

A super-sized new home towers over its older next-door neighbor.

The builders and buyers of these giant homes are callous to community and environmental concerns. Preserving an old Dallas neighborhood's rich architectural history and green landscape is of little importance to them. For example, most McMansions occupy an extremely large footprint, leaving little or no yard space. Original homes in my neighborhood occupied about a third of their rectangular lot. This design permitted a sizable back yard with room for a small one-car garage as well as an inviting front lawn where children could play. By contrast, mega homebuilders show no appreciation for conventional site planning. They employ bulldozers to flatten the lot and uproot native trees. Their goal is to make room for as much house as possible, raking in more profit with each square foot. Furthermore, each tall fortress has a wide cold, concrete driveway leading to the grandiose two-Tahoe garage, equivalent to nearly half the size of my one-story house.

Ross 4

What was once a grassy lawn is now paved with concrete.

Only ten years ago pecan trees, the official state tree of Texas, and flowering magnolias graced every lawn on my block. These beautiful native trees, some over a century old, shaded our homes from the harsh Texas sun and our sidewalks from the triple-digit, summer heat. There is no way the new home owners' landscaping can replace what is lost. The charm of the neighborhood is being destroyed.

Aside from changing the face of my neighborhood, these monster houses, many selling for half a million or more, have skyrocketed property taxes and pushed out many older, lower-income, long-time residents. As a result, several senior citizens and other long-time residents of Lakewood have been forced to sell their homes and move to apartments. Many custom homeowners argue that more expensive, larger homes positively contribute to a neighborhood by increasing the resale value of smaller, older homes. This may be true to a certain extent. However, from a wider perspective,

Transition into another reason

Ross 5

short-term gains in resale prices are no compensation for
the irreversible harm done to our neighborhoods.

But the destruction of a neighborhood is only half the story.
These over-sized homes, and others like them everywhere, are
irresponsible from a larger environmental perspective. According
to Peter Davey, editor of the *Architectural Review,* "Buildings
[residential and commercial combined] take up rather more
than half of all our energy use: they add more to the pollution
of the atmosphere than transport and manufacture combined."
Not only is pollution a consequence of this surge in residential
structure size, but also the building of larger homes drains
our natural resources, such as lumber. The National Resource
Defense Council notes that forested areas, necessary for
absorbing greenhouse gas emissions, are being depleted by the
super-sizing trend in residential building:

> Almost every one of these new, large homes is made
> out of wood—roughly three-quarters of an acre of
> forest. Much of the destructive logging around the
> world is fueled by our demand for housing. . . .
> Many houses today are still built using outdated,
> inefficient construction methods. About one-sixth of
> the wood delivered to a construction site is never
> used, but simply hauled away as waste. And much of
> the wood that goes into the frame of a house is
> simply unnecessary. ("How to Build")

Obviously, residential construction must "go green" in an
effort to save valuable resources and conserve energy. But
what does it mean to "go green"? As Earth Advantage, a green
building certification organization, explains: "Green building
entails energy efficiency, indoor air quality, durability and
minimal site impact" (Kaleda). However, whether a home can
be designated as "green" depends on more than just

Double-space
blocked quotations;
use no quotation
marks

Period ends
sentence. Ellipses of
three dots indicates
material omitted

With block form,
period goes before
parenthetical
citation

Ross 6

energy-efficient construction methods and materials. According to Martin John Brown, an ecologist and independent consultant, green homebuilding is being used to describe a wide range of residential construction, and not all homes should qualify. Essentially, while some homebuilders are selling "environmentally-friendly" design, the epic scale of these new homes outweighs any ecological benefits provided through materials and construction methods. So, size does matter. A recent article in the *Journal of Industrial Energy,* published by M.I.T. Press, reports that a 1,500 square foot house with "mediocre energy-performance standards" will consume far less energy than a 3,000 square foot house with all the latest energy-saving materials and details (Wilson 284). In Boston, a house rated "poor" in terms of energy standards used 66% less energy than one rated "good" but twice the size (Wilson 282).

For articles by reporters or staff writers, rather than experts and authorities, their names can be cited parenthetically only

Brown argues that practically minded, ecologically conscious homebuilding should be part of our overall effort to decrease our consumption of limited resources and energy. Evidence from the Department of Energy supports his claim: "From 1985 to 2002, total residential energy consumption per capita climbed eight percent, and residential consumption for the nation—the figure most relevant to global effects like carbon dioxide (CO_2) emissions—climbed 32 percent" (Brown 23).

Unfortunately, many Americans who can afford it won't stop buying environmentally irresponsible, un-humble abodes. Their motives may stem from the competitive nature of consumer society. When people see their neighbors driving a new car, they think they need to buy a new one too. This is called "keeping up with the Joneses." Discussing the super-sized house, best-selling author Gregg Easterbrook has coined a new phrase, "call and raise the Joneses." As he explains it,

Ross 7

In call-and-raise-the-Joneses, Americans feel compelled
not just to match the material possessions of others,
but to stay ahead. Bloated houses . . . arise from a
desire to call-and-raise-the-Joneses—surely not from a
belief that a seven-thousand-square-foot house that
comes right up against the property setback line
would be an ideal place in which to dwell. (140)

Daniel Chiras, the author of *The Natural House: A Complete
Guide to Healthy, Energy-Efficient, Environmental Homes,*
warns: "People tell themselves that if they can afford a
10,000-square-foot house, then that's what they should have
. . . but I wonder if the earth can afford it" (qtd. in Iovine).

Fortunately, other Americans are starting to recognize
the folly of buying more space than they need. A survey by
Lowe's and Harris Interactive found that "46% of
homeowners admit to wasting up to half of their home"
("Are McMansions Giving Way"). Felicia Oliver of
Professional Builder magazine suggests that the marriage of
conservation and construction is the next natural step in the
evolution of residential building. One example of a builder
taking this step is the Cottage Company in Seattle, which
specializes in "finely detailed and certified-green" houses of
between 1,000 and 2,000 square feet. Company co-owner
Linda Pruitt says Cottage Company houses "'live as big' as
McMansions because they're better designed, with features
like vaulted ceilings and abundant built-ins. 'It's kind of like
the design of a yacht,' she says. The theme is quality of
space, not quantity" (qtd. in Brown 24).

Even Richard Moe of the National Trust for Historic
Preservation admits that responsible new construction has a
place in older neighborhoods:

---

*Cite author of
article, not speaker.
Use "qtd." to
indicate quotation
appeared in the
source*

*If no author, use
shortened form of
title
Shows possible
solution to problem*

Ross 8

Trees tower over this stretch of original modest-scale homes in
Lakewood Heights, reminding us of what is being lost.

No one is saying that homebuyers shouldn't be able to
alter or expand their home to meet their needs, just as
no one is saying that older neighborhoods should be
frozen in time like museum exhibits. A neighborhood is a
living thing, and change is both inevitable and desirable.
The challenge is to manage change so that it respects
the character and distinctiveness that made these
neighborhoods so appealing in the first place.

This is the challenge that must be met in my own
neighborhood. If new construction and additions are as
architecturally interesting as the older homes and
comparable with them in size and footprint, preserving lawns
and trees, the neighborhood can retain its unique character.

Jessie Sackett, a member of the U.S. Green Building
Council, writes: "Owning a home is the cornerstone of the

Conclusion returns
to idea used in
introduction

Ross 9

American dream. Recently, however, we've realized that keeping that dream alive for future generations means making some changes to how we live today" (36). We must ensure that the American Dream doesn't translate into a horrific nightmare for our planet or future generations. Therefore, I ask would-be homebuyers to consider only the more conscientious construction in both urban and suburban areas. When we demand more modest and responsible homebuilding, we send a clear message: younger generations will know that we value our planet and our future more than we value excessive personal living space.

- - - - - - - - - - - - - - [separate page] - - - - - - - - - - - - - -

Works Cited

"Are McMansions Giving Way to Smaller, Cozier Homes?" *Coatings World.* Aug. 2004: 12. *Academic OneFile.* Web. 12 Jan. 2007.

Brown, Martin John. "Hummers on the Homefront: At 4,600 Square Feet, Is It an Eco-House?" *E, The Environmental Magazine.* Sept–Oct 2006: 23–24. *Academic OneFile.* Web. 6 Oct. 2006.

Davey, Peter. "Decency and Forethought: It Is Foolish to Behave As If We as a Race Can Go on Treating the Planet As We Have Been Doing Since the Industrial Revolution." *The Architectural Review* 213.1281 (2003): 36–37. *Academic OneFile.* Web. 18 Oct. 2006.

Easterbrook, Gregg. *The Progress Paradox: How Life Gets Better While People Feel Worse.* New York: Random House, 2003. Print.

"How to Build a Better Home: A New Approach to

Use alphabetical order according to author's last name or if no author, according to first word in title, ignoring articles (a, an, the)

Double-space in and between entries

Ross 10

Homebuilding Saves Trees and Energy—and Makes for
Economical, Comfortable Homes." *National Resources
Defense Council.* 22 July 2004. Web. 22 Oct. 2006.

Iovine, Julie V. "Muscle Houses Trying to Live Lean; Solar
Panels on the Roof, Five Cars in the Garage." *The New
York Times.* 30 Aug. 2001: B9. *Academic OneFile.* Web.
18 Oct. 2006.

Kaleda, Colleen. "Keeping It 'Green' with Panels and More."
The New York Times. 15 Oct. 2006: 11. *Academic
OneFile.* Web. 22 Oct. 2006.

Moe, Richard. "Battling Teardowns, Saving Neighborhoods."
The National Trust for Historic Preservation. 28 June
2006. Web. 23 Jan. 2007.

Oliver, Felicia. "The Case for Going Green." *Professional
Builder* (1993). 2.5 (2006): 38. *Academic OneFile.* Web.
6 Oct. 2006.

Sackett, Jessie. "The Green American Dream: LEED for
Homes Is Currently Being Piloted." *The LEED Guide:
Environmental Design & Construction.* 9.6 (2006): 36+.
Academic OneFile. Web. 18 Oct. 2006.

Wilson, Alex, and Jessica Boehland. "Small Is Beautiful: U.S.
House Size, Resource Use, and the Environment." *Journal
of Industrial Energy.* 9.1 (Winter/Spring 2005): 277–287.
Academic Search Complete. Web. 17 Feb. 2007.

CHAPTER 7

Ethical Writing and Plagiarism

WHY ETHICS MATTER

To write well, you need to be informed about your topic, which means doing research into what others have already said about it. You will want to put some of these ideas into your papers, but it is unethical to do so in a way that does not give credit to the source.

By citing your sources, you also earn your reader's respect. Readers are more likely to accept your views if you project good character, what the ancient rhetoricians called *ethos*. Honesty is part of good character. Part of writing honestly is distinguishing your ideas from the ideas of others.

The news has been filled in recent years with stories about unethical writers, people who have been caught using other writers' words and ideas without citing the source. One university president who borrowed too freely in a convocation speech was forced to resign. Recently, some history professors' books were found to contain long passages taken word-for-word from sources, the result—they claimed—of careless note-taking. Whether deliberate or accidental, such mistakes can destroy a person's career.

Plagiarism by students also has become an increasing problem, partly as a result of the Internet. Students may plagiarize by accident, not realizing

www.mhhe.com/**crusius**

For more information on plagiarism, go to:

Research > Plagiarism

that material that is so easy to copy and paste from the Web must be treated as a quotation and cited as a source. The Internet has also become part of the solution to this problem: Professors using programs like Turnitin.com can check submitted work for originality. At schools using this software, plagiarism dropped by 82%.*

For students, the consequences of plagiarizing are severe, ranging from failure on the writing project to failure in the course and even to suspension or expulsion from the university. Many universities will indicate on a student's transcript if there has been an honor violation, something that potential employers will see.

The purpose of this chapter is to help you avoid plagiarizing.

WHAT PLAGIARISM IS

We like the definition of plagiarism on Fairfield University's online honor tutorial because it includes the various kinds of media that count as sources and must be acknowledged when you draw from them. See Concept Close-Up, on the next page, to read this definition.

As we explain in Chapter 6, "Writing Research-Based Arguments," you must document the sources of all direct quotations, all paraphrased ideas taken from sources, and even information paraphrased from sources, unless it is "common knowledge."

A good definition of *common knowledge* comes from Bruce Ballenger's excellent book *The Curious Researcher:* "Basically, common knowledge means facts that are widely known and about which there is no controversy."† If you already knew something that shows up in your research, that is a good indication that it is common knowledge, but you also have to consider whether your *readers* would already know it. If your readers know less about your topic than you do, it is good to cite the source, especially if the information might surprise them.

THE ETHICS OF USING SOURCES

There are five major kinds of violations of ethics in using sources.

Purchasing a Paper

A simple Internet browser search for most topics will turn up services that offer pre-written essays for sale. These services claim that the essays are merely "examples" of what could be written on the topic, but we all know better. In almost every arena of life, people are ruthlessly trying to make a

---

*"Largest Study of Cheating in the World Reveals 82% Drop in Plagiarism After Using Turnitin.com for Five or More Years." *PR Newswire.* Oct. 4, 2006.

†Bruce Ballenger, *The Curious Researcher: A Guide to Writing Research Papers,* 3rd ed. (Boston: Allyn and Bacon, 2001), 236.

CONCEPT CLOSE-UP

Plagiarism: The Presentation or Submission of Another's Work as Your Own

Plagiarism includes summarizing, paraphrasing, copying, or translating words, ideas, artworks, audio, video, computer programs, statistical data, or any other creative work, without proper attribution.

Plagiarism can be deliberate or accidental. It can be partial or complete. No matter which, the penalties are often similar. Understanding what constitutes plagiarism is your first step to avoiding it.

SOME ACTS OF PLAGIARISM:

- Copying and pasting from the Internet without attribution
- Buying, stealing, or ghostwriting a paper
- Using ideas or quotations from a source without citation
- Paraphrasing an author too lightly

"What Constitutes Plagiarism?" by Ramona Islam, Senior Reference Librarian and Instruction Coordinator at Fairfield University. Reprinted with permission.

---

buck off the gullible or the desperate. These services are counting on college students to take the bait. It's a bad idea for all these reasons:

- You learn nothing about writing, so you are cheating yourself.
- College professors can find the same essays by searching the Internet and by using more sophisticated search engines designed by textbook publishers to help them find plagiarism.
- The paper will be a poor fit with the prompt your teacher has given you, and the style of the writing will not match previous examples of your own voice and style—red flags professors easily detect.
- Some of these papers are poorly written, often filled with generalizations, bad thinking, and errors of grammar and punctuation.

Using a Paper Found Online

Many college professors and high school teachers have class Web sites where they post the best work of their students. These papers will often turn up in online searches. Do not be tempted to use these papers or parts of them without citing them, and that includes giving the qualifications of the author.

Using Passages from Online Sources without Citing the Source

It is easy to copy and paste material from the Internet, and much of it is not protected by copyright. Nevertheless, to take passages, sentences, or even

CONCEPT

Understanding the Ethics of Plagiarism

A student who plagiarizes faces severe penalties: a failing grade on a paper, perhaps failure in a course, even expulsion from the university and an ethics violation recorded on his or her permanent record. Outside of academe, in the professional world, someone who plagiarizes may face public humiliation, loss of a degree, rank, or job, perhaps even a lawsuit. Why is plagiarism such a serious offense?

Plagiarism is theft. If someone takes our money or our car, we rightly think that person should be punished. Stealing ideas or the words used to express them is no less an act of theft.

Plagiarism is a breach of ethics. In our writing, we are *morally obligated* to distinguish between our ideas, information, and language and somebody else's ideas, information, and language. Human society cannot function without trust and integrity—hence the strong condemnation of plagiarism.

Plagiarism amounts to taking an unearned and unfair advantage. You worked hard to get that "B" on the big paper in your political science class. How would you feel if you knew that another student had simply purchased an "A" paper, thereby avoiding the same effort? At the very least, you would resent it. You should report it. Plagiarism is not just a moral failure with potentially devastating consequences for an individual. *Plagiarism, like any form of dishonesty, damages human society and hurts everyone.*

---

phrases or single significant words from another text is plagiarism. Significant words express strong judgment or original style, such as metaphors.

Compare the source text below with the uses of it. It comes from an interview with Al Gore about his film *An Inconvenient Truth*. The interview appeared in *Sierra* magazine, found on the Sierra Club Web site.*

> **Sierra:** In your movie, you cite U.S. determination in World War II as an example of the kind of resolve we need to confront global warming. But it took the attack on Pearl Harbor to galvanize the country. Are we going to have a similar moment in this crisis?
>
> **Gore:** Obviously, we all hope it doesn't come to that, but for hundreds of thousands of people in New Orleans, that moment has already been reached. And for millions of people in Africa's Sahel, that moment has already been reached with the disappearance of Lake Chad. For an untold number of species, it has been reached. The challenge for the rest of us is to connect the dots and see the picture clearly. H. G. Wells

---

*Pat Joseph, "Start by Arming Yourself with Knowledge: Al Gore Breaks Through with His Global-Warming Message." *Sierra*. Sept.-Oct. 2006. Oct. 21, 2006 <http://www.sierraclub.org/sierra/200609/interview.asp>.

wrote that "history is a race between education and catastrophe." And this is potentially the worst catastrophe in the history of civilization. The challenge now is to seize our potential for solving this crisis without going through a cataclysmic tragedy that would be the climate equivalent of wartime attack. And it's particularly important because, by the nature of this crisis, when the worst consequences begin to manifest themselves, it will already be too late.

Unethical use of source:

> It will take an environmental crisis to galvanize the country into confront-ing the problem of global warming, and for hundreds of thousands of people in New Orleans, that moment has already been reached. The challenge for the rest of us is to connect the dots and see the picture clearly. H. G. Wells wrote that "history is a race between education and catastrophe." And this is potentially the worst catastrophe in the history of civilization, so we must step up our efforts to learn about global warming and the means to keep it in check.

In this example, the writer has made no reference to the source of the words or ideas. This is wholesale theft of another's words and ideas. This kind of borrowing from sources is every bit as unethical as buying a paper online and turning it in as your own writing.

Ethical use of source:

> There are two routes to discovering the need to confront the problem of global warming, as Al Gore explained to *Sierra* magazine. We can wait for catastrophes like Hurricane Katrina, or we can learn from other environmental crises that are occurring around the globe and take action now. Quoting H. G. Wells, who said that "history is a race between educa-tion and catastrophe," Gore argues that we need to get educated because global warming is "potentially the worst catastrophe in the history of civilization. . . ." (Joseph).

The ethical way to use a source is

- to integrate paraphrase and direct quotation into a paragraph of your own, and
- to cite the source.

Notice that good paraphrasing does not borrow either the language or the sentence pattern of the original text. The source is cited and the style of the sentences is the student's own.

Inadequate Paraphrasing

Paraphrasing is tricky because paraphrases must be *entirely* your own words, not a mixture of your words and the words of the source. Even if you cite the source, it is plagiarism to borrow words and phrases from another author.

Therefore, you must put quotation marks around sentences, parts of sentences, and even significant words taken directly from another text.

Here is a source text, and on page 173 is the picture, to which the examples of paraphrase that follow refer:

> Subversive masculine modes in the second half of this century began with the tee-shirts and blue jeans of rural laborers, later adopted by rebellious urban youth.
>
> —Anne Hollander, *Sex and Suits* (New York: A. A. Knopf, 1994)

Unethical use of source:

> Marlon Brando symbolizes the subversive masculine mode of the second half of the twentieth century with the tee-shirts and blue jeans of rural laborers (Hollander 186).

Even though the student cited his source, this is plagiarism because his sentence contains words from the source without quotation marks. This example illustrates the most common kind of unintentional plagiarism. This passage also fails to identify Hollander as the interpreter of the image.

To avoid this accidental plagiarism:

- When taking notes, highlight in color any wording that you copy directly from a source.

- When paraphrasing, study the original passage but then put it aside when you write your paraphrase, so that you will not be tempted to use the wording of the source. Then go back and check your paraphrase for accuracy and for originality of expression. As the ethical version below shows, any quoted parts must be treated as quotations.

Ethical use of source:

> According to art historian Anne Hollander, Marlon Brando's tee-shirt and blue jeans illustrate a rebellious kind of late-twentieth-century masculinity, a look originally associated with "rural laborers" (186).

This version has reworded the sentence into an adequate paraphrase and used quotation marks around a phrase taken word for word from Hollander. It also identifies Hollander as an art historian, which establishes her credibility. When you tell your readers something about your source, you increase the credibility of your own writing.

Paraphrasing Ideas or Information without Naming the Source

Although it is not necessary to cite sources of commonly available information, such as the percentage of high school graduates who go to college, you must give credit when a source presents someone's idea, interpretation, or opinion, or when the information would be difficult for your readers to

Marlon Brando in A Streetcar Named Desire, *1951.*

verify on their own. If in doubt, it is always better to cite. The source text below comes from a book about the college experience:

> Many [college] seniors single out interdisciplinary classes as the courses that meant the most to them. As a corollary, they cite faculty members who, while expert in their own fields, are able to put the fields in proper perspective. Students find this important. They believe that the real world, and the way people think about the world, does not divide neatly into categories called history, chemistry, literature, psychology, and politics.
>
> —Richard J. Light, *Making the Most of College: Students Speak Their Minds* (Cambridge: Harvard UP, 2001)

Unethical use of source:

> Studies have shown that college students find interdisciplinary courses the most meaningful. They also prefer professors who can think outside the box of their own areas of academic specialization.

Richard Light's research led him to this information; he deserves credit for his work.

Ethical use of source:

> In interviews with seniors at Harvard, where he teaches, Richard Light found that college students say that interdisciplinary courses are the most meaningful. They also prefer professors who can think outside the box of their own areas of academic specialization (126).

By citing Light as the source of this information, the writer has also added credibility to his or her own essay.

When Opinions Coincide

Students often ask what to do when they have an idea, opinion, or interpretation and then encounter that same idea, opinion, or interpretation as they are doing research. For example, after looking into the problem of global warming, a student could easily come to the conclusion that rising temperatures and ocean levels could become a threat to civilization. Reading the *Sierra* interview with Al Gore, that student sees that she and Gore share the opinion that global warming "is potentially the worst catastrophe in the history of civilization." If the student doesn't use Gore's exact words, is it plagiarism to use the opinion without citing him? A classic book on the subject of research, *The Craft of Research*, advises the cautious approach: "In the world of research, priority counts not for everything, but for a lot. If you do not cite that prior source, you risk having people think that you plagiarized it, even though you did not."* You do not have to check to see that all of your own ideas are not already out there; however, if you encounter one of your own in a source, you should acknowledge that source.

THE ETHICS OF GIVING AND RECEIVING HELP WITH WRITING

Writing is not a solitary act. Most professional writers seek feedback from colleagues, editors, family, and friends, and they thank those who have contributed in the acknowledgments section of the book. Students benefit from help with their projects—in conferences with their instructors, peer exchanges with other students in class, and visits to their campus's tutorial services. Whether you are giving help or receiving it, you need to realize that inappropriate help is also plagiarism because it involves using someone else's ideas and language. If someone tells you what to write, rewrites your work for you, or even proofreads or "edits" your work, that is plagiarism, because you are using someone else's work as if it were your own. Likewise, it is

---

*Wayne C. Booth, Gregory Colomb, and Joseph M. Williams, *The Craft of Research*. (Chicago: University of Chicago Press, 2003), 203.

unethical for you to provide such help to anyone else, a practice known as "facilitating plagiarism" and equally punishable at most schools.

The following list describes three unethical ways of giving and receiving help.

1. **Having someone "ghostwrite" your paper.** College campuses attract unscrupulous people who offer to "help" students with their writing. It is dangerous to use an off-campus tutor because his or her primary interest is income, not education.

2. **Having someone edit your paper for style.** It is plagiarism to have someone else change your wording and word choices for you. Your instructor will teach you about elements of style and illustrate principles of editing. This textbook covers such material in Appendix A.

   After you have used this advice to edit your own paper, it is okay to ask someone else to point out passages that need more attention and even to explain why those passages are wordy or unclear. But it is up to you to improve the expression.

3. **Having someone proofread your paper for grammar and punctuation.** As with editing for style, proofreading is your responsibility. You

B. Smaller

"My parents didn't write it—they just tweaked it."

plagiarize if you hand your paper to someone else to "clean it up," whether as a favor or for money. Many students need help with proofreading, and your instructor or on-campus tutorial service can offer instruction that will help you catch errors in the future.

ETHICAL WRITING AND GOOD STUDY HABITS

Good study habits are central to ethical writing.

- **Do not procrastinate.** Students who procrastinate are more likely to make the kind of careless errors that lead to accidental plagiarism. They are also more likely to use intentional plagiarism as the only way to meet a deadline.

- **Take careful notes.** Use your notebook or notecards to write about your sources, being sure to distinguish your own ideas from the material you copy directly or paraphrase. Use quotation marks around any words you take directly from a source.

- **Ask your instructor about proper sources of help with your writing.** Avoid using untrained family members and friends as tutors. If your school has a writing center, take advantage of the tutors there.

- **Work on improving your reading skills.** Good reading skills will empower you to use sources more confidently. Read Chapter 2, "Reading an Argument," for advice on how to improve your comprehension and analysis of texts.

The Aims of
Argument

THE AIMS OF ARGUMENT

CHAPTER 8

Joining the Conversation: Arguing to Inquire

In Chapter 2, "Reading an Argument," and Chapter 3, "Analyzing an Argument," we offered what you need to respond critically to any argument you encounter. Chapter 4 took you through the process of writing a critique, an application of what you learned in Chapters 2 and 3.

What you learned in these chapters applies to arguing to inquire. However, inquiry is different from responding to single arguments. **Inquiry** *is joining a conversation, an ongoing exchange of opinions about some controversial topic,* and therefore involves many arguments advanced by many people.

To join any conversation, you have to know already or become familiar with what is going on. This is the case whether you are talking in a group, posting on a blog, working on a term paper, drafting a business proposal, or composing a letter to your mayor or city council. In short, *having something to say depends on knowing what others have said.* It depends on *comparing perspectives,* analyzing and evaluating existing viewpoints.

What Is Synthesis?

All the genres that use comparisons *synthesize*—a Greek word that means "putting together." Typically the views you encounter in comparing perspectives are at odds with one another enough to make point-by-point reconciliation impossible. In other words, no one could fashion a single, consistent view out of everything they say. Therefore, aim for a *partial synthesis,* selecting what you consider the best insights from each, combining them with your own insights, thereby creating a new perspective. The result is your viewpoint, matured and refined by open and thoughtful engagement with the viewpoints of others.

WHAT IS COMPARING PERSPECTIVES?

Many situations call for written comparisons of people's perspectives on a problem, issue, or question. Money managers compare stock analysts' reports; land developers compare architectural concepts for a new building; government administrators compare reports from advocacy groups; a consumer compares product reviews. Among many others, genres that compare perspectives include

- Book reviews that evaluate two or three recently published books on the same topic
- Market research that analyzes the results of in-depth interviews to find patterns and commonalities in consumers' preferences and attitudes
- Introductions to articles in the sciences that provide overviews of past research
- Exploratory essays that question and evaluate the viewpoints of other people writing on the same topic

WHY WRITE TO COMPARE PERSPECTIVES?

All researched writing begins with reading and comparing other people's perspectives on a topic. Writing out this exploration helps us to

- Sort out the specific points being discussed
- See where opinions intersect and diverge
- Pin down, point by point, the differences and similarities
- Reflect on the points under debate
- Formulate our own view

Put another way, what do you do *after* you find sources for a paper? The answer is, compare perspectives, without which you cannot make sense out of them or use them to say anything yourself. Comparing perspectives, then, is an essential part of doing research for anything you write.

HOW DOES COMPARING PERSPECTIVES WORK?

Writing that compares perspectives usually proceeds by asking and answering a series of questions about the readings selected for comparison.

The Art of Questioning: What to Ask When Comparing Perspectives

1. What is the central question addressed in all the readings?

2. What are the key terms or concepts used in discussing this question, and how do the writers define these terms? Is there disagreement about the meaning of key terms?

3. What do the authors have to say about the question, and where do their answers agree or disagree on points in common? When perspectives disagree, how do you assess the arguments of each author? Whose views have more validity, and why?

4. What conclusions or insights into the central question have you been able to reach as a result of comparing perspectives on it?

Of these four questions, the third is especially important. Locate the points of agreement; they will reveal the *current state of informed opinion.* Locate the points where there is disagreement; they will reveal the *live issues,* what is currently in dispute. We must know both to join a conversation—what is accepted as true, and what people are arguing about.

The Writer as Inquirer

In addition to the perspectives you read, you will probably have a perspective of your own on the central question you are investigating. Acknowledge it, but keep an open mind as you read through others' opinions. Read all perspectives with an equally critical stance. You will be reading arguments, but *you will be arguing to inquire, writing an exploration.* Your paper should open with the central question to explore, not with your own thesis on the question.

It is important to keep the central question open and to present all views fairly and accurately. Use your own thinking to evaluate the views. Keeping a question open does not mean accepting everything you read. Give reasons for saying what you accept as the better perspective as you work through the points of agreement and disagreement. Expect your exploration to lead you to a more informed viewpoint than you had before writing.

Which Character Should Sports Develop?

ANDY RUDD

Andy Rudd is a psychologist on the faculty at Florida State University. The following selection is the opening from a much longer article on the relationship of sports and character. It is widely assumed that participation in sports builds character in young people. If it does, Rudd asks, what kind of character does it build? As you read, identify the differing informed opinions Rudd presents. Where do you stand on this issue, and what might you add to the conversation?

ABSTRACT

For years, strong claims have been made that sport builds character. Despite such claims, a "winning at all cost" mentality can frequently be seen within all of sport. The reason for this paradox may relate to confusion around what it means to demonstrate character. The purpose of this article is to show that there are indeed two distinct types of character that are espoused in the sport milieu. One type is related to social values (social character) the other related to moral values (moral character). Following an explication and comparison of these types of character, a recommendation is made for a needed emphasis towards the development of moral character.

INTRODUCTION

In his *A Way Out of Ethical Confusion,* Zeigler (2004) asks the question: "What character do we seek for people?" He refers to Commager's 1966 list of 12 traits— i.e., "common denominators"—that can be attributed to Americans. In this list are many traits, some of which apply directly to the topic of sport's relationship to character. These are self-confidence; materialism; complacency bordering occasionally on arrogance; cultivation of the competitive spirit; and indifference to, and exasperation with laws, rules, and regulations" (p. 7). Zeigler believes that the situation deteriorated further by the end of the 20th century. In the dedication to this work, he states: "I believe there is an urgent need to challenge the underlying human values and norms that have determined the direction the United States is heading in the 21st century" (p. iii). This comment, if true, has significance in a search for an answer to the topic at hand. Which "character" should sport develop?

Typically when an athlete or team at any level of sport is considered to have displayed character, the word "character" is associated with a host of values such as teamwork, loyalty, self-sacrifice, perseverance, work ethic, and mental toughness. As a specific example, a high school athletic director defined an athlete's character as "a willingness to try no matter what the situation. An attempt to continually improve; a willingness to give all up for the cause; and sacrificing without expectations." In another example, a high school coach asserted: "Character is the belief in self-worth and your own work ethic. . . ." (Rudd, 1999).

In professional sport, character has been defined similarly. For instance, consider a newspaper article that headlined, "The Arizona Diamondbacks Attribute Their Success to Character." Specifically, the article highlighted the Diamondbacks as players who work hard and don't complain about salaries (Heyman, 2000). Consider also an issue of *Sports Illustrated* in which New England Patriots' Troy Brown commented on former teammate Drew Bledsoe's ability to play with a broken finger and lead his team to victory. Brown stated, "It showed a lot of character" (Zimmerman, 2001, p. 162).

A convention in science articles, abstracts help researchers decide whether an article is relevant to their research without having to read the article itself.

First paragraph "frames" the article by answering key questions: What is character as Americans understand and value it? How does character relate to sports? How does character developed by sports relate to the future of American values?

This article uses APA notational conventions. Use it as a model for papers you write that require APA style.

Specifies what character means in sports, as generally understood by athletic directors and coaches. Author must establish this understanding of character to serve as a contrast with "moral character" in paragraph 4.

4   However, in contrast to the notion that an athlete of character is one who displays values such as teamwork, loyalty, self-sacrifice, perseverance, work ethic, and mental toughness, sport scholars in the area of character development have defined character with a different set of values. Sport scholars, including sport philosophers and sport psychologists, more commonly define an athlete of character as one who is honest, fair, responsible, respectful, and compassionate (Arnold, 1999; Beller & Stoll, 1995; Gough, 1998; Shields & Bredemeier, 1995). For example, Arnold (1999) states, "In terms of moral goodness, or what I refer to as moral character, it involves a life that complies with such virtues as justice, honesty, and compassion" (p. 42).

Specifies what author means by "moral character" and contrasts it with "social character." This is the second perspective the article develops.

5   It does indeed seem, therefore, that there are two distinct definitions of character maintained by two camps. The first camp consists of coaches, administrators, and players who may typically define character with social values such as teamwork, loyalty, self-sacrifice, and perseverance. This could be designated as "social character." The second camp consists of sport scholars, and people of earlier generations still alive, who typically define character with moral values such as honesty, fairness, responsibility, compassion, and respect. This is commonly referred to by many of them as "moral character." The existence of these two camps, each with their respective definitions of character, suggests that there is confusion and disagreement concerning the definition of character in sport. (Of course, there may be some "in the middle" who accept an overlapping, possibly conflicting set of values to describe the term "character.")

Summarizes the social versus moral character contrast. It is weighted to favor moral character.

Anticipates objection: That the contrast between social and moral character is too sharp, as if there is no middle ground. Author concedes that the values can be combined.

6   As a result of the above, the differences in the way character is defined may provide strong evidence why many feel there is a lack of sportsmanship in competitive sport today. Similarly, these same people decry the "winning-at-all-cost" mentality that seems to prevail in athletics (see, for example, "A Purpose," 1999; Hawes, 1998; Spencer, 1996). Many coaches, athletic administrators, and parents may indeed place such a premium on social values such as teamwork, loyalty, self-sacrifice, and work ethic that they forget, or at least downplay, any emphasis on time-honored moral values such as honesty, fairness, responsibility, and respect.

Points to a commonly recognized problem in contemporary sports that makes the author's research and conclusions relevant, worth reading and studying.

7   The purpose of this paper is to define and discuss in detail two types of character (moral and social) that are espoused by two distinct groups in the sport milieu. The ramifications of the "social character view" in sport are explained below. At the same time, what the author feels is the need for greater emphasis on the development of moral character in sport and physical education will also be discussed.

Prepares the reader for the rest of the article by stating what the author is doing and why.

REFERENCES

Arnold, P. (1994). Sport and moral education. *The Journal of Moral Education, 23*(1), 75–89.

Beller, J. M., & Stoll, S. K. (1995). Moral reasoning of high school student athletes and general students: An empirical study versus personal testimony. *Pediatric Exercise Science, 7*(4), 352–363.

Gough, R. (1998). A practical strategy for emphasizing character development in sport and physical education. *Journal of Physical Education, Recreation, & Dance, 69*(2), 18–23.

Hawes, K. (1998). Sportsmanship: Why should anybody care? *NCAA news,* pp. 1, 18.

Heyman, J. (2000, May 22). They're 'good guys, good players.' *Statesman Journal,* p. 3B.

A purpose pitch. (1999, May 17). *Sports Illustrated, 90,* 24.

Rudd, A. (1999). [High school coaches' definitions of character]. Unpublished raw data.

Shields, D., & Bredemeier, B. (1995). *Character development and physical activity.* Champaign, IL: Human Kinetics.

Spencer, A. F. (1996). Ethics in physical and sport education. *Journal of Physical Education, Recreation & Dance, 67*(7), 37–39.

Zeigler, E. F. (2004). *A way out of ethical confusion.* Victoria, Canada: Trafford.

Zimmerman, P. (2001, September 3). New England Patriots. *Sports Illustrated, 95*(9), 162–163.

> Note APA "References" section, rather than the MLA "Works Cited" list. See Chapter 6, pages 148–156 for more on APA conventions.

QUESTIONS FOR DISCUSSION

1. Notice that the Rudd reading is organized around questions addressed by various writers rather than around what each writer says, taken up one by one. Why does organizing around questions work so well?

2. One of the keys to responding to anything we read, including exploratory writing, is to evaluate it according to our own experience. What have you learned from participating in sports or from observing sports events? Does your experience mirror what this article says?

READINGS

To demonstrate the process of exploring perspectives, we present three readings with different views on whether narcissism is increasing in Western culture, particularly among young people.

> See Chapter 2, "Reading an Argument," pages 15–30, for more on preparing to read any challenging text.

Take time to consider the topic and your first response to it. In this case, what is narcissism? A good place to find in-depth definitions is the *Oxford English Dictionary (OED)*. As defined by the *OED*, *narcissism* is:

1. Excessive self-love or vanity; self-admiration, self-centredness.

2. *Psychol.* The condition of gaining emotional or erotic gratification from self-contemplation, sometimes regarded as a stage in the normal

Figure 8.1
Narcissus contemplating his own image
Bridgeman Art Library/Getty Images

psychological development of children which may be reverted to in adulthood during mental illness.

The term *narcissism* alludes to a character in Greek mythology. (See Figure 8.1.) The *OED* defines Narcissus as:

> *Greek Mythol.* (The name of) a beautiful youth who fell in love with his own reflection in water and pined to death. Hence (allusively): a person characterized by extreme self-admiration or vanity; a narcissist.

FOLLOWING THROUGH

What examples of excessive self-love have you observed, either in your own life or in the media? What kind of behavior do you consider narcissistic? What conditions might contribute to such behavior?   •

The Paradox of Narcissism

JOHN F. SCHUMAKER

> This selection comes from *In Search of Happiness: Understanding an Endangered State of Mind.* John F. Schumaker is a clinical psychologist who lives in Australia and has published nine books on issues of culture and mental health. As you read, consider the concepts of self-esteem, happiness, and consumer culture Schumaker introduces and how he uses them to compare perspectives on narcissism.

1   While walking through the local Botanical Gardens recently, a woman wearing a "Love Yourself" T-shirt jogged past me. T-shirts like that were non-existent in the 1960s, when they all read "Love" or "Love One Another." But preachers of self-love are everywhere today. There are even numerous books extolling the virtues of self-love, including Peter McWilliams's *Love 101: To Love Oneself Is the Beginning of a Lifelong Romance.* The subtitle of that book is actually a tongue-in-cheek comment once made by Oscar Wilde. But it seems that many people have come to take that idea literally.

2   Today the self-esteem movement is in full swing. As an arm of feel-good culture, this movement has persuaded us that it is not good enough to feel good within ourselves. We must also feel good *about* ourselves. It has grown in force to the extent that it has reshaped childhood education. Teachers in recent years have been trained that a high level of self-esteem is the child's passport to happiness and success in life, as well as to a good education. Less and less emphasis is being paid to self-discipline, hard work, integrity, and helping students gain realistic appraisals of themselves. Instead, young people are being told automatically that they are infinitely talented, phenomenally creative, and erupting with potential in any area that takes their fancy. One zealous school in Alabama went so far as placing banners over all bathroom mirrors that read "You are now looking at one of the most special people in the whole world."

3   Young people find themselves in a culture that tells us to feel good about ourselves regardless of what we are as people. It does not matter if we are spoiled, selfish, indifferent, wasteful, or cruel. We have done our best to make self-esteem unconditional. But many education theorists are now conceding that the self-esteem extravaganza is proving to be a dismal failure in terms of education and personality development.

4   For instance, it was once thought that high self-esteem was crucial for effective leadership, social skills, and cooperation. The same was said about the ability to resist risky, anti-social, and self-destructive behaviours such as drug taking, smoking, drinking, and unsafe sex. But in all the cases, high self-esteem offers no advantages. In fact, research shows that high self-esteem increases people's likelihood to experiment and to take chances, which can make them more vulnerable to certain problems.

5   Once considered to be essential for advanced social skills and interpersonal effectiveness, high self-esteem has been shown to give no additional edge in these areas as well. It can even impair social judgement and conscience development. Recent research has found that "self-enhancers" with highly favourable views of themselves were more prone to acts of aggression such as bullying. They were also more inclined toward irritating behaviour patterns such as bragging, being overly opinionated, and interrupting others in conversation.

6   Those with high self-esteem appear to have their trumped-up pride hurt more easily, which can trigger in them hostility and other reactions that turn people off. High self-esteem individuals find themselves even more alienated from others when they are not able to conceal their elevated perception of themselves. While high self-esteem leads people to perceive themselves to be more popular and socially adept than other people, this does not correspond to reality when others are asked to rate them. While it is still promoted as a happiness helper, it has become clear that high self-esteem is not all that it was once cracked up to be.

7   . . . The notion that we are not worthy of being happy unless we are big, and full of ourselves, is a thoroughly Western one. Happiness in modern Western culture unfolds in the context of individualism. So it follows that our perceptions of ourselves would be crucial in judging our own degree of happiness. If we are self-satisfied, we are likely to say that we are satisfied with life. This contrasts with collectivist cultures where happiness is tied to cooperation and social harmony, and to being a worthwhile and valued member of the group. In such settings, less effort would be put into self-enhancement, and more into group-enhancement, as a pathway to happiness.

8   The worst problem comes when self-esteem becomes completely blown out of proportion to the extent that it gives way to narcissism. Unwarranted self-esteem may in many respects be a forerunner of the modern type of "unwarranted happiness" that has been criticised because it is not founded on anything substantial. In this regard, the type of narcissism and unjustified self-esteem that prevails today is quite interesting in light of the history of the self-esteem movement, which many say was begun by Los Angeles psychotherapist and corporate consultant

Dr Nathaniel Branden. While he tried to soften our negative connotations about self-centredness, he was careful to distinguish between healthy and unhealthy types of self-attention. He professed self-esteem that was built on the recognition of the need for love, healthy relationships, and spiritual awareness that he called "soulfulness." Since its origins, the self-esteem movement has given way to unbridled me-ism that lacks much scope for a meaningful shared happiness.

9 | The ego has become so artificially inflated in today's cultural climate that the idea of being famous is seen as a requirement for happiness. Local fame is no longer enough. Fame seekers want the whole world as their audience, which may in part be a reaction to the absence of true carers in their local environments. If nobody around me cares, maybe I can get the whole world to care. As our need for affection has been relocated to the public sphere, wooing the mass media has become a popular form of courtship. Ignored people of every description are coming out of the woodwork to set world records or be the first to unicycle blindfolded across the Utah salt flats or leapfrog a thousand beer barrels in less than fifteen minutes.

10 | The familiar cry "Look at me!" of the neglected child begging for parental attention has spread across the entire Western world as people have become increasingly invisible. For many, fame is imagined to be the only touch that can soothe their gnawing separation anxiety. The problem from a happiness standpoint is that there are very few winners in the fame game. As desperate as we are to be seen and recognised, getting anonymous fans is no easy task. Yet the quest for fame has become inseparable from the quest for happiness.

11 | This trend is eating away at people's prospects for happiness by way of condemning them to almost certain disappointment. They become slaves to a public that is largely a fiction propagated by Hollywood-style hype. The lucky few who make it into the limelight often fall prey to their anxieties about the fickleness of their unknown worshippers, not to mention the loss of privacy and the relationship breakdowns that are part of the package. Despite this, the desire for public fame grows more powerful as our local worlds continue to weaken as a source of recognition. Mixed in with our own ambitions for fame is a trend to bow down further and further to those who have already become famous.

12 | Consumer culture has a large investment in narcissism, just as it does with fame. A lot has been said about today's culture of narcissism, but almost always from a negative point of view. The upside of narcissism is that it is always associated with a high degree of entitlement that sways people to think that they deserve to have things—lots of things. The advertising industry is geared toward selling on the back of rising narcissism. Some of it is blatant, such as commercials that blurt out various messages to the effect ". . . because you deserve it." Others are subtler at selling things as part of people's growing desire to romance themselves. As narcissism becomes a dominant personality trait, the person gradually becomes shallower and loses the ability to feel deeply for other people. This too increases consumption potential by making people more accepting of the fictionalised world of objects.

13   The perfect psychological incubator for narcissism is a combination of overindulgence and neglect, which is the story for so many people growing up under modern cultural conditions. It is also the classic condition for the emergence of sociopaths whose main attribute is an absence of social conscience. Narcissists, like sociopaths, experience little guilt, or sense of sin. But sin is not good for the economy. As the cult of the individual has gradually made narcissism acceptable, the sense of sin has been overtaken by the feeling that one has the right to do whatever it takes to satisfy oneself and to feel good.

14   The sins that remain in our culture of narcissism are largely sins against oneself. We feel that we have done something wrong if we have not gotten the most for ourselves, done the most, or made the most of our opportunities. Other than that, the old-fashioned sins that stemmed from offending others or God are virtually obsolete. The worst sin today is to deprive oneself, which once again is music to the ears of a consumer economy. While feelings of being a sinful person can tarnish happiness, the wholesale erasure of social responsibility can be even more destructive to one's prospects for happiness.

15   An unceasing preoccupation with personal happiness is in many ways an expression of narcissism. Or at least this is the case with a large percentage of happiness seekers who are looking for happiness by way of what they can draw toward themselves, rather than what they can share with others. Jean-Jacques Rousseau once alluded to narcissism in saying that "man's nature is not fully mature until it becomes social." One could say the same thing about happiness; that is, happiness is not fully mature until it becomes social.

16   The myth of Narcissus is a tragic one. Because he will not surrender himself, Narcissus blows his chances with the beautiful nymph Echo, only to be cursed by an unrelenting self-devotion that robs him of his vigour and beauty. His beloved self never returns his affections, and finally he pines to death, leaving in his place only a lonely flower to preserve his memory. Fittingly, the tale lacks a happy ending. Yet it could be argued that narcissism is not a bad plan of attack. Put yourself first at all times and devote your full energies to feeling good. But narcissism has little to offer by way of happiness, or even self-love. Societies that generate narcissism among their members are dysfunctional ones that have lost sight of the reciprocal nature of human happiness.

17   The unofficial labels "middle-class narcissism" and "normal narcissism" have been used to describe the garden variety of narcissism that is generated by modern consumer culture, which has removed all taboos on selfishness in order to stimulate consumption. As a personality structure, collective narcissism has some advantages since it allows people in a hyper-competitive environment to exploit others without guilt. At the same time, it promotes a low tolerance for frustration that destroys relationships. People often end up fluctuating between expressions of hostility and ungainly attempts to get the approval of others.

Changes in Narcissism

JEAN M. TWENGE

Jean M. Twenge is Associate Professor of Psychology at San Diego State University. This selection is from *Generation Me: Why Today's Young Americans Are More Confident, Assertive, Entitled—and More Miserable Than Ever Before* (Free Press, 2006). Notice the number and variety of sources Twenge cites. What do the number and variety of sources Twenge cites reveal about her position on the prevalence of narcissism in today's society?

1   Narcissism is one of the few personality traits that psychologists agree is almost completely negative. Narcissists are overly focused on themselves and lack empathy for others, which means they cannot see another person's perspective. (Sound like the last clerk who served you?) They also feel entitled to special privileges and believe that they are superior to other people. As a result, narcissists are bad relationship partners and can be difficult to work with. Narcissists are also more likely to be hostile, feel anxious, compromise their health, and fight with friends and family. Unlike those merely high in self-esteem, narcissists admit that they don't feel close to other people.

2   All evidence suggests that narcissism is much more common in recent generations. In the early 1950s, only 12% of teens aged 14 to 16 agreed with the statement "I am an important person." By the late 1980s, an incredible 80%—almost seven times as many—claimed they were important. Psychologist Harrison Gough found consistent increases on narcissism items among college students quizzed between the 1960s and the 1990s. GenMe students were more likely to agree that "I would be willing to describe myself as a pretty 'strong' personality" and "I have often met people who were supposed to be experts who were no better than I." In other words, those other people don't know what they're talking about, so everyone should listen to me.

3   In a 2002 survey of 3,445 people conducted by Joshua Foster, Keith Campbell, and me, younger people scored considerably higher on the Narcissistic Personality Inventory, agreeing with items such as "If I ruled the world it would be a better place," "I am a special person," and "I can live my life anyway I want to." (These statements evoke the image of a young man speeding down the highway in the world's biggest SUV, honking his horn, and screaming, "Get out of my way! I'm important!") This study was cross-sectional, though, meaning that it was a one-time sample of people of different ages. For that reason, we cannot be sure if any differences are due to age or to generation; however, the other studies of narcissism mentioned previously suggest that generation plays a role. It is also interesting that narcissism scores were fairly high until around age 35, after which they decreased markedly. This is right around the cutoff between GenMe and previous generations.

4   Narcissism is the darker side of the focus on the self, and is often confused with self-esteem. Self-esteem is often based on solid relationships with others, whereas narcissism comes from believing that you are special and more important than other people. Many of the school programs designed to raise self-esteem probably raise narcissism instead. Lillian Katz, a professor of early childhood

education at the University of Illinois, wrote an article titled "All About Me: Are We Developing Our Children's Self-Esteem or Their Narcissism?" She writes, "Many of the practices advocated in pursuit of [high self-esteem] may instead inadvertently develop narcissism in the form of excessive preoccupation with oneself." Because the school programs emphasize being "special" rather than encouraging friendships, we may be training an army of little narcissists instead of raising kids' self-esteem.

5   Many young people also display entitlement, a facet of narcissism that involves believing that you deserve and are entitled to more than others. A scale that measures entitlement has items like "Things should go my way," "I demand the best because I'm worth it," and (my favorite) "If I were on the *Titanic,* I would deserve to be on the *first* lifeboat!" A 2005 Associated Press article printed in hundreds of news outlets labeled today's young people "The Entitlement Generation." In the article, employers complained that young employees expected too much too soon and had very high expectations for salary and promotions.

Teachers have seen this attitude for years now. One of my colleagues said his students acted as if grades were something they simply deserved to get no matter what. He joked that their attitude could be summed up by "Where's my A? I distinctly remember ordering an A from the catalog." Stout, the education professor, lists the student statements familiar to teachers everywhere: "I need a better grade," "I deserve an A on this paper," "I *never* get B's." Stout points out that the self-esteem movement places the student's feelings at the center, so "students learn that they do not need to respect their teachers or even earn their grades, so they begin to believe that they are entitled to grades, respect, or anything else . . . just for asking."

6   Unfortunately, narcissism can lead to outcomes far worse than grade grubbing. Several studies have found that narcissists lash out aggressively when they are insulted or rejected. Eric Harris and Dylan Klebold, the teenage gunmen at Columbine High School, made statements remarkably similar to items on the most popular narcissism questionnaire. On a videotape made before the shootings, Harris picked up a gun, made a shooting noise, and said "Isn't it fun to get the respect we're going to deserve?" (Chillingly similar to the narcissism item. "I insist upon getting the respect that is due me.") Later, Harris said, "I could convince them that I'm going to climb Mount Everest, or I have a twin brother growing out of my back. I can make you believe anything" (virtually identical to the item "I can make anyone believe anything I want them to"). Harris and Klebold then debate which famous movie director will film their story. A few weeks after making the videotapes, Harris and Klebold killed thirteen people and then themselves.

7   Other examples abound. In a set of lab studies, narcissistic men felt less empathy for rape victims, reported more enjoyment when watching a rape scene in a movie, and were more punitive toward a woman who refused to read a sexually arousing passage out loud to them. Abusive husbands who threaten to kill their wives—and tragically sometimes do—are the ultimate narcissists. They see everyone and everything in terms of fulfilling their needs, and become very angry and aggressive when things don't go exactly their way. Many workplace shootings occur after an employee is fired and decides he'll "show" everyone how powerful he is.

8   The rise in narcissism has very deep roots. It's not just that we feel better about ourselves, but that we even think to ask the question. We fixate on self-esteem, and unthinkingly build narcissism, because we believe that the needs of the individual are paramount. This will stay with us even if self-esteem programs end up in the dustbin of history.

QUESTIONS FOR DISCUSSION

1. How would you summarize Twenge's perspective on the topic of narcissism? How does it compare with Schumaker's?

2. Twenge is a psychology professor—a teacher and researcher. How might her profession affect her purpose and audience?

Generation Y and the New Myth of Narcissus

DUNCAN GREENBERG

At the time he wrote this column for his campus newspaper, the *Yale Herald,* Duncan Greenberg was a senior.

1   In our 10 or 20 years of existence as an age group, we've been called a lot of things, but "narcissistic" is the slur *du jour.* A controversial study at San Diego State University, which trickled down to papers this week, found that "30 percent more college students showed 'elevated narcissism' in 2006 compared with 1982." The study was authored by Jean Twenge, the cynic behind the book *Generation Me: Why Today's Young Americans Are More Confident, Assertive, Entitled—and More Miserable Than Ever Before.* Twenge consolidated data from 25 years of surveys and found—or claimed to find—that the Millennials had reached unhealthy heights of self-esteem.

2   To you and me, narcissism remains an elusive term. But words have different meanings in common parlance than in academic jargon, and there is a general consensus in the psychology community as to the symptoms of "narcissism." Some of the more familiar characteristics, as defined by the Mayo Clinic, include a "need for constant praise," a "grandiose sense of one's own abilities or achievements," a "lack of empathy for other people," and an "expectation of special treatment."

3   Twenge's study hasn't been published yet, but newspaper articles give us glimpses of her methodology: In an annual poll conducted for 25 years, students were asked if they agreed with statements like, "If I ruled the world, it would be a better place," "I think I am a special person," and "I can live my life any way I want to." Each student's answers were ranked on a scale from egocentric to empathetic.

4   Having circumscribed the malady, though, we are left with the problem of diagnosis. You can't just flat-out ask people if they're narcissistic (a true narcissist will never admit it); your only hope is to trick your subject into signing off on

statements that indirectly expose his inflated ego. That's why psychologists use oblique and ambiguous statements like, "I think I am a special person." The downside of obliquity, however, is questionable results.

5   Take the second question for example: if someone thinks he's special, does that make him a narcissist? Isn't everyone "special," in the etymologically related sense of "species," implying a unique combination of color, shape, and size? And where exactly is the line between narcissism and self-confidence? Given our high achievement and low rates of violence, maybe we Millennials are entitled to some self-esteem. Remember, surveys are like a house of mirrors: You can appear fat or thin, tall or short, depending on which study you happen to be looking at. UCLA's annual report, "The American Freshman National Norms for 2006," for example, paints a radically different picture. Its finding? "A record number [of college freshmen]—83 percent— say they volunteered at least occasionally during their senior year of high school."

6   Either we're narcissistic, or we're compassionate—we can't be both. But rather than reconcile the two studies, Twenge dismisses the redeeming evidence, arguing that more and more high schools require students to meet a not-for-profit quota— the drive to do community service, she suggests, is coming from without, not from within. Admittedly, as university acceptance rates have fallen, students have turned increasingly to volunteer work to gild their applications. But if you eliminate competitive pressure from the equation, two-thirds of college freshman still believe it is "essential or very important to help others who are in difficulty, the highest percentage in a quarter century." I'm not calling Twenge a quack, but for every study that supports her point, there's another that contradicts it. And the fact of the matter is that when it comes to giving back, we've more than done our part.

7   "Okay," the critics say, "maybe you're not selfish, but you're self-absorbed." True, Millennials have been known to flaunt their lives on YouTube and MySpace. But it's not as if our predecessors didn't get attention other ways—you're telling me the hippie and grunge movements weren't attempts to attract eyeballs by raising eyebrows. Besides, while there's no denying that YouTube and MySpace are perfect outlets for the world's narcissists, vanity is not the only trait those websites cater to. Would YouTube be worth $1.65 billion to Google if users only posted videos of themselves without so much as a glance at others' postings? Critics get hung up on the egotism of the prefixes "my" and "you," but these sites are only successful because they're about other people—about meeting other people, about seeing what hidden talents other people have. Social networking, whether virtual or in person, is always going to entail a little window-dressing; the quasi-narcissistic practice of putting one's best foot forward in social settings is hardly confined to cyberspace.

8   In a recent *Los Angeles Times* editorial, William Strauss and Neil Howe ["Will the Real Gen Y Please Stand Up?" 2 March 2007] hit upon a baffling phenomenon: "Whenever youth behavior seems clearly positive, critics cynically find a way to dismiss it." Maybe these critics begrudge us our youth, maybe they mistake young-looking bodies for immature minds—your guess is as good as mine. For not only do we care about what other people think, seeking the approval of our peers through YouTube ratings and FaceBook friend requests, but we care about how other people feel, volunteering for heroic causes on unprecedented scale. Yes, we

feel entitled—to a world without terrorism and global warming and to politicians who will take these scourges seriously. And, no, we don't need constant praise—but a little positive feedback, when we deserve it, would be nice.

QUESTIONS FOR DISCUSSION

1. Greenberg was prompted to write this column by a news story about research by Jean Twenge into the topic of narcissism. How does his description of the research compare to Twenge's perspective?

2. What arguments and evidence does Greenberg give to refute Twenge's conclusions? Which author do you find more credible?

CLAIMING VOICE IN COMPARING PERSPECTIVES

Voice must adapt to convention, the norms certain genres typically observe. For example, the reading, "Which Character Should Sports Develop?" by Andy Rudd comes from a science journal. Convention dictates that authors avoid the first person—that is, the use of "I"—because science writing wants to sound objective, as if the judgments made are free of bias and passion.

Nevertheless, authors do express their point of view in scientific writing. For example, in the Rudd reading, the author points out that

> Sport scholars, including sport philosophers and sport psychologists, more commonly define an athlete of character as one who is honest, fair, responsible, respectful, and compassionate (Arnold, 1999; Beller & Stoll, 1995; Gough, 1998; Shields & Bredemeier, 1995).

The voice sounds neutral and objective, but actually the author is favoring what he calls "moral character" over what he calls "social character" by identifying the first with "sports scholars" rather than the coaches with which he associates "winning at all costs." He also cites in parenthesis names and professional publications associated with the moral view of character, which he does not provide for the social view of character. There are subtle ways of expressing your point of view, then, even when convention prevents you from saying "I think that . . ." or "This view is dangerous and that view is healthy."

Because the objective voice is a common convention for writing in many college courses and professional settings, learning how to make this voice work for you is important.

THE ASSIGNMENT

Read at least two perspectives addressing a topic you care about. In an essay explore the perspectives by noting where different authors address the same or similar questions, and compare their answers. Decide which views seem most valid and which have deepened your own understanding of the topic and its relevance to your life.

Topic and Focus

Pick a topic of current interest on which many people are expressing their views. The point is to explore the views, examine and question them carefully. Keep your mind open until you have explored the viewpoints, then draw your conclusions.

Audience

Think of your audience as people interested in your topic but who have not read what you have read. Consequently, you will need to tell your readers enough about each view for them to know who says what, using quotations and paraphrases as needed.

Voice and Style

Imagine that you are participating in a conversation with your readers about the perspectives and your opinions of them. You should sound fair, thoughtful, and receptive, willing to ponder points of view you do not find persuasive but which may contain valuable points or insights. Be willing also to look for problems in perspectives you do find persuasive.

Writing Assignment Suggestions

Comparing perspectives is a common occurrence in our everyday lives. For a film you have seen or a performance you have attended, find two or more reviews of substantial length, and compare the reviewers' interpretations and evaluations. Conclude by explaining how reading the perspectives added to your ideas about the film. If your library has a collection of history text-books, find ones from different time periods and compare their treatments of events or people. Have "the facts" changed? How has interpretation of the facts changed?

CHOOSING A TOPIC

Your instructor may assign a topic and readings arguing from different perspectives about it. If not, here are some possibilities for finding topics.

- *Reading and research.* Most authors will mention the names of people who agree and disagree with their point of view. For example, a news article about Jean Twenge also mentioned a psychologist whose work disputed Twenge's conclusions. To bring that perspective into your comparison, do an Internet or library database search of that person's name.

- *Library databases.* Research the topic in an index to periodicals, such as Academic OneFile (see Chapter 6, pages 110–112). The advantage is that you will find readings grouped according to topic and time, some of which will likely refer to each other.

Strategies for Comparing Perspectives

With each reading

1. Paraphrase or summarize the main points
2. Find the questions each point answers
3. Write down your response to each point
4. Keep track of connections across perspectives
5. Maintain an exploratory stance

We take you through these five steps, showing why they are worth doing and how they work with the narcissism topic.

- *Internet discussions.* If you find a reading on the Internet, it will often link you to what other writers have said. Online journals and magazines often contain lengthy comments in which readers exchange opinions with the original author and with each other.

EXPLORING YOUR TOPIC

Before reading, begin by clarifying key definitions as we did with narcissism, using a good dictionary. Write to record your own viewpoints on the topic. Then, move on to explore the perspectives through your selection of readings.

Paraphrase or Summarize the Main Points

See Chapter 6, pages 127–133, for guidance on paraphrasing and summarizing.

Paraphrasing or summarizing will help you digest the ideas and talk about them in your own voice. Mark the major subdivisions (paragraphs that discuss the same point) as you read. For each subdivision, put the main point in your own words. Reread the first two paragraphs of the Schumaker reading, "The Paradox of Narcissism," reproduced below and compare them with our student, Ian Fagerstrom's, paraphrase.

I. Schumaker, Paragraphs 1–2

> While walking through the local Botanical Gardens recently, a woman wearing a "Love Yourself" T-shirt jogged past me. T-shirts like that were non-existent in the 1960s, when they all read "Love" or "Love One Another." But preachers of self-love are everywhere today. There are even numerous books extolling the virtues of self-love, including Peter McWilliams's *Love 101: To Love Oneself Is the Beginning of a Lifelong Romance.* The subtitle of that book is actually a tongue-in-cheek comment once made by Oscar Wilde. But it seems that many people have come to take that idea literally.
>
> Today the self-esteem movement is in full swing. As an arm of feel-good culture, this movement has persuaded us that it is not good

enough to feel good within ourselves. We must also feel good about ourselves. It has grown in force to the extent that it has reshaped childhood education. Teachers in recent years have been trained that a high level of self-esteem is the child's passport to happiness and success in life, as well as to a good education. Less and less emphasis is being paid to self-discipline, hard work, integrity, and helping students gain realistic appraisals of themselves. Instead, young people are being told automatically that they are infinitely talented, phenomenally creative, and erupting with potential in any area that takes their fancy. One zealous school in Alabama went so far as placing banners over all the bathroom mirrors that read "You are now looking at one of the most special people in the whole world."

Ian's Paraphrase of Schumaker's Paragraphs 1–2

Schumaker compares self-love now to the 1960's to show a change in focus. He also makes the point that the schools have worked too hard to bring up kids' self esteem at the expense of old-fashioned values like hard work.

FOLLOWING THROUGH

Mark up the text of one of the readings to indicate its subdivisions. For each subdivision, write a paraphrase of its main point or points. As a class, discuss what students selected as main points and compare your paraphrases. •

Turn Main Points into Questions

Turn the main points into questions by asking, What question is this an answer to? Turning the main points into questions will help you in two ways: (1) *to connect the readings,* because writers will address the same questions; and (2) *to organize your paper,* because exploratory writing is structured around questions. These are the questions the main points in Ian's paraphrase of Paragraphs 1–2 answer:

- Has there been an increase in narcissism? Schumaker says yes.
- What has caused this increase? Schumaker says a cause is the self-esteem movement in the schools.

FOLLOWING THROUGH

In groups of two or three, take paraphrases or quotations that the group agrees represent key points in the reading. As we have illustrated, rephrase the point to show what question the author is addressing. •

Paraphrase and Comment

Write informally, such as in your notebook or on a class discussion board, to respond to the main points in each reading. Draw on your own experiences to test the merit of the author's ideas.

Here is an example of a notebook entry in response to Schumaker's reading. Notice how Ian moves back and forth between quoted and paraphrased passages in the text and his own response to the passages. To show the texture of moving from what the text says to what Ian says back, we have bolded the references to Schumaker's text.

> Shumaker seems to be very cynical about self-esteem, without pointing out that self-esteem in moderation is actually not a bad thing. **He says that "high self-esteem is not all that it was once cracked up to be" (169) and shows a correlation between people with high self-esteem and negative traits like risky sexual behavior, bragging, and hostility when they think they have been slighted.** Yes, I agree that too-high self-esteem is detrimental to happiness, but he could at least say that moderate self-esteem isn't bad. Without some self-esteem, I would not push myself to take on new challenges. Sure, **Western culture says that we always need to feel good about ourselves (169),** but he could at least admit that positive self-worth doesn't automatically lead to narcissism. He says, **"Societies that generate narcissism among their members are dysfunctional ones that have lost sight of the reciprocal nature of human happiness" (173).** This is a good point because individualism won't ever result in true happiness, but why can't he talk about people who balance self-worth with respect and love for others?

As you read other perspectives, write more comparative notebook entries. In a notebook entry responding to more than one reading, show how both provide answers to a single question, either agreeing or disagreeing. If you organize these informal comparisons around questions in common, you will be creating material to use in the rough draft.

◎◎ FOLLOWING THROUGH

As you read and reread each of the perspectives, record key points in a reading and interact with them by stating your own evaluations of the text, connections with the topic, and comparisons to other readings.

Create a comparative grid to map your comparisons. When reading to compare what different authors have to say on similar topics, focus on where they agree and disagree on the same points. If you look at the list of questions raised in the first reading, you will see whether the second reading addresses any of the same questions. A comparative grid makes these connections easier to see. Review the following comparative grid to get a sense of how the points made about narcissism in the Schumaker and Twenge essays compare.   •

Question	Schumaker	Twenge
What is narcissism? How does it compare with self-esteem?	Paragraph 8	Paragraphs 1, 4
Is narcissism greater today than in the past?	Paragraphs 1, 3, 9	Paragraphs 2–3, 5–6
Is high self-esteem a good thing or a bad thing?	Paragraphs 3–6	Paragraph 4
If narcissism is increasing, what is contributing to this change?	Paragraphs 2, 9–13	Paragraphs 4, 9
What effects does narcissism have on personality and behavior?	Paragraphs 5–6, 9, 11, 15, 17	Paragraphs 1, 7–8

◎◎ FOLLOWING THROUGH

Print out the online worksheet in Connect to make an idea grid of the passages and ideas that connect across the readings as the answers address similar questions. This will also serve as an aid in organizing your draft.   •

Keep Track of Connections across Perspectives

As you read a second or third person's perspective, try one or more of these suggestions to help keep control over your sources:

- Annotate each reading with references to page numbers in other sources that address the same questions.
- Use color-coded highlighters to mark passages addressing the same questions in different readings.
- Consult previous informal writings often to recall ideas already responded to. Add quotes and paraphrases from new sources as they relate to points already explored.
- Add to your idea grid if you prefer this way of tracking ideas across sources.

Maintain an Exploratory Stance

It is important not to limit your observations to personal experience; doing this will limit your ability to compare effectively. For example, on the question of what causes narcissism, Twenge says that elementary schools praise kids who have done nothing to deserve praise. Some students said, "She's wrong; that didn't happen at my school. We had to work for our A's." A more exploratory stance would be to say, "While some schools may give kids false praise, in my experience I haven't seen it." And then you could go on to say more about how your schools did not have grade inflation, allowed students to fail, and so on. But you might also ask other students what their experiences have been at their schools. Inquiry, comparing perspectives, is all about opening your mind to the way others see the world. Doing so will enhance your own point of view.

DRAFTING YOUR PAPER

Drafting the essay for this project should not be difficult if you have been doing informal writing as you explored the sources. Read through your material again, and then consider the following advice.

Planning the Draft

Before you start drafting you need a plan to give your paper focus, purpose, and organization. For your introduction, you could

- open with your own view before reading. In the body and conclusion, indicate how your thinking changed.
- open with the question that is the focus of your exploration. State it clearly and explain its importance.
- open with one of the main questions that cut across the readings, such as "Some people think narcissism is a growing problem. Is it?" You could move directly into your paper this way.

You also need to mention the writers whose viewpoints you are exploring. You could devote one paragraph to background for all of them, citing full names, credentials, titles of the works you read, and main points. Or you could save this information for the body of your paper, introducing the authors as you bring them into your discussion.

The Art of Questioning: Planning the Body

Do not try to cover every point that comes up in the readings. *Be selective;* explore a few questions in depth. Choose ones you wrote most about in the informal writing you did.

Take up the general questions first and then more specific ones. It wouldn't make sense to look at the role of schools in creating narcissists before taking up the questions "What is narcissism?" and "Is it increasing?"

Bear in mind that you need not agree with a viewpoint to explore interesting questions it raises. You could say, "While I see Greenberg's position on my generation as more realistic than Twenge's, is there anything valid in her idea that American culture encourages self-absorption?" Once you have worked out your answers to these questions, start drafting your paper.

Organizing around Questions

A paper that synthesizes ideas from multiple authors needs to be organized around the questions that cut across the readings, *not around the readings themselves*. If you devote the first part of your paper to just one author's views, the second to the second author's views, and so on, your paper will read like a summary rather than an exploration. Here are some suggestions for organizing around questions.

- Check the lists of questions you have made for each perspective. Put these lists together now and identify questions that appear in multiple readings.

- Consider whether narrowing the focus of your exploration might help. An exploration of narcissism, for instance, might deal only with the difference between healthy self-esteem and genuine narcissism.

- Based on length requirements for the paper and how much you have to say about the questions, select the ones you intend to address.

- Order the questions logically. For example, a definition question makes more sense at the paper's beginning. Discuss causes, then effects.

- Plan on multiple paragraphs for each question. You could, for instance, devote one paragraph to one source's answer, and another to what the others say on the same question.

- Create transitions so that your reader will know when discussion of one question is over and another is beginning.

Development and Organization

The Best Practices box above summarizes a key point about structure in comparing perspectives.

REVISING YOUR DRAFT

Revising this kind of paper usually involves improving the organization, looking more closely at the perspectives to make your exploration more specific, and including more of your own reactions to the authors' views. The Best Practices box on page 201 provides a checklist to help you revise your paper.

When you have limited time to revise a paper, you have to prioritize. Take care of the bigger problems first, the ones that alter your essay substantially. If smaller problems remain, solve as many as you can in the time you have.

The following excerpts from Ian Fagerstrom's draft focus on three problems his peer reviewers found, common problems your draft also may have.

1. One large paragraph addressed two questions rather than one.

> Does narcissism create unhappiness, and more important, is narcissism a growing problem? Schumaker, concerned that happiness is an

The paragraph answers two questions: about effects of narcissism and whether there has been an increase in narcissism. This causes loss of focus and makes the paragraph too long.

Revision Checklist for Comparing Perspectives

The checklist moves in descending order, from the major challenges of the project to concerns in every piece of formal writing.

1. *How much did you explore?* Exploring means entertaining a question. To entertain a question is to hold it open and consider it thoughtfully. If you disputed a point before considering its merits, revise and give it a chance.

2. *How well did you represent the ideas of all the authors?* Did you draw on the sources enough to represent their views accurately and fully?

3. *How well did you work quotations into your paper?* Set them up rather than drop them in, and follow up with explanation and commentary about context as needed.

4. *How well did you organize the paper?* Check to see that you are focusing on one question at a time.

5. *How well did you respond to the sources?* Use specifics to show exactly what you agreed or disagreed with and why.

6. *How smoothly did the sentences flow?* Each sentence sets up the reader's expectations for the one coming next. Read your draft aloud, listening for places where flow could be improved.

7. *Did you introduce the authors adequately?* Provide full name on first mention and something about their credentials.

"endangered state of mind," does well to show that narcissism will lead to a false sense of happiness. Coming from the belief that you must surround yourself with good people to be happy, I completely agree with his point that "happiness is almost impossible if one is unable to escape the prison of self-interest" (175). Considering that happiness is typically the goal of one's life, Schumaker has effectively proved that narcissism ends any chances of that. He does not make any convincing points about it being a significant problem, though—just illustrating with an example of a woman wearing a "love yourself" T-shirt. What does that prove? Twenge says in an interview with National Public Radio that if you are narcissistic, "you may be happy—probably very happy—with how you feel about yourself, but you're going to end up in the long run alienating other people" ("Study"). So they would agree that narcissism really leads to a false kind of happiness that would not be satisfying. In fact, Twenge shows the even darker side of narcissism. Much more than just unhappiness, she believes that in extreme cases narcissism can lead to hostility and aggression of the worst kind, including murder (70–71).

Sidebar annotations:

Addresses first question.

Addresses second question.

Addresses first question.

The paragraph was too long and not unified. In the revised version, Ian uses three focused paragraphs: 4, 5, and 6.

2. Ian did not mention Twenge's use of the NPI (Narcissistic Personality Inventory). In this excerpt, Ian refers to data misinterpretation, but he does not say what the data are.

Ian hasn't mentioned what data he is referring to. In the revised version, he added what he needed. See paragraph 2 in the revised version.

Jean M. Twenge, an Associate Professor of Psychology at San Diego State University and author of *Generation Me*, also tends to put the young generation in a negative light, accusing us of being obsessed with ourselves and putting the blame for it on the schools, media, and parents. She believes narcissism is on the rise, almost an epidemic. To put things back in perspective, Duncan Greenberg, an undergraduate student at Yale, wrote an editorial in his campus newspaper, "Generation Y and the New Myth of Narcissus." He would confront both Schumaker and Twenge and say that narcissism is actually not a problem at all, instead a misinterpretation of data. He takes the opposition and points out that our generation is actually more empathetic than most. So, on most issues, the two psychologists would agree, and Greenberg would disagree.

3. In many places, Ian needed to refer to the texts more specifically.

The cliché about "going down the drain" doesn't get at Schumaker's real concern. See paragraph 2 for a better paraphrase.

There are many perspectives on the topic, some more critical than others. John F. Schumaker, a clinical psychologist and author of *In Search of Happiness*, has a very negative view on it all, arguing that American society is basically going down the drain because of narcissism, saying that it "is an unfulfilling experience that sets the stage for rage and eventual despair" (175).

REVISED STUDENT EXAMPLE
Comparison of Perspectives on Narcissism

IAN FAGERSTROM

You will notice that Ian added a fourth reading, a National Public Radio interview with Twenge. Multiple readings can represent the same perspective so long as a participant in the conversation does not change his or her position. Twenge was interviewed about new research supporting her views on narcissism.

Ian leads into his exploration with a natural voice and shows his connection to the topic.

Living in a bustling city like Dallas, going to a college with many affluent students, and watching the TV every once in a while, I see self-absorbed people everywhere I turn. Many students get caught up in the appealing idea of being special. It's a good feeling to be at the top of the class, or the one with the newest iPod. So strong is the desire to be special that self-absorption or narcissism has become a much-discussed topic.

There are many perspectives on it, some more critical than others. John Schumaker, a clinical psychologist and author of *In Search of Happiness*, has a very negative view, arguing that Americans are much less happy than they could be because of their focus on themselves. He says that narcissism "is an unfulfilling experience that sets the stage for rage and eventual despair" (175). While he may acknowledge the positives of healthy self-esteem based in relationships, he is more interested in the downside of high self-esteem.

3   Jean M. Twenge, an Associate Professor of Psychology at San Diego State University and author of *Generation Me,* also tends to put the young generation in a negative light, accusing us of being obsessed with ourselves and putting the blame for it on the self-esteem movement in the schools, media, and parents. She believes narcissism is on the rise, almost an epidemic, as indicated by college students' responses over the years to a psychological survey known as the Narcissistic Personality Inventory (NPI). To put things back in perspective, though, Duncan Greenberg, an undergraduate student at Yale, wrote an editorial in his campus newspaper, "Generation Y and the New Myth of Narcissus." He would confront both Schumaker and Twenge and say that narcissism is actually not a problem at all, instead a misinterpretation of the NPI data. He points out that our generation is actually more empathetic than most. So, on most issues, the two psychologists would agree, and Greenberg would disagree.

4   To fully understand what these authors are saying, we must first know how they are defining narcissism. For Schumaker, narcissism consists of "self-esteem . . . completely blown out of proportion" as well as "unwarranted self-esteem" (170). Although he does not necessarily equate high self-esteem with narcissism, he mentions that certain types of high self-esteem are potentially dangerous. His definition leaves room for misinterpretation and could be used to label many people as narcissists.

5   Twenge describes narcissists as "overly focused on themselves"; they are people who "feel entitled to special privileges and believe that they are superior . . ." (*Generation,* 68). She carefully makes the distinction between high self-esteem and narcissism. She notes that people with high self-esteem feel close to others; narcissists, on the other hand, do not (69). Greenberg wisely uses the Mayo Clinic's definition to define it; traits such as "a need for constant praise" in addition to an "expectation of special treatment" succinctly embody narcissistic tendencies. Instead of trying to make his own definition, he goes with a well-known and respected authority. Still, the Mayo Clinic definitions in Greenberg are similar to the traits Twenge describes; their definitions are the same but they reach different conclusions about the existence of narcissism as a problem.

6   So with these definitions in mind, is narcissism becoming increasingly problematic? Schumaker does not really give evidence to show that rising narcissism is a serious problem. He doesn't have any evidence; he just makes good points that it is a negative trait. While Twenge may have some hard evidence with her survey, saying that 30 percent more college students score above average on the NPI than in 1982 ("Study"), Greenberg makes some compelling points to challenge her findings. He argues that the survey tricks people with "oblique and ambiguous" statements most people would agree with. What's wrong with feeling that you are special? As Greenberg asks, "if someone thinks he's special, does that make him a narcissist? Isn't everyone 'special,' in the etymologically related sense of 'species,' implying a unique combination of color, shape, and size?" He actually goes to the other end of the spectrum by saying that our generation may be "entitled to some

This wording is more specific than the cliché "going down the drain."

Ian realized that he had to refer to the survey here to make his later references to it clear.

The second paragraph introduces all three perspectives, one option for introducing them.

Ian leads into his first point of comparison: How do the authors define narcissism?

This paragraph synthesizes definitions and compares similarities.

This section of the paper will address the question: Is narcissism really becoming more prevalent?

Ian revised paragraph 2 to include information about Twenge's research, so he can refer to it again here without confusing his readers.

self-esteem." Greenberg is savvy enough about surveys to realize that for every Twenge argument, there is probably another survey to refute it with. He does this by citing the UCLA survey of first-year students, which shows that they are volunteering "in record numbers" for community service. I agree with Greenberg: young people cannot be both empathetic and narcissistic.

7

The focus of this section of the exploration is: What are the consequences or effects of narcissism on a person?

Whether narcissism is increasing or not, these authors do show that it will lead to a false sense of happiness or worse. Coming from the belief that you must surround yourself with good people to be happy, I completely agree with Schumaker's point that "happiness is almost impossible if one is unable to escape the prison of self-interest" (175). Considering that happiness is typically the goal of one's life, Schumaker has effectively proved that narcissism ends any chances of that. Twenge says in an interview with National Public Radio that if you are narcissistic, "you may be happy—probably very happy—with how you feel about yourself, but you're going to end up in the long run alienating other people" ("Study"). So they would agree that narcissism really leads to a false kind of happiness that would not be satisfying.

8

This paragraph is further development of Twenge's answer to the question about the effects of narcissism.

Ian clearly explains Twenge's point but shows why he reaches a different conclusion.

In fact, Twenge shows the even darker side of narcissism. Much more than just unhappiness, she believes that in extreme cases narcissism can lead to hostility and aggression of the worst kind, including murder (*Generation* 70–71). She uses the example of the Columbine shooters and their video where they make comments about getting the respect they deserve. While this is certainly scary to think about, I would disagree with her here and say that these boys actually had very little self-esteem to begin with. It was their lack of an ego rather than an inflated one that led them to kill thirteen people and commit suicide. Twenge bases her conclusion on the similarities between what the boys said on their video and what some of the items on the NPI say. But that is not enough evidence to make a diagnosis. It simply shows their desire for power after being bullied by other students. Twenge may scare people away from narcissism here, which is not a bad intention, but I believe that her reasoning is flawed.

Whatever definition of narcissism is used, everyone will agree that it is in no way a healthy behavior and will lead to unhappiness, just as in the myth of Narcissus. The main question still remains: Is narcissism on the rise? With many interpretations of data, people refute each other using the same evidence, and given the persistent bickering, the question may never be answered. Personally, at first I was inclined to accept Twenge's argument that schools, media, and parents are going too far in telling children they are the best, most special kids ever ("Study"). And Schumaker is right that some societies encourage narcissistic tendencies, very true in the consumer-society of the United States. But I am not so pessimistic as Twenge and Schumaker about the future, based on my generation's values.

10

I tend to agree with Greenberg that Generation Y is not as narcissistic as generations before us. He makes a valid point when he says that older generations often dismiss positive youth behavior. Whenever a younger generation is praised for something, the older generations put us down, call us spoiled and scoff at us. I have met my fair share of narcissists, but it is hard to prove that it is such a big problem that we need to name my generation "Generation Me."

WORKS CITED

Greenberg, Duncan. "Generation Y and the New Myth of Narcissus." Editorial. *The Yale Herald,* 8 Mar. 2007. Web. 20 Feb. 2007. Print.

Schumaker, John F. *In Search of Happiness: Understanding an Endangered State of Mind.* Westport, CT: Praeger, 2007. Print.

Twenge, Jean M. *Generation Me: Why Today's Young Americans Are More Confident, Assertive, Entitled—and More Miserable Than Ever Before.* New York: Free Press, 2006. Print.

"Study Sees Rise of Narcissism among College Students." Interview by Alex Chadwick and Luke Burbank. *Day to Day.* Natl. Public Radio. WNYC, New York, 27 Feb. 2007. *NPR.org.* Web. 19 Feb. 2008.

CHAPTER SUMMARY

This chapter has given you practice in essential skills for other writing assignments in this course and others. You learned that people's perspectives are answers to questions, and that careful reading uncovers the questions that serve as threads, weaving the conversation together, even if authors do not refer to each other directly. Finding the questions at issue is essential to any research project and to making your own arguments.

CHAPTER 9

Making Your Case: Arguing to Convince

The last chapter ended where inquiry ends—with the attempt to formulate a position, an opinion that we can assert with some confidence. When our aim shifts from inquiring to convincing, everything changes.

The most significant change is in audience. In inquiry, our audience consists of our fellow inquirers—friends, classmates, and teachers we can talk with face to face. We seek assurance that our position is at least plausible and defensible. In convincing, however, our audience consists of readers whose positions differ from our own or who have no position at all. The audience changes from a small, inside group that helps us develop our argument to a larger, public audience who will either accept or reject it.

As the audience changes, so does the situation or need for argument. Inquiry is a cooperative use of argument; convincing is more competitive. We pit our cases against the cases of others to win the assent of readers who will compare the various arguments and ask, Who makes the best case?

From Inquiry to Convincing

Inquiry ———————⟶	Convincing
Intimate audience	Public readership
Cooperative	Competitive
Earns a conviction	Argues a thesis
Seeks a case convincing *to us*	Makes a case convincing *to them,* the readers

We take the position we discovered through inquiry and turn it into a thesis supported by a case designed to gain the assent of a specific group of readers.

Because of the change in audience and situation, our thinking becomes more strategic, calculated to influence readers. In inquiry, we find out what we can believe in; in convincing, we make a case readers can believe in. What we find compelling in inquiry will sometimes also convince readers, but *in convincing we must adapt our reasoning to appeal to their beliefs, values, and self-interest.* Convincing, however, does not mean abandoning the work of inquiry. Our version of the truth, our conviction, gained through inquiry, is what we argue for.

WHAT IS A CASE?

A *case* develops your opinion about a controversial issue or question. The result is an argument with three levels of assertion:

1. A central contention or **claim,** also called a thesis.

    Example: College costs are unjustifiably high.

2. One or more reasons that explain or justify the claim.

    Example: They have increased much more than inflation over the last thirty years.

3. Appropriate evidence to back up each reason.

    Example: Data comparing the cost of living in general with increases in tuition and fees over the last thirty years.

WHY MAKE A CASE?

We make cases to do the following:

1. *Influence the thinking of others.* CEOs make cases for decisions they have made to their Board of Directors and stockholders; lawyers make cases to convince judges or a jury; special interest groups make cases to bring their causes to the attention of communities and civic leaders.

Visualizing the Structure of a Case

The **thesis** answers the question, *What are you asserting or claiming?*

Reasons explain or justify the thesis; they answer the question, *Why do you hold this thesis?*

Evidence backs up each reason; it answers the question, *What information confirms your reasoning?*

2. *Avoid violence.* Reason together or fight: these are the alternatives—hence, the Chinese proverb, "He who strikes the first blow has lost the argument." Nothing less than peaceful resolution of differences is at stake in arguing well.

3. *Learn what we really think.* In college, making cases is part of the learning process. We all have casual opinions we have never thought through. How good are they? Do they stand up to what is known about a subject in dispute? If not, we need to modify our opinion or alter what we think entirely. Reasoning is a way of learning that can change us profoundly.

HOW DOES MAKING A CASE WORK?

Cases combine structure with strategy. The structure is the three-part division of reasoning: thesis, reasons, and evidence. The strategy is what you do to *connect with your readers,* to make what you have to say convincing to other

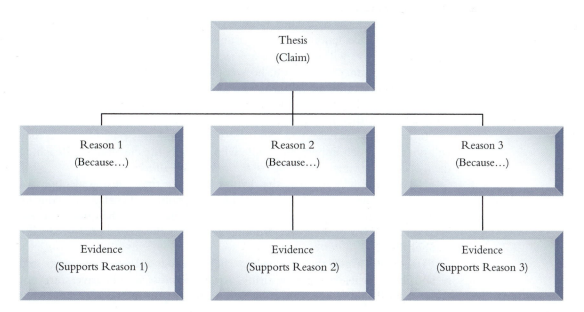

Key Questions for Case-Making

1. Who is your target audience?
2. What preconceptions and biases might they hold about your topic?
3. What claim do you want your readers to accept?
4. What reasons are likely to appeal to this audience?
5. How should you arrange these reasons for maximum impact on your target audience?
6. How might you introduce your case?
7. How might you conclude it?
8. How can you gain the trust and respect of your audience?

Convincing is audience centered. Every choice we make must be made with the target audience in mind.

---

people. See the Concept Close-Up, "Key Question for Case-Making" to understand the concerns of strategic thinking in general. The following example should also help.

Many people, including some college presidents, are in favor of lowering the drinking age from twenty-one to eighteen. The concern is binge drinking, which they partly blame on the current drinking age. Breaking the law is part of the appeal of underaged drinking. Universities cannot advocate responsible drinking when many undergraduates are not supposed to drink at all.

Organizations such as MADD, Mothers against Drunk Driving, support the twenty-one legal age. They point to thousands of people who die each year in traffic accidents caused by drunk drivers. Lower the drinking age, they say, and you will only make a serious problem worse.

Given the range of opinion, how could you make a good case favoring legal access to alcohol at eighteen? The most common reason offered is based on consistency. If young adults are old enough to fight in Afghanistan or Iraq, shouldn't they be old enough to drink legally?

In making your case, you can offer reasons like this one. However, they will not have much impact on people who support the current law. Reaching them requires strategy, *thinking as the other side thinks.*

Here is one way to cross the divide. All agree that abusing alcohol is a big problem. They differ on how to reduce the problem. Legalize and educate is one way; prohibit by law and strictly enforce the law is the other. In making a case in favor of the lower drinking age, stress the shared goal—reducing alcohol abuse.

You could argue that age is not the issue but rather moderation and responsibility whenever people drink. After all, most drunk drivers are not under legal drinking age. But moderation and responsibility is exactly what the current law cannot promote. Prohibition hardly encourages moderation and responsibility; on the contrary, it drives underaged drinking underground, out of sight but hardly out of common practice. You could go on to support MADD's well-developed measures for preventing drunk driving, such as encouraging designated drivers. You could advocate that universities devote more effort and time to educating college students about drinking. Such is strategy in case-making, without which any case you make can only strengthen the adherence of people who already share your position.

The Art of Questioning: Examining Your Audience's Beliefs

You cannot reach everyone. But you can reach many people, at least enough to get them to reconsider what they think. The problem is not that reasoning lacks power but that its power depends on coming up with ways to appeal to people who do not already agree with you.

Begin by asking these two questions:

- What are the opinions of people who differ from me?
- Why do they hold these opinions?

Based on this understanding, then ask,

- Are there goals, values, attitudes, or beliefs that I share with those who differ from me?
- Can I agree with at least some of what they say?
- What exactly do I need to change in their viewpoint to move them toward my position?

In short, *you need to find the common ground you share with those you want to convince.* In this way you can reduce the "us versus them" mentality that makes reasoning seem so frustrating and pointless.

READINGS

We begin with a recent contribution to a long-standing dispute—teaching evolution in public schools—that remains controversial enough in the United States to result in court cases.

Optimism in Evolution

OLIVIA JUDSON

Educated at Stanford and Oxford, Olivia Judson is a biologist at Imperial College, in London. She's best known for her book, *Dr. Tatiana's Sex Advice to All Creation,* an international best-seller that deals in an engaging way with the role of sex in evolution. She writes a weekly blog on evolutionary biology called "The Wild Side," accessible on the *New York Times* Web site.

The following column appeared in the *New York Times,* August 13, 2008. As you read, note how well Judson structures her case for teaching evolution in all beginning biology classes.

When the dog days of summer come to an end, one thing we can be sure of is that the school year that follows will see <u>more fights over the teaching of evolution and whether intelligent design, or even Biblical accounts of creation, have a place in America's science classrooms.</u>

Reminds readers of the conflict of opinion.

In these arguments, evolution is treated as an abstract subject that deals with the age of the earth or how fish first flopped onto land. It's discussed as though it were an optional, quaint and largely irrelevant part of biology. <u>And a common consequence of the arguments is that evolution gets dropped from the curriculum entirely.</u>

Indicates what's at stake, why this topic matters.

3   This is a travesty.

4   It is also dangerous.

5   <u>Evolution should be taught—indeed, it should be central to beginning biology classes—for at least three reasons.</u>

States thesis or central claim, signals reader to expect three-part defense of the thesis.

<u>First,</u> it provides a powerful framework for investigating the world we live in. Without evolution, biology is merely a collection of disconnected facts, a set of descriptions. <u>The astonishing variety of nature, from the tree shrew that guzzles vast quantities of alcohol every night to the lichens that grow in the Antarctic wastes, cannot be probed and understood.</u> Add evolution—and it becomes possible to make inferences and predictions and (sometimes) to do experiments to test those predictions. All of a sudden patterns emerge everywhere, and apparently trivial details become interesting.

Numbers reasons to help readers identify them.

Note use of specific examples of "astonishing variety."

The second reason for teaching evolution is that the subject is immediately relevant here and now. The impact we are having on the planet is causing other organisms to evolve—and fast. And I'm not talking just about the obvious examples: <u>widespread resistance to pesticides among insects; the evolution of drug resistance in the agents of disease, from malaria to tuberculosis; the possibility that, say, the virus that causes bird flu will evolve into a form that spreads easily from person to person.</u> The impact we are having is much broader.

Makes first point forcefully: that nature cannot be understood without evolution.

For instance, we are causing animals to evolve just by hunting them. The North Atlantic cod fishery has caused the evolution of cod that mature smaller and younger than they did 40 years ago. Fishing for grayling in Norwegian lakes has caused a similar pattern in these fish. Human trophy hunting for bighorn rams has caused the population to evolve into one of smaller-horn rams. (All of which, incidentally, is in line with evolutionary predictions.)

Reminds readers of well-known examples of evolution caused by human activity.

Use of transitional phrase.

Conversely, hunting animals to extinction may cause evolution in their former prey species. Experiments on guppies have shown that, without predators, these fish evolve more brightly colored scales, mature later, bunch together in shoals less and lose their ability to suddenly swim away from something. Such changes can happen in fewer than five generations. If you then reintroduce some predators, the population typically goes extinct.

Another use of a transitional word or phrase.

<u>Thus,</u> a failure to consider the evolution of other species may result in a failure of our efforts to preserve them. And, perhaps, to preserve ourselves from

diseases, pests and food shortages. In short, evolution is far from being a remote and abstract subject. A failure to teach it may leave us unprepared for the challenges ahead.

11   The third reason to teach evolution is more philosophical. It concerns the development of an attitude toward evidence. <u>In his book, "The Republican War on Science," the journalist Chris Mooney argues persuasively that a contempt for scientific evidence—or indeed, evidence of any kind—has permeated the Bush administration's policies, from climate change to sex education, from drilling for oil to the war in Iraq.</u> A dismissal of evolution is an integral part of this general attitude.

Cites authority to back up her reason.

12   Moreover, since the science classroom is where a contempt for evidence is often first encountered, it is also arguably where it first begins to be cultivated. A society where ideology is a substitute for evidence can go badly awry. <u>(This is not to suggest that science is never distorted by the ideological left; it sometimes is, and the results are no better.)</u>

Acknowledges that distortion of science is not limited to the political right.

13   But for me, the most important thing about studying evolution is something less tangible. It's that the endeavor contains a profound optimism. It means that when we encounter something in nature that is complicated or mysterious, such as the flagellum of a bacteria or the light made by a firefly, we don't have to shrug our shoulders in bewilderment.

14   Instead, we can ask how it got to be that way. And if at first it seems so complicated that the evolutionary steps are hard to work out, we have an invitation to imagine, to play, to experiment and explore. To my mind, this only enhances the wonder.

Good conclusion that stresses the author's personal view and refutes the notion that evolution takes away from the wonder and beauty of nature.

QUESTIONS FOR DISCUSSION

1. When you took your first biology class, was evolution taught as the foundation of the discipline, or as "an optional, quaint, and largely irrelevant part of biology" (paragraph 2)? How did you feel about evolution then? What is your view now?

2. Judson calls the failure to teach evolution a "travesty"—that is, a gross misrepresentation of something. Does she establish that leaving evolution out of biological instruction distorts the discipline? How?

3. She also calls the failure to teach evolution "dangerous." What in her article confirms that statement?

Strategies Used in Case-Making: Structure and Readership

There could not be a clearer example of how to structure an effective case, one easy for a reader to follow:

Thesis: Evolution should be central to beginning biology classes

   Reason 1: It provides a powerful framework for investigation.

      Evidence: moving beyond "disconnected facts" to "inferences and predictions"

Reason 2: Evolution is relevant to the here and now.

Evidence: drug resistance in microbes, the impact of hunting, evolution in species whose prey goes extinct, and so on

Reason 3: Teaching evolution encourages a respect for evidence.

Evidence: reference to *The Republican War on Science,* the ignoring or suppression of scientific evidence

You can learn much about how to structure a case from Judson's article, including how to develop individual reasons in support of a thesis. Note that the second reason takes four paragraphs (7–10) to explain and support and that she devotes two paragraphs (11–12) to her third reason. *Follow her example, and don't think of each reason as corresponding to a single paragraph.* Reasons often require more than one paragraph to explain and support.

Another feature of the article worth your attention is how to *frame* (provide a context for) a case and how to *close* or conclude a case. Note that Judson has a four-paragraph introduction that precedes her thesis, stated in paragraph 5. The opening paragraphs explain why she is making her case for teaching evolution—because too often it either is not taught or not taught well. Readers need to know *why* you are making a case, the context that makes a case worth making.

Her two-paragraph conclusion (13–14) is a good example of something much better than a summarizing "in conclusion" close. She says that evolution "contains a profound optimism" and "enhances the wonder" of studying nature. It is these positive attitudes that opponents of evolution say teaching evolution destroys. Her conclusion, therefore, addresses an objection the other side has raised.

In addition to its structure, the Judson article offers an important insight into *selecting an appropriate readership* for any case you make. On one hand, Judson is not writing for her fellow biologists. With very few exceptions, they agree with her already. On the other hand, she also makes no effort to convince those unalterably opposed to teaching evolution. Instead, she is making her case for those who may think teaching evolution does not matter much or for those who support equal time for evolution and creationism.

You should do likewise in conceiving readers for the cases you make. Depending on the topic and your position on it, there will always be a segment of readers unalterably opposed to what you have to say. Ignore them and address an audience capable of responding to your reasoning.

CLAIMING VOICE IN ARGUING A CASE

Traditionally, the voice of arguing a case has been linked to **middle style,** in contrast to the plain style of informing and the passionate style of some public speaking, designed to arouse emotions in an audience. What does middle style sound like? Here it is in a passage from the reading that follows, an argument advocating prison reform:

> Prison has a role in public safety, but it is not a cure-all. Its value is limited, and its use should be limited to what it does best: isolating young criminals long enough to give them a chance to grow up and get a grip on their impulses.

Read these sentences aloud and you can hear the voice of middle style: It states its position clearly, directly, and forcefully. It is more formal than relaxed chatting with a friend, but not as formal as a speech from President Obama or an emotional sermon from the pulpit on Sunday.

You can miss middle style in two ways. On one hand, you may have been taught to keep your opinions out of your writing. Clearly the advice does not apply to arguing a case because the thesis you are defending *is* your opinion. On the other hand, resist being influenced by the phony, overheated sensationalism of much talk radio and TV. Argument is not name-calling, insults, outrageous claims, or partisan bickering—all designed to increase ratings. Argument is the calm voice of reason, of opinions stated precisely and defended well. It is one of the voices most admired and respected at universities, in business meetings, in community gatherings, and wherever productive interaction among people occurs.

Why Prisons Don't Work

WILBERT RIDEAU

Wilbert Rideau was convicted of murder at age nineteen, and spent over forty years of his life in Louisiana State Penitentiary at Angola. He edited the prison newspaper and became an award-winning journalist and one of the best-known convicts ever in the United States.

As you read his article, pay special attention to how Rideau depicts the problem of how we deal with criminals in the United States and to the solution he proposes. Note also his use of cause-and-effect reasoning, common in case-making.

1   I was among thirty-one murderers sent to the Louisiana State Penitentiary in 1962 to be executed or imprisoned for life. We weren't much different from those we found here, or those who had preceded us. We were unskilled, impulsive, and uneducated misfits, mostly black, who had done dumb, impulsive things—failures, rejects from the larger society. Now a generation has come of age and gone since I've been here, and everything is much the same as I found it. The faces of the prisoners are different, but behind them are the same impulsive, uneducated, unskilled minds that made dumb, impulsive choices that got them into more trouble than they ever thought existed. The vast majority of us are consigned to suffer and die here so politicians can sell the illusion that permanently exiling people to prison will make society safe.

2   Getting tough has always been a "silver bullet," a quick fix for the crime and violence that society fears. Each year in Louisiana—where excess is a way of

life—lawmakers have tried to outdo each other in legislating harsher mandatory penalties and in reducing avenues of release. The only thing to do with criminals, they say, is get tougher. They have. In the process, the purpose of prison began to change. The state boasts one of the highest lockup rates in the country, imposes the most severe penalties in the nation, and vies to execute more criminals per capita than anywhere else. This state is so tough that last year, when prison authorities here wanted to punish an inmate in solitary confinement for an infraction, the most they could inflict on him was to deprive him of his underwear. It was all he had left.

3   If getting tough resulted in public safety, Louisiana citizens would be the safest in the nation. They're not. Louisiana has the highest murder rate among states. Prison, like the police and the courts, has a minimal impact on crime because it is a response after the fact, a mop-up operation. It doesn't work. The idea of punishing the few to deter the many is counterfeit because potential criminals either think they're not going to get caught or they're so emotionally desperate or psychologically distressed that they don't care about the consequences of their actions. The threatened punishment, regardless of its severity, is never a factor in the equation. But society, like the "incorrigible" criminal it abhors, is unable to learn from its mistakes.

4   Prison has a role in public safety, but it is not a cure-all. Its value is limited, and its use should also be limited to what it does best: isolating young criminals long enough to give them a chance to grow up and get a grip on their impulses. It is a traumatic experience, certainly, but it should be only a temporary one, not a way of life. Prisoners kept too long tend to embrace the criminal culture, its distorted values and beliefs; they have little choice—prison is their life. There are some prisoners who cannot be returned to society—serial killers, serial rapists, professional hit men, and the like—but the monsters who need to die in prison are rare exceptions in the criminal landscape.

5   Crime is a young man's game. Most of the nation's random violence is committed by young urban terrorists. But because of long, mandatory sentences, most prisoners here are much older, having spent fifteen, twenty, thirty, or more years behind bars, long past necessity. Rather than pay for new prisons, society would be well served by releasing some of its older prisoners who pose no threat and using the money to catch young street thugs. Warden John Whitley agrees that many older prisoners here could be freed tomorrow with little or no danger to society. Release, however, is governed by law or by politicians, not by penal professionals. Even murderers, those most feared by society, pose little risk. Historically, for example, the domestic staff at Louisiana's Governor's mansion has been made up of murderers, hand-picked to work among the chief-of-state and his family. Penologists have long known that murder is almost always a once-in-a-lifetime act. The most dangerous criminal is the one who has not yet killed but has a history of escalating offenses. He's the one to watch.

6   Rehabilitation can work. Everyone changes in time. The trick is to influence the direction that change takes. The problem with prisons is that they don't do more to rehabilitate those confined in them. The convict who enters prison illiterate will

probably leave the same way. Most convicts want to be better than they are, but education is not a priority. This prison houses 4,600 men and offers academic training to 240, vocational training to a like number. Perhaps it doesn't matter. About 90 percent of the men here may never leave this prison alive.

7   The only effective way to curb crime is for society to work to prevent the criminal act in the first place, to come between the perpetrator and crime. Our youngsters must be taught to respect the humanity of others and to handle disputes without violence. It is essential to educate and equip them with the skills to pursue their life ambitions in a meaningful way. As a community, we must address the adverse life circumstances that spawn criminality. These things are not quick, and they're not easy, but they're effective. Politicians think that's too hard a sell. They want to be on record for doing something now, something they can point to at reelection time. So the drumbeat goes on for more police, more prisons, more of the same failed policies.

8   Ever see a dog chase its tail?

QUESTIONS FOR DISCUSSION

1. According to Rideau, why doesn't the possibility of prison deter criminal acts?

2. What does he say prisons do best? What roles should they play in our society's effort to cope with criminals? Do his proposals make sense, given his analysis of cause and effect? Why or why not?

3. What does Rideau contend would truly be effective in reducing crime, especially the violent crime we fear most? What would have to change to pursue the course of action he favors?

FOLLOWING THROUGH

In groups of two or three, look over Rideau's argument with an eye to **case structure**. Write up an outline of its claim and reasons. Beneath each reason, jot down something about the evidence that he uses to support it. Compare your group's decisions about Rideau's case structure with the outline of at least one other group. Where did you find consensus about the argument's structure? If you found disagreement about structure, how might that be explained or reconciled?   •

Strategies Used in Case-Making: Problem-Solution, Cause-and-Effect Reasoning

The difficulty in solving any problem resides in understanding it, which is why cause-and-effect reasoning dominates problem-solution cases. Fail to grasp the causes of a problem and you will also fail to solve it. It sounds simple, but of course it is not.

Rideau shows us clearly why understanding a problem can be so difficult. First, there is prejudice, often rooted in common sense. Get tough with crime?—certainly, we say. It seems so reasonable that our politicians outdo each other trying to be the toughest. But as Rideau explains, getting tough is only a "mop-up operation" (paragraph 3) after the criminal has been caught and convicted. Do we feel safer when violent criminals receive long prison terms and, in some cases, life without parole? We do, yet murder and other violent crimes are daily news items, and the cost of locking up so many people for so long imposes a huge burden on taxpayers.

With most problems, understanding depends on getting beyond gut reactions and common sense. Ask, *What is really going on?* Answering it requires cool, dispassionate analysis of the information we have. Drawing on his own long experience, Rideau sees a pattern: "Crime is a young man's game," especially the violent crime we fear most (paragraph 5). If this is so, prisons should "[isolate] young criminals long enough to give them a chance to grow up and get a grip on their impulses" (paragraph 4). If this is so, rehabilitation requires more effort; otherwise, paroled prisoners will not be equipped to rejoin society as productive, law-abiding citizens. If this is so, it makes no sense to keep older prisoners in jail for so long, well past their impulsive youth. If this is so, "coming between the perpetrator and the crime"—that is, working with young people in the neighborhoods where so much of the violent crime occurs—is about the only effective way to *prevent* crime, as opposed to reacting to it after it occurs.

The Rideau article shows how problem-solution, cause-and-effect case-making works: Analyze what you know to identify the cause or causes of a problem. The solution, then, follows from understanding the cause: If crime is a young man's game, everything Rideau proposes makes sense.

A Plan for Reducing American Dependence on Foreign Oil

T. BOONE PICKENS

T. Boone Pickens is an internationally prominent Texas oil man, investor, and philanthropist, who recently used his money and influence to bring the following proposal to the attention of all Americans through newspaper spreads and Internet postings.

We took the following argument from his Web site. The selection preserves the formatting of the Web site. As you read, pay special attention to the use of graphics as an efficient way of presenting evidence and to the use of font size and bold print as a way of calling attention to key points.

THE PLAN

1 America is addicted to foreign oil.

2 It's an addiction that threatens our economy, our environment and our national security.

3 | It touches every part of our daily lives and ties our hands as a nation and a people.

4 | The addiction has worsened for decades and now it's reached a point of crisis.

5 | **In 1970, we imported 24% of our oil. Today it's nearly 70% and growing.**

6 | Oil prices have come down from the staggering highs of last summer, but lower prices have not reduced our dependence on foreign oil or lessened the risks to either our economy or our security.

7 | If we are depending on foreign sources for nearly 70% of our oil, we are in a precarious position in an unpredictable world.

8 | In addition to putting our security in the hands of potentially unfriendly and unstable foreign nations, we spent $475 billion on foreign oil in 2008 alone. That's money taken out of our economy and sent to foreign nations, and it will continue to drain the life from our economy for as long as we fail to stop the bleeding.

9 | Projected over the next 10 years the cost will be $10 trillion—it will be the greatest transfer of wealth in the history of mankind.

10 | Can't we just produce more oil?

11 | America uses a lot of oil. Every day 85 million barrels of oil are produced around the world.

12 | And 21 million of those are used here in the United States.

13 | That's 25% of the world's oil demand. Used by just 4% of the world's population.

14 | Consider this: America imports 12 million barrels a day, and Saudi Arabia only produces 9 million a day. Is there really more undiscovered oil here than in all of Saudi Arabia?

15 | World oil production peaked in 2005. Despite growing demand and an unprecedented increase in prices, oil production has fallen over the last three years. Oil is getting more expensive to produce, harder to find and there just isn't enough of it to keep up with demand.

16 | The simple truth is that cheap and easy oil is gone.

17 | **But America is focused on another crisis: The economy.**

18 | All Americans are feeling the effects of our recent downturn. And addressing this problem is the top priority of our nation. This is more than bailing out a bank, an insurance firm or a car company. The American economy is huge and has many facets.

19 | To make a real and lasting impact we must seek do more than create new jobs and opportunities today, we must build the platform on which our economy can continue to grow for decades to come.

20 | There is nothing more important to the present and future of our economy than energy. Any effort to address our economic problems will require a thorough understanding of this issue and willingness to confront our dependence on foreign oil and what domestic resources we can use.

21 | It is a crisis too large to be addressed by piecemeal steps. We need a plan of action on scale with the problems we face. That is the spirit in which the Pickens Plan was conceived. The Pickens Plan is a collection of steps that together form a comprehensive approach to America's energy needs.

The Pickens Plan

22 There are several pillars to the Pickens Plan:

- Create millions of new jobs by building out the capacity to generate up to 22 percent of our electricity from wind. And adding to that with additional solar capacity.
- Building a 21st century backbone electrical grid.
- Providing incentives for homeowners and the owners of commercial buildings to upgrade their insulation and other energy saving options.
- Using America's natural gas to replace imported oil as a transportation fuel.

23 While dependence on foreign oil is a critical concern, it is not a problem that can be solved in isolation. We have to think about energy as a whole, and that begins by considering our energy alternatives and thinking about how we will fuel our world in the next 10 to 20 years and beyond.

New Jobs from Renewable Energy and Conservation

24 Any discussion of alternatives should begin with the 2007 Department of Energy study showing that building out our wind capacity in the Great Plains—from northern Texas to the Canadian border—would produce 138,000 new jobs in the first year, and more than 3.4 million new jobs over a ten-year period, while also producing as much as 20 percent of our needed electricity.

25 Building out solar energy in the Southwest from western Texas to California would add to the boom of new jobs and provide more of our growing electrical needs—doing so through economically viable, clean, renewable sources.

26 To move that electricity from where it is being produced to where it is needed will require an upgrade to our national electric grid. A 21st century grid which will, as

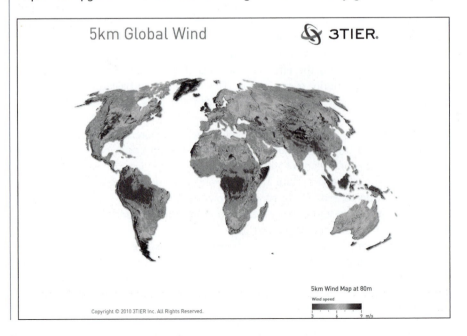

5km Global Wind   3TIER

5km Wind Map at 80m

Wind speed

3   6   9 m/s

technology continues to develop, deliver power where it is needed, when it is needed, in the direction it is needed, will be the modern equivalent of building the Interstate Highway System in the 1950's.

27 Beyond that, tremendous improvements in electricity use can be made by creating incentives for owners of homes and commercial buildings to retrofit their spaces with proper insulation.

28 Studies show that a significant upgrading of insulation would save the equivalent of one million barrels of oil per day in energy by cutting down on both air conditioning costs in warm weather and heating costs in winter.

A Domestic Fuel to Free Us from Foreign Oil

29 Conserving and harnessing renewable forms of electricity not only has incredible economic benefits, but is also a crucial piece of the oil dependence puzzle. We should continue to pursue the promise of electric or hydrogen powered vehicles, but America needs to address transportation fuel today. Fortunately, we are blessed with an abundance of clean, cheap, domestic natural gas.

30 Currently, domestic natural gas is primarily used to generate electricity. It has the advantage of being cheap and significantly cleaner than coal, but this is not the best use of our natural gas resources.

31 By generating electricity from wind and solar and conserving the electricity we have, we will be free to shift our use of natural gas to where it can lower our need for foreign oil—helping President Obama reach his goal of zero oil imports from the Middle East within ten years—by replacing diesel as the principal transportation fuel for heavy trucks and fleet vehicles.

32 Nearly 20% of every barrel of oil we import is used by 18-wheelers moving goods burning imported diesel. An over-the-road truck cannot be moved using current battery technology. Fleet vehicles like buses, taxis, express delivery trucks, and municipal and utility vehicles (any vehicle which returns to the "barn" each night

2010 Civic GX Sedan

The Honda Civic GX Natural Gas Vehicle is the cleanest internal-combustion vehicle in the world according to the EPA.

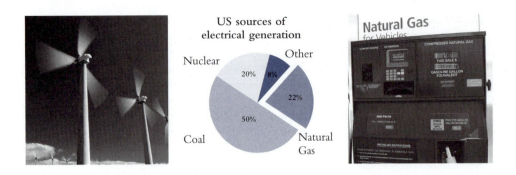

US sources of electrical generation

where refueling is a simple matter) should be replaced by vehicles running on clean, cheap, domestic natural gas rather than imported gasoline or diesel fuel.

A Plan that Brings It All Together

33   Natural gas is not a permanent or complete solution to imported oil. It is a bridge fuel to slash our oil dependence while buying us time to develop new technologies that will ultimately replace fossil transportation fuels. Natural gas is the critical puzzle piece that will help us keep more of the $350 to $450 billion every year at home, where it can power our economy and pay for our investments in wind energy, a smart grid and energy efficiency.

34   It is this connection that makes The Pickens Plan not just a collection of good ideas, but a plan. By investing in renewable energy and conservation, we can create millions of new jobs. New alternative energies allow us to shift natural gas to transportation; securing our economy by reducing our dependence on foreign oil, and keeping more money at home to pay for the whole thing.

How Do We Get It Done?

35   The Pickens Plan is a bridge to the future—a blueprint to reduce foreign oil dependence by harnessing domestic energy alternatives, and to buy us time to develop even greater new technologies.

36   Building new wind generation facilities, conserving energy and better utilizing our natural gas resources can replace more than one-third of our foreign oil imports in 10 years. But it will take leadership.

37   We're organizing behind the Pickens Plan now to ensure our voices will be heard.

38   Together with President Obama and the new Congress, we can take down the old barriers and provide energy security for generations to come, while helping dig out of the recession we are in today.

39   As our new President has said, "Yes, we can." And together, as never before, we will.

QUESTIONS FOR DISCUSSION

1.   Cases made online or in other popular, mass media like television and newspapers usually observe special conventions. Describe the conventions in this Web site posting. In your view do they work well to communicate the message? Why or why not?

2. This short article uses five graphics, including several types—photographs, a map, and a pie graph. In case-making, graphics present evidence efficiently and memorably. What evidence do the graphics in this piece provide? What statements in the article do they support?

3. The T. Boone Pickens Web site makes no effort to conceal his personal stake in the plan. He is heavily invested in natural gas and wind power. In your view, does being up front strengthen or weaken his case?

Strategies in Case-Making: Lines of Reasoning

Compare the structure of this case with Judson's in "Optimism in Evolution" (pages 211–213). Judson's is the typical case: State a thesis; defend it with three or four reasons; support each reason with evidence. It works well when your thesis is a single claim, such as "Evolution should be central to beginning biology classes."

In contrast, the Pickens Plan is an example of a case composed of two or more claims or theses, each requiring explanation and evidence. The Pickens Plan makes three claims:

- We must reduce our dependence on foreign oil. (claim 1)
- We can do this by exploiting domestic wind power for generating electricity. (claim 2)
- We can also substitute domestic supplies of natural gas for the gasoline and diesel we are currently using in vehicles. (claim 3)

The three claims are linked together by the contrast between *foreign* crude oil and *domestic* wind energy and natural gas.

Each part of the Pickens Plan also develops differently from Judson's single-thesis case. Think of it as answers to your questions as you read, and the logic is easy to follow. Here is the logic for claim 1, which establishes the problem:

What is the problem your plan would solve?

Answer: America's addiction to foreign oil.

Is that really such a big problem?

Answer: Yes. We import 70% of our oil. It threatens our economy, environment, and national security.

Why not just produce more oil domestically?

Answer: There is not enough to satisfy the current demand. The era of cheap and easy oil is gone.

This way of arguing a point works by anticipating your readers' questions and answering them one by one. The secret to arguing this way is *to imagine what your readers will think based on what you have just said.* If you say that America is addicted to foreign oil, your reader will think, So what? Where's the harm? Then, when you answer that question, your reader will think, Why not produce more domestic oil? When you indicate that doing so will not solve the problem, that brings one line of reasoning to a close, and you are ready to move on to the solutions you advocate.

FOLLOWING THROUGH

In class do with the rest of the Pickens case what we did above with claim 1, establishing the problem. What sequence of questions is being answered in the solution parts of the case?

Then address this question: Is the reasoning as a whole convincing? Why or why not? •

FOLLOWING THROUGH

Each of the topics addressed in the readings in this chapter—teaching evolution, prison reform, and the energy crisis—is debated vigorously online, especially in blogs and in e-mail responses to Web postings and print publications. Why not weigh in on the subject that interests you the most? If you have a blog, post a response to one of the readings, or make your own short case on the subject. If you do not maintain a blog, compose an e-mail response to one of the authors, or get a conversation going online with other members of your class via e-mail or Blackboard or any other online means for exchanging viewpoints and ideas.

The best way to learn to make cases is to get involved in real arguments on genuine issues. You also may find your topic for this chapter's assignment this way. •

THE ASSIGNMENT

Make a case that seeks to convince readers to accept your central claim or thesis about any controversial topic, problem, issue, or question. "Controversial" means that various positions or stances are possible—not necessarily that the subject has received media attention. It can address anything from something as personal and local as a family dilemma or a campus concern to something as impersonal and global as U.S. relations with China.

Topic and Focus

Whatever your topic is, avoid thinking in pro–con, us versus them ways. Despite how they are depicted in the media, even highly polarized issues like abortion are not simply "pro-life" versus "pro-choice." Strongly antiabortion cases, for instance, usually allow abortion in instances of rape, incest, or when the woman's life is in danger, and many people labeled "pro-choice" don't oppose reasonable restrictions on abortion after the first trimester. *Think in terms of many possible stances.*

Most topics also consist of many controversial issues. Consider limiting your case to one of them. For instance, standardized testing in public schools raises many issues, including what subject areas should be tested, how standardized testing affects coverage of a subject, what to do about schools that do not meet standards, and how to control cheating. You can easily locate many other areas for debate in newspapers and Web searches.

Audience

Cases aim at two audiences: people weakly inclined to agree and those tending toward another stance but open to reason. Your case should strengthen the adherence of those favorably disposed to your thesis by giving them good reasons and strong evidence they may have lacked before. Those good reasons and strong evidence also may appeal to readers entertaining other positions, but reaching them requires strategy (see pages 210–211).

Voice and Style

Cases aim for assent to a thesis. They want to secure agreement by advancing good reasons based on current, accurate information about the topic.

Your voice should be dispassionate, calm, and fair. Treat other positions and arguments with respect, even as you show that your evidence and reasons are more compelling.

Writing Assignment Suggestions

The paper could be written in many possible genres: an editorial, a posting on a Web site, a magazine article, a text for a speech, an open letter to some group of people, a personal letter, and so on. You might consider writing in one of these genres if your topic and readership seem appropriate and your instructor approves.

A wide range of topics are of interest to college students: college costs, living conditions on campus, and avoiding excessive debt in personal finances; cultural and social issues, such as the impact of electronic communication on how people live and relate to other people, computer gaming, rap music, the behavior of people at sporting events, controversial films, TV shows, and advertisements; political issues, such as counterterrorism policy, the use of torture in interrogating persons suspected of terrorist activity, health care, energy policy, global warming, and immigration. Perhaps your topic can be one of these or related to one of them.

CHOOSING A TOPIC

Often the best topics come from problems and issues you have experienced directly as a student, voter, friend, parent, resident in a foreign country, participant in a sport or other activity—in short, something you have lived. Maybe you are involved in a club, volunteer organization, or student activity that deserves more recognition or support. Maybe you attended a campus event and heard a controversial speaker with a viewpoint you responded to strongly. Civic activities, internships, and jobs can also be rich sources of topics for case-making. Here are some possibilities for finding topics.

- *Class readings.* Class readings can suggest topics for case-making, especially if the readings themselves are cases, like the examples in this chapter. For instance, after reading the Pickens Plan, you may have your own ideas about how to reduce American dependence on foreign oil.

- *Local news or observation.* Read your local and campus newspapers for issues and problems of concern to your community. Take a walk around your neighborhood or campus with an eye for problems that need solutions, such as wasted energy in offices, dorms, and classrooms.
- *Internet discussions.* If you keep a blog, you probably have a store of observations about issues that concern you, things you would like to convince others to see as you do. Also try visiting blogs concerned with public issues, such as National Public Radio's "Blog of the Nation," based on topics from its radio program *Talk of the Nation.*

EXPLORING YOUR TOPIC

The best approach to exploring a topic depends on many variables: how much you know about the topic already, whether you have participated in debates or discussions about it previously, how much time you have to produce the paper, and so on. Let's assume the situation many students face in their classes: an assigned topic about which you know little or nothing.

The Art of Questioning: Find the Issues

An **issue** is a point of controversy always or frequently discussed when a particular topic arises. For any topic, begin by asking, What are the questions that people disagree about when discussing this topic? For instance, the primary purpose of prisons is always an issue when prison reform is discussed. Some see prisons primarily as punishment for crime; others see them primarily as institutions that should rehabilitate criminals.

◎◎ FOLLOWING THROUGH

Relying on general knowledge, list the issues connected with the topic. The key question is, *What do people argue about whenever this topic is discussed?*

Assign each issue to a group of between two and four students for research and further exploration. Each group should report its results to the class. Here are some key questions class discussion might address:

Did you encounter issues in your group that you were not aware of before research?

What knowledge about the issues struck you as most important?

Given what you know now, what would you like to know more about?

After the discussion is over, consider your view of the topic now. If you had no opinion before discussing the issues, are you beginning to form one now? If you had a strong opinion, is it changing significantly?

Order the Issues (Stasis)

Discussing the issues is an important step in exploring a controversial topic. Ordering them can help as well, beginning with the most elementary of questions and moving through to subsequent issues. As an example, here is one way of ordering the issues involved in committing American troops to a foreign country:

- Are vital American interests at stake?

  If you say no, make a case against committing the troops. If you say yes, move on to the next question.

- Have nonmilitary alternatives been exploited fully?

  If you say no, make a case for increased diplomatic effort or some other measure not requiring American troops on the ground. If you say yes, move on to the next question.

- Do the announced objectives make sense?

  If you say no, make a case for changing the objectives. If you say yes, move on to the next question.

- Can we realize our objectives in a reasonable amount of time with minimal loss of lives?

  If you say yes, make a case for military intervention. If you say no, make a case against it based on impracticality.

Ordering the issues in this way is sometimes called **stasis,** a word that means "stop" or "stay." That is, if you think a proposed military intervention would not secure vital national interests, you stop with the first question and make a case against it. If you think nonmilitary options have not been pursued far enough, you argue for more diplomacy, economic sanctions, or some other alternative. You stay with the second question—and so on, through the whole list.

You can order the issues connected with any controversial topic this way. Doing so can help you see how the issues relate to one another and on what key questions opinion divides. It can clarify your own thinking as you work toward an opinion or assess the one you have.

◎◉ FOLLOWING THROUGH

Cases require a *considered opinion*—that is, an opinion *thought through carefully*. Consequently, after finding and ordering the issues, you need to decide what your opinion is on the issue you chose to address. Your opinion may change as you write and assess your first draft, but you cannot write a draft at all without committing to an opinion.

In a blog post or notebook entry, state your opinion and the reasons you have for holding it.

Doing Team Research

Sometimes instructors want you to do research on your own. When that is part of the assignment, do not use the team approach suggested here. Otherwise a team approach is best because there is so much information on nearly all topics.

Here are the steps in a team approach to research:

1. Form small groups based on sharing the same opinion.

2. Share all information you have already, so that everyone in the group has the same knowledge base.

3. Make a list of the information you lack.

4. Divide the items on the needed information list among group members and set a deadline for getting the research done.

5. Get together to share and discuss the implications of the new research materials.

The team approach to research is the norm in business settings, community organizations, government, and often in advanced academic work. The advantages are obvious: sharing the work burden and having people with whom to discuss the results.

Do More Research

The amount of research needed to argue a case depends on such variables as the nature of the topic, how much you know about it already, and what the assignment requires.

Even thought-through opinions need to confront "the facts," current, reliable knowledge about a topic. For controversial topics, the problem is rarely lack of sources. If you use the resources for finding information discussed in Chapter 6, "Writing Research-Based Arguments," you can count on finding much more than you will have time to read.

Therefore, let the opinion you formed after considering the issues dictate the direction for further research. You can then look only for sources relevant to it and take notes (see pages 127–128 for how to do this) only on those sources that provide the best information. You can pass over many articles and book chapters because the titles alone indicate they will not be relevant. Others you can eliminate with a quick, partial reading; the title turns out to be more promising than the content. You can concentrate on what is left, the articles that are most relevant, and among these, the few that are outstanding, most authoritative, recent, and detailed in offering reliable information. (See pages 116–121 for estimating how reliable a source is.)

The Best Practices box offers an approach to research that can make it more efficient yet.

Analyze Your Sources: Information versus Interpretation

Research materials on controversial topics typically are arguments backed by information used as evidence. Consequently, you need to distinguish information from the "spin" or interpretation the writer and his or her sources supply. For example, it is a fact that in a recent year about 6,200 people died in Mexico as a result of the traffic in narcotics. Citing this figure, some writers argue that American tourists should avoid Mexico. There is no reason to doubt the 6,200 figure, but the interpretation is far from certain—drug-related violence seldom involves American tourists, and many destinations in Mexico are no more risky than some of our own cities.

It is also important to distinguish information from speculation. Facts are uncontested, established pieces of data. How the stock market performed over the last month is a matter of fact, as measured, for example, by the Dow Jones average. Speculations are at most probabilities and possibilities. How the stock market will perform over the next year is anyone's guess. When relevant to your opinion, you *must* engage the facts; speculation you can ignore or use if it supports your opinion.

In general, despite what people sometimes say, the facts cannot speak for themselves. *Facts have to be interpreted, put into a context where they have meaning.* For example, newspapers are in significant financial trouble in the United States. Does this mean, as some people claim, that Americans are less well informed about current events than they were thirty years ago, when papers were in much better shape? Or does it mean that people are getting the news from other sources—online, for instance? It is hard to say, but in any case the decline of newspapers, a fact beyond dispute, must be interpreted to have meaning and significance.

Finally, above all, *strive to maintain intellectual independence from the view your source has of the subject.* Avoid distorting or misrepresenting the information in a source to fit what you want to believe, but feel free to interpret the information your own way, as you see the subject. For instance, you may support screening passengers before boarding commercial airliners as a necessary counterterrorism measure. If so, you cannot ignore considerable evidence that screening often fails to detect prohibited items that could be used for a terrorist act. Instead of ignoring or denying the evidence, argue instead that screening technology must improve.

Start Your Working Bibliography

As you do research, maintain a complete list of your sources, including all information you will need for the concluding bibliography or works cited page. (See examples of the various types of entries for these pages on pages 139–148.) Doing this as you work can save having to relocate the sources later.

Keep the bibliographical information with your drafts, bearing in mind that revision and rewriting usually result in dropping and adding source material.

Ponder a Key Question: Is My Opinion Defensible?

You are about to make your case, so address the following question coolly and apart from how strongly you are committed to the opinion you had before research: Given what I know now, can I make a good case for my opinion?

One outcome is that current knowledge makes your opinion impossible or very difficult to defend. Change your opinion to accord with the evidence.

More commonly, research yields another result. Your opinion is still defensible, but you need to modify it some to allow for information you lacked prior to research. Perhaps you did not know that the flu vaccine developed each year is never 100% effective. You could still make a case in favor of a more aggressive vaccination campaign. You need only admit that the inoculation is not uniformly reliable. There is still overwhelming evidence of its benefit to public health—of the approximately 36,000 Americans who die from the flu each year, a high percentage did not receive the vaccine.

The Art of Questioning: Assessing Your Opinion from Research Results

Cases are public arguments and therefore must respect what is known about a topic. Ask these questions as you adjust your opinion to the evidence you have gathered:

1. What facts and expert opinion best support my position?
2. What did I learn from research that challenges my position? Do I need to rethink or modify it?
3. What further information should I seek?

Some people believe that arguments require that they take a stand and hold it regardless of what the available evidence says. They elevate saying what they think over responding to the evidence, and often they appeal to honesty to justify their behavior.

We urge a sharply different attitude. Case-making is a rational process, and part of being rational is changing your mind or modifying your opinion as you learn more about a subject. This process is not dishonest. On the contrary, admitting that "I used to believe this, but now that I know more I believe that instead" requires not only being honest with yourself and other people but also being open to experience, which is necessary for intellectual growth and maturity.

PREPARING TO WRITE

Some writers prefer to go straight to drafting, working out their cases in several drafts. We recommend going through the following steps first, which most writers find helpful:

1. State your opinion as a claim or thesis.
2. "Unpack" (analyze) the thesis to determine what you must argue to defend it adequately.
3. State the reasons you will use to explain or justify your thesis.
4. Select and order the evidence you will use to back up each reason.

These steps, described in more detail below, yield a **brief,** an outline of your case. Add ideas for an introduction and a conclusion and you have all you need to guide your first draft.

State Your Opinion as a Thesis

You are still exploring your opinion when your write a first draft of your case because the ultimate test of any opinion is how strong a case you can make for it. However, your first draft will be stronger if you attempt to state your opinion as a thesis before you begin drafting. An opinion is a general stance or point of view. For instance, in the second reading in this chapter (pages 215–217), Wilbert Rideau believes that our prison system is not working because politics rather than reason and an adequate understanding of crime and criminals controls it. That is his opinion. In contrast, his thesis is much more specific: "Society would be well served by releasing some of its older prisoners who pose no threat and using the money to catch young street thugs" (paragraph 5).

In preparing to write a case, the advantage of a thesis over an opinion is a *sharper focus, with carefully selected key terms.* It is worth your time and effort to work toward a thesis before you draft.

Writing Defensible Claims

- Your claim is a statement you'll defend, not just a description of something that is factual.

  Not a claim: Student debt for government loans has grown to over $20,000 for the average graduate, a heavy burden for young people just entering the workplace.

  Claim: The economy as a whole would benefit if the federal government would forgive student debts for higher education, which now average over $20,000 per graduate.

The first in this pair describes a problem. The second proposes a solution for doing something about the problem.

- The claim should be focused and specific, and directed at a readership.

  Too general: Many professors do not know how to make effective use of technology in teaching.

  Better: Professors who use presentation technology such as PowerPoint too often stifle creativity and student involvement in the class.

The second example in this pair is more refined, indicating specific directions that the argument will take. The more specific your claim, the easier it will be to decide what your paper will include.

- Some claims may need to be qualified.

  Too absolute: Professors should openly state their opinions on political issues in classes where such opinions are relevant to course content.

Qualified: Provided that students are encouraged to discuss their own opinions freely, professors should be able to openly state their opinions on political issues so long as the issue is relevant to course content.

Think of objections your readers might have to your claim and revise it to eliminate the possible objection.

FOLLOWING THROUGH

Any opinion can be expressed in many thesis statements. If you are having difficulty formulating yours or hesitating between or among two or more possibilities, post a blog entry or send an e-mail to your instructor or to some other appropriate person that lays out your thought process and asks for feedback. Just writing the blog or e-mail can help you think things through and make a good decision. Any feedback you receive can help you even more. •

Unpack Your Thesis

To "unpack" a thesis means to detect the key terms that make the assertion. Judson's thesis, "Evolution should be central to beginning biology classes," contains terms that demand that the argument show why evolution is *central*, rather than a theory one can explain and discuss at one meeting and then ignore. It will also show why biology classes must start with evolution as a foundation.

As another example, consider the thesis: "*Huckleberry Finn* should be required reading in all American high schools." To defend the thesis adequately requires addressing all the key terms: why this *particular book* should be a *required* title on American literature lists and why *high school* is the best place to teach it.

The Art of Questioning: Thinking about Reasons

The reasoning that led you to your claim will supply the reasons you will offer to explain and justify it to your reader. In listing your reasons, however, you can avoid potential problems by thinking carefully about the following questions:

- Does the statement of each reason say exactly what I mean to say? The wording of your reason or reasons matters as much as the wording of your thesis.
- Do I need all the reasons I am thinking of using? As a general rule, two or three reasons are better than four or five because they are easier for the reader to remember. *Concentrate on developing your best reasons well rather than offering all the reasons you can think of.*
- Does each reason clearly connect to the thesis by either explaining or justifying it? Imagine your reader asking this question, "Why do you believe your thesis?" Each reason should answer this question.

- Are there advantages in developing my reasons in a particular order? In general, begin and end your argument with your strongest reasons. But also consider the possibility that one reason will lead naturally to another, and therefore should come first.

- If you have more than one reason, are they consistent with each other? Make sure, for instance, that your first reason does not contradict your third reason.

Arrange Your Evidence under Each Reason

Just as the reasons that led you to your thesis are the reasons you will develop to convince your readers, so the information you found in research that led you to your reasons or confirmed them will supply the evidence. Arrange the evidence you have under each reason.

The Art of Questioning: Thinking about Evidence

Select and order your evidence in response to the following questions:

- What kind of evidence does each reason require? For example, if you are arguing for making cell phone use by drivers illegal, one of your main reasons will be the link of cell phone use with accidents. You will need data, facts and figures, to back it up. If you also argue that such a law would not restrict personal freedom unduly, you will need other kinds of evidence, such as pointing out that banning cell phones is no more restrictive than laws against driving while intoxicated.

- How much evidence do I need? The answer is, *Enough to overcome the degree of resistance your reader is likely to have.* Many Americans, for instance, assume that the federal government is already too big, too intrusive, and too expensive. Defending any proposal that would increase its role requires significant evidence for both need and positive results.

- Have I mixed evidence types when I can? For example, when a reason requires hard data, you must supply it. But if you also have a statement from a respected expert confirming your reason, consider using it as well. Some readers are convinced more by authoritative statements than by hard data. You could also offer anecdotes, stories from people involved in an event, to confirm a reason. Stories from wounded soldiers who have served in Afghanistan or Iraq, for example, can be used to argue for improvements in Veteran Administration hospitals. Many people find testimony more convincing than any other kind of evidence.

- Have I selected the best pieces of evidence from all that I could use? Just as it is better to develop two or three reasons well than four or five poorly, so it is better to offer two or three strong pieces of evidence than four or five that vary in quality. More is not necessarily better, and too much evidence can confuse and overburden your reader.

BEST PRACTICES

The Brief in Sum

1. A position or general outlook on a topic is not a thesis. A **thesis** is a carefully worded claim that your entire essay backs up with reasons and evidence. Experiment with various ways of stating your thesis until it says *exactly* what you want it to say and creates the least resistance in your readers.

2. Be willing to give up or modify significantly a thesis you find you cannot support with good reasons and strong evidence that appeal *to your readers*. We must argue a thesis that fits the available **evidence**.

3. Create a specific audience profile. We are always trying to convince some definite group of possible readers. What are the age, gender, and economic status of your target audience? What interests, beliefs, and values might they bring to your topic and thesis?

4. Unpack your thesis to discover what you must argue. If you say, for instance, that *Huckleberry Finn* should be *required* reading in high school, you must show why *this particular novel* should be an experience shared by all American high school students. It will not be enough to argue that it is a good book.

5. Select your reasons based on what you must argue to defend your thesis combined with what you should say given your audience's prior knowledge, preconceptions, prejudices, and interests.

6. Be prepared to try out different ways of ordering your reasons. The order that seemed best in your brief might not work best as you draft and redraft your essay.

Student Example: Noelle Alberto's Brief

See Best Practices, "The Brief in Sum" for a checklist of the thinking that needs to go into preparing a brief.

Here is an example of a brief from a student urging her fellow students to stop multitasking when they study. Note its three-level structure: the claim is the thesis or statement your paper defends; each reason is subordinate to the thesis because it explains why you hold your thesis; each piece of evidence is subordinate to the reason it supports.

Claim: **Multitasking between recreational technology and studying impairs students' learning and does not prepare them for the real world of work.**

> *Reason: Multitasking increases the amount of time spent studying.*
>
> > *Evidence:* Homework takes twice as long to complete with multitasking. (Source: Tugend)
> >
> > *Evidence:* Switching tasks makes you have to relearn information to get back on track. (Source: Hamilton)

Reason: Multitasking impairs the brain's abilities to learn and store information.

> *Evidence:* It prevents students from being able to store information learned through studying. (Sources: Rosen, Jarmon)

Reason: Multitasking is poor preparation for the workplace.

> *Evidence:* Businesses don't want people who multitask; they want people who prioritize. (Source: LPA)

> *Evidence:* Multitasking decreases production ability of workers. (Source: Rosen)

Reason: *Multitasking promotes shallow rather than deep thinking.*

> *Evidence:* Ability to pay attention to one thing at a time is a mark of mature thinking. (Source: Rosen)

DRAFTING YOUR PAPER

Using your brief as a guide, write your first draft.

Development and Organization

Start by orienting your reader, providing what she or he needs to know to understand your topic and why it is significant. Establish the point of view toward the topic you have and want your reader to share. Make your own position clear. The Best Practices box offers suggestions to help you as you write.

Student Example: Excerpts from Noelle's Draft

The introduction from Noelle's first draft illustrates a common problem with arguments. It opens with generalizations that do not grab the reader's attention and show how the topic of the paper will matter to them.

> Long before the computer, people have always needed to multitask. Mothers dressed their children while getting ready for work and making breakfast. Men drank their morning coffee and ate breakfast on their drive to work. Multitasking has long been a part of our society, and now, technology has granted us new means of multitasking. This multitasking is now crucial to the younger generation's way of life, but it may be hurting them academically.

Noelle did a good job of creating a context for her case against multitasking, and her thesis is clearly stated in the last sentence. However, she could have used a specific example to connect with her intended audience, college and high school students. By using a source, she was able to revise her introduction (see page 238) to engage her readers better immediately.

Drafting Your Case

1. Openers are important. Start your essay by putting your case in context. For example, Judson (page 211) opens hers by referring to the beginning of a school year, when how to teach biology is immediately relevant.

2. Your reader may need background information to understand your case. Part of this will come from establishing the context in the opening, but sometimes additional information your reader lacks or may not remember will be necessary. Pickens (page 219) provides a good example of needed background information in developing his first claim: "America is addicted to foreign oil." Most of his readers are aware of our dependence on foreign crude, but probably not of its full consequences: $700 billion going out of the country to feed our habit every year, $10 trillion over the next ten years, "the greatest transfer of wealth in the history of mankind." Information like this not only provides needed background but also catches reader attention.

3. Cases do not have to deal with opposing points of view. However, if there is an obvious objection to your case you think most readers will think of, better mention it and show why the objection does not hold. Pickens provides good examples of anticipating and responding to objections. For instance, he explains why we cannot overcome our addiction to foreign oil by pumping more domestically (page 219).

4. Consider using visuals as an efficient way to convey evidence. Again, Pickens provides a good example of how effective photos, maps, and graphs can be.

5. Avoid summary, "in conclusion," conclusions. Strive instead for a memorable "parting shot," something with impact. Rideau's "Ever see a dog chase its tail?" is a good example, but you can use, for instance, a well-worded quotation followed by commentary of your own.

6. Strive to maintain throughout your essay the voice described in the assignment—dispassionate, calm, and fair—and the middle style case-making favors: simple, forceful statements that allow the thesis and its supporting reasons and evidence to stand out for your reader.

Another common problem in arguments is using sources to support and develop points, but not using enough from the source to make the evidence clear and convincing. Here is an example that is not easy to follow.

> David Meyer, a professor at University of Michigan, found that when you switch to a new task, the parts of the brain that are no longer being used "start shutting things down—like neural connections to important information" (Hamilton). The work you were focusing on isn't as understandable, and when you finally get back to it you "will have to repeat much of the process that created [the information] in the first place" (Hamilton).

Revision Checklist for Arguing a Case

1. Who is the target audience? How is the case framed—introduced—to reach that audience? Does the writer keep this audience in mind throughout the essay?

2. Locate the claim as stated or implied. Is it held consistently throughout the essay?

3. Locate the reasons that explain and justify the claim. Does the writer focus on one reason at a time, staying with it until it is completely developed? How effectively does each reason appeal to the audience? Is each reason clearly connected to the thesis it defends?

4. Do you detect a logical progression in the ordering of the reasons, so that the first reason leads to the second, the second to the third, and so on? Is there a better way to order the reasons? Can you find weak reasons that should be cut? Can you suggest reasons not included that would make the case stronger?

5. How much will the audience resist each reason? Is there sufficient evidence to overcome the resistance? Is the evidence for each reason clear and relevant to the reason it supports?

6. Do you see a better way to order the evidence for any of the reasons?

7. Look at the conclusion. How does it clinch the case, leaving the reader with something memorable? Can you see a way to make the conclusion more forceful?

The source actually gave a much more detailed description of the problem Noelle describes above. See the revised version of this passage (paragraph 3 on page 238).

To catch this kind of revision problem, ask a friend to read your draft and to be completely honest about where you may not have been clear enough in explaining evidence from a source.

REVISING YOUR DRAFT

Write a brief assessment of your first draft. Exchange your draft and assessment with at least one other student and help each other decide what needs improvement.

The revision questions in the Best Practices box should help you assess your own and your partner's draft.

Formulate a Plan to Guide Your Revision

The plan can be a single sentence or two: "I'll cut this, rearrange that, and add a section here." The important thing is to have a definite, clear idea of what you want to do and what moves you will make to get the results you want.

REVISED STUDENT EXAMPLE
Multitasking: A Poor Study Habit

NOELLE ALBERTO

1   A recent National Public Radio program described the study habits of a modern teenager, Zach Weinberg of Chevy Chase, Maryland. On a typical evening, he worked on French homework while visiting his e-mail and Facebook, listening to iTunes, messaging a friend, and playing an online word puzzle (Hamilton). According to the story, Zach is a successful student, but many studies of multitasking suggest that he could be better if he focused on one thing at a time. While human beings are capable of doing two things at once if one of those things does not require much attention, like driving and drinking your morning coffee, there are some things that require a single focus, like school work. Multitasking between studies and recreational technology is not an effective way to study.

2   One misconception that students may have about their multitasking is that they are saving time. Some say that they feel they get more done in a shorter amount of time, but they are actually not doing two things at once. They are switching from one task to another, and constant task switching takes more time. Gloria Mark of the University of California, Irvine conducted a study in which business workers were interrupted while working on a project. Each time, it took them about 25 minutes to return their attention to the original project (Turgend). In study terms, if you interrupt yourself to check your e-mail, a chapter that would take thirty minutes to read straight through could take much longer.

Paragraph gives more evidence for the first reason.

3   What happens when people shift from one demanding task to another? David Meyer, a professor at University of Michigan, found that when you switch to a new task, the parts of the brain that are no longer being used "start shutting things down—like neural connections to important information." If a student is studying French and stops to shop online, the neural connections to the French homework start to shut down. To restore full understanding, Meyer says the student "will have to repeat much of the process that created [the connections] in the first place" (qtd. in Hamilton).

A transitional paragraph wrapping up the first reason.

4   This frequent reconnecting to prior levels of focus and understanding is a waste of time. It is time lost that could be used more efficiently. If students eliminated technological distractions during study time, they would be able to complete more work in a shorter amount of time with greater understanding. There is always time to socialize after homework and studying has been completed.

Second reason.

Another misconception is that multitasking prepares you for the business world. "Able to multitask" used to be considered a positive on employee résumés. However, the researchers found that "extreme multitasking—information overload—costs the U.S. economy $650 billion a year in lost productivity" (Rosen 106). A study conducted at the University of London found that "workers distracted by e-mail and phone calls suffer a fall in IQ more than twice that found in marijuana smokers" (qtd. in Rosen 106). Employers, therefore, do not value multitasking. Now, according to the U.S. Departments of Labor and Education, businesses want an employee who "selects goal-relevant activities, ranks them, allocates time, and prepares and follows schedules" ("Skills and Competencies"). If multitasking is difficult and harmful in the business world, it has no place in university work either.

6   Besides wasted time and money, another unfortunate effect of multitasking is serious damage to students' ability to learn. Studies by psychology professor Russell Poldrack show that multitasking makes "learning . . . less flexible and more special-ized, so you cannot retrieve the information as easily" (qtd. in Rosen 107). Studies of blood flow in the brain show why. When people are task-switching, they use the "striatum, a region of the brain involved in learning new skills" (Rosen 107). In contrast, people who are not multitasking "show activity in the hippocampus, a region involved in storing and recalling information" (Rosen 108). Amy Jarmon, Dean at Texas Tech's School of Law, recalls a study comparing two groups of students in a large lecture class. One group of students was allowed to use laptops in class; they performed much more poorly on a memory quiz of lecture content than students not permitted to use laptops. Students who checked their e-mail and updated their Web pages during class did not recall information as well because they were not using the hippocampus.

Third reason.

7   Finally, if students get into the habit of multitasking, they could miss out on developing a personality trait prized by highly successful people. Christine Rosen calls the trait "a finely honed skill for paying attention" (109). The great British scientist Sir Isaac Newton said his discoveries owed "more to patient attention than to any other talent." The American psychologist William James wrote that the ability to pay attention marked the difference between a mature and an immature person: "The faculty of voluntarily bringing back a wandering attention, over and over again . . . is the very root of judgment, character, and will" (qtd. in Rosen 109). Maturity means recognizing that there is "a time and place for everything." When I go to the library to study, I leave my computer behind so that I will not be tempted to multitask. After an hour of focused school work, I have accomplished a great deal.

Fourth reason. This is the last reason because it has weight in showing how multitasking undermines intel-lectual potential.

Brings personal experience into the paper.

8   Multitasking is now part of every student's life. The facts indicate that we need to resist it more. It is not as helpful as many people think, and its very appeal is part of the problem. It is inefficient, reduces intelligence, and impairs recall. To think deeply rather than shallowly, we need to concentrate. Therefore, the best approach is to divide study time from social time. Focusing on one thing at a time will produce better outcomes now and in the future.

WORKS CITED

Hamilton, Jon. "Multitasking Teens May Be Muddling Their Brains." *NPR.* National Public Radio, 9 Oct. 2008. Web. 7 Apr 2009.

Jarmon, Amy L. "Multitasking: Helpful or Harmful? Multitasking Has Been Shown to Slow Learning and Reduce Efficiency." *Student Lawyer* 36.8 (April 2008): 30(5). *Academic OneFile.* Web. 23 Mar. 2009.

Rosen, Christine. "The Myth of Multitasking," *The New Atlantis* 20 (Spring 2008) 105–110. Print.

"Skills and Competencies Needed to Succeed in Today's Workplace." North Central Regional Education Laboratory, Learning Point Associates. N.d. Web. 7 April 2009.

Tugend, Alina. "Multitasking Can Make You Lose . . . Um . . . Focus." *The New York Times.* 25 Oct. 2008. Web. 23 Mar. 2009.

CHAPTER SUMMARY

Go back and review the steps you went through in writing this paper, concentrating on what happened when you were preparing to write. Pay special attention to testing your opinion. No matter what the subject or whether you are writing an argument or not, the method and attitude always apply. Internalize it. Make it a part of how you encounter new information and new experience. It boils down to this: Take time to form an opinion on controversial issues you hear and read about. But be constantly open to revising your opinion when you encounter anything new and relevant. Only in this way can your understanding of life and the world deepen and mature.

You know people who seem to gain almost instant respect from others, people who are listened to—part of this special quality is knowing what you think while remaining open to changing what you think. The impact of such people is not surprising at all: When people offer considered and well-informed opinions, they influence others who lack them. That is not only how it is but how it should be.

Motivating Action: Arguing to Persuade

We can define persuasion as "convincing plus" because, in addition to reason, three other forms of appeal receive conscious attention: appeals to the writer's character, to the emotions of the audience, and to style, the artful use of language. These three forms of appeal usually are present in case-making but in need of development for full persuasive impact, which means everything you learned in Chapter 9 remains relevant. We are building on Chapter 9 to help you understand and control persuasion's wider range of appeals.

WHAT IS PERSUASION?

Have you ever advocated change in an existing policy or way of doing something at school, in your dormitory or apartment complex, on your job, or at a community meeting? If so, you know about the potential power of persuasion. *Persuasion asks us to do something*—spend money, give money, join a demonstration, recycle, vote, enlist, convict, or acquit. For this reason, we call persuasion "appealing for action."

Persuasion joins a case to other ways of moving people to act, especially by gaining their trust and confidence and by arousing emotions favorable to the action advocated. In a moment, we will look at the means of persuasion,

NCEPT

When Should You Persuade?

Pay close attention to what your course assignments call for because the full range of persuasive appeal is not always appropriate. The more purely intellectual your topic and the more academic your audience, the more you should emphasize logical appeal, or making a good case. A clear thesis, supported by good reasons and backed by solid evidence, is usually what professors want.

When the issue is public, matters of policy or right and wrong, persuasion's fuller range of appeal is appropriate. Making an argument for the creation of a homeless shelter in your community requires establishing your good character and personal involvement with the project as well as appealing to the emotions of your readers. *Persuasion appeals to the whole person:* mind, emotion, the capacity for trust and cooperation, even the virtue of saying things well.

College assignments calling for persuasion will often ask you to take knowledge gained from a course and use it to persuade others who lack it. For example, using what you learned from a course in environmental science, you might write an article urging Americans to buy smaller, fuel-efficient automobiles to reduce carbon dioxide emissions and consumption of oil.

---

often called forms of appeal. First, consider the issue of appropriateness, when to convince and when to persuade, especially in college writing.

WHY WRITE TO PERSUADE?

Persuasion brings about change in the world, whether in national or local politics, in neighborhoods, on campus, in the workplace, or in personal relationships. For example, persuasion can:

- Sway elected officials to favor one policy over another
- Induce people and nations to resolve conflicts peacefully rather than by violent means
- Affect business decisions of all kinds, including how to promote a product or service
- Influence college officials who set tuition rates and housing costs on campus

No other kind of writing has more practical impact. If you want to make a difference in a world that needs to change in many ways, learning how to persuade other people is the key.

HOW DOES PERSUASION WORK?

Getting people to take action requires more than a good case. That's why the ancient Greek philosopher Aristotle identified three kinds of appeal: to reason (*logos*); to the character of the speaker (*ethos*); and to the emotions

The Four Forms of Appeal

Form	Function	Presence in Text
Reason	Logical cogency	Your case; any supported contention
Character	Personal appeal	Indications of author's status and values
Emotion	Appeals to feelings	Concrete descriptions, moving images
Style	Appeals through language	Word choice, sentence structure, metaphor

Essentially, persuasion differs from convincing in seeking action, not just agreement; it integrates rational appeal with other ways to influence people.

---

of the listeners (*pathos*). In all three, you adapt what you are advocating to the interests, beliefs, and values of a target audience.

In the readings that follow this section, you will see the appeals at work in an ad and two articles, all finished texts. Let us consider them at the other end of the writing process, as a *heuristic* (learning device) for coming up with something to say.

To save money and for other reasons, Americans are looking for alternatives to cars. One of these alternatives is the motorcycle or scooter. Suppose you were writing an essay with the title, "Getting Around on Two Wheels." What might you say?

Starting with logos, or the appeal to reason, you could argue that

- Motorcycles cost far less than cars to buy and maintain.
- They use on average about one-third as much gas.
- They take up only about half as much parking space.
- With proper training and equipment, they are not as dangerous to operate as many people think.

Motorcycles could help solve many problems, including reduction in traffic, greenhouse gas emissions, and American dependence on foreign crude oil.

How could you use pathos, or emotional appeal? The main value here is the fun of motorcycling. Motorcycles are the mechanical horse—you do not drive them, you ride them—and it should be fairly easy to appeal to the American love for freedom and adventure.

Finally, how could you appeal to ethos, or character? If you are a motorcyclist yourself, you could draw on your own experience. If not, interview friends who ride and cite what they say: you can borrow ethos from others.

The Art of Questioning: What Really Persuades Us?

Many people say they are persuaded by reasons and evidence. That is, logos matters most. Aristotle thought that ethos might be more powerful: if we think that a writer is intelligent, well informed, trustworthy, and has genuine concern for our needs, we will tend to believe most of what that person says. Look at advertising and you will probably conclude that pathos is the prime persuader. Nearly all ads appeal to emotions and attitudes most of all.

What do you think? Consider the last important decision you made. How did you persuade yourself to do one thing rather than another? If someone tried to persuade you, what kinds of appeal did they use? Which of these appeals had the most impact on the decision you made?

READINGS

The following readings will help you see in more detail how persuasion works and what you can do when you encounter a situation that calls for persuasion.

Subaru Advertisement

1 Advertising is one of the most common examples of moving people to action. We can learn a great deal about persuasion by studying advertisers' creative use of

http://www.subaru.com/dearsubaru/index.html

rhetorical appeals, both verbal and visual, to targeted audiences. This advertisement from Subaru's Web site illustrates all of the appeals Aristotle identified as contributing to effective persuasion.

2   Although Subaru also advertises in print magazines, appealing to specific readerships like mountain-bike riders, this advertisement is well designed for people who use the Internet to investigate possible automobile choices. The links in the menu across the top enable readers to see the range of vehicles, specifics about Subaru cars, pricing, and dealerships—all good basic information. However, this particular page moves beyond informing to persuading because of its emotional and ethical appeals aimed at people accustomed to the social networking and collaboration made possible by Web 2.0.

3   The ad invites owners and potential buyers to interact personally with the company and with each other by posting pictures of themselves with their cars and brief testimonials about why they love their Subaru. It is an emotional appeal to be part of a group of happy and fun-loving people swapping their stories. Sharing is emphasized in the text: "Share your love. . . ." "Share your story."

4   The ad also appeals logically to Internet shoppers who routinely check out other consumers' reviews and opinions about a product. Buyers' testimonials about good mileage, safety, and performance are good reasons and evidence that would also move the reader to choose this line of cars.

5   Subaru also displays its corporate ethos, or character, in this promotion by showing that it cares about its customers and the pleasure they get from driving their cars. The corporate image is friendly and unpretentious, a company for sporty, adventurous, outdoor lovers. "Share the love" is a theme in Subaru advertisements, referring to Subaru's philanthropic efforts on behalf of five major national charities. Market research told Subaru that its customers are likely to be committed to charitable causes.

6   Finally, the visuals and layout of the advertisement contribute to the message of personal connection, fun, and adventure. The featured visual looks like a letter with its salutation, "Dear Subaru." The letter's message is the car itself with its balloons, flowing streamers, and "Just Married" sign. These details visually depict the words in the caption at the lower right. The compilation of pictures and stories are a slightly less cluttered version of a Facebook page, completing the appeal to a targeted audience of connected, fun-loving people.

FOLLOWING THROUGH

Find an advertisement that you think is effective for its target audience. Who is the audience? Analyze how the ad appeals to ethos, pathos, and logos. Describe the visual and verbal appeals to style.   •

Consuming Faith

TOM BEAUDOIN

"Consuming Faith" was published in *Tikkun,* the journal of a socially progressive organization that publishes interfaith perspectives on issues of justice, preservation of the environment, and political freedom.

Tom Beaudoin is professor of theology at Santa Clara University in California. The essay comes from his book, *Consuming Faith: Integrating Who We Are with What We Buy* (Sheed and Ward, 2004). As you read this essay, think about your own consumer behavior and your relationship to the people who produce the items you purchase.

1   In December, several Honduran women came to Boston College. They were on a speaking tour of New England universities, talking about their work back home sewing shirts for a major brand that many of my students wore.

2   These women told stories that anyone familiar with the global sweatshop workforce will find painfully predictable: verbal abuse, beastly wages, forbidden unions, forced overtime, no holidays, no health insurance or other benefits, the inability to save money so their children can break out of this life, and transportation and food costs that ate up four hours' wages every day. And the workforce consisted entirely of young women, aged 15 to 30.

3   I was outraged, because these women worked for a company that I knew had turned enormous profits. It was not as if the company was going to go broke if it had even minimally met the meager requests of these women. I was outraged because many of my students wore this clothing brand and I hated that they were paying this corporation to brand themselves at these women's expense [. . .] . And I was outraged because I was reminded that this corporation got away with it because I myself spent so many years not doing my part to stop such practices. I had paid lots of money to be a foot soldier for my favorite brands of shoes, jeans, and shirts—even coffee.

4   For me, the turning point came when I started seeing the faces of the women making my favorite brands. I had read a story several years ago about impoverished coffee farmers who harvest coffee beans for wealthy American coffee companies, and saw a picture of one of their faces on the Web or in the paper. I ended up pulling my favorite brands out of my closet and tracking down who made "my" brands, where they were produced, and the conditions under which they were put together. With the exception of my branded sport coat produced in Toronto under Canadian labor laws, the rest of my favorite brands were assembled by non-American faces that were forbidden to join unions, had to submit to pregnancy tests, and were kept in poverty by American companies that had almost eliminated the cost of labor, while avoiding paying any taxes at all due to breaks from the host countries where the factories were placed. Not that any of them volunteered this information. Most of the companies gave me public relations blowback and legal-speak and some outright lied to me. I had to turn to independent reportage to find out exactly what I was supporting, and whose faces I was affecting, by my purchase of my favorite brands. When I called the corporate headquarters of my local outpost of a coffee

chain to see if I could travel—at my own expense—to South America to take pictures of the farmers who harvested my coffee and post them in the store, I got a firm and unequivocal "no." Why did so many of my favorite coffee and clothing brands want to hide the faces of those who made my stuff?

5   I was beginning to see that there were relationships in which I was an involved but irresponsible partner—economic relationships. Just as any other common relationship we have has both pleasures and responsibilities (whether as spouse, friend, or co-worker), so do my economic relationships, I was beginning to see. By enjoying my branded jeans, I was necessarily in relationship with the women who made them. They had done their part by making clothes that protected me and brought me pleasure. What was my obligation to them? What was my part of the relationship?

6   This raised the question for me: how central are economic relationships to faith? Are my economic relationships secondary to who I am before God, or central? The popular picture of Christianity today, unfortunately, does not show the best face of my faith on this issue. As a Catholic Christian, I notice the way Christianity is portrayed in the media, and how it portrays itself in its own advertising, and what I see lately is a religion too often indifferent to war, over interested in individual morality, and defensive about its own institutional abuses. One would almost think that this public image of religiosity was mandated by the Christian scriptures. However, when I turned back to scripture to see how Jesus of Nazareth dealt with economics, I was shocked at what I found. Jesus very seldom talks about God's final judgment, about "heaven" and "hell," but when he does, as his way of talking about what is most important in a life of spiritual maturity before God, he does something interesting. He almost always talks about intimacy with God in the next life as bound up with one's economic relationships in this life. He speaks of a wealthy man who ignores a poor man at his gate finding himself later in hell, crying out to the poor man for help. He talks about those who use their resources of time and money to visit prisoners and clothe the naked as going on to a final happiness with God, and those who do not as having failed to love God and live a truly human life. Jesus was not focused on whom one is sleeping with, whether one has properly obeyed religious authorities, or how religious institutions can preserve themselves. He saw economic relationships as ultimate expressions of one's true faith. Responsibility for the other is where and how one ought to live in relationship to that gracious and mysterious power that sustains us, which he intimately called his "Father."

7   For me, the Jewishness of Jesus' concern for the other is present in a more recent idiom in the philosophy of Emmanuel Levinas. For Levinas, we are everywhere and in each moment dependent on and responsible to others. To be human is to be responsible for the other, whose well-being my very existence may be threatening. This obligation to others is encountered and symbolized in the face-to-face relationship. The faces of others represent persons genuinely different from us, exposed to us. The vulnerability of the human face presents us with the claim: do not kill me. In a sense, Levinas says, the face says to us "do not deface me"; allow me, it says, my otherness and exposure without violation, shame, or indifference.

8 But what if we are systematically excluded, in a brand economy, from seeing the faces of the others who inhabit our lives? What if your local branded coffee shop does not want you to even see the faces of those who harvest your coffee? Would we not think of our brands differently if we had in view the faces of those who make our stuff?

9 A more human brand economy would be a more holy one, one in which we take responsibility for our economic relationships, for the well-being of the faces who make our stuff. In a better world, the brands themselves will better manage the economic relationships between producers and consumers that they steward. In a better world, we will each think and even pray about our obligations to our economic relationships. In a better world, brands will try to talk us into purchasing them because they give their workers in China, Indonesia, or El Salvador a living wage, holidays, overtime pay, child care, and health insurance. Whether you are more with Jesus of Nazareth or Levinas of Lithuania, this better world is possible. If only we made economics a part of the discourse of spiritual maturity today, it would begin to happen.

QUESTIONS FOR DISCUSSION

1. Beaudoin uses word pattern repetition to appeal to the readers' emotions. Reread the selection and locate some examples. Why does he employ this strategy in those places rather than others? How effective is it for his intended audience?

2. The article attempts to overcome a common dissociation: probably most people see religion and economics as separate and at most weakly related. Does it succeed? Are you persuaded to pull them together? Why or why not?

Strategies Used for Appealing for Action

Beaudoin wants to persuade his readers to see their consumer choices as part of their religious practice. He tailors his argument to his audience (1) by giving them religious reasons for knowing more about the conditions in which goods are produced and (2) by refusing to buy from companies that exploit and abuse their workers.

We can learn something about strategy in appealing for action by examining how Beaudoin arranged the parts of his essay. Like many persuasive writers, he does not present his claim and reasons at the start of the essay but leads the readers gradually to the argument, which does not begin until about the midpoint. Beaudoin's essay falls into three parts:

1. The introductory narrative about the Honduran women. (paragraphs 1–3)

   > Stories based on personal experience are often good openings. Beaudoin connects with his readers by assuming that they already know and disapprove of sweatshop conditions. But they are still buying the products, not "doing [their] part."

2. The story of his attempts to find out more about his brand-name goods. (paragraph 4)

> This section, also a narrative, builds up Beaudoin's ethos because it shows his long-term concern for and dedication to finding out about the workers.

3. The argument that responsible economic relationships are central to living a spiritual life. (paragraphs 5–9)

> This section is a case based on reasons and evidence. Paragraph 5 gives his first reason: Economic relationships entail responsibility just like other relationships. Then, in paragraphs 6–9, he argues that this relationship is religious. He asks, "[H]ow central are economic relationships to faith?" He answers this question by showing that economic relationships are central to religious identity (*the claim*). He justifies the claim with this reason: Both Christianity and Judaism see economic responsibility for others as integral to faith. He supports the reason with evidence from two sources, the Bible and the writings of the Jewish philosopher Emmanuel Levinas.

The Factories of Lost Children

KATHARINE WEBER

Katharine Weber's subject matter and claim are similar to Beaudoin's in the previous essay, but she bases her argument on tragic incidents involving child labor. It was originally published in the *New York Times*.

How does Weber's use of persuasion differ from that found in the Beaudoin essay? As you read, consider which argument is more appealing to you and why.

1   Ninety-five years ago, March 25 also fell on a Saturday. At 4:40 p.m. on that sunny afternoon in 1911, only minutes before the end of the workday, a fire broke out on the eighth floor of the Asch Building, a block east of Washington Square in Manhattan.

2   The Triangle Waist Company occupied the top three floors of the 10-story building. There, some 600 workers were employed in the manufacture of ladies' shirtwaists, most of them teenage girls who spoke little English and were fresh off the boat from Russia, the Austro-Hungarian Empire and Italy. The fire, probably caused by a carelessly tossed match or cigarette butt (there were perhaps 100 men working at the Triangle), engulfed the premises in minutes.

3   The factory owners and the office staff on the 10th floor, all but one, escaped onto the roof and climbed to an adjacent building on Waverly Place. But on the eighth and ninth floors, the workers were trapped by a deadly combination of highly combustible materials, workrooms crowded by dense rows of table-mounted sewing machines, doors that were locked or opened inward, inadequate fire escapes, and the lack of any plan or instruction.

4   Before the first horse-drawn fire engines arrived at the scene, girls—some holding hands, in twos and threes—had already begun to jump from the windows. The hundred-foot drop to the cobbled street was not survivable. The firemen deployed their nets, but the force of gravity drove the bodies of the girls straight through to the pavement, and they died on impact.

5   The ladders on the fire trucks were raised quickly, but the New York City Fire Department of 1911 was not equipped to combat fires above six stories—the limit of those ladders. The top floors of the Asch Building, a neo-Renaissance "fireproof" warehouse completed in 1901 in full compliance with building codes, burned relentlessly.

6   The workers trapped near the windows on the eighth and ninth floors made the fast and probably instinctive choice to jump instead of burning or suffocating in the smoke. The corpses of the jumpers, by some estimates as many as 70, could at least be identified. But the bodies of most of those who died inside the Triangle Waist Company—trapped by the machinery, piled up on the wrong side of doors, heaped in the stairwells and elevator shafts—were hideously charred, many beyond recognition.

7   Before 15 minutes had elapsed, some 140 workers had burned, fallen from the collapsing fire escapes, or jumped to their deaths. Several more, critically injured, died in the days that followed, putting the official death toll at 146.

8   But what happened to the children who were working at the Triangle Waist Company that afternoon?

9   By most contemporary accounts, it was common knowledge that children were usually on the premises. They were hidden from the occasional inspectors, but underage girls, as young as 9 or 10, worked in most New York garment factories, sewing buttons and trimming threads. Where were they on this particular Saturday afternoon?

10   There are no descriptions of children surviving the fire. Various lists of those who died 95 years ago today—140 named victims plus six who were never identified (were some of those charred remains children?)—include one 11-year-old, two 14-year-olds, three 15-year-olds, 16 16-year-olds, and 14 17-year-olds. Were the ages of workers, living and dead, modified to finesse the habitual violation of child labor laws in 1911? How many children actually died that day? We will never know. And now 1911 is almost beyond living memory.

11   But we will also never know how many children were among the dead on May 10, 1993, in Thailand when the factory of the Kader Industrial Toy Company (a supplier to Hasbro and Fisher-Price) went up in flames. Most of the 188 workers who died were described as teenage girls.

12   We will never know with any certainty how many children died on Nov. 25, 2000, in a fire at the Chowdhury Knitwear and Garment factory near Dhaka, Bangladesh (most of the garments made in Bangladesh are contracted by American retailers, including Wal-Mart and the Gap), where at least 10 of the 52 trapped in the flames by locked doors and windows were 10 to 14 years old.

13   And we will never know how many children died just last month, on Feb. 23, in the KTS Composite Textile factory fire in Chittagong, Bangladesh. The official

death toll has climbed into the 50's, but other sources report that at least 84 workers lost their lives. It's a familiar story: crowded and unsafe conditions, locked exits, hundreds of undocumented female workers as young as 12, a deadly fire. There may never be another tragic factory fire in America that takes the lives of children. We don't lock them into sweatshops any more. There are child labor laws, fire codes.

14   But as long as we don't question the source of the inexpensive clothing we wear, as long as we don't wonder about the children in those third world factories who make the inexpensive toys we buy for our own children, those fires will occur and young girls and boys will continue to die. They won't die because of natural catastrophes like monsoons and earthquakes; they will die because it has become our national habit to outsource, and these days we outsource our tragedies, too.

Strategies Used for Appealing for Action

Detailed arguments are not the only way of being persuasive. Weber shows us how effective narrative can be. It serves the following persuasive purposes:

- It establishes her credibility and ethos with a wealth of detailed information. Readers feel she knows what she is talking about and has the welfare of other people foremost in her concerns.

- In paragraphs 4, 6, and 7, she appeals to pathos well, drawing her readers into this tragic incident with powerful images of brutal, unnecessary deaths.

- In these same paragraphs, she also appeals to the readers' ethics, knowing they would not tolerate such conditions in New York today.

Effective narratives depend on *telling detail,* on statements of fact that imply the writer's judgments without stating them. For instance,

- Many of the workers "were fresh off the boat from Russia, the Austrio-Hungarian Empire and Italy."

  Implication: They were expendable. There was a ready supply of labor on the next boat.

- "The factory owners and the office staff on the 10th floor, all but one, escaped."

  Implication: The people that mattered survived. The bosses would not lock themselves or valued employees inside, where they could not escape.

- "The New York City Fire Department of 1911 was not equipped to combat fires above six stories. . . . The top floors of the Asch Building [were] completed in 1901 in full compliance with building codes."

  Implication: You cannot depend on authorities to prevent tragedies or respond to unfolding disasters adequately.

Tell your readers what they need to know and they will draw the conclusions you want them to make.

In the concluding paragraph, Weber makes a summarizing case, stating her claim and her reason in one sentence: "As long as we don't question the source of the inexpensive clothing we wear, as long as we don't wonder about the children in those third world factories who make the inexpensive toys we buy for our own children, those fires will occur and young girls and boys will continue to die." The case brings her general point home, linking her narrative of a past event to present concerns.

◎◎ FOLLOWING THROUGH

Using the analysis of Beaudoin as a model (pages 248–249), break up into small groups, assign the roles of recorder and reporter, and investigate the following questions:

- Why do you think the author organized her material the way she did?

- In paragraphs 11–13 Weber shifts attention from the past to the present. Does the shift work; that is, do you find the connections to the present persuasive? If so, why? If not, why not?

Share the results of your work with the class and discuss how each group's answers differed. Address this question at some point in your class dialogue: What strategies does Weber use that we can use in our own way?   •

CLAIMING VOICE IN APPEALING FOR ACTION

Appealing for action or persuasion is in part the calm voice of reason described in Chapter 9: your opinion stated clearly, directly, forcefully, with confidence. To this persuasion adds the *controlled passion* of emotional appeal, designed to arouse *appropriate* feelings in your readers.

Look at paragraphs 10–14 in Katharine Weber's "The Factories of Lost Children." Here is the voice of controlled passion:

> We will never know with any certainty how many children died on Nov. 25, 2000, in a fire at the Chowdhury Knitwear and Garment factory near Dhaka, Bangladesh (most of the garments made in Bangladesh are contracted by American retailers, including Wal-Mart and the Gap), where at least 10 of the 52 trapped in the flames by locked doors and windows were 10 to 14 years old. (paragraph 12)

She gives the reader the terrible facts, including the role of American companies in allowing the conditions that result in tragic loss of children's lives. She does not have to say, "This is outrageous, intolerable"; the facts say it for her.

Furthermore, she cites several tragic instances in paragraphs 10–14, all linked together by the repeated statement, "We will never know how many children died." This is how you arouse appropriate emotions in readers and how the voice of controlled passion should sound. Moving people to act requires using this voice as well as the calm voice of reasoning.

THE ASSIGNMENT

Write an essay on any controversial topic that asks your readers to take action. "Controversial" for this assignment means that various courses of action are possible, genuine choice exists. In some cases, you might advocate doing nothing when other people want to take action or stop doing something that causes more harm than benefit.

Topic and Focus

Your topic may grow out of readings or discussion of current events in your class, or your instructor may have you choose your own topic. Whatever happens, distinguish topics from possible focuses within them. For instance, "illegal immigration" is a highly controversial topic, ideal for persuasion because so many courses of action are possible. However, illegal immigration covers too much ground for anything less than a book. You might focus, for example, on the fences being constructed along the U.S.–Mexico border. Or, because many people here illegally overstay their visas, you might focus on the visa process itself. *Find some part of the topic you can handle in the space you have.*

Audience

Think of your audience as people weakly inclined toward your position, weakly opposed, or uncommitted. Within these possibilities, consider two questions: Who can take action? Which audience can I relate to best? Choose your audience based on how you answer these questions.

Voice and Ethos

Persuasion favors middle style, neither ultra-formal (as in a legal brief) nor informal and off-hand (like an e-mail to a friend). You should sound like someone talking about a serious topic to people you do not know well. The readings provide good examples of middle style and the voice that goes with it.

Good character, or ethos, always matters in writing, but especially in persuasion because you are asking your readers to trust you enough to take action. Be sincere. Project confidence. Show respect for your audience.

Writing Assignment Suggestions

This paper could be written in many possible genres: an editorial, a personal letter, a magazine article, a text for a speech, and so on. You might consider one of these genres, especially if your topic and audience seem appropriate and your instructor approves.

Our students have written on the following topics: U.S. policy in Iraq and Afghanistan; immigration issues, especially border control; all issues connected with "going green"; and many issues connected with consumer society. Be sure to consider local issues as well, including what is going on where you work, where you live, and in organizations to which you belong.

CHOOSING A TOPIC

Persuasive topics arise from *exigency;* that is, *the need for action.* If you are choosing your own topic, pick one you care about and are personally invested in enough to take action yourself. You can then draw on what moves you to motivate your readers to act as you do. Here are some possible places to find topics.

- *Class readings.* Class readings can suggest topics for persuasion, especially if the readings themselves are persuasive, like the examples in this chapter. For instance, if the sweatshop problem interests you, begin by finding out about the labor practices of the companies that make the clothing you and your friends wear.

- *Reading in other classes.* In a political science class, for example, you might study how presidential candidates are selected by the Democratic and Republican parties. The process is highly controversial and many proposals for reform have been advanced. Perhaps one of the reforms struck you as especially desirable. Do some more reading about it; perhaps you have found your topic.

- *Local news or observation.* Read your local and campus newspapers for issues and problems of concern to your community. Take a walk around your neighborhood or campus, looking for problems that need solutions, such as wasted energy in offices, dorms, and classrooms.

- *Internet discussions.* If you keep a blog, you probably have a store of observations about issues that concern you, things you would like to see changed. Or visit blogs on issues of public concern, such as "The Opinionator" at the *New York Times,* which gathers opinions from publications all over the world.

EXPLORING YOUR TOPIC

Whether your topic is assigned or you chose your own, all or some of the following activities can help you gain a better initial sense of your paper.

The Art of Questioning: Focus, Audience, and Need

Consider these questions:

- Can you handle the topic in the space you have? If not, how might you limit the topic?

- What audience do you wish to reach? Usually there are several appropriate choices. Consult the Concept Close-Up, "Audience Analysis," when you have identified your audience.

- How can you establish a need for taking action? See the next section to grasp the importance of need in persuasive writing.

Your answers to these questions may change as you work on your paper. Asking them now, however, can help you gain a sense of focus, audience, and purpose, always important in writing well.

Audience Analysis

To understand any audience we hope to persuade, we must know *both* what separates us from them *and* what common ground we share.

We may **differ** from our audience in:

Kind of Difference	Example
Assumptions	Western writers assume that separation of church and state is normal; some Muslim audiences do not make the distinction.
Principles	Most conservative writers believe in the principle of the open market; labor audiences often believe in protecting American jobs from foreign competition.
Value rankings	Some writers value personal freedom over duty and obligation; some audiences place duty and obligation above personal freedom.
Ends and means	Writer and audience may agree about purpose (for example, making America safe from terrorism) but disagree about what policies will best accomplish this end.
Interpretation	Some writers understood the September 11, 2001, attacks as acts of war; some audiences saw them as criminal acts that demanded legal rather than military measures.
Consequences	Some writers think making divorce harder would keep more couples together; some audiences think it would only promote individual unhappiness.

We may **share** with our audience:

Kind of Identification	Example
Local identity	Students and teachers at the same university
Collective identity	Citizens of the same state or the same nation
Common cause	Improving the environment
Common experience	Pride in the success of American Olympic athletes
Common history	Respect for soldiers who have died defending the United States

Essentially, we must understand differences to discover how we need to argue; we must use the resources of identification to overcome differences separating us from our readers.

Establishing Need

Sometimes the need for action is so widely and well understood that it is hardly necessary to mention it. We need a cure for cancer, for instance. Usually, however, need cannot be taken for granted. Consider global warming: Attitudes toward it range from casual dismissal to taking it as the biggest long-term problem we face. If you are trying to persuade an audience to take action to reduce global warming, you must devote a significant portion of your paper to establishing the damage global warming has done already and will do in the next decade or so.

In contrast, sometimes people think that a need to act exists when you think the best course is to do nothing or postpone taking action. When you face such a situation, your entire paper will be devoted to showing that no compelling need to act exists or that no immediate action is required.

In any case, thinking about need—the motivation for action—matters. The temptation is to imagine that everyone sees the need as you do, which is rarely the case.

⊚⊚ FOLLOWING THROUGH

Jot down your first ideas about topic, focus, audience, and need. If you have the beginnings of a case in mind—your claim, reasons, and evidence—write them down as well. Include whatever insights you have gained from personal experience. These entries will help shape your first ideas.   •

Doing Research

If the assignment calls for research, use the techniques for finding and evaluating sources (pages 99–121) to find articles, books, and online materials about or related to your topic. Arguments require evidence, and research will help with this as well as with refining and developing your thinking.

⊚⊚ FOLLOWING THROUGH

Break out into pairs or groups of three to discuss your ideas for the persuasive paper. Assess each other's choice of topics, focus within the topics, choice of audience, and your ideas for moving the audience to take action. At the end of your discussion, evaluate the comments made about your ideas and use them to refine your topic.   •

PREPARING TO WRITE

Exploring your topic is a good first step in preparing to write. Some writers go straight to drafting, preferring to work out what they have to say in chunks that they eventually piece together to form a complete first draft. Most, however, need more preparation before drafting. We suggest beginning with the key questions listed in the Best Practices box, "Key Questions for Preparing to Write."

⊚⊚ FOLLOWING THROUGH

Write answers to the seven questions in the Best Practices box. Exchange them with a partner via e-mail or in small group sessions in or out of class to help refine and develop your ideas for and approaches to the first draft.   •

Key Questions for Preparing to Write

1. What do you want your readers to do?

2. Who are your readers? Describe them as specifically as you can. What about them will be relevant to your argument? Consider age, religion, income bracket, occupation, political orientation, education, and gender.

3. Reader awareness is important: How much will they know about the problem, question, or issue you intend to address? What is their likely attitude?

4. Why do you care about this topic? What makes you a credible writer on behalf of your position?

5. What is the best reason you can give your readers for doing what you want them to do? State it as a sentence. Do you have a second reason in mind?

6. What additional ideas do you have for appealing to your readers? What values and beliefs can you appeal to?

7. If your topic requires more than general knowledge and personal experience, what sources have you found to support your argument? What additional material might you need?

Thinking More about Persuasive Appeals

Dig deeper into the appeals to logic, character, and emotion. Thinking them through now helps many writers build up confidence, energy for drafting, and a more detailed plan to guide the first draft.

The Appeal through Logos: Deciding on a Claim and Reasons

You know what you want your readers to do; try formulating it as a claim. These suggestions will help.

1. Your claim is a statement you will defend, not just a description of something factual.

   Not a claim: Students are choosing majors based on future income instead of interests and abilities.

   Claim: Students should find a major that excites their desire to learn rather one that promises only financial rewards.

2. The claim should be focused and specific, and directed at a readership.

   Too general: Parents need to be stricter.

   Better: Parents need to teach children to be sensitive to other people when they are in restaurants, stores, and other public places.

3. The claim uses concrete nouns and verbs, rather than vague and indirect wording, to make its point.

   Vague: One's natural abilities cannot grow into an established intelligence unless a person learns how to control his or her attention and concentration.

Better: Even highly talented people need to learn to control attention and concentration to develop their full potential.

4. Some claims may need to be qualified.

Too absolute: High schools need a vocational track.

Qualified: Except for high schools where all students go on to college, a high-quality vocational track should exist.

◎◎ FOLLOWING THROUGH

Share several versions of the claim you have in mind by an e-mail exchange with one or several other students. Ask for feedback using questions taken from the peer review questions in the Best Practices box on page 263. Modify the claim as you draft and revise using this feedback. •

Developing Reasons for Your Claim

Once you have a working version of the claim, begin to formulate reasons for it—why your readers should take the action you are arguing for. Focus on the fit between reasons and the values and beliefs of your readers.

The Best Practices box, "Places to Find Audience-Based Reasons" (page 259), provides some places to look for reader-oriented reasons.

Making a Brief of Your Case

The brief is a concise version of a logical argument. It has three levels:

1. The claim, what you want your readers to do.

2. A reason or reasons explaining why.

3. Evidence to support each reason.

Briefs can help in preparing to write, but keep in mind that new ideas will come to you as you draft. Also bear in mind that a brief is not a plan for the whole paper, only its logical appeal. Beaudoin postponed his argument until the midpoint of his essay (pp. 247–248, paragraphs 6–9); Weber presented her evidence first (p. 251, paragraph 14), then the claim and reasons.

Student Example: Natsumi Hazama's Brief

A student in one of our classes, Natsumi Hazama, wrote a persuasive paper urging Asian parents not to push their children so hard in school. Here is the brief she developed for her argument:

Claim: Asian-American parents need to moderate their demands for high career goals and obedience to parents, allowing their children to find goals and challenges that are right for them.

Reason: Too much pressure can lead to depression and even suicide.

Places to Find Audience-Based Reasons

- In the audience's *beliefs and values.* Think about their politics and the values of their culture or subculture.

- In *traditions* and traditional texts. What books, ceremonies, ideas, places, and people do they revere?

- In *expert opinion and data.* Draw on the reasoning of qualified experts your audience will respect—mention them by name and cite their credentials. Construct reasons from information and statistics taken from sources your readers will know and trust.

- In comparisons or *analogies* your audience would accept. Analogies work because they liken the less familiar to the more familiar and known. Those who oppose genetic engineering, for example, often reason that altering human genes is like altering nature—it has bad side effects.

- In establishing *cause and effect.* If you can show that the action you would like the audience to take will lead to positive consequences, you have a good reason. Of course, you will need evidence to show that the cause-and-effect relationship exists.

> *Evidence:* CNN.com article on college student suicides; *Chronicle of Higher Education* online article about depression and suicide at Cornell
>
> *Reason:* Over-protective parenting does not prepare children for the independence of college life.
>
> *Evidence:* Asian Outlook Web site quotes
>
> *Reason:* Students will be more successful at careers they prefer, not the limited choices of engineering and medicine preferred by their parents.
>
> *Evidence:* My personal experience
>
> *Reason:* Constant pressure to do better rather than praise for what has been accomplished leads to low self-esteem.
>
> *Evidence:* Class reading by Csikszentmihalyi.

Note that Natsumi's brief "blocks out" (separates into clear, distinct points) what she intends to say. No matter how closely related they are, *do not allow your reasons to run together.* Note also that she uses both statements from experts and personal experience as evidence. The experts lend authoritative support for her argument, whereas personal experience makes it more concrete and demonstrates firsthand knowledge.

FOLLOWING THROUGH

In your notebook, outline the logical case you will make. If possible, include supporting evidence for each reason.

The Appeal through Ethos: Presenting Good Character

Ethos is self-presentation. In general, you should

- Sound informed and engaged with your topic
- Show awareness of your readers' views
- Treat competing courses of action with respect, but show that yours is better
- Refer to your values and beliefs, your own ethical choices
- When appropriate, reinforce your ethos by citing information and expert testimony from sources your readers respect and trust

A more specific list of ideas for establishing good ethos follows.

The Art of Questioning: Establishing Ethos with Your Readers

1. Do you have a shared local identity—as members of the same organization, the same institution, the same town or community, the same set of beliefs?

2. Can you get your audience to see that you and they have a common cause or perspective?

3. Are there experiences you might share? These might include dealing with siblings, helping friends in distress, caring for ailing family members, struggling to pay debts, or working hard for something.

4. Can you connect through a well-known event or cultural happening, perhaps a movie, book, a political rally, something in the news?

◎◎ FOLLOWING THROUGH

Write about what attitudes you could convey in your paper that will show your good character and values. What can you talk about that will get these appeals across to your readers?

The Appeal through Pathos: Using Emotional Appeals

Sharing your own emotions is the most honest way to appeal to your audience's feelings. However, simply saying what your feelings are will not arouse emotion in others. How can you arouse emotions?

Show the audience the *concrete images and facts* that aroused the feelings in you. Beaudoin listed the indignities suffered by the Honduran women he interviewed. Likewise, Weber described the bodies of the burned workers in the Triangle fire, "trapped by the machinery, piled up on the wrong side of doors, heaped in the stairwells and elevator shafts . . . hideously charred, many beyond recognition."

In short, give your readers a verbal picture. You can often give them visual images as well, such as photographs.

◎◎ FOLLOWING THROUGH

Do a free writing of ideas for specifics details and images that moved you. Make lists of what you recall. Visit or revisit places relevant to your topic and take notes or pictures.

DRAFTING YOUR PAPER

By now you have generated many ideas for appealing to your readers. As you move toward drafting, focus attention on two main concerns:

- Voice, how you want to sound to your reader
- A plan to guide the draft

Voice

Voice is always important in writing because people react subconsciously to the "sound" of your prose. In persuasion it is especially important because voice helps to create ethos.

Write with passion and conviction, but also sound reasonable, mature, courteous, and responsible. The readings at the beginning of this chapter are good examples of voice in persuasion. Read aloud the first page or two of the Beaudoin and Weber essays, concentrating only on the impression you have of the writer's character. Then join in the following discussion.

◎◎ FOLLOWING THROUGH

In small groups of two or three people, explore these questions:

1. How is Weber's voice like Beaudoin's? How are they different?
2. Beaudoin wrote in first person (uses "I"), whereas Weber favors third person. Is your sense of the author's presence different in Beaudoin? If so, how would you describe the difference?

Development and Organization

Here are answers to some common questions that will help you with both development and organization of your paper.

1. *How might I open the paper?*

Here are some possibilities:

- An anecdote (short narrative) based on your own experience or something you found in a source
- A surprising fact or opinion relevant to your topic
- A question that will stimulate reader interest
- A description of a person or place relevant to your claim
- A memorable quotation, with commentary from you

Introductions are often more than one paragraph, and your claim can appear anywhere in the paper.

2. *What background material should I provide?*

Here are two principles:

- Offer *only* what your readers need
- Place it just before the section or sections of your essay where the background is relevant

3. *Where will I show my connection to the topic?*

The introduction is often a good place. Beaudoin's first four paragraphs (p. 246) describe his awakening to a sense of economic responsibility. He wanted his readers to see his personal commitment to the topic.

4. *Will I present opposing views, and, if so, where?*

How you handle opposing views depends on your reader's relationship to them. If you think your readers will believe them, the best strategy is to engage the opposing views first in several paragraphs. Otherwise handle them after your case and with less space devoted to them.

5. *How will I order my reasons?*

If your case has three or more reasons, starting and ending with your stronger ones is good strategy. In developing your reasons, remember that multiple paragraphs are often necessary to develop a reason.

6. *What visuals might I use, and where should they go?*

For example, a student who wrote against wearing fur added much to the pathos of her argument by including photographs of animals injured by trappers.

7. *How will I conclude my paper?*

Try one of these ending strategies:

- Look back at your introduction. Perhaps some idea you used there to attract your reader's attention could come into play again—a question you posed has an answer, or a problem you raised has a solution.
- Think about the larger context of your argument. For example, Beaudoin puts his argument about responsible consuming into the larger context of a more humane world.
- End with a well-worded quotation, and follow it up with comments of your own.
- Repeat an idea you used earlier in the essay, but with a twist. Weber took the word "outsource" and used it in a new way: people "will die because it has become our national habit to outsource, and these days we outsource our tragedies, too."

REVISING YOUR DRAFT

Writing is revising. Most first drafts need big changes on the way to completion. They need parts taken out, new parts added, and parts rearranged.

Revision Checklist for Appealing for Action

Take the point of view of someone reading your paper. Ask these questions to assess it.

1. Is it clear what the author wants the readers to do? Where is it stated most clearly? Is this the best place to state it?

2. Does the paper have a shape and sense of direction? Does it have parts that clearly play their individual roles in making the argument? Could you make any suggestions for arranging the parts to make it easier to follow?

3. Do the reasons for taking this action stand out as reasons? Are they good reasons for the intended audience? Is there a better way to order the reasons?

4. Has the author given enough evidence to support each reason?

5. Has the author shown awareness of and sympathy for the audience's perspective?

6. Are the individual paragraphs unified, and is their contribution to the section in which they appear clear?

7. Can you hear the author's voice in this paper? Do you think the readers would find it appealing? Does the author show personal connection with the topic?

8. Where do you see the author using emotional appeals? Are they appropriate? Do they move you?

9. Do you have suggestions to improve the introduction and the conclusion?

10. Has the author smoothly integrated the sources used or just dropped them in?

The strongest revisions begin with assessing the draft yourself. Put it aside for a day or two. Then go back and give it a critical reading.

Getting Feedback from Others

It always helps to have someone else look at your draft. Be sure that the person understands the assignment and the target audience before they read. Share the Revision Checklist in the Best Practices box with your reader.

◎◎ FOLLOWING THROUGH

After getting a second opinion, formulate a revision strategy:

1. Decide what you think the useful criticisms and comments are. Reassess your self-criticisms—do you still see the same problems?

2. Make a list of specific items you intend to work on. "The first point on page 3 needs more development" is an example of what we mean by specific.

3. Divide your list into two categories: big revisions that will change all or much of the paper and smaller revisions requiring only adding, deleting, or rewriting a paragraph or two.

4. Ponder the best order for doing big revisions. For example, suppose that you need to rearrange the order of your reasons and improve your tone throughout. Rearrange first because attending to tone will require changing many sentences, and each sentence revision can have an impact on the flow of ideas from sentence to sentence.

5. Finalize your plan with a step-by-step list. Usually the spot revisions can be done in any order, but tackle the ones requiring most work first, leaving the easier ones for last.

Practicing Revision

A revised draft of Natsumi Hazama's paper appears on pages 266–268. To see how revision improved it, read the following excerpts from her first draft.

Paragraph 1

> One night in 1990, Eliza Noh got off the phone with her sister in college. Eliza knew her sister was depressed and something bad might happen. She sat down to write a letter to support and encourage her. But it was too late. By the time the letter arrived, her sister was dead. She had taken her own life. Eliza believed that too much pressure to succeed contributed to her sister's death. This tragedy led Noh to pursue a career in studying the effects of pressure on Asian-American students.

Paragraph 7

> Low self-esteem can be a result of too much pressure to be at the top. According to Mihaly Csikszentmihalyi, goals can determine a person's level of self-esteem. Because Asian-Americans' goals are set so high by parents, these students tend to have lower self-esteem (Csikszentmihalyi, 23). A 24-year-old Korean rock star named Jeong-Hyun Lim has turned into a global phenomenon from his rock rendition of Pachelbel's Canon (Lam). Some call him a second Jimi Hendrix and his YouTube video has been viewed more than 24 million times (Lam). But when interviewers ask him to rate himself he said 50 or 60 out of 100 and is always thinking that he needs to improve (Lam). This is an example of a stereotypical Asian.

Compare the first draft's introduction with the introduction to the final version of the paper (page 266). Do you agree that opening with Natsumi's own story is more effective? The original opening was moved to paragraphs 12–13; do you think this arrangement is better?

⊚⊚ FOLLOWING THROUGH

Look at the opening of your own draft. Why did you choose to open the paper as you did? If you are not happy with the opening, do you see material elsewhere in the draft that might work better? If not, review the opening strategies discussed on page 261 and try one of those instead.   •

Revising to Bring Out the Structure of the Argument

Here is a body paragraph from Natsumi's first draft, offering a reason and evidence in support of her claim:

> Dr. Henry Chung, assistant vice president for student health at New York University and executive director of the NYU student Health Center, says "Asian-American/Asian students, especially males, are under unique pressures to meet high expectations of parents by succeeding in such traditional predetermined careers as medicine and engineering" (qtd. in Ramanujan). Asian students feel that even though they aren't interested in these fields they must major in them and they end up stressing themselves out. Because students major in fields that they aren't interested in they end up not doing as well in school as they could. If you don't have a passion for your job you feel like you are working twice as hard with loads of work on your shoulders.

This paragraph was revised to become paragraph 10 in the final version (page 267). Compare them. In the revised version, how has the argument emerged better in the opening sentence? How has it been better supported?

⊚⊚ FOLLOWING THROUGH

Look over the body paragraphs of your draft. Open with a point of your own; use your sources to support and develop it. Look over your entire draft. How could revising make your reasons stand out more?   •

Revising to Improve Incorporation of Quoted Material

Using sources responsibly means not only citing the source but also identifying the source by name. Natsumi noticed that she was not always clear about whose words were in quotation marks. Here is an example of the problem:

Draft Version

> Also when kids come to college they receive conflicting messages. "The message at home is that their priority should be to look after their parents and take care of their families" ("Mental"). But the message you get at college and from your friends is that you need to learn to think for yourself and be who you are and do what is best for you. This is a different value than the Asian culture so Asian students feel guilty for not doing what they are supposed to be doing ("Mental").

See Chapter 6, "Writing Research-Based Arguments," for more on this important research skill.

Revised Version

As the underlined phrases show, identifying your sources by name and qualifications not only helps your reader understand who is saying what but also increases the authority of the quoted statements.

According to Diem Nguyen, a UC Davis student affairs officer, when Asian-American students come to college, they sometimes end up partying too much because they are not used to this freedom (qtd. in "Mental"). Also, when kids come to college they receive conflicting messages. Nadine Tang, a psychotherapist who has counseled students at UC Berkeley, says they get the message at home that family is their top priority, but the message at college is "to be who you are, learn to be yourself and do what is best for you. . . . You feel guilty for not doing what you're supposed to and not fulfilling your obligations" (qtd. in "Mental").

⊙⊚ FOLLOWING THROUGH

If you are using the words of someone quoted in your source, are you *identifying the actual speaker of the words* as well as citing the source? If not, identify them as Natsumi did in the revised version above.   •

REVISED STUDENT EXAMPLE
Is Too Much Pressure Healthy?

NATSUMI HAZAMA

1   Growing up in an Asian-American family, I was raised to stay close to my family and always to strive to be number one in my class. My parents were both born in Japan and came to America for my father's work. My father was a very intelligent man who wanted me to go into either medicine or engineering. My parents also made me go to Japanese School every Saturday to learn to read and write my native tongue. Going to school six days a week left no time for a social life. The girls at my English school would always have sleepover parties on Friday nights, but I was studying for my next Japanese test. I excelled in school, but that wasn't good enough. Even if I scored a 98 on my math test, my parents would say, "Why didn't you get a 100?"

2   When I was in 8th grade, my father was diagnosed with colon cancer. He grew very ill, and my parents actually knew that he was dying but didn't tell my sister and me. One week, all my relatives from Japan flew in; at the end of that week he passed away. It was a horrible experience, but my mother, sister, and I helped each other, and with the support of all of our family and friends we got through it.

3   Starting high school was completely different. Because my mother knew growing up without a father was hard enough, she just wanted me to be happy. Coming home with a few B's on my report card was okay now. My mother didn't pressure me to get good grades; she basically let me do whatever I wanted. I wasn't in the top 10% of my class, didn't get straight A's, or take all AP courses. However, I was completely satisfied with my high school experience. I was part of the nationally

ranked cheerleading team. I had higher self-esteem. I would give anything to have my father still alive, but I have learned to think for myself and to set my own goals.

4   My situation before the death of my father is common among Asian-American families. I understand it is part of my culture, which I value. However, Asian-American parents need to moderate their demands and allow their children to find goals and challenges that are right for them.

5   Wenju Shen and Weimin Mo, experts on educating Asian-Americans, describe our ways as rooted in Confucianism: "The Confucian ethical code . . . holds that the first loyalty is to the family, even above their allegiance to their country and religion."

6   This closeness to family can bring pressures. In an Asian family the most important thing is to always keep your "face." "Face" means family pride. "Family" means not only immediate relatives, extended relatives, dead ancestors, but also anyone with my last name. To fail in any obligation to the family is to "lose face" and bring shame to myself, my parents, my relatives, and all my ancestors.

7   While family should be important, this cultural pressure to succeed helps to create harmful stereotypes. As Shen and Mo point out, the "whiz kid" stereotype of Asian-American students encourage their parents to maintain practices "not compatible with the values and beliefs of American society." Asian-American parents need to learn how to balance obligations to the family with the more individual values of Americans.

8   A more balanced approach to parenting will lead children to more fulfilling lives. Mihaly Csikszentmihalyi, a psychologist at the University of Chicago, is noted for his work on happiness, creativity, and subjective well-being. His book, *Finding Flow*, describes the kind of family that leads children to develop their full potential: "they combine discipline with spontaneity, rules with freedom, high expectations with unstinting love. An optimal family system is complex in that it encourages the unique individual development of its members while uniting them in a web of affective ties" (88). Asian-American parents should raise their children more like this. Too much parental pressure hinders what Csikszentmihalyi calls "flow," a state of mind where the person is fully engaged in what he or she is doing for its own sake (29–32).

9   For most Asian students, college is their first significant time away from home. Because they aren't used to the freedom of college life, they sometimes end up partying too much.

10   They also receive conflicting messages. Nadine Tang, a psychotherapist who has counseled students at UC Berkeley, says the message at home is that family matters most, but the message at college is "be who you are, learn to be yourself and do what is best for you. . . . You feel guilty for not doing what you're supposed to and not fulfilling your obligations" (qtd. in "Mental").

11   That is what life is all about, fulfilling your own potential, as Csikszentmihalyi says. Unfortunately, even if Asian-American students receive excellent grades in school, they tend to have lower self-esteem than other students (Csikszentmihalyi 24). I think this is so because their parents never praise them. Asian-American parents see success as a duty, so children should not receive praise; instead they are told to do even better and aim still higher (Shen).

12   Along with bringing home straight "A's," parents also urge their children to major in a subject that they see as respectable. Dr. Henry Chung, assistant vice president

for student health at New York University and executive director of the Health Center, points out that "Asian-American/Asian students, especially males, are under unique pressures to meet high expectations of parents by succeeding in such traditional predetermined careers as medicine and engineering" (qtd. in Ramanujan). Even if these fields are not areas of strength or interest, Asian-American students feel that they must major in them. Their grades may start to slip, but as Nguyen at Berkeley says, "Some stay in these majors because they think that they need to. They're reluctant to leave because their parents don't understand: 'If you're not a doctor or engineer, then what are you?'" (qtd. in "Mental").

13   The result can be destructive to a student's mental health, often leading to anxiety and depression. These problems are more common in Asian-American students than in the general population ("Mental"). When Asian-American students are unhappy, they usually don't seek help, even though the best way to recover is to get counseling. Chung at NYU explains that in Asian culture "suffering and working hard are accepted as part of life, a cultural paradigm" (Ramanujan). Asian-American students don't get counseling because discussing emotional problems is a sign of weakness ("Mental"). They also do not tell their parents about their problems. A psychologist at Baylor University, Dr. Dung Ngo, says, "The line of communication in an Asian culture goes one way. It's communicated from the parents downward" (qtd. in Cohen). If students can't express their anger and frustration, it turns into helplessness; they feel like there is no way out.

14   Suicide is therefore common among Asian-American students. According to CNN, Asian American women age 15–24 have the highest suicide rate of any ethnic group. Suicide is the second-leading cause of death (Cohen). At Cornell University between 1996 and 2006 there were 21 suicides; 13 of these were Asian or Asian-American students (Ramanujan).

15   CNN tells the story of how Eliza Noh, a professor of Asian-American studies at California State University at Fullerton, decided to devote her studies to depression and suicide among Asian-American women. One night in 1990, she had been talking to her sister, a college student, on the telephone. She knew her sister was depressed. She sat down to write a letter to encourage her. It was too late. By the time the letter arrived, she had taken her life. Noh believes that the pressure to succeed contributed to her sister's death (Cohen).

16   I have lived both sides, with pressure and without. Living without pressure has enabled me think for myself and be happier. Asian-American parents need to give their children support and encouragement, allow them to make their own decisions about goals, and most of all, stop pressuring them so much.

WORKS CITED

Cohen, Elizabeth. "Push to Achieve Tied to Suicide in Asian-American Women." *CNN.com Health.* 16 May 2007. Web. 1 April 2008.

Csikszentmihalyi, Mihaly. *Finding Flow: The Psychology of Engagement with Everyday Life.* New York City: Basic Books, 1997. Print.

"Mental Health of Asian Youth a Growing Concern." *Asian Outlook—Challenges for Today's Asian American Students.* Asian Pacific Fund. Fall/Winter 2007. Web. 15 April 2008.

Ramanujan, Krishna. "Health Expert Explains Asian and Asian-American Students' Unique Pressures to Succeed." *Chronicle Online.* The Chronicle of Higher Education. 19 March 2006. Web. 22 Feb. 2008.

Shen, Wenju, and Weimin Mo. "Reaching Out to Their Cultures: Building Communication with Asian American Families." N. p. (1990) ERIC. Web. 15 April 2008.

CHAPTER SUMMARY

In this assignment, you learned to combine logical appeal (logos) with ethos, pathos, and style to move an audience to action. You will use what you have learned over and over, in college, at work, and in the community.

What you learn from persuasion applies to other kinds of writing. For instance, how you present yourself—your ethos—makes a difference. We are always writing to reach others even when moving readers to act is not on our mind.

Resolving Conflict: Arguing to Mediate

Private citizens can avoid the big conflicts that concern politicians and activist groups: debates over gay marriage, abortion, taxes, foreign policy, and so on. However, we cannot hide from all conflict. Family members have different preferences about budgeting, major purchases, where to go on vacation, and much else. Furthermore, if you care about what goes on beyond your front door, you will find conflict close to home. The school down the street, for example, wants to expand its athletic stadium. Some parents support the decision because their children play sports at the school. Others oppose it because they think the expansion will bring more traffic, noise, and bright lights to the neighborhood.

One way to resolve conflict is through reasoned arguments. The chapters on convincing and persuading show how appeals to logic and emotion can change minds. But what if we cannot change someone's mind or impose our will in other ways?

Some conflicts do not have to be resolved. The Republican husband can live happily with the Democratic wife. Other conflicts are resolved by compromise. We can go to the mountains this year, the seashore the next. Compromise is better than shouting matches, but it does not result in a common understanding.

CONCEPT CLOSE-UP

Characteristics of Mediation

1. Aims to resolve conflict between opposing and usually hardened positions, often because action of some kind must be taken.

2. Aims to reduce hostility and promote understanding between or among conflicting parties; preserving human relationships and promoting communication are paramount.

3. Like inquiry, mediation involves dialogue and requires that one understand all positions and strive for an open mind.

4. Like convincing, mediation involves making a case that appeals to all parties in the controversy.

5. Like persuasion, mediation depends on the good character of the negotiator and on sharing values and feelings.

6. Mediation depends on conflicting parties' desire to find solutions to overcome counterproductive stalemates.

Essentially, mediation comes into play when convincing and persuading have resulted in sharply differing viewpoints. The task is first to understand the positions of all parties involved and second to uncover a mediating position capable of producing consensus and a reduction in hostility.

This chapter presents mediation as argument whose aim is to resolve conflict by thinking more critically about it. People too often see disputes uncritically by simplifying them to their extreme positions, pro and con. *Mediation aims to move disputants beyond the polarized thinking that makes conflicts impossible to resolve.*

MEDIATION AND THE OTHER AIMS OF ARGUMENT

Mediation uses the other three aims of argument: inquiry, convincing, and persuading. Like inquiry, it examines the range of positions on an issue. Mediation requires knowledge of case structure. The mediator scrutinizes the arguments offered by all sides. A mediatory essay must also present a well-reasoned case of its own. Finally, like persuasion, mediation considers the values, beliefs, and assumptions of the people who hold the conflicting positions. Mediators must appeal to all sides and project a character all sides will trust and find attractive.

In short, mediation requires the mediator to rise above a dispute, including his or her own preferences, to see what is reasonable and right in conflicting positions. The mediator's best asset is wisdom.

THE PROCESS OF MEDIATION

Mediation takes place more often in conversation, through dialogue with the opposing sides, than in writing. But essays can mediate by attempting to argue for middle ground in a conflict. Mediation begins where all arguments should—with inquiry.

MEDIATION AND ROGERIAN ARGUMENT

Arguing to mediate resembles an approach to communication developed by a psychologist, Carl Rogers (1902–1987). In "Communication: Its Blocking and Its Facilitation," he urged people in conflict to listen carefully and with empathy to each other as a first step toward resolving differences. The second step is to go beyond listening in an effort to understand one another's background. Finally, a third step is for each person involved in a dispute to state the position of his or her opponents in a way the opponents agree is accurate and fair. The total approach reduces misunderstanding and helps to clarify what the genuine points of difference are, thus opening up the potential to resolve conflict.

In their textbook *Rhetoric: Discovery and Change* (1970), Richard Young, Alton Becker, and Kenneth Pike outlined four stages for Rogerian argument:

1. An introduction to the problem and a demonstration that the opponent's position is understood

2. A statement of the contexts in which the opponent's position may be valid

3. A statement of the writer's position, including the contexts in which it is valid

4. A statement of how the opponent's position would benefit if he were to adopt elements of the writer's position. If the writer can show that the positions complement each other, that each supplies what the other lacks, so much the better.[1]

Our approach to mediation draws on Rogerian argument. As a mediator, rather than a participant in a dispute, you need to consider the validity of opposing positions, including the personal backgrounds of the people involved. In light of these backgrounds, you look for what is good and right in each position.

Rather than face-to-face oral arguments, in this chapter you will be reading written arguments on a controversial issue and exploring them to uncover

---

[1]This summary of the four stages comes from Douglas Brent, "Rogerian Rhetoric: An Alternative to Traditional Rhetoric," *Argument Revisited, Argument Redefined: Negotiating Meaning in the Composition Classroom,* ed. Barbara Emmel, Paula Resch, and Deborah Tenney (Thousand Oaks, CA: Sage, 1996) <http://www.acs.ucalgary.ca/~dabrent/art/rogchap.html>.

exactly how and why their authors disagree. Instead of sitting around a table with parties in conflict as mediators do, you will write a mediatory essay proposing a point of view designed to appeal to both sides.

A Conflict to Mediate

The United States is a nation of immigrants, but recently the immigrant population includes a wider array of races, ethnicities, religions, and cultures than in the past. The result is a population less white and less Protestant. Should we become a multicultural nation or maintain a single culture based on the original northern European settlers?

Some people argue that the influx of diverse people should have no impact on the traditional Eurocentric identity of America. According to this position, America has a distinctive and superior culture, traceable to the Puritan settlers and based more broadly on Western civilization. This culture is the source of our nation's strength. To keep it strong, newcomers need to assimilate, adopting its values and beliefs. In other words, people holding this position advocate the melting-pot metaphor. Because they believe cultural differences should dissolve as new immigrants become "true Americans," they oppose multiculturalism. We have chosen a recent essay by Roger Kimball, an art critic and editor at the conservative journal *The New Criterion*, to represent the assimilationist position.

Opponents argue that newcomers should preserve their distinctive cultures, taking pride in being Mexican, Chinese, African, and so on. Their metaphor is the mosaic, with each culture remaining distinct but contributing to the whole. We have chosen an essay by Elizabeth Martínez to represent the multiculturalist perspective. Martínez is a Chicana writer and an activist on issues of social justice, including racism and women's rights.

Understanding the Positions

Any attempt to mediate positions requires an understanding of opposing cases. Printed below are the two arguments, followed by our analyses.

Institutionalizing Our Demise: America vs. Multiculturalism

ROGER KIMBALL

The following abridged article appeared in *The New Criterion* (June 2004). Roger Kimball's books include *The Long March: How the Cultural Revolution of the 1960s Changed America* (Encounter, 2000) and *Tenured Radicals: How Politics Has Corrupted Our Higher Education* (HarperCollins, 1990).

There is no room in this country for hyphenated Americanism. When I refer to hyphenated Americans, I do not refer to naturalized Americans. Some of the very best Americans I have ever known were naturalized Americans, Americans born abroad. But a hyphenated American is not an American at all. This is just as true of the man who puts "native" before the hyphen as of the man who puts German or Irish or English or French before the hyphen.

—Theodore Roosevelt, 1915

1   It is often said that the terrorist attacks of September 11 precipitated a new resolve throughout the nation. There is some truth to that. Certainly, the extraordinary bravery of the firefighters and other rescue personnel in New York and Washington, D.C., provided an invigorating spectacle—as did Todd "Let's roll" Beamer and his fellow passengers on United Airlines Flight 93. Having learned from their cell phones what had happened at the World Trade Center and the Pentagon, Beamer and his fellows rushed and overpowered the terrorists who had hijacked their plane. As a result, the plane crashed on a remote Pennsylvania farm instead of on Pennsylvania Avenue. Who knows how many lives their sacrifice saved?

2   The widespread sense of condign outrage—of horror leavened by anger and elevated by resolve—testified to a renewed sense of national purpose and identity after 9/11. Attacked, many Americans suddenly (if temporarily) rediscovered the virtue of patriotism. At the beginning of his remarkable book *Who Are We? The Challenges to America's National Identity* (2004), the Harvard political scientist Samuel Huntington recalls a certain block on Charles Street in Boston. At one time, American flags flew in front of a U.S. Post Office and a liquor store. Then the Post Office stopped displaying the flag, so on September 11, 2001, the flag was flying only in front of the liquor store. Within two weeks, seventeen American flags decorated that block of Charles Street, in addition to a huge flag suspended over the street close by. "With their country under attack," Huntington notes, "Charles Street denizens rediscovered their nation and identified themselves with it."

3   Was that rediscovery anything more than a momentary passion? Huntington reports that within a few months, the flags on Charles Street began to disappear. By the time the first anniversary rolled around in September 2002, only four were left flying. True, that is four times more than were there on September 10, 2001, but it is less than a quarter of the number that populated Charles Street at the end of September 2001.

4   There are similar anecdotes from around the country—an access of flag-waving followed by a relapse into indifference. Does it mean that the sudden upsurge of patriotism in the weeks following 9/11 was only, as it were, skin deep? Or perhaps it merely testifies to the fact that a sense of permanent emergency is difficult to maintain, especially in the absence of fresh attacks. Is our sense of ourselves as Americans patent only when challenged? "Does it," Huntington asks, "take an Osama bin Laden . . . to make us realize that we are Americans? If we do not experience recurring destructive attacks, will we return to the fragmentation and eroded Americanism before September 11?"

5   One hopes that the answer is No. . . . But I fear that for every schoolchild standing at attention for the National Anthem, there is a teacher or lawyer or judge or politician or ACLU employee militating against the hegemony of the dominant

culture, the insupportable intrusion of white, Christian, "Eurocentric" values into the curriculum, the school pageant, the town green, etc., etc. . . .

6   The threat shows itself in many ways, from culpable complacency to the corrosive imperatives of "multiculturalism" and political correctness. . . . In essence, as Huntington notes, multiculturalism is "anti-European civilization. . . . It is basically an anti-Western ideology.". . . [W]herever the imperatives of multiculturalism have touched the curriculum, they have left broad swaths of anti-Western attitudinizing competing for attention with quite astonishing historical blindness. Courses on minorities, women's issues, the Third World proliferate; the teaching of mainstream history slides into oblivion. "The mood," Arthur Schlesinger wrote in *The Disuniting of America* (1992), his excellent book on the depredations of multiculturalism, "is one of divesting Americans of the sinful European inheritance and seeking redemptive infusions from non-Western cultures."

7   A profound ignorance of the milestones of American culture is one predictable result of this mood. The statistics have become proverbial. Huntington quotes one poll from the 1990s showing that while 90 percent of Ivy League students could identify Rosa Parks, only 25 percent could identify the author of the words "government of the people, by the people, for the people." (Yes, it's the Gettysburg Address.) In a 1999 survey, 40 percent of seniors at fifty-five top colleges could not say within half a century when the Civil War was fought. Another study found that more high school students knew who Harriet Tubman was than knew that Washington commanded the American army in the revolution or that Abraham Lincoln wrote the Emancipation Proclamation. Doubtless you have your own favorite horror story.

8   But multiculturalism is not only an academic phenomenon. The attitudes it fosters have profound social as well as intellectual consequences. One consequence has been a sharp rise in the phenomenon of immigration without—or with only partial—assimilation: a dangerous demographic trend that threatens American identity in the most basic way. These various agents of dissolution are also elements in a wider culture war: the contest to define how we live and what counts as the good in the good life. Anti-Americanism occupies such a prominent place on the agenda of the culture wars precisely because the traditional values of American identity—articulated by the Founders and grounded in a commitment to individual liberty and public virtue—are deeply at odds with the radical, de-civilizing tenets of the "multiculturalist" enterprise.

9   To get a sense of what has happened to the institution of American identity, compare Robert Frost's performance at John F. Kennedy's inauguration in 1961 with Maya Angelou's performance thirty-two years later. As Huntington reminds us, Frost spoke of the "heroic deeds" of America's founding, an event, he said, that with "God's approval" ushered in "a new order of the ages." By contrast, Maya Angelou never mentioned the words "America" or "American." Instead, she identified twenty-seven ethnic or religious groups that had suffered repression because of America's "armed struggles for profit," "cynicism," and "brutishness.". . .

10   A favorite weapon in the armory of multiculturalism is the lowly hyphen. When we speak of an African-American or Mexican-American or Asian-American these

days, the aim is not descriptive but deconstructive. There is a polemical edge to it, a provocation. The hyphen does not mean "American, but hailing at some point in the past from someplace else." It means "only provisionally American: my allegiance is divided at best.". . . The multicultural passion for hyphenation is not simply a fondness for syntactical novelty. It also bespeaks a commitment to the centrifugal force of anti-American tribalism. The division marked by the hyphen in African-American (say) denotes a political stand. It goes hand-in-hand with other items on the index of liberal desiderata—the redistributive impulse behind efforts at "affirmative action," for example. . . .

11   Multiculturalism and "affirmative action" are allies in the assault on the institution of American identity. As such, they oppose the traditional understanding of what it means to be an American—an understanding hinted at in 1782 by the French-born American farmer J. Hector St. John de Crèvecoeur in his famous image of America as a country in which "individuals of all nations are melted into a new race of men." This crucible of American identity, this "melting pot," has two aspects. The negative aspect involves disassociating oneself from the cultural imperatives of one's country of origin. One sheds a previous identity before assuming a new one. One might preserve certain local habits and tastes, but they are essentially window-dressing. In essence one has left the past behind in order to become an American citizen.

12   The positive aspect of advancing the melting pot involves embracing the substance of American culture. The 1795 code for citizenship lays out some of the formal requirements.

> I do solemnly swear (1) to support the Constitution of the United States; (2) to renounce and abjure absolutely and entirely all allegiance and fidelity to any foreign prince, potentate, state, or sovereignty of whom or which the applicant was before a subject or citizen; (3) to support and defend the Constitution and the laws of the United States against all enemies, foreign and domestic; (4) to bear true faith and allegiance to the same; and (5) (A) to bear arms on behalf of the United States when required by law, or (B) to perform noncombatant service in the Armed Forces of the United States when required by law. . . .

For over two hundred years, this oath had been required of those wishing to become citizens. In 2003, Huntington tells us, federal bureaucrats launched a campaign to rewrite and weaken it.

13   I shall say more about what constitutes the substance of American identity in a moment. For now, I want to underscore the fact that this project of Americanization has been an abiding concern since the time of the Founders. "We must see our people more Americanized," John Jay declared in the 1780s. Jefferson concurred. Teddy Roosevelt repeatedly championed the idea that American culture, the "crucible in which all the new types are melted into one," was "shaped from 1776 to 1789, and our nationality was definitely fixed in all its essentials by the men of Washington's day."

14   It is often said that America is a nation of immigrants. In fact, as Huntington points out, America is a country that was initially a country of *settlers*. Settlers

precede immigrants and make their immigration possible. The culture of those mostly English-speaking, predominantly Anglo-Protestant settlers defined American culture. Their efforts came to fruition with the generation of Franklin, Washington, Jefferson, Hamilton, and Madison. The Founders are so denominated because they founded, they inaugurated a state. Immigrants were those who came later, who came from elsewhere, and who became American by embracing the Anglophone culture of the original settlers. The English language, the rule of law, respect for individual rights, the industriousness and piety that flowed from the Protestant work ethic—these were central elements in the culture disseminated by the Founders. And these were among the qualities embraced by immigrants when they became Americans. "Throughout American history," Huntington notes, "people who were not white Anglo-Saxon Protestants have become Americans by adopting America's Anglo-Protestant culture and political values. This benefited them and the country."

15   Justice Louis Brandeis outlined the pattern in 1919. Americanization, he said, means that the immigrant "adopts the clothes, the manners, and the customs generally prevailing here . . . substitutes for his mother tongue the English language" and comes "into complete harmony with our ideals and aspirations and cooperate[s] with us for their attainment." Until the 1960s, the Brandeis model mostly prevailed. Protestant, Catholic, and Jewish groups, understanding that assimilation was the best ticket to stability and social and economic success, eagerly aided in the task of integrating their charges into American society.

16   The story is very different today. In America, there is a dangerous new tide of immigration from Asia, a variety of Muslim countries, and Latin America, especially from Mexico. The tide is new not only chronologically but also in substance. First, there is the sheer matter of numbers. More than 2,200,000 legal immigrants came to the U.S. from Mexico in the 1990s alone. The number of illegal Mexican immigrants is staggering. So is their birth rate. Altogether there are more than 8 million Mexicans in the U.S. Some parts of the Southwest are well on their way to becoming what Victor Davis Hanson calls "Mexifornia," "the strange society that is emerging as the result of a demographic and cultural revolution like no other in our times." A professor of Chicano Studies at the University of New Mexico gleefully predicts that by 2080 parts of the Southwest United States and Northern Mexico will join to form a new country, "La Republica del Norte."

17   The problem is not only one of numbers, though. Earlier immigrants made—and were helped and goaded by the ambient culture to make—concerted efforts to assimilate. Important pockets of these new immigrants are not assimilating, not learning English, not becoming or thinking of themselves primarily as Americans. The effect of these developments on American identity is disastrous and potentially irreversible.

18   Such developments are abetted by the left-wing political and educational elites of this country, whose dominant theme is the perfidy of traditional American values. Hence the passion for multiculturalism and the ideal of ethnic hyphenation that goes with it. This has done immense damage in schools and colleges as well as in

betrayal of truth

the population at large. By removing the obligation to master English, multiculturalism condemns whole subpopulations to the status of permanent second-class
citizens. . . .

19   As if in revenge for this injustice, however, multiculturalism also weakens the
social bonds of the community at large. The price of imperfect assimilation is
imperfect loyalty. Take the movement for bilingualism. Whatever it intended in
theory, in practice it means *not* mastering English. It has notoriously left its supposed
beneficiaries essentially monolingual, often semi-lingual. The only *bi* involved is a
passion for bifurcation, which is fed by the accumulated resentments instilled by
the anti-American multicultural orthodoxy. Every time you call directory assistance
or some large corporation and are told "Press One for English" and "Para español
oprime el numero dos" it is another small setback for American identity. . . .

20   We stand at a crossroads. The future of America hangs in the balance.
Huntington outlines several possible courses that the country might take, from the
loss of our core culture to an attempt to revive the "discarded and discredited racial
and ethnic concepts" that, in part, defined pre-mid-twentieth century America.
Huntington argues for another alternative. If we are to preserve our identity as a
nation we need to preserve the core values that defined that identity. This is a
point that the political philosopher Patrick, Lord Devlin made in his book *The
Enforcement of Morals* (1965):

> [S]ociety means a community of ideas; without shared ideas on politics, morals, and
> ethics no society can exist. Each one of us has ideas about what is good and what is
> evil; they cannot be kept private from the society in which we live. If men and
> women try to create a society in which there is no fundamental agreement about
> good and evil they will fail; if having based it upon a common set of core values, they
> surrender those values, it will disintegrate. For society is not something that can be
> kept together physically; it is held by the invisible but fragile bonds of common beliefs
> and values. . . . A common morality is part of the bondage of a good society, and
> that bondage is part of the price of society which mankind must pay.

What are those beliefs and values? They embrace several things, including religion.
You wouldn't know it from watching CNN or reading *The New York Times,* but
there is a huge religious revival taking place now, affecting just about every part
of the globe except Western Europe, which slouches towards godlessness almost
as fast as it slouches towards bankruptcy and demographic collapse. (Neither Spain
nor Italy are producing enough children to replace their existing populations, while
the Muslim birthrate in France continues to soar.)

21   Things look different in America. For if America is a vigorously secular country—
which it certainly is—it is also a deeply religious one. It always has been. Tocqueville
was simply minuting the reality he saw around him when he noted that "[o]n my
arrival in the United States the religious aspect of the country was the first thing
that struck my attention." As G. K. Chesterton put it a century after Tocqueville,
America is "a nation with the soul of a church." Even today, America is a country
where an astonishing 92 percent of the population says it believes in God and
80 to 85 percent of the population identifies itself as Christian. Hence Huntington's
call for a return to America's core values is also a call to embrace the religious

principles upon which the country was founded, "a recommitment to America as a deeply religious and primarily Christian country, encompassing several religious minorities adhering to Anglo-Protestant values, speaking English, maintaining its cultural heritage, and committed to the principles" of political liberty as articulated by the Founders. . . . Huntington is careful to stress that what he offers is an "argument for the importance of Anglo-Protestant culture, not for the importance of Anglo-Protestant people." That is, he argues not on behalf of a particular ethnic group but on behalf of a culture and set of values that "for three and a half centuries have been embraced by Americans of all races, ethnicities, and religions and that have been the source of their liberty, unity, power, prosperity, and moral leadership."

22   American identity was originally founded on four things: ethnicity, race, ideology, and culture. By the mid-twentieth century, ethnicity and race had sharply receded in importance. Indeed, one of America's greatest achievements is having eliminated the racial and ethnic components that historically were central to its identity. Ideology—the package of Enlightened liberal values championed by the Founders—[is] crucial but too thin for the task of forging or preserving national identity by themselves. ("A nation defined only by political ideology," Huntington notes, "is a fragile nation.") Which is why Huntington, like virtually all of the Founders, explicitly grounded American identity in religion. . . .

23   Opponents of religion in the public square never tire of reminding us that there is no mention of God in the Constitution. This is true. Neither is the word "virtue" mentioned. But both are presupposed. For the American Founders, as the historian Gertrude Himmelfarb points out, virtue, grounded in religion, was presumed "to be rooted in the very nature of man and as such . . . reflected in the *moeurs* of the people and in the traditions and informal institutions of society." It is also worth mentioning that if the Constitution is silent on religion, the Declaration of Independence is voluble, speaking of "nature's God," the "Creator," "the supreme judge of the world," and "divine Providence.". . . Benjamin Rush, one of the signers of the Declaration of Independence, summed up the common attitude of the Founders toward religion when he insisted that "[t]he only foundation for a useful education in a republic is to be laid in religion. Without it there can be no virtue, and without virtue there can be no liberty, and liberty is the object of all republican governments." George Washington concurred: "Reason and experience both forbid us to expect that national morality can prevail in exclusion of religious principles."

24   No nation lasts forever. An external enemy may eventually overrun and subdue it; internal forces of dissolution and decadence may someday undermine it, leaving it prey to more vigorous competitors. Sooner or later it succumbs. The United States is the most powerful nation the world has ever seen. Its astonishing military might, economic productivity, and political vigor are unprecedented. But someday, as Huntington reminds us, it too will fade or perish as Athens, Rome, and other great civilizations have faded or perished. Is the end, or the beginning of the end, at hand?

25   So far, the West—or at least the United States—has disappointed its self-appointed undertakers. How do we stand now, at the dawn of the twenty-first

century? It is worth remembering that besieged nations do not always succumb to the forces, external or internal, that threaten them. Sometimes, they muster the resolve to fight back successfully, to renew themselves. Today, America faces a new external enemy in the form of militant Islam and global terrorism. That minatory force, though murderous, will fail in proportion to our resolve to defeat it. Do we still possess that resolve? Inseparable from resolve is self-confidence, faith in the essential nobility of one's regime and one's way of life. To what extent do we still possess, still practice that faith?

Reinventing "America": Call for a New National Identity

ELIZABETH MARTÍNEZ

> Elizabeth Martínez has written six books, including one on Chicano history. This essay comes from her 1998 book, *De Colores Means All of Us: Latina Views for a Multi-Colored Century.*

1 For some 15 years, starting in 1940, 85 percent of all U.S. elementary schools used the Dick and Jane series to teach children how to read. The series starred Dick, Jane, their white middle-class parents, their dog Spot and their life together in a home with a white picket fence.

2   "Look, Jane, look! See Spot run!" chirped the two kids. It was a house full of glorious family values, where Mom cooked while Daddy went to work in a suit and mowed the lawn on weekends. The Dick and Jane books also taught that you should do your job and help others. All this affirmed an equation of middle-class with whiteness with virtue.

3   In the mid-1990s, museums, libraries and 80 Public Broadcasting Service (PBS) stations across the country had exhibits and programs commemorating the series. At one museum, an attendant commented, "When you hear someone crying, you know they are looking at the Dick and Jane books." It seems nostalgia runs rampant among many Euro-Americans: a nostalgia for the days of unchallenged White Supremacy—both moral and material—when life was "simple."

4   We've seen that nostalgia before in the nation's history. But today it signifies a problem reaching a new intensity. It suggests a national identity crisis that promises to bring in its wake an unprecedented nervous breakdown for the dominant society's psyche.

5   Nowhere is this more apparent than in California, which has long been on the cutting edge of the nation's present and future reality. Warning sirens have sounded repeatedly in the 1990s, such as the fierce battle over new history textbooks for public schools, Proposition 187's ugly denial of human rights to immigrants, the 1996 assault on affirmative action that culminated in Proposition 209, and the 1997 move to abolish bilingual education. Attempts to copycat these reactionary measures have been seen in other states.

6   The attack on affirmative action isn't really about affirmative action. Essentially it is another tactic in today's war on the gains of the 1960s, a tactic rooted in

Anglo resentment and fear. A major source of that fear: the fact that California will almost surely have a majority of people of color in 20 to 30 years at most, with the nation as a whole not far behind.

7 Check out the February 3, 1992, issue of *Sports Illustrated* with its double-spread ad for *Time* magazine. The ad showed hundreds of newborn babies in their hospital cribs, all of them Black or brown except for a rare white face here and there. The headline says, "Hey, whitey! It's your turn at the back of the bus!" The ad then tells you, read *Time* magazine to keep up with today's hot issues. That manipulative image could have been published today; its implication of shifting power appears to be the recurrent nightmare of too many potential Anglo allies.

8 Euro-American anxiety often focuses on the sense of a vanishing national identity. Behind the attacks on immigrants, affirmative action and multiculturalism, behind the demand for "English Only" laws and the rejection of bilingual education, lies the question: with all these new people, languages and cultures, what will it mean to be an American? If that question once seemed, to many people, to have an obvious, universally applicable answer, today new definitions must be found. But too often Americans, with supposed scholars in the lead, refuse to face that need and instead nurse a nostalgia for some bygone clarity. They remain trapped in denial.

9 An array of such ostriches, heads in the sand, began flapping their feathers noisily with the publication of Allan Bloom's 1987 best-selling book, *The Closing of the American Mind.* Bloom bemoaned the decline of our "common values" as a society, meaning the decline of Euro-American cultural centricity (shall we just call it cultural imperialism?). Since then we have seen constant sniping at "diversity" goals across the land. The assault has often focused on how U.S. history is taught. And with reason, for this country's identity rests on a particular narrative about the historical origins of the United States as a nation.

THE GREAT WHITE ORIGIN MYTH

10 Every society has an origin narrative that explains that society to itself and the world with a set of stories and symbols. The origin myth, as scholar-activist Roxanne Dunbar Ortiz has termed it, defines how a society understands its place in the world and its history. The myth provides the basis for a nation's self-defined identity. Most origin narratives can be called myths because they usually present only the most flattering view of a nation's history; they are not distinguished by honesty.

11 Ours begins with Columbus "discovering" a hemisphere where some 80 million people already lived but didn't really count (in what became the United States, they were just buffalo-chasing "savages" with no grasp of real estate values and therefore doomed to perish). It continues with the brave Pilgrims, a revolution by independence-loving colonists against a decadent English aristocracy and the birth of an energetic young republic that promised democracy and equality (that is, to white male landowners). In the 1840s, the new nation expanded its size by almost one-third, thanks to a victory over that backward land of little brown people called Mexico. Such has been the basic account of how the nation called the United States of America came into being as presently configured.

12   The myth's omissions are grotesque. It ignores three major pillars of our nationhood: genocide, enslavement and imperialist expansion (such nasty words, who wants to hear them?—but that's the problem). The massive extermination of indigenous peoples provided our land base; the enslavement of African labor made our economic growth possible; and the seizure of half of Mexico by war (or threat of renewed war) extended this nation's boundaries north to the Pacific and south to the Rio Grande. Such are the foundation stones of the United States, within an economic system that made this country the first in world history to be born capitalist.

13   Those three pillars were, of course, supplemented by great numbers of dirt-cheap workers from Mexico, China, the Philippines, Puerto Rico and other countries, all of them kept in their place by White Supremacy. In history they stand alongside millions of less-than-supreme white workers and sharecroppers.

14   Any attempt to modify the present origin myth provokes angry efforts to repel such sacrilege. In the case of Native Americans, scholars will insist that they died from disease or wars among themselves, or that "not so many really did die." At worst it was a "tragedy," but never deliberate genocide, never a pillar of our nationhood. As for slavery, it was an embarrassment, of course, but do remember that Africa also had slavery and anyway enlightened white folk finally did end the practice here.

15   In the case of Mexico, reputable U.S. scholars still insist on blaming that country for the 1846–48 war. Yet even former U.S. President Ulysses Grant wrote in his memoirs that "[w]e were sent to provoke a fight [by moving troops into a disputed border area] but it was essential that Mexico should commence it [by fighting back]" (*Mr. Lincoln's General: Ulysses S. Grant, an illustrated autobiography*). President James Polk's 1846 diary records that he told his cabinet his purpose in declaring war as "acquiring California, New Mexico, and perhaps other Mexican lands" (*Diary of James K. Polk 1845–49*). To justify what could be called a territorial drive-by, the Mexican people were declared inferior; the U.S. had a "Manifest Destiny" to bring them progress and democracy.

16   Even when revisionist voices expose particular evils of Indian policy, slavery or the war on Mexico, they remain little more than unpleasant footnotes; the core of the dominant myth stands intact. PBS's eight-part documentary series of 1996 titled "The West" is a case in point. It devoted more than the usual attention to the devastation of Native Americans, but still centered on Anglos and gave little attention to why their domination evolved as it did. The West thus remained the physically gorgeous backdrop for an ugly, unaltered origin myth.

17   In fact, "The West" series strengthens that myth. White Supremacy needs the brave but inevitably doomed Indians to silhouette its own inevitable conquest. It needs the Indian-as-devil to sustain its own holy mission. Remember Timothy Wight, who served as pastor to Congress in the late 1700s and wrote that, under the Indians, "Satan ruled unchallenged in America" until "our chosen race eternal justice sent." With that self-declared moral authority, the "winning of the West" metamorphosed from a brutal, bloody invasion into a crusade of brave Christians marching across a lonely, dangerous landscape.

RACISM AS LINCHPIN OF THE U.S. NATIONAL IDENTITY

18 A crucial embellishment of the origin myth and key element of the national identity has been the myth of the frontier, analyzed in Richard Slotkin's *Gunfighter Nation,* the last volume of a fascinating trilogy. He describes Theodore Roosevelt's belief that the West was won thanks to American arms, "the means by which progress and nationality will be achieved." That success, Roosevelt continued, "depends on the heroism of men who impose on the course of events the latent virtues of their 'race.'" Roosevelt saw conflict on the frontier producing a species of virile "fighters and breeders" who would eventually generate a new leadership class. Militarism thus went hand in hand with the racialization of history's protagonists.

19 No slouch as an imperialist, Roosevelt soon took the frontier myth abroad, seeing Asians as Apaches and the Philippines as Sam Houston's Texas in the process of being seized from Mexico. For Roosevelt, Slotkin writes, "racial violence [was] the principle around which both individual character and social organization develop." Such ideas have not remained totally unchallenged by U.S. historians, nor was the frontier myth always applied in totally simplistic ways by Hollywood and other media. (The outlaw, for example, is a complicated figure, both good and bad.) Still, the frontier myth traditionally spins together virtue and violence, morality and war, in a convoluted, Calvinist web. That tortured embrace defines an essence of the so-called American character—the national identity—to this day.

20 The frontier myth embodied the nineteenth-century concept of Manifest Destiny, a doctrine that served to justify expansionist violence by means of intrinsic racial superiority. Manifest Destiny saw Yankee conquest as the inevitable result of a confrontation between enterprise and progress (white) versus passivity and backwardness (Indian, Mexican). "Manifest" meant "God-given," and the whole doctrine is profoundly rooted in religious conviction going back to the earliest colonial times. In his short, powerful book *Manifest Destiny: American Expansion and the Empire of Right,* Professor Anders Stephanson tells how the Puritans reinvented the Jewish notion of chosenness and applied it to this hemisphere so that territorial expansion became God's will. . . .

MANIFEST DESTINY DIES HARD

21 The concept of Manifest Destiny, with its assertion of racial superiority sustained by military power, has defined U.S. identity for 150 years. Only the Vietnam War brought a serious challenge to that concept of almightiness. Bitter debate, moral anguish, images of My Lai and the prospect of military defeat for the first time in U.S. history all suggested that the long-standing marriage of virtue and violence might soon be on the rocks. In the final years of the war the words leaped to mind one day: this country is having a national nervous breakdown.

22 Perhaps this is why the Vietnam War continues to arouse passions today. Some who are willing to call the war "a mistake" still shy away from recognizing its immorality or even accepting it as a defeat. A few Americans have the courage to conclude from the Vietnam War that we should abandon the idea that our identity rests on being the world's richest, most powerful and indeed *best* nation. Is it possible that the so-called Vietnam syndrome might signal liberation from a crippling

self-definition? Is it possible the long-standing belief that "American exceptionalism" had made freedom possible might be rejected someday?

23   The Vietnam syndrome is partly rooted in the fact that, although other societies have also been based on colonialism and slavery, ours seems to have an insatiable need to be the "good guys" on the world stage. That need must lie at least partially in a Protestant dualism that defines existence in terms of opposites, so that if you are not "good" you are bad, if not "white" then Black, and so on. Whatever the cause, the need to be seen as virtuous, compared to someone else's evil, haunts U.S. domestic and foreign policy. Where on earth would we be without Saddam Hussein, Qaddafi, and that all-time favorite of gringo demonizers, Fidel Castro? Gee whiz, how would we know what an American really is?

24   Today's origin myth and the resulting concept of national identity make for an intellectual prison where it is dangerous to ask big questions about this society's superiority. When otherwise decent people are trapped in such a powerful desire not to feel guilty, self-deception becomes unavoidable. To cease our present falsification of collective memory should, and could, open the doors of that prison. When together we cease equating whiteness with Americanness, a new day can dawn. As David Roediger, the social historian, has said, "[Whiteness] is the empty and therefore terrifying attempt to build an identity on what one isn't, and on whom one can hold back."

25   Redefining the U.S. origin narrative, and with it this country's national identity, could prove liberating for our collective psyche. It does not mean Euro-Americans should wallow individually in guilt. It does mean accepting collective responsibility to deal with the implications of our real origin. A few apologies, for example, might be a step in the right direction. In 1997, the idea was floated in Congress to apologize for slavery; it encountered opposition from all sides. But to reject the notion because corrective action, not an apology, is needed misses the point. Having defined itself as the all-time best country in the world, the United States fiercely denies the need to make a serious, official apology for anything. . . . To press for any serious, official apology does imply a new origin narrative, a new self-image, an ideological sea change.

26   Accepting the implications of a different narrative could also shed light on today's struggles. In the affirmative-action struggle, for example, opponents have said that that policy is no longer needed because racism ended with the Civil Rights Movement. But if we look at slavery as a fundamental pillar of this nation, going back centuries, it becomes obvious that racism could not have been ended by 30 years of mild reforms. If we see how the myth of the frontier idealized the white male adventurer as the central hero of national history, with the woman as sunbonneted helpmate, then we might better understand the dehumanized ways in which women have continued to be treated. A more truthful origin narrative could also help break down divisions among peoples of color by revealing common experiences and histories of cooperation.

27   A new origin narrative and national identity could help pave the way to a more livable society for us all. A society based on cooperation rather than competition, on the idea that all living creatures are interdependent and that humanity's goal

should be balance. Such were the values of many original Americans, deemed "savages." Similar gifts are waiting from other despised peoples and traditions. We might well start by recognizing that "America" is the name of an entire hemisphere, rich in a stunning variety of histories, cultures and peoples—not just one country.

28   The choice seems clear, if not easy. We can go on living in a state of massive denial, affirming this nation's superiority and virtue simply because we need to believe in it. We can choose to believe the destiny of the United States is still manifest: global domination. Or we can seek a transformative vision that carries us forward, not backward. We can seek an origin narrative that lays the groundwork for a multicultural, multinational identity centered on the goals of social equity and democracy. We do have choices.

29   There is little time for nostalgia. Dick and Jane never were "America," they were only one part of one community in one part of one country in one part of one continent. Yet we have let their image define our entire society and its values. Will the future be marked by ongoing denial or by steps toward a new vision in which White Supremacy no longer determines reality? When on earth will we transcend the assumptions that imprison our minds?

30   At times you can hear the clock ticking.

Analysis of the Writers' Positions

The first step in resolving conflict is to understand what the parties are claiming and why. Below is our paraphrase of Kimball's and Martínez's arguments.

Kimball's Position   He opposes multiculturalism and wants to preserve an American identity based in Anglo-Protestant culture.

> *Thesis:* Multiculturalism weakens America by keeping people of different cultures from assimilating to the core values of America's Anglo-Protestant identity.
>
>> *Reason:* Educational multiculturalism degrades traditional American values and ignores mainstream history and culture.
>>
>>> *Evidence:* Opinions of Samuel Huntington and Arthur Schlesinger Jr. Examples of college students' ignorance about history. Maya Angelou's speech at Clinton's inauguration.
>>
>> *Reason:* Multiculturalism "weakens the social bond" by denying that immigrants need to assimilate to the language and values of the dominant culture.
>>
>>> *Evidence:* Rise of hyphenization. Rise of non-English-speaking communities. Calls for affirmative action, which violates the idea of success based on merit.
>>
>> *Reason:* America should be defined by one culture and nationality, not many.
>>
>>> *Evidence:* Quotations from de Crèvecoeur on the "new race of men." Quotations from Theodore Roosevelt, John Jay, Thomas

Jefferson, Benjamin Franklin. The 1795 oath of allegiance for citizenship.

Reason: The single, unifying identity of America should be based in Anglo-Saxon Protestant Christianity.

Evidence: Religious beliefs of original settlers. Historian Himmelfarb on American virtue as deeply rooted in religion. Quotes from Founding Fathers on relation of virtue to religion. Huntington on the need for national identity based in religion.

Martínez's Position   She wants to replace traditional Anglo-American identity with a multicultural one.

Thesis: The United States needs to discard its "white supremacist" identity.

Reason: It's based on racism, genocide, and imperialist expansion.

Evidence: The "origin myth" in common accounts of U.S. history. The historical record of slavery, takeover of Native American land, wars of expansion. Primary sources such as Presidents Grant and Polk. Theodore Roosevelt's statements about racial superiority. Historian Richard Slotkin's analysis of frontier myth.

Reason: It's based on a false sense of moral superiority and favor in the eyes of God.

Evidence: Professor Anders Stephanson on the concept of Manifest Destiny. Protestant moral dualism—seeing the world in terms of good and evil. Social historian David Roediger on the Anglo sense of superiority.

Reason: America will be a more fair and democratic country if we revise our identity to acknowledge Anglo faults and adopt the values of non-Anglo cultures.

Evidence: Racism and sexism not eliminated. The valuable gifts of other cultures, such as cooperation over competition.

FOLLOWING THROUGH

If you and some of your classmates have written arguments taking opposing views on the same issue, prepare briefs of your respective positions to share with one another. (You might also create briefs of your opponents' positions to see how well you have understood one another's written arguments.)

Alternatively, write briefs summarizing the opposing positions offered in several published arguments as a first step toward mediating these viewpoints.   •

Locating the Areas of Agreement and Disagreement

Differences over Facts

Most conflicts result from interpreting facts differently rather than disagreement about the facts themselves. For example, in the arguments of Kimball and Martínez, we see agreement on many factual points:

- Whites are becoming the minority in some parts of the United States.
- Assimilation has meant conformity to a culture defined by Anglo-Protestant values.
- Christianity has played a large role in America's sense of identity.

If a mediator finds disagreement over facts, he or she needs to look into them and provide evidence from credible sources that would resolve the disagreement.

◎◎ FOLLOWING THROUGH

For the arguments you are mediating, make a list of facts that the authors both accept. Note facts offered by one side but denied or not considered by the other. Where your authors do not agree on the facts, do research to decide how valid the facts cited on both sides are. Explain the discrepancies. If your class is mediating the same conflict, compare your findings.   •

Differences over Interests, Values, and Interpretations

Facts alone cannot resolve entrenched disputes such as the debate over multiculturalism. For example, a history lesson about white settlers' treatment of Native Americans would not change Kimball's mind. Nor would a lesson in Enlightenment philosophy alter what Martínez thinks. When we attempt to mediate, *we have to look into why people hold the positions they do.* Like persuasion, mediation looks at the contexts of a dispute.

To identify these differences, we can ask questions similar to those that are useful in persuasion for identifying what divides us from our audience (see the Best Practices box, "Questions for Understanding Difference," page 289). We apply below the questions about difference to Kimball's and Martínez's positions.

Is the Difference a Matter of Assumptions? Every argument has assumptions—unstated assertions that the audience must share to find the reasoning valid and persuasive. Kimball assumes that Anglo-Protestant culture is moral; therefore, he does not show how Christianity has made America a moral nation. Martínez disputes the very assumption that America is moral. But she also makes assumptions. She assumes that the "origin narrative" of the white man's conquest and exploitation is the sole basis for the nation's past and present identity. This assumption allows her to argue that the culture of the United States is simply white supremacist.

1. Is the difference a matter of *assumptions?*
2. Is the difference a matter of *principle?*
3. Is the difference a matter of *values* or a matter of having the same values but giving them different *priorities?*
4. Is the difference a matter of *ends* or *means?*
5. Is the difference a matter of *implications* or *consequences?*
6. Is the difference a matter of *interpretation?*
7. Is the difference a result of *personal background, basic human needs,* or *emotions?*

To our list of questions about difference in persuasive writing, we add this last question because mediators must look not just at the arguments but also at the disputants as people with histories and feelings. Mediators must take into account such basic human needs as personal security, economic well-being, and a sense of belonging, recognition, and control over their lives.

These two assumptions show polarized thinking—one assumes that Anglo-Protestant values are all good, the other that Anglo-Protestant values are all evil. Such polarized assumptions are common in disputes because, as philosopher of ethics Anthony Weston explains, we polarize not just to simplify but to justify: "We polarize . . . to be able to picture ourselves as totally justified, totally right, and the 'other side' as totally unjustified and wrong."[2] It is precisely this tactic that mediation must resist and overcome.

Is the Difference a Matter of Principle? By principles, we mean informal rules that guide our actions, like the "rule" in sales: "The customer is always right." Kimball's principle is patriotism: Americans should be undivided in loyalty and allegiance to the United States. Martínez's principle is fairness and justice for all, which means rewriting the origin narrative, admitting past mistakes, and recognizing the richness and morality of all the cultures that make up America. A mediator might ask, Can we be patriotic *and* self-critical? Must we repudiate the past entirely to fashion a new national identity?

Is the Difference a Matter of Values or Priorities? The principles just discussed reflect differing priorities. In the post–9/11 world, Kimball is concerned with America's strength on the world stage, whereas Martínez concentrates more on America's compassion in its domestic policies. This is a significant difference because Martínez supports programs like affirmative

---

[2]Anthony Weston, *A Practical Companion to Ethics* (New York: Oxford, 2005) 50.

action and multicultural education, the very policies Kimball claims weaken our social bonds. Once we see this difference, we can see the dispute in the context of liberal and conservative opinion in general. Kimball is arguing for a national identity acceptable to conservatives, Martínez for one acceptable to liberals. But what we need, obviously, is something that can cross this divide and appeal to most Americans.

Is the Difference a Matter of Ends or Means?   Martínez and Kimball have different ends in mind, so they also have different means to achieve the ends. For Martínez, a multicultural identity is the means to a more fair and livable society for all. For Kimball, a common identity in Anglo-Protestant culture is the means to remaining "the most powerful nation the world has ever seen." A mediator could reasonably ask: Couldn't we have both? Couldn't the United States be a powerful nation that is also fair and livable for all its citizens?

Is the Difference a Matter of Implications or Consequences?   The mediator has to consider what each side fears will happen if the other side prevails. Kimball fears that multiculturalism will lead Americans to self-doubt, loss of confidence. He also forecasts a large population of "permanent second-class citizens" if subgroups of the population do not assimilate. Martínez fears continuing oppression of minorities if our national self-conception does not change to fit our country's actual diversity. The mediator must acknowledge the fears of both sides while not permitting either to go unquestioned. Fear is a powerful motivator that must be confronted squarely.

Is the Difference a Matter of Interpretation?   A major disagreement here is over how to interpret the values of Anglo-Protestant culture. To Kimball, these values are "individual liberty and public virtue" (paragraph 8), "the rule of law" (paragraph 14), "respect for individual rights" (paragraph 14), devotion to God and a strong work ethic (paragraph 14). In contrast, Martínez interprets Anglo-Protestant values as a belief in whites' moral superiority and favor in the eyes of God (paragraph 20) that enabled them to see their own acts of "genocide, enslavement, and imperialist expansion" (paragraph 12) as morally acceptable and even heroic (paragraph 19). These interpretations stem from the different backgrounds of the writers, which we consider next.

Is the Difference a Matter of Personal Background, Basic Human Needs, or Emotions?   When mediating between positions, it is a good idea to go to the library or an online source for biographical information about the authors. It will pay off with insight into why they disagree.

Kimball and Martínez obviously come from very different backgrounds that are representative of others who hold the same positions they do. For example, as a white male with the financial means to have attended Yale, Kimball represents the group that has benefited most from the traditional national identity. His conservative views have pitted him against liberal academics and social activists.

Martínez identifies herself as a Chicana, an American woman of Mexican descent (her father was an immigrant). She is an activist for social justice and heads the Institute for MultiRacial Justice in San Francisco and has taught women's studies and ethnic studies in the California State University system. She knows the burden of discrimination from personal experience and from her work and research. As a proponent of bilingual and multicultural education, she sees people like Kimball as the opposition.

◉◉ FOLLOWING THROUGH

If you are mediating among printed arguments, write an analysis based on applying the questions in the Best Practices box on page 289 to two or more arguments. Write out your analysis in list form, as we did in analyzing the differences between Kimball and Martínez.   •

Finding Creative Solutions: Exploring Common Ground

Using critical thinking to mediate means looking closely at what people want and why they want it. It also means seeing the dispute in larger contexts. For example, the dispute over national identity is part of a larger debate between liberals and conservatives over social policy and education.

Mediation cannot reach everyone. Some people hold extreme views that reason cannot touch. An example would be the professor Kimball cites who predicts that the southwestern United States and northern Mexico will eventually become a new and separate country. Mediation between this person and Kimball is about as likely as President Obama and Osama bin Laden having dinner together. But mediators can bring reasonable people closer together by trying to arrive at creative solutions that appeal to some of the interests and values of all parties.

The ethicist Anthony Weston suggests trying to see conflict in terms of what each side is right about.[3] He points to the debate over saving owls in old-growth forests versus logging interests that employ people. Preserving the environment and endangered species is good, but so is saving jobs. If jobs could be created that use wood in craft-based ways, people could make a living without destroying massive amounts of timber. This solution is possible if the parties cooperate—but not if corporations are deadlocked with radical environmentalists, neither willing to concede anything or give an inch.

Mediators should aim for "win-win" solutions, which resolve conflict by dissolving it. The challenge for the mediator is keeping the high ground and looking for the good and reasonable in what each side wants.

---

[3]Weston, *Practical Companion* 56.

Exploring Common Ground
in the Debate over National Identity

To find solutions for the national identity–multiculturalism dispute, we used our list of questions for understanding difference to find interests and values Kimball and Martínez might share or be persuaded to share. Here, in sum, is what we found.

Both want Americans to know their history. Kimball is right. It is a disgrace that college students cannot recognize a famous phrase from the Gettysburg Address. But they need to know that *and* the relevance of Harriet Tubman to those words. Martínez is right also that history should not be propaganda for one view of events. The history of all nations is a mix of good and bad.

Neither Kimball nor Martínez wants a large population of second-class citizens, living in isolated poverty, not speaking English, not seeing themselves as Americans, and not having a say in the democratic process. Martínez's multiculturalism would "break down divisions among peoples of color by revealing common experiences and histories of cooperation" with the goal of "social equity and democracy." She would be more likely, however, to achieve her goal if she considered white men and women *as participants* in this multicultural discussion. To exclude whites keeps people of color where they too often are—on the margins, left out. Kimball needs to be reminded that failure to assimilate is not typically a choice. As in the past, assimilation works only when educational and economic opportunities exist. Kimball needs to look into solutions to the problem of poverty among immigrants.

There is agreement too on the need for a national identity. Martínez calls for "a new identity." But asking what culture should provide it is the wrong question. Concentrating on the values themselves will help everyone see that most values are shared across races and cultures. For example, Martínez takes Anglo-Protestant culture as competitive, not cooperative. We need to recall that early Protestant settlers also valued community. The Puritans tried to establish utopian communities devoted to charity. Kimball's "Protestant" work ethic can be found in every ethnic group—for example, in the predominantly Catholic Mexican laborers who do backbreaking work in agriculture and construction.

Finally, what agreement could be reached about assimilation? Kimball suggests that immigrants follow Justice Louis Brandeis's advice—adopting "the clothes, the manners, and the customs generally prevailing here." But would such advice mean that what "prevails" here is based in Protestantism and Anglo-Saxon culture? A more realistic idea of "Americanization" comes from our third writer, Bharati Mukherjee, who suggests in her mediatory essay that "assimilation" is a two-way transformation, with immigrants and mainstream culture interacting, influencing each other. Such a conception *requires* both the preservation of tradition Kimball wants and the respect for diversity Martínez wants.

◎◎ FOLLOWING THROUGH

Either in list form or as an informal exploratory essay, find areas of agreement between the various positions you have been analyzing. End your list or essay with a summary of a position that all sides might accept.   •

THE MEDIATORY ESSAY

The common human tendency in argument is to polarize—to see conflict as "us" versus "them." That is why mediation is necessary: to move beyond polarized thinking. An example of mediation in the multiculturalism debate appears below. The essay's author is the novelist Bharati Mukherjee. She was born into a wealthy family in Calcutta but became an American citizen. She is now Distinguished Professor of English at the University of California at Berkeley.

There is no single model for a mediatory essay. In this case, Mukherjee's essay mediates by making a case against both radical extremes, one way of seeking to bring people together on the remaining middle ground.

Beyond Multiculturalism:
A Two-Way Transformation

BHARATI MUKHERJEE

1   The United States exists as a sovereign nation with its officially stated Constitution, its economic and foreign policies, its demarcated, patrolled boundaries. "America," however, exists as image or idea, as dream or nightmare, as romance or plague, constructed by discrete individual fantasies, and shaded by collective paranoias and mythologies.

2   I am a naturalized U.S. citizen with a certificate of citizenship; more importantly, I am an American for whom "America" is the stage for the drama of self-transformation. I see American culture as a culture of dreamers, who believe material shape (which is not the same as materialism) can be given to dreams. They believe that one's station in life—poverty, education, family background—does not determine one's fate. They believe in the reversal of omens; early failures do not spell inevitable disaster. Outsiders can triumph on merit. All of this happens against the backdrop of the familiar vicissitudes of American life.

3   I first came to the United States—to the state of Iowa, to be precise—on a late summer evening nearly thirty-three years ago. I flew into a placid, verdant airport in Iowa City on a commercial airliner, ready to fulfill the goals written out in a large, lined notebook for me by my guiltlessly patriarchal father. Those goals were unambiguous: I was to spend two years studying Creative Writing at Paul Engle's unique Writers Workshop; then I was to marry the perfect Bengali bridegroom selected by my father and live out the rest of a contented, predictable life in the city of my birth, Calcutta. In 1961, I was a shy, pliant, well-mannered, dutiful young daughter from a very privileged, traditional, mainstream Hindu family that believed women should be

protected and provided for by their fathers, husbands, sons, and it did not once occur to me that I might have goals of my own, quite distinct from those specified for me by my father. I certainly did not anticipate then that, over the next three decades, Iowans—who seemed to me so racially and culturally homogeneous—would be forced to shudder through the violent paroxysms of a collective identity in crisis.

4   When I was growing up in Calcutta in the fifties, I heard no talk of "identity crisis"—communal or individual. The concept itself—of a person not knowing who she or he was—was unimaginable in a hierarchical, classification-obsessed society. One's identity was absolutely fixed, derived from religion, caste, patrimony, and mother tongue. A Hindu Indian's last name was designed to announce his or her forefathers' caste and place of origin. A Mukherjee could *only* be a Brahmin from Bengal. Indian tradition forbade inter-caste, inter-language, inter-ethnic marriages. Bengali tradition discouraged even emigration; to remove oneself from Bengal was to "pollute" true culture.

5   Until the age of eight, I lived in a house crowded with forty or fifty relatives. We lived together because we were "family," bonded by kinship, though kinship was interpreted in flexible enough terms to include, when necessary, men, women, children who came from the same *desh*—which is the Bengali word for "homeland"— as had my father and grandfather. I was who I was because I was Dr. Sudhir Lal Mukherjee's daughter, because I was a Hindu Brahmin, because I was Bengali-speaking, and because my *desh* was an East Bengal village called Faridpur. I was encouraged to think of myself as indistinguishable from my dozen girl cousins. Identity was viscerally connected with ancestral soil and family origins. I was first a Mukherjee, then a Bengali Brahmin, and only then an Indian.

6   Deep down I knew, of course, that I was not quite like my girl cousins. Deeper down, I was sure that pride in the purity of one's culture has a sinister underside. As a child I had witnessed bloody religious riots between Muslims and Hindus, and violent language riots between Bengalis and Biharis. People kill for culture, and die of hunger. Language, race, religion, blood, myth, history, national codes, and manners have all been used, in India, in the United States, are being used in Bosnia and Rwanda even today, to enforce terror, to "otherize," to murder.

7   I do not know what compelled my strong-willed and overprotective father to risk sending us, his three daughters, to school in the United States, a country he had not visited. In Calcutta, he had insisted on sheltering us from danger and temptation by sending us to girls-only schools, and by providing us with chaperones, chauffeurs, and bodyguards.

8   The Writers Workshop in a quonset hut in Iowa City was my first experience of coeducation. And after not too long, I fell in love with a fellow student named Clark Blaise, an American of Canadian origin, and impulsively married him during a lunch break in a lawyer's office above a coffeeshop.

9   That impulsive act cut me off forever from the rules and ways of upper-middle-class life in Bengal, and hurled me precipitously into a New World life of scary improvisations and heady explorations. Until my lunchtime wedding, I had seen myself as an Indian foreign student, a transient in the United States. The five-minute ceremony in the lawyer's office had changed me into a permanent transient.

10   Over the last three decades the important lesson that I have learned is that in this era of massive diasporic movements, honorable survival requires resilience, curiosity, and compassion, a letting go of rigid ideals about the purity of inherited culture.

11   The first ten years into marriage, years spent mostly in my husband's *desh* of Canada, I thought myself an expatriate Bengali permanently stranded in North America because of a power surge of destiny or of desire. My first novel, *The Tiger's Daughter,* embodies the loneliness I felt but could not acknowledge, even to myself, as I negotiated the no-man's-land between the country of my past and the continent of my present. Shaped by memory, textured with nostalgia for a class and culture I had abandoned, this novel quite naturally became my expression of the *expatriate consciousness.*

12   It took me a decade of painful introspection to put the smothering tyranny of nostalgia into perspective, and to make the transition from expatriate to immigrant. I have found my way back to the United States after a fourteen-year stay in Canada. The transition from foreign student to U.S. citizen, from detached onlooker to committed immigrant, has not been easy.

13   The years in Canada were particularly harsh. Canada is a country that officially— and proudly—resists the policy and process of cultural fusion. For all its smug rhetoric about "cultural mosaic," Canada refuses to renovate its national self-image to include its changing complexion. It is a New World country with Old World concepts of a fixed, exclusivist national identity. And all through the seventies when I lived there, it was a country without a Bill of Rights or its own Constitution. Canadian official rhetoric designated me, as a citizen of non-European origin, one of the "visible minority" who, even though I spoke the Canadian national languages of English and French, was straining "the absorptive capacity" of Canada. Canadians of color were routinely treated as "not real" Canadians. In fact, when a terrorist bomb, planted in an Air India jet on Canadian soil, blew up after leaving Montreal, killing 329 passengers, 90 percent of whom were Canadians of Indian origin, the prime minister of Canada at the time, Brian Mulroney, cabled the Indian prime minister to offer Canada's condolences for India's loss, exposing the Eurocentricity of the "mosaic" policy of immigration.

14   In private conversations, some Canadian ambassadors and External Affairs officials have admitted to me that the creation of the Ministry of Multiculturalism in the seventies was less an instrument for cultural tolerance, and more a vote-getting strategy to pacify ethnic European constituents who were alienated by the rise of Quebec separatism and the simultaneous increase of non-white immigrants.

15   The years of race-related harassments in a Canada without a Constitution have politicized me, and deepened my love of the ideals embedded in the American Bill of Rights.

16   I take my American citizenship very seriously. I am a voluntary immigrant. I am not an economic refugee, and not a seeker of political asylum. I am an American by choice, and not by the simple accident of birth. I have made emotional, social, and political commitments to this country. I have earned the right to think of myself as an American.

17 But in this blood-splattered decade, questions such as who is an American and what is American culture are being posed with belligerence and being answered with violence. We are witnessing an increase in physical, too often fatal, assaults on Asian Americans. An increase in systematic "dot-busting" of Indo-Americans in New Jersey, xenophobic immigrant-baiting in California, minority-on-minority violence during the south-central Los Angeles revolution.

18 America's complexion is browning daily. Journalists' surveys have established that whites are losing their clear majority status in some states, and have already lost it in New York and California. A recent *Time* magazine poll indicated that 60 percent of Americans favor limiting *legal* immigration. Eighty percent of Americans polled favor curbing the entry of undocumented aliens. U.S. borders are too extensive and too porous to be adequately policed. Immigration, by documented and undocumented aliens, is less affected by the U.S. Immigration and Naturalization Service, and more by wars, ethnic genocides, famines in the emigrant's own country.

19 Every sovereign nation has a right to formulate its immigration policy. In this decade of continual, large-scale diasporic movements, it is imperative that we come to some agreement about who "we" are now that the community includes oldtimers, newcomers, many races, languages, and religions; about what our expectations of happiness and strategies for its pursuit are; and what our goals are for the nation.

20 Scapegoating of immigrants has been the politicians' easy instant remedy. Hate speeches fill auditoria, and bring in megabucks for those demagogues willing to profit from stirring up racial animosity.

21 The hysteria against newcomers is only minimally generated by the downturn in our economy. The panic, I suspect, is unleashed by a fear of the "other," the fear of what Daniel Stein, executive director of the Federation for American Immigration Reform, and a champion of closed borders, is quoted as having termed "cultural transmogrification."

22 The debate about American culture has to date been monopolized by rabid Eurocentrists and ethnocentrists; the rhetoric has been flamboyantly divisive, pitting a phantom "us" against a demonized "them." I am here to launch a new discourse, to reconstitute the hostile, biology-derived "us" versus "them" communities into a new *consensual* community of "we."

23 All countries view themselves by their ideals. Indians idealize, as well they should, the cultural continuum, the inherent value system of India, and are properly incensed when foreigners see nothing but poverty, intolerance, ignorance, strife, and injustice. Americans see themselves as the embodiments of liberty, openness, and individualism, even when the world judges them for drugs, crime, violence, bigotry, militarism, and homelessness. I was in Singapore when the media was very vocal about the case of an American teenager sentenced to caning for having allegedly vandalized cars. The overwhelming local sentiment was that caning Michael Fay would deter local youths from being tempted into "Americanization," meaning into gleefully breaking the law.

24 Conversely, in Tavares, Florida, an ardently patriotic school board has legislated that middle school teachers be required to instruct their students that American

culture—meaning European-American culture—is inherently "superior to other foreign or historic cultures." The sinister, or at least misguided, implication is that American culture has not been affected by the American Indian, African American, Latin American, and Asian American segments of its population.

25 The idea of "America" as a nation has been set up in opposition to the tenet that a nation is a collection of like-looking, like-speaking, like-worshiping people. Our nation is unique in human history. We have seen very recently, in a Germany plagued by anti-foreigner frenzy, how violently destabilizing the traditional concept of nation can be. In Europe, each country is, in a sense, a tribal homeland. Therefore, the primary criterion for nationhood in Europe is homogeneity of culture, and race, and religion. And that has contributed to blood-soaked balkanization in the former Yugoslavia and the former Soviet Union.

26 All European Americans, or their pioneering ancestors, gave up an easy homogeneity in their original countries for a new idea of Utopia. What we have going for us in the 1990s is the exciting chance to share in the making of a new American culture, rather than the coerced acceptance of either the failed nineteenth-century model of "melting pot" or the Canadian model of the "multicultural mosaic."

27 The "mosaic" implies a contiguity of self-sufficient, utterly distinct culture. "Multiculturalism" has come to imply the existence of a central culture, ringed by peripheral cultures. The sinister fallout of official multiculturalism and of professional multiculturalists is the establishment of one culture as the norm and the rest as aberrations. Multiculturalism emphasizes the differences between racial heritages. This emphasis on the differences has too often led to the dehumanization of the different. Dehumanization leads to discrimination. And discrimination can ultimately lead to genocide.

28 We need to alert ourselves to the limitations and the dangers of those discourses that reinforce an "us" versus "them" mentality. We need to protest any official rhetoric or demagoguery that marginalizes on a race-related and/or religion-related basis any segment of our society. I want to discourage the retention of cultural memory if the aim of that retention is cultural balkanization. I want to sensitize you to think of culture and nationhood *not* as an uneasy aggregate of antagonistic "them" and "us," but as a constantly re-forming, transmogrifying "we."

29 In this diasporic age, one's biological identity may not be the only one. Erosions and accretions come with the act of emigration. The experiences of violent unhousing from a biological "homeland" and rehousing in an adopted "homeland" that is not always welcoming to its dark-complected citizens have tested me as a person, and made me the writer I am today.

30 I choose to describe myself on my own terms, that is, as an American without hyphens. It is to sabotage the politics of hate and the campaigns of revenge spawned by Eurocentric patriots on the one hand and the professional multiculturalists on the other, that I describe myself as an "American" rather than as an "Asian-American." Why is it that hyphenization is imposed only on non-white Americans? And why is it that only non-white citizens are "problematized" if they choose to

describe themselves on their own terms? My outspoken rejection of hyphenization is my lonely campaign to obliterate categorizing the cultural landscape into a "center" and its "peripheries." To reject hyphenization is to demand that the nation deliver the promises of the American Dream and the American Constitution to *all* its citizens. I want nothing less than to invent a new vocabulary that demands, and obtains, an equitable power-sharing for all members of the American community.

31   But my self-empowering refusal to be "otherized" and "objectified" has come at tremendous cost. My rejection of hyphenization has been deliberately misrepresented as "race treachery" by some India-born, urban, upper-middle-class Marxist "green card holders" with lucrative chairs on U.S. campuses. These academics strategically position themselves as self-appointed spokespersons for their ethnic communities, and as guardians of the "purity" of ethnic cultures. At the same time, though they reside permanently in the United States and participate in the capitalist economy of this nation, they publicly denounce American ideals and institutions.

32   They direct their rage at me because, as a U.S. citizen, I have invested in the present and the future rather than in the expatriate's imagined homeland. They condemn me because I acknowledge erosion of memory as a natural result of emigration; because I count that erosion as net gain rather than as loss; and because I celebrate racial and cultural "mongrelization." I have no respect for these expatriate fence-straddlers who, even while competing fiercely for tenure and promotion within the U.S. academic system, glibly equate all evil in the world with the United States, capitalism, colonialism, and corporate and military expansionism. I regard the artificial retentions of "pure race" and "pure culture" as dangerous, reactionary illusions fostered by the Eurocentric and the ethnocentric empire builders within the academy. I fear still more the politics of revenge preached from pulpits by some minority demagogues. . . .

33   As a writer, my literary agenda begins by acknowledging that America has transformed *me.* It does not end until I show that I (and the hundreds of thousands of recent immigrants like me) am minute by minute transforming America. The transformation is a two-way process; it affects both the individual and the national cultural identity. The end result of immigration, then, is this two-way transformation: that's my heartfelt message.

34   Others often talk of diaspora, of arrival as the end of the process. They talk of arrival in the context of loss, the loss of communal memory and the erosion of an intact ethnic culture. They use words like "erosion" and "loss" in alarmist ways. I want to talk of arrival as gain. . . .

35   What excites me is that we have the chance to retain those values we treasure from our original cultures, but we also acknowledge that the outer forms of those values are likely to change. In the Indian American community, I see a great deal of guilt about the inability to hang on to "pure culture." Parents express rage or despair at their U.S.-born children's forgetting of, or indifference to, some aspects of Indian culture. Of those parents, I would ask: What is it we have lost if our children are acculturating into the culture in which we are living? Is it so terrible that our children are discovering or inventing homelands for themselves? Some first-generation Indo-Americans, embittered by overt anti-Asian racism and by

unofficial "glass ceilings," construct a phantom more-Indian-than-Indians-in-India identity as defense against marginalization. Of them I would ask: Why not get actively involved in fighting discrimination through protests and lawsuits?

36   I prefer that we forge a national identity that is born of our acknowledgment of the steady de-Europeanization of the U.S. population; that constantly synthesizes—fuses—the disparate cultures of our country's residents; and that provides a new, sustaining, and unifying national creed.

Analyzing Mukherjee's Essay

Let's see what we can learn about how to appeal to audiences in mediatory essays. We'll look at ethos (how Mukherjee projects good character), pathos (how she arouses emotions favorable to her case), and logos (how she wins assent through good reasoning).

Ethos: Earning the Respect of Both Sides

Mediatory essays are not typically as personal as this one. But the author is in an unusual position, which makes the personal relevant. By speaking in the first person and telling her story, Mukherjee seeks the goodwill of people on both sides. She presents herself as patriotic, a foreigner who has assimilated to American ways, clearly appealing to those on Kimball's side. But she is also a "person of color," who's been "tested" by racial prejudices in the United States, clearly appealing to Martínez's side. She creates negative ethos for the radical extremists in the identity debate, depicting them as lacking morality and/or honesty. That is why she cites the violence committed by both whites and minorities, the scapegoating by politicians pandering to voter fears, the hypocrisy of professors who live well in America while denouncing its values. She associates her own position with words like *commitment, compassion, consensus, equality,* and *unity.*

By including her own experiences in India and Canada and her references to Bosnia, Rwanda, Germany, and the former Soviet Union, Mukherjee is able to place this American debate in a larger context—parts of the world in which national identity incites war and human rights violations.

Pathos: Using Emotion to Appeal to Both Sides

Appealing to the right emotions can help to move parties in conflict to the higher ground of consensus. Mukherjee displays a range of emotions, including pride, anger, and compassion. In condemning the extremes on both sides, her tone becomes heated. She uses highly charged words like *rabid, demagogues, scapegoaters, fence-straddlers,* and *reactionaries* to describe them. Her goal is to distance the members of her audience who are reasonable from those who are not, so her word choice is appropriate and effective.

Patriotism is obviously emotional. Mukherjee's repeated declaration of devotion to her adopted country stirs audience pride. So does the contrast with India and Canada and the celebrating of individual freedom in the United States.

Her own story of arrival, nostalgia, and transformation arouses compassion and respect because it shows that assimilation is not easy. She understands the reluctance of Indian parents to let their children change. This shows her ability to empathize.

Finally, she appeals through hope and optimism. Twice she describes the consensus she proposes as *exciting*—and also fresh, new, vital, alive—in contrast to the rigid and inflexible ethnic purists.

Logos: Integrating Values of Both Sides

Mukherjee's thesis is that the opposing sides in the national identity debate are two sides of the wrong coin: the mistaken regard for ethnic purity. Making an issue of one's ethnicity, whether it be Anglo, Chicano, Indian-American, or whatever, is not a means to harmony and equality. Instead, America needs a unifying national identity that blends the ever-changing mix of races and cultures that make up our population.

Mukherjee offers reasons to oppose ethnic "purity":

Violence and wars result when people divide according to ethnic and religious differences. It creates an "us" versus "them" mentality.

The multicultural Canadian program created second-class, marginal populations.

Hyphenization in America makes a problem out of non-whites in the population.

We said that mediation looks for the good in each side and tries to show what they have in common. Mukherjee shows that her solution offers gains for both sides, a "win-win" situation. She concedes that her solution would mean some loss of "cultural memory" for immigrants, but these losses are offset by the following gains:

The United States would be closer to the strong and unified nation that Kimball wants because *everyone's* contributions would be appreciated.

The cultural barriers between minorities would break down, as Martínez wants. This would entail speaking to each other in English, but being free to maintain diverse cultures at home.

The barriers between "Americans" and hyphenated Americans would break down, as both Kimball and Martínez want. In other words, there would be assimilation, as Kimball wants, but not assimilation to one culture, which Martínez strongly resists.

By removing the need to prove one's own culture superior, we could all recognize the faults in our past as well as the good things. We would have no schools teaching either the superiority or the inferiority of any culture.

Emphasizing citizenship instead of ethnicity is a way of standing up for and demanding equal rights and equal opportunity, helping to bring about the social justice and equality Martínez seeks.

> The new identity would be "sustaining," avoiding future conflicts
>   because it would adapt to change.

Mukherjee's essay mediates by showing that a definition of America based on either one ethnic culture or many ethnic cultures is not satisfactory. By dropping ethnicity as a prime concern, both sides can be better off and freer in pursuit of happiness and success.

QUESTIONS FOR DISCUSSION

Look over the essays by Elizabeth Martínez and Roger Kimball. Do you think either of them would find Bharati Mukherjee's essay persuasive? What does Mukherjee say that might cause either of them to relax their positions about American identity? Do you think any further information might help to bring either side to Mukherjee's consensus position? For example, Kimball mentions the "Letter from an American Farmer" by de Crèvecoeur, who describes Americans as a new "race" of blended nationalities, leaving behind their ties and allegiances to former lands. How is Crèvecouer's idea of the "new race" similar to Mukherjee's?

Writing a Mediatory Essay

Prewriting

In preparing to write a mediatory essay, you should work through the steps described on pages 286–293. Prepare briefs of the various conflicting positions, and note areas of disagreement; think hard about the differing interests of the conflicting parties, and respond to the questions about difference on page 289.

Give some thought to each party's background—age, race, gender, and so forth—and how it might contribute to his or her viewpoint on the issue.

Describe the conflict in its full complexity, not just its polar opposites. Try to find the good values in each position: You may be able to see that people's real interests are not as far apart as they might seem. You may be able to find common ground.

At this point in the prewriting process, think of some solutions that would satisfy at least some of the interests on all sides. It might be necessary for you to do some additional research. What do you think any of the opposing parties might want to know more about in order to accept your solution?

Finally, write up a clear statement of your solution. Can you explain how your solution appeals to the interests of all sides?

Drafting

There is no set form for the mediatory essay. As with any argument, the important thing is to have a plan for arranging your points and to provide clear signals to your readers. One logical way to organize a mediatory essay is in three parts:

> *Overview of the conflict.* Describe the conflict and the opposing
>   positions in the introductory paragraphs.

Discussion of differences underlying the conflict. Here your goal is to make all sides more sympathetic to one another and to sort out the important real interests that must be addressed by the solution.

Proposed solution. Here you make a case for your compromise position, giving reasons why it should be acceptable to all—that is, showing that it does serve at least some of their interests.

Revising

When revising a mediatory essay, you should look for the usual problems of organization and development that you would be looking for in any essay to convince or persuade. Be sure that you have inquired carefully and fairly into the conflict and that you have clearly presented the cases for all sides, including your proposed solution. At this point, you also need to consider how well you have used the persuasive appeals:

The appeal to character. Think about what kind of character you have projected as a mediator. Have you maintained neutrality? Do you model open-mindedness and genuine concern for the sensitivities of all sides?

The appeal to emotions. To arouse sympathy and empathy, which are needed in mediation, you should take into account the emotional appeals discussed on pages 299–300. Your mediatory essay should be a moving argument for understanding and overcoming difference.

The appeal through style. As in persuasion, you should put the power of language to work. Pay attention to concrete word choice, striking metaphors, and phrases that stand out because of repeated sounds and rhythms.

www.mhhe.com/**crusius**

For help editing your essay, go to:

Editing

For suggestions about editing and proofreading, see Appendix A.

AN ESSAY ARGUING TO MEDIATE

The following mediatory essay was written by Angi Grellhesl, a first-year student at Southern Methodist University. Her essay examines opposing views on the institution of speech codes at various U.S. colleges and its effect on freedom of speech.

Mediating the Speech Code Controversy

ANGI GRELLHESL

1   The right to free speech has raised many controversies over the years. Explicit lyrics in rap music and marches by the Ku Klux Klan are just some examples that test the power of the First Amendment. Now, students and administrators are questioning if, in fact, free speech ought to be limited on university campuses. Many schools have instituted speech codes to protect specified groups from harassing speech.

2   Both sides in the debate, the speech code advocates and the free speech advocates, have presented their cases in recent books and articles. Columnist Nat Hentoff argues strongly against the speech codes, his main reason being that the codes violate students' First Amendment rights. Hentoff links the right to free speech with the values of higher education. In support, he quotes Yale president Benno Schmidt, who says, "Freedom of thought must be Yale's central commitment. . . . [U]niversities cannot censor or suppress speech, no matter how obnoxious in content, without violating their justification for existence . . . " (qtd. in Hentoff 223). Another reason Hentoff offers against speech codes is that universities must teach students to defend themselves in preparation for the real world, where such codes cannot shield them. Finally, he suggests that most codes are too vaguely worded; students may not even know they are violating the codes (216).

3   Two writers in favor of speech codes are Richard Perry and Patricia Williams. They see speech codes as a necessary and fair limitation on free speech. Perry and Williams argue that speech codes promote multicultural awareness, making students more sensitive to the differences that are out there in the real world. These authors do not think that the codes violate First Amendment rights, and they are suspicious of the motives of those who say they do. As Perry and Williams put it, those who feel free speech rights are being threatened "are apparently unable to distinguish between a liberty interest on the one hand and, on the other, a quite specific interest in being able to spout racist, sexist, and homophobic epithets completely unchallenged—without, in other words, the terrible inconvenience of feeling bad about it" (228).

4   Perhaps if both sides trusted each other a little more, they could see that their goals are not contradictory. Everyone agrees that students' rights should be protected. Hentoff wishes to ensure that students have the right to speak their minds. He and others on his side are concerned about freedom. Defenders of the codes argue that students have the right not to be harassed, especially while they are getting an education. They are concerned about opportunity. Would either side really deny that the other's goal had value?

5   Also, both sides want to create the best possible educational environment. Here the difference rests on the interpretation of what benefits the students. Is the best environment one most like the real world, where prejudice and harassment occur? Or does the university have an obligation to provide an atmosphere where potential victims can thrive and participate freely without intimidation?

www.mhhe.com/**crusius**

For many additional examples of student writing, go to:

Writing

6   I think it is possible to reach a solution that everyone can agree on. Most citizens want to protect constitutional rights; but they also agree that those rights have limitations, the ultimate limit being when one person infringes on the rights of others to live in peace. All sides should agree that a person ought to be able to speak out about his or her convictions, values, and beliefs. Most people can see a difference between that protected speech and the kind that is intended to harass and intimidate. For example, there is a clear difference between expressing one's view that Jews are mistaken in not accepting Christ as the son of God, on the one hand, and yelling anti-Jewish threats at a particular person on the other. Could a code not be worded in such a way as to distinguish between these two kinds of speech?

7   Also, I don't believe either side would want the university to be an artificial world. Codes should not attempt to ensure that no one is criticized or even offended. Students should not be afraid to say controversial things. But universities do help to shape the future of the real world, so shouldn't they at least take a stand against harassment? Can a code be worded that would protect free speech and prevent harassment?

8   The current speech code at Southern Methodist University is a compromise that ought to satisfy free speech advocates and speech code advocates. It prohibits hate speech at the same time that it protects an individual's First Amendment rights.

9   First, it upholds the First Amendment by including a section that reads, "[D]ue to the University's commitment to freedom of speech and expression, harassment is more than mere insensitivity or offensive conduct which creates an uncomfortable situation for certain members of the community" (*Peruna* 92). The code therefore should satisfy those, like Hentoff, who place a high value on the basic rights our nation was built upon. Secondly, whether or not there is a need for protection, the current code protects potential victims from hate speech or "any words or acts deliberately designed to disregard the safety or rights of another, and which intimidate, degrade, demean, threaten, haze, or otherwise interfere with another person's rightful action" (*Peruna* 92). This part of the code should satisfy those who recognize that some hurts cannot be permitted. Finally, the current code outlines specific acts that constitute harassment: "Physical, psychological, verbal and/or written acts directed toward an individual or group of individuals which rise to the level of 'fighting words' are prohibited" (*Peruna* 92).

10   The SMU code protects our citizens from hurt and from unconstitutional censorship. Those merely taking a position can express it, even if it hurts. On the other hand, those who are spreading hatred will not be protected. Therefore, all sides should respect the code as a safeguard for those who use free speech but a limitation on those who abuse it.

WORKS CITED

Hentoff, Nat. "Speech Codes on the Campus and Problems of Free Speech." *Debating P.C.* Ed. Paul Berman. New York: Bantam, 1992. 215–24.

Perry, Richard, and Patricia Williams. "Freedom of Speech." *Debating P.C.* Ed. Paul Berman. New York: Bantam, 1992. 225–30.

Peruna Express 1993–1994. Dallas: Southern Methodist U, 1993.

CHAPTER SUMMARY

We often must deal as constructively as we can with sharp differences of opinion, where people taking opposing positions seem unable or unwilling to explore ways to reduce or eliminate conflict. Sometimes efforts at mediation fail, no matter how skillful the mediator is. However, as you have seen in this chapter, mediation is possible and can result in agreement on a course of action satisfactory to all parties. Mediating involves understanding the positions of all sides, finding common ground, defusing hostilities among the contending sides, and making a good case for the course of action the mediator advocates. It involves, that is, everything you have learned in this book about using argument to inquire, convince, and persuade.

A Brief Guide to Editing and Proofreading

Editing and proofreading are the final steps in creating a finished piece of writing. Too often, however, these steps are rushed as writers race to meet a deadline. Ideally, you should distinguish between the acts of revising, editing, and proofreading. Because each step requires that you pay attention to something different, you cannot reasonably expect to do them well if you try to do them all at once.

Our suggestions for revising appear in each of Chapters 8–11 on the aims of argument. *Revising* means shaping and developing the whole argument with an eye to audience and purpose; when you revise, you are ensuring that you have accomplished your aim. *Editing,* on the other hand, means making smaller changes within paragraphs and sentences. When you edit, you are thinking about whether your prose will be a pleasure to read. Editing improves the sound and rhythm of your voice. It makes complicated ideas more accessible to readers and usually makes your writing more concise. Finally, *proofreading* means eliminating errors. When you proofread, you correct everything you find that will annoy readers, such as misspellings, punctuation mistakes, and faulty grammar.

In this appendix, we offer some basic advice on what to look for when editing and proofreading. For more detailed help, consult a handbook on grammar and punctuation and a good book on style, such as Joseph Williams's *Ten Lessons in Clarity and Grace* or Richard Lanham's *Revising Prose*. Both of these texts guided our thinking in the advice that follows.

EDITING

Most ideas can be phrased in a number of ways, each of which gives the idea a slightly distinctive twist. Consider the following examples:

In New York City, about 74,000 people die each year.

In New York City, death comes to one in a hundred people each year.

Death comes to one in a hundred New Yorkers each year.

www.mhhe.com/**crusius**

For a wealth of online editing resources, check out the tools grouped under:

Editing

www.mhhe.com/**crusius**

To take a diagnostic test covering editing skills, go to:

Editing > Diagnostic Test

To begin an article on what becomes of the unknown and unclaimed dead in New York, Edward Conlon wrote the final of these three sentences. We can only speculate about the possible variations he considered, but because openings are so crucial, he almost certainly cast these words quite deliberately.

For most writers, such deliberation over matters of style occurs during editing. In this late stage of the writing process, writers examine choices made earlier, perhaps unconsciously, while drafting and revising. They listen to how sentences sound, to patterns of rhythm both within and among sentences. Editing is like an art or craft; it can provide you the satisfaction of knowing you've said something gracefully and effectively. To focus on language this closely, you will need to set aside enough time following the revision step.

In this section, we discuss some things to look for when editing your own writing. Don't forget, though, that editing does not always mean looking for weaknesses. You should also recognize passages that work well just as you wrote them, that you can leave alone or play up more by editing passages that surround them.

Editing for Clarity and Conciseness

Even drafts revised several times may have wordy and awkward passages; these are often places where a writer struggled with uncertainty or felt less than confident about the point being made. Introductions often contain such passages. In editing, you have one more opportunity to clarify and sharpen your ideas.

Express Main Ideas Forcefully

Emphasize the main idea of a sentence by stating it as directly as possible, using the two key sentence parts (*subject* and *verb*) to convey the two key parts of the idea (*agent* and *act*).

As you edit, first look for sentences that state ideas indirectly rather than directly; such sentences may include (1) overuse of the verb *to be* in its various forms (*is, was, will have been,* and so forth), (2) the opening words "There is . . ." or "It is . . . ," (3) strings of prepositional phrases, or (4) many vague nouns. Then ask, "What is my true subject here, and what is that subject's action?" Here is an example of a weak, indirect sentence:

> It is a fact that the effects of pollution are more evident in lower-class neighborhoods than in middle-class ones.

The writer's subject is pollution. What is the pollution's action? Limply, the sentence tells us its "effects" are "evident." The following edited version makes pollution the agent that performs the action of a livelier verb, "fouls." The edited sentence is more specific—without being longer.

> *Pollution* more frequently *fouls* the air, soil, and water of lower-class neighborhoods than of middle-class ones.

Editing Practice   The following passage about a plan for creating low-income housing contains two weak sentences. In this case, the weakness results from wordiness. (Note the overuse of vague nouns and prepositional phrases.) Decide what the true subject is for each sentence, and make that word the subject of the verb. Your edited version should be much shorter.

> As in every program, there will be the presence of a few who abuse the system. However, as in other social programs, the numbers would not be sufficient to justify the rejection of the program on the basis that one person in a thousand will try to cheat.

Choose Carefully between Active and Passive Voice

Active voice and passive voice indicate different relationships between subjects and verbs. As we have noted, ideas are usually clearest when the writer's true subject is also the subject of the verb in the sentence—that is, when it is the agent of the action. In the passive voice, however, the agent of the action appears in the predicate or not at all. Rather than acting as agent, the subject of the sentence *receives* the action of the verb.

www.mhhe.com/**crusius**

For more coverage of voice, go to:

Editing > Verb and Voice Shifts

The following sentence is in the passive voice:

> The air of poor neighborhoods is often fouled by pollution.

There is nothing incorrect about the use of the passive voice in this sentence, and in the context of a whole paragraph, passive voice can be the most emphatic way to make a point. (Here, for example, it allows the word *pollution* to fall at the end of the sentence, a strong position.) But, often, use of the passive voice is not a deliberate choice at all; rather, it's a vague and unspecific way of stating a point.

Consider the following sentences, in which the main verbs have no agents:

> It *is believed* that dumping garbage at sea is not as harmful to the environment as *was* once *thought.*

> Ronald Reagan *was considered* the "Great Communicator."

Who thinks such dumping is not so harmful? environmental scientists? industrial producers? Who considered former president Reagan a great communicator? speech professors? news commentators? Such sentences are clearer when they are written in the active voice:

> Some environmentalists believe that dumping garbage at sea is not as harmful to the environment as they used to think.

> Media commentators considered Ronald Reagan the "Great Communicator."

In editing for the passive voice, look over your verbs. Passive voice is easily recognized because it always contains (1) some form of *to be* as a helping verb and (2) the main verb in its past participle form (which ends in *-ed, -d, -t, -en,* or *-n,* or in some cases may be irregular: *drunk, sung, lain,* and so on).

When you find a sentence phrased in the passive voice, decide who or what is performing the action; the agent may appear after the verb or not at all. Then decide if changing the sentence to the active voice will improve the sentence as well as the surrounding passage.

Editing Practice

1. The following paragraph from a student's argument needs to be edited for emphasis. It is choking with excess nouns and forms of the verb *to be,* some as part of passive constructions. You need not eliminate all passive voice, but do look for wording that is vague and ineffective. Your edited version should be not only stronger but shorter as well.

   Although emergency shelters are needed in some cases (for example, a mother fleeing domestic violence), they are an inefficient means of dealing with the massive numbers of people they are bombarded with each day. The members of a homeless family are in need of a home, not a temporary shelter into which they and others like them are herded, only to be shuffled out when their thirty-day stay is over to make room for the next incoming herd. Emergency shelters would be sufficient if we did not have a low-income housing shortage, but what is needed most at present is an increase in availability of affordable housing for the poor.

2. Select a paragraph of your own writing to edit; focus on using strong verbs and subjects to carry the main idea of your sentences.

Editing for Emphasis

When you edit for emphasis, you make sure that your main ideas stand out so that your reader will take notice. Following are some suggestions to help.

Emphasize Main Ideas by Subordinating Less Important Ones

Subordination refers to distinctions in rank or order of importance. Think of the chain of command at an office: the boss is at the top of the ladder, the middle management is on a lower (subordinate) rung, the support staff is at an even lower rung, and so on.

In writing, subordination means placing less important ideas in less important positions in sentences in order to emphasize the main ideas that should stand out. Writing that lacks subordination treats all ideas equally; each idea may consist of a sentence of its own or may be joined to another idea by a coordinator (*and, but,* and *or*). Such a passage follows with its sentences numbered for reference purposes.

(1) It has been over a century since slavery was abolished and a few decades since lawful, systematic segregation came to an unwilling halt. (2) Truly, blacks have come a long way from the darker days that lasted for more than three centuries. (3) Many blacks have

entered the mainstream, and there is a proportionately large contingent of middle-class blacks. (4) Yet an even greater percentage of blacks are immersed in truly pathetic conditions. (5) The inner-city black poor are enmeshed in devastating socioeconomic problems. (6) Unemployment among inner-city black youths has become much worse than it was even five years ago.

Three main ideas are important here—that blacks have been free for some time, that some have made economic progress, and that others are trapped in poverty—and of these three, the last is probably intended to be the most important. Yet, as we read the passage, these key ideas do not stand out. In fact, each point receives equal emphasis and sounds about the same, with the repeated subject-verb-object syntax. The result seems monotonous, even apathetic, though the writer is probably truly disturbed about the subject. The following edited version, which subordinates some of the points, is more emphatic. We have italicized the main points.

> *Blacks have come a long way* in the century since slavery was abolished and in the decades since lawful, systematic segregation came to an unwilling halt. Yet, although many blacks have entered the mainstream and the middle class, *an even greater percentage is immersed in truly pathetic conditions*. To give just one example of these devastating socioeconomic problems, *unemployment among inner-city black youths is much worse now than it was even five years ago*.

Although different editing choices are possible, this version plays down sentences 1, 3, and 5 in the original so that sentences 2, 4, and 6 stand out.

As you edit, look for passages that sound wordy and flat because all the ideas are expressed with equal weight in the same subject-verb-object pattern. Then single out your most important points, and try out some options for subordinating the less important ones. The key is to put main ideas in main clauses and modifying ideas in modifying clauses or phrases.

Modifying Clauses Like simple sentences, modifying clauses contain a subject and verb. They are formed in two ways: (1) with relative pronouns and (2) with subordinating conjunctions.

Relative pronouns introduce clauses that modify nouns, with the relative pronoun relating the clause to the noun it modifies. There are five relative pronouns: *that, which, who, whose,* and *whom.* The following sentence contains a relative clause:

> Alcohol advertisers are trying to sell a product *that is by its very nature harmful to users.*
>
> —Jason Rath (student)

Relative pronouns may also be implied:

> I have returned the library book [that] *you loaned me.*

Relative pronouns may also be preceded by prepositions, such as *on, in, to,* or *during:*

> Drug hysteria has created an atmosphere *in which civil rights are disregarded.*

Subordinating conjunctions show relationships among ideas. It is impossible to provide a complete list of subordinating conjunctions in this short space, but here are the most common and the kinds of modifying roles they perform:

> To show time: *after, as, before, since, until, when, while*
>
> To show place: *where, wherever*
>
> To show contrast: *although, though, whereas, while*
>
> To show cause and effect: *because, since, so that*
>
> To show condition: *if, unless, whether, provided that*
>
> To show manner: *how, as though*

By introducing it with a subordinating conjunction, you can convert one sentence into a dependent clause that can modify another sentence. Consider the following two versions of the same idea:

> Pain is a state of consciousness, a "mental event." It can never be directly observed.

> *Since pain is a state of consciousness, a "mental event,"* it can never be directly observed.
>
> —Peter Singer, *"Animal Liberation"*

Modifying Phrases Unlike clauses, phrases do not have a subject and a verb. Prepositional phrases and infinitive phrases are most likely already in your repertoire of modifiers. (Consult a handbook if you need to review these.) Here, we remind you of two other useful types of phrases: (1) participial phrases and (2) appositives.

Participial phrases modify nouns. Participles are created from verbs, so it is not surprising that the two varieties represent two verb tenses. The first is present participles ending in *-ing:*

> *Hoping to eliminate harassment on campus,* many universities have tried to institute codes for speech and behavior.

> The desperate Haitians fled here in boats, *risking all.*
>
> —Carmen Hazan-Cohen (student)

The second is past participles ending in *-ed, -en, -d, -t,* or *-n:*

> Women themselves became a resource, *acquired by men much as the land was acquired by men.*
>
> —Gerda Lerner

Linked more to the Third World and Asia than to the Europe of America's racial and cultural roots, Los Angeles and Southern California will enter the 21st century as a multi-racial and multicultural society.

—Ryszard Kapuscinski

Notice that modifying phrases should immediately precede the nouns they modify.

An *appositive* is a noun or noun phrase that restates another noun, usually in a more specific way. Appositives can be highly emphatic, but more often they are tucked into the middle of a sentence or added to the end, allowing a subordinate idea to be slipped in. When used like this, appositives are usually set off with commas:

Rick Halperin, *a professor at Southern Methodist University,* noted that Ted Bundy's execution cost Florida taxpayers over six million dollars.

—Diane Miller (student)

Editing Practice

1. Edit the following passage as needed for emphasis, clarity, and conciseness, using subordinate clauses, relative clauses, participial phrases, appositives, and any other options that occur to you. If some parts are effective as they are, leave them alone.

    The monetary implications of drug legalization are not the only reason it is worth consideration. There is reason to believe that the United States would be a safer place to live if drugs were legalized. A large amount of what the media has named "drug-related" violence is really prohibition-related violence. Included in this are random shootings and murders associated with black-market transactions. Estimates indicate that at least 40 percent of all property crime in the United States is committed by drug users so they can maintain their habits. That amounts to a total of 4 million crimes per year and $7.5 billion in stolen property. Legalizing drugs would be a step toward reducing this wave of crime.

2. Edit a paragraph of your own writing with an eye to subordinating less important ideas through the use of modifying phrases and clauses.

Vary Sentence Length and Pattern

Even when read silently, your writing has a sound. If your sentences are all about the same length (typically fifteen to twenty words) and all structured according to a subject-verb-object pattern, they will roll along with the monotonous rhythm of an assembly line. Obviously, one solution to this problem is to open some of your sentences with modifying phrases and clauses, as we discuss in the previous section. Here we offer some other strategies, all of which add emphasis by introducing something unexpected.

1. Use a short sentence after several long ones.

   [A] population's general mortality is affected by a great many factors over which doctors and hospitals have little influence. For those diseases and injuries for which modern medicine can affect the outcome, however, which country the patient lives in really matters. Life expectancy is not the same among developed countries for premature babies, for children born with spina bifida, or for people who have cancer, a brain tumor, heart disease, or chronic renal failure. *Their chances of survival are best in the United States.*

   —John Goodman

2. Interrupt a sentence.

   The position of women in that hippie counterculture was, *as a young black male leader preached succinctly,* "prone."

   —Betty Friedan

   Symbols and myths—*when emerging uncorrupted from human experience*—are precious. Then it is the poetic voice and vision that informs and infuses—*the poet-warrior's, the prophet-seer's, the dreamer's*—reassuring us that truth is as real as falsehood. And ultimately stronger.

   —Ossie Davis

3. Use an intentional sentence fragment. The concluding fragment in the previous passage by Ossie Davis is a good example.

4. Invert the order of subject-verb-object.

   Further complicating negotiations is the difficulty of obtaining relevant financial statements.

   —Regina Herzlinger

   This creature, with scarcely two thirds of man's cranial capacity, was a fire user. Of what it meant to him beyond warmth and shelter, we know nothing; with what rites, ghastly or benighted, it was struck or maintained, no word remains.

   —Loren Eiseley

Use Special Effects for Emphasis

Especially in persuasive argumentation, you will want to make some of your points in deliberately dramatic ways. Remember that just as the crescendos stand out in music because the surrounding passages are less intense, so the special effects work best in rhetoric when you use them sparingly.

Repetition Deliberately repeating words, phrases, or sentence patterns has the effect of building up to a climactic point. Here is an example from the conclusion of an argument linking women's rights with environmental reforms:

> Environmental justice goes much further than environmental protection, a passive and paternalistic phrase. *Justice requires that* industrial nations pay back the environmental debt incurred in building their wealth by using less of nature's resources. *Justice prescribes that* governments stop siting hazardous waste facilities in cash-poor rural and urban neighborhoods and now in the developing world. *Justice insists that* the subordination of women and nature by men is not only a hazard; it is a crime. *Justice reminds us that* the Earth does not belong to us; even when we "own" a piece of it, we belong to the Earth.
>
> —H. Patricia Hynes

Paired Coordinators Coordinators are conjunctions that pair words, word groups, and sentences in a way that gives them equal emphasis and that also shows a relationship between them, such as contrast, consequence, or addition. In grade school, you may have learned the coordinators through the mnemonic *FANBOYS,* standing for *for, and, nor, but, or, yet, so.*

Paired coordinators emphasize the relationship between coordinated elements; the first coordinator signals that a corresponding coordinator will follow. Some paired coordinators are:

both _____ and _____
not _____ but _____
not only _____ but also _____
either _____ or _____
neither _____ nor _____

The key to effective paired coordination is to keep the words that follow the marker words as grammatically similar as possible. Pair nouns with nouns, verbs with verbs, prepositional phrases with prepositional phrases, and whole sentences with whole sentences. (Think of paired coordination as a variation on repetition.) Here are some examples:

> Feminist anger, or any form of social outrage, is dismissed breezily—*not* because it lacks substance *but* because it lacks "style."
>
> —Susan Faludi

> Alcohol ads that emphasize "success" in the business and social worlds are useful examples *not only* of how advertisers appeal to people's envy *but also* of how ads perpetuate gender stereotypes.
>
> —Jason Rath (student)

Emphatic Appositives While an appositive (a noun or noun phrase that restates another noun) can subordinate an idea, it can also emphasize an idea if it is placed at the beginning or the end of a sentence, where it will command attention. Here are some examples:

> *The poorest nation in the Western hemisphere,* Haiti is populated by six million people, many of whom cannot obtain adequate food, water, or shelter.
>
> —Sneed B. Collard III

> [Feminists] made a simple, though serious, ideological error when they applied the same political rhetoric to their own situation as women versus men: *too literal an analogy with class warfare, racial oppression.*
>
> —Betty Friedan

Note that at the end of a sentence, an appositive may be set off with a colon or a dash.

Emphatic Word Order The opening and closing positions of a sentence are high-profile spots, not to be wasted on weak words. The following sentence, for example, begins weakly with the filler phrase "there are":

> *There are* several distinctions, all of them false, that are commonly made between rape and date rape.

A better version would read:

> My opponents make several distinctions between rape and date rape; all of these are false.

Even more important are the final words of every paragraph and the opening and closing of the entire argument.

Editing Practice

1. Select one or two paragraphs from a piece of published writing you have recently read and admired. Be ready to share it with the class, explaining how the writer has crafted the passage to make it work.

2. Take a paragraph or two from one of your previous essays, perhaps even an essay from another course, and edit it to improve clarity, conciseness, and emphasis.

Editing for Coherence

Coherence refers to what some people call the "flow" of writing; writing flows when the ideas connect smoothly, one to the next. In contrast, when writing is incoherent, the reader must work to see how ideas connect and must infer points that the writer, for whatever reason, has left unstated.

Incoherence is a particular problem with writing that contains an abundance of direct or indirect quotations. In using sources, be careful always to lead into the quotation with some words of your own, showing clearly how this new idea connects with what has come before.

Because finding incoherent passages in your own writing can be difficult, ask a friend to read your draft to look for gaps in the presentation of ideas. Here are some additional suggestions for improving coherence.

Move from Old Information to New Information

Coherent writing is easy to follow because the connections between old information and new information are clear. Sentences refer to previously introduced information and set up reader expectations for new information to come. Notice how every sentence fulfills your expectations in the following excerpts from an argument on animal rights by Steven Zak.

> The credibility of the animal-rights viewpoint . . . need not stand or fall with the "marginal human beings" argument.

Next, you would expect to hear why animals do not have to be classed as "marginal human beings"—and you do:

> Lives don't have to be qualitatively the same to be worthy of equal respect.

At this point you might ask upon what else we should base our respect. Zak answers this question in the next sentence:

> One's perception that another life has value comes as much from an appreciation of its uniqueness as from the recognition that it has characteristics that are shared by one's own life.

Not only do these sentences fulfill reader expectations, but each also makes a clear connection by referring specifically to the key idea in the sentence before it, forming an unbroken chain of thought. We have italicized the words that accomplish this linkage and connected them with arrows.

> The credibility of the animal-rights viewpoint . . . need not stand or fall with the *"marginal human beings"* argument.

> Lives don't have to be *qualitatively the same* to be worthy of *equal respect.*

> One's perception that *another life has value* comes as much from an *appreciation of its uniqueness* as from the recognition that it has characteristics that are shared by one's own life.

> One can imagine that the lives of various kinds of animals *differ radically.* . . .

In the following paragraph, reader expectations are not so well fulfilled:

> We are presently witness to the greatest number of homeless families since the Great Depression of the 1930s. The cause of this phenomenon is a shortage of low-income housing. Mothers with children as young as two weeks are forced to live on the street because there is no room for them in homeless shelters.

Although these sentences are all on the subject of homelessness, the second leads us to expect that the third will take up the topic of shortages of low-income housing. Instead, it takes us back to the subject of the first sentence and offers a different cause—no room in the shelters.

Looking for ways to link old information with new information will help you find problems of coherence in your own writing.

Editing Practice

1. In the following paragraph, underline the words or phrases that make the connections back to the previous sentence and forward to the next, as we did earlier with the passage from Zak.

    The affluent, educated, liberated women of the First World, who can enjoy freedoms unavailable to any women ever before, do not feel as free as they want to. And they can no longer restrict to the subconscious their sense that this lack of freedom has something to do with—with apparently frivolous issues, things that really should not matter. Many are ashamed to admit that such trivial concerns—to do with physical appearance, bodies, faces, hair, clothes—matter so much. But in spite of shame, guilt, and denial, more and more women are wondering if it isn't that they are entirely neurotic alone but rather that something important is indeed at stake that has to do with the relationship between female liberation and female beauty.

    —Naomi Wolf

2. The following student paragraph lacks coherence. Read through it, and put a slash (/) between sentences expressing unconnected ideas. You may try to rewrite the paragraph, rearranging sentences and adding ideas to make the connections tighter.

    Students may know what AIDS is and how it is transmitted, but most are not concerned about AIDS and do not perceive themselves to be at risk. But college-age heterosexuals are the number-one high-risk group for this disease (Gray and Sacarino 258). "Students already know about AIDS. Condom distribution, public or not, is not going to help. It just butts into my personal life," said one student surveyed. College is a time for exploration and that includes the discovery of sexual freedom. Students, away from home and free to make their own decisions for maybe the first time in their lives, have a "bigger than life" attitude. The thought of dying is the farthest from their minds. Yet at this point in their lives, they are most in need of this information.

Use Transitions to Show Relationships between Ideas

Coherence has to be built into a piece of writing; as we discussed earlier, the ideas between sentences must first cohere. However, sometimes readers need help in making the transition from one idea to the next, so you must provide signposts to help them see the connections more readily. For example, a transitional word like *however* can prepare readers for an idea in contrast to the one before it, as in the second sentence in this paragraph. Transitional words can also highlight the structure of an argument ("These data will show three things: first . . . , second . . . , and third . . ."), almost forming a verbal path for the reader to follow. Following are examples of transitional words and phrases and their purposes:

To show order: *first, second, next, then, last, finally*

To show contrast: *however, yet, but, nevertheless*

To show cause and effect: *therefore, consequently, as a result, then*

To show importance: *moreover, significantly*

To show an added point: *as well, also, too*

To show an example: *for example, for instance*

To show concession: *admittedly*

To show conclusion: *in sum, in conclusion*

The key to using transitional words is similar to the key to using special effects for emphasis: Don't overdo it. To avoid choking your writing with these words, anticipate where your reader will genuinely need them, and limit their use to these instances.

Editing Practice   Underline the transitional words and phrases in the following passage of published writing:

When people believe that their problems can be solved, they tend to get busy solving them.

On the other hand, when people believe that their problems are beyond solution, they tend to position themselves so as to avoid blame. Take the woeful inadequacy of education in the predominantly black central cities. Does the black leadership see the ascendancy of black teachers, school administrators, and politicians as an asset to be used in improving those dreadful schools? Rarely. You are more likely to hear charges of white abandonment, white resistance to integration, conspiracies to isolate black children, even when the schools are officially desegregated. In short, white people are accused of being responsible for the problem. But if the youngsters manage to survive those awful school systems and achieve success, leaders want to claim credit. They don't hesitate to attribute that success to the glorious Civil Rights movement.

—William Raspberry

PROOFREADING

Proofreading is truly the final step in writing a paper. After proofreading, you ought to be able to print your paper out one more time; but if you do not have time, most instructors will be perfectly happy to see the necessary corrections done neatly in ink on the final draft.

Following are some suggestions for proofreading.

Spelling Errors

If you have used a word processor, you may have a program that will check your spelling. If not, you will have to check your spelling by reading through again carefully with a dictionary at hand. Consult the dictionary whenever you feel uncertain. Note also that spell checkers can be unreliable; a word that is spelled correctly but is the wrong word won't be caught. You might consider devoting a special part of your writer's notebook to your habitual spelling errors: some students always misspell *athlete,* for example, whereas others leave the second *n* out of *environment.*

Omissions and Jumbled Passages

Read your paper out loud. Physically shaping your lips around the words can help locate missing words, typos (*saw* instead of *was*), or the remnants of some earlier version of a sentence that did not get fully deleted. Place a caret (^) in the sentence and write the correction or addition above the line, or draw a line through unnecessary text.

Punctuation Problems

Apostrophes and commas give writers the most trouble. If you have habitual problems with these, you should record your errors in your writer's notebook.

Apostrophes

Apostrophe problems usually occur in forming possessives, not contractions, so here we discuss only the former. If you have problems with possessives, you may also want to consult a good handbook or seek a private tutorial with your instructor or your school's writing center.

Here are the basic principles to remember.

www.mhhe.com/**crusius**

For some additional help using apostrophes, go to:

Editing > Apostrophes

1. Possessive pronouns—*his, hers, yours, theirs, its*—never take an apostrophe.

2. Singular nouns become possessive by adding *-'s.*

    A single parent's life is hard.

    A society's values change.

    Do you like Mr. Voss's new car?

3. Plural nouns ending in *-s* become possessive by simply adding an apostrophe.

    Her parents' marriage is faltering.

    Many cities' air is badly polluted.

    The Joneses' house is up for sale.

4. Plural nouns that do not end in *-s* become possessive by adding *-'s.*

    Show me the women's (men's) room.

    The people's voice was heard.

If you err by using apostrophes where they do not belong in nonpossessive words ending in *-s*, remember that a possessive will always have a noun after it, not some other part of speech such as a verb or a preposition. You may even need to read each line of print with a ruler under it to help you focus more intently on each word.

Commas

Because commas indicate a pause, reading your paper aloud is a good way to decide where to add or delete them. A good handbook will elaborate on the following basic principles. The example sentences have been adapted from an argument by Mary Meehan, who opposes abortion.

1. Use a comma when you join two or more main clauses with a coordinating conjunction.

   Main clause, conjunction (and, but, or, nor, so, yet) *main clause.*

   Feminists want to have men participate more in the care of children, but abortion allows a man to shift total responsibility to the woman.

2. Use a comma after an introductory phrase or dependent clause.

   Introductory phrase or clause, main clause.

   To save the smallest children, the Left should speak out against abortion.

3. Use commas around modifiers such as relative clauses and appositives unless they are essential to the noun's meaning. Be sure to put the comma at both ends of the modifier.

   _____, *appositive,* _____

   _____, *relative clause,* _____

   One member of the 1972 Presidential commission on population growth was Graciela Olivarez, a Chicana who was active in civil rights and antipoverty work. Olivarez, who later was named to head the Federal Government's Community Services Administration, had known poverty in her youth in the Southwest.

4. Use commas with a series.

   ___x___, ___y___, and ___z___

   The traditional mark of the Left has been its protection of the underdog, the weak, and the poor.

Semicolons

Think of a semicolon as a strong comma. It has two main uses.

1. Use a semicolon to join two main clauses when you choose not to use a conjunction. This works well when the two main clauses are closely related or parallel in structure.

   Main clause; main clause.

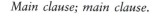
www.mhhe.com/**crusius**

For some additional coverage of comma use, go to:

Editing > Commas

www.mhhe.com/**crusius**

For more coverage of semicolons, go to:

Editing > Semicolons

Pro-life activists did not want abortion to be a class issue; they wanted to end abortion everywhere, for all classes.

As a variation, you may wish to add a transitional adverb to the second main clause. The adverb indicates the relationship between the main clauses, but it is not a conjunction, so a comma preceding it would not be correct.

Main clause; transitional adverb (however, therefore, thus, moreover, consequently), *main clause.*

When speaking with counselors at the abortion clinic, many women change their minds and decide against abortion; however, a woman who is accompanied by a husband or boyfriend often does not feel free to talk with the counselor.

2. Use semicolons between items in a series if any of the items themselves contain commas.

___,___ ; ___,___ ; ___,___

A few liberals who have spoken out against abortion are Jesse Jackson, a civil rights leader; Richard Neuhaus, a theologian; the comedian Dick Gregory; and politicians Mark Hatfield and Mary Rose Oakar.

Colons

www.mhhe.com/**crusius**

For some additional help using colons, go to:

Editing > Colons

The colon has two common uses.

1. Use a colon to introduce a quotation when both your own lead-in and the words quoted are complete sentences that can stand alone. (See the section in Chapter 6 entitled "Incorporating and Documenting Source Material" for more on introducing quotations.)

Main clause in your words: "Quoted sentence(s)."

Mary Meehan criticizes liberals who have been silent on abortion: "If much of the leadership of the pro-life movement is right-wing, that is due largely to the default of the Left."

2. Use a colon before an appositive that comes dramatically at the end of a sentence, especially if the appositive contains more than one item.

Main clause: appositive, appositive, and appositive.

Meehan argues that many pro-choice advocates see abortion as a way to hold down the population of certain minorities: blacks, Puerto Ricans, and other Latins.

Grammatical Errors

Grammatical mistakes can be hard to find, but once again we suggest reading aloud as one method of proofing for them; grammatical errors tend not to "sound right" even if they look like good prose. Another suggestion is to recognize your habitual errors and then look for particular grammatical structures that lead you into error.

Introductory Participial Phrases

Constructions such as these often lead writers to create dangling modifiers. To avoid this pitfall, see the discussion of participial phrases earlier in this appendix. Remember that an introductory phrase dangles if it is not immediately followed by the noun it modifies.

> *Incorrect:* Using her conscience as a guide, our society has granted each woman the right to decide if a fetus is truly a "person" with rights equal to her own.

(Notice that the implied subject of the participial phrase is "each woman," when in fact the subject of the main clause is "our society"; thus, the participial phrase does not modify the subject.)

> *Corrected:* Using her conscience as a guide, each woman in our society has the right to decide if a fetus is truly a "person" with rights equal to her own.

Paired Coordinators

If the words that follow each of the coordinators are not of the same grammatical structure, then an error known as nonparallelism has occurred. To correct this error, line up the paired items one over the other. You will see that the correction often involves simply adding a word or two to, or deleting some words from, one side of the paired coordinators.

> not only _____ but also _____
>
> *Incorrect:* Legal abortion not only protects women's lives, but also their health.
>
> *Corrected:* Legal abortion protects not only women's lives but also their health.

Split Subjects and Verbs

If the subject of a sentence contains long modifying phrases or clauses, by the time you get to the verb you may make an error in agreement (using a plural verb, for example, when the subject is singular) or even in logic (for example, having a subject that is not capable of being the agent that performs the action of the verb). Following are some typical errors:

> The *goal* of the courses grouped under the rubric of "Encountering Non-Western Cultures" *are* . . .

Here the writer forgot that *goal*, the subject, is singular.

> During 1992, *the Refugee Act of 1980,* with the help of President Bush and Congress, *accepted* 114,000 immigrants into our nation.

www.mhhe.com/crusius

For additional coverage of agreement, go to:

Editing > Subject/Verb Agreement

The writer here should have realized that the agent doing the accepting would have to be the Bush administration, not the Refugee Act. A better version would read:

> During 1992, the Bush administration accepted 114,000 immigrants into our nation under the terms of the Refugee Act of 1980.

Proofreading Practice   Proofread the following passage for errors of grammar and punctuation.

> The citizens of Zurich, Switzerland tired of problems associated with drug abuse, experimented with legalization. The plan was to open a central park, Platzspitz, where drugs and drug use would be permitted. Many European experts felt, that it was the illegal drug business rather than the actual use of drugs that had caused many of the cities problems. While the citizens had hoped to isolate the drug problem, foster rehabilitation, and curb the AIDS epidemic, the actual outcome of the Platzspitz experiment did not create the desired results. Instead, violence increased. Drug-related deaths doubled. And drug users were drawn from not only all over Switzerland, but from all over Europe as well. With thousands of discarded syringe packets lying around, one can only speculate as to whether the spread of AIDS was curbed. The park itself was ruined and finally on February 10, 1992, it was barred up and closed. After studying the Swiss peoples' experience with Platzspitz, it is hard to believe that some advocates of drug legalization in the United States are urging us to participate in the same kind of experiment.

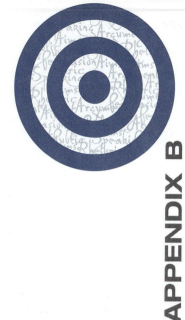
Fallacies—and Critical Thinking

Arguments, like [people], are often pretenders.

—Plato

Throughout this book we have stressed how to argue well, accentuating the positive rather than dwelling on the negative, poor reasoning and bad arguments. We would rather say "do this" than "do not do that." We would rather offer good arguments to emulate than bad arguments to avoid. In stressing the positive, however, we have not paid enough attention to an undeniable fact. Too often unsound arguments convince too many people who should reject them. This appendix addresses a daily problem—arguments that succeed when they ought to fail.

Traditionally, logicians and philosophers have tried to solve this problem by exposing "fallacies," errors in reasoning. About 2,400 years ago, the great ancient Greek philosopher Aristotle was the first to do so in *Sophistical Refutations.* "Sophistry" means reasoning that *appears* to be sound. Aristotle showed that such reasoning only seems sound and therefore should not pass critical scrutiny. He identified thirteen common errors in reasoning. Others have since isolated dozens more, over a hundred in some recent treatments.

We respect this ancient tradition and urge you to learn more about it. Irving M. Copi's classic textbook, *Introduction to Logic,* offers an excellent discussion. It is often used in beginning college philosophy courses. However, our concern is not philosophy but arguments about public issues, where a different notion of fallacy is more useful. Let's start, then, with how we define it.

WHAT IS A FALLACY?

Our concern is arguing well, both skillfully and ethically, and arguments have force through *appeals to an audience.* Therefore, we define *fallacy* as "the misuse of an otherwise common and legitimate form of appeal."

A good example is the appeal to authority, common in advancing evidence to defend reasons in an argument. If I am writing about flu epidemics, for instance, I may cite a scientist studying them at the national Centers for Disease Control to support something I have said. As long as I report what he or she said accurately, fully, and without distortion, I have used the appeal to authority correctly. After all, I am not a flu expert and this person is—it only makes sense to appeal to his or her authority.

But suppose that my authority's view does not represent what most experts believe—in fact most leading authorities reject it. Perhaps I just do not know enough to realize that my authority is not in the mainstream. Or perhaps I do know, but for reasons of my own I want my audience to think a minority view is the majority view. It does not matter whether I intend to deceive or not—if I present my authority in a misleading way, I have misused the appeal to authority. I have committed a fallacy in the meaning we are giving it here.

Here is the point of our definition of fallacy: There is nothing wrong with the appeal to authority itself. Everything depends on how it is used in a particular case. That is why fallacies must be linked with critical thinking. Studying fallacies can lead to mindless "fallacy hunts" and to labeling all instances of a kind of appeal as fallacious. Fallacies are common, but finding them requires *thinking through any appeal that strikes us as suspect for some reason*. We have to decide in each case whether to accept or reject the appeal—or more often, how much we should let it influence our thinking.

WHY ARE FALLACIES SO COMMON?

Fallacies are common because they are deeply rooted in human nature. We must not imagine that we can eliminate them. But we can understand some of their causes and motivations and, with that understanding, increase our critical alertness.

We have distinguished unintended fallacies from intentional ones. We think most fallacies are not meant to deceive, so let's deal with this bigger category first. Unintentional fallacies can result from not knowing enough about the subject, which we may not realize for a number of reasons:

- *Inaccurate reporting or insufficient knowledge.* Arguments always appeal to the facts connected with a controversial question. Again, as with the appeal to authority, there is nothing wrong with appealing to what is known about something. It is hard to imagine how we would argue without doing so. But we have to get the facts right and present them in a context of other relevant information.

  So, for example, experts think that about 300,000 undocumented, foreign-born people immigrate to the United States each year. Not 3,000 or 30,000, but 300,000, and not per month or decade, but annually. The first way we can misuse the appeal to facts is not to report the information accurately. Mistakes of this kind occur often. Magazines and newspapers frequently acknowledge errors in their stories from previous issues.

If we cite the correct figure, 300,000 per year, to support a contention that the Border Patrol is not doing its job, we would be guilty of a fallacy if we did not know that about half of these immigrants come legally, on visas, and simply stay. They are not the Border Patrol's problem. So, even if we cite information accurately, we can still misrepresent what it means or misinterpret it. Accuracy is important but not enough by itself to avoid fallacies. We have to double-check our facts and understand what the facts mean.

- *Holding beliefs that are not true.* If what we do not know can hurt us, what we think we know that is false does more damage. We pick up such beliefs from misinformation that gets repeated over and over in conversation and the media. For example, many Americans equate Islam with Arabs. But most Muslims are not Arabs, and many Arabs are not Muslims. The linkage is no more than a popular association. Furthermore, many terrorists are neither Arabs nor Muslims—we just do not hear about them much. Unfortunately, even when informed people point out the facts just mentioned, they tend not to register or be forgotten quickly. Such is the hold of incorrect beliefs on the minds of many people.

- *Stubbornly adhering to a belief despite massive counterevidence.* At one time most climate scientists resisted the notion that human activities could influence the weather, much less cause global warming. But as more and more evidence accumulated, the overwhelming majority eventually came to agree that carbon dioxide emissions, especially from vehicles and power-generating plants, are the major cause of global warming. But dissenters still exist, and not all of them are being paid by oil companies. Some may sincerely feel that natural variation in the Earth's climate is the real cause of global warming. Some may enjoy the role of outsider or maverick. Some may say that often the majority opinion turns out to be wrong, which is true enough, and somebody needs to play the skeptic. Whatever the motivation may be, the dissenters are brushing aside an enormous amount of evidence. Their fallacious arguments have helped to convince too many Americans that we do not have a problem when we do. We cite this example to show that fallacies are not restricted to popular arguments. Scientists can be as stubborn as anyone. It is human nature, against which no degree of expertise can protect us.

- *Dodging issues we do not understand or that disturb or embarrass us.* The issues that immigration, both legal and illegal, raise, for example, are more often avoided or obscured than confronted. People talk about immigrants becoming "good Americans" and worry about whether the latest wave can or will "assimilate." But what is a "good American"?

The question is rarely posed. Exactly what does "assimilate" involve? Again, few ask the question. Thus, arguments about this subject often dodge the important questions connected with it. In many cases those making these arguments do so while thinking they are confronting it.

If you recognize yourself and people you know in some or all of these causes and motivations that drive fallacious arguments, welcome to the club. We are all guilty. Without meaning to, we all get the facts wrong; we all pick up notions we take to be true that are not; and we all are at times stubborn and evasive.

Fortunately, unintended fallacies usually have telltale signs we can learn to detect, such as these:

- the reported fact that seems unlikely or implausible
- the interpretation that reduces a complex problem to something too simple to trust
- the belief that does not fit what we know of the world and our own experience
- the argument that strains too hard to downplay or explain away data that would call it into question
- the argument that dances around issues rather than confronting them

The good news is that unintended fallacies are seldom skillful enough to fool us often or for long. They tend to give themselves away once we know what to look for and care enough to exercise our natural critical capacity.

The bad news is that arguments coldly calculated to deceive, although less common than arguments that mislead unintentionally, are often much harder to detect. What makes the problem especially tough is that deceit comes too often from people we want and even need to trust. Why? Why do people sometimes set out to deceive others? We think the philosopher and brilliant fallacy hunter Jeremy Bentham had the best answer. He called the motivation "interest-begotten prejudice." What did he mean?

He meant that all human beings have interests they consider vital—status, money, and power they either have and seek to protect or strive to acquire. As a direct result of these interests, their outlook, thinking, and of course their arguments are shot through with prejudices, unexamined judgments about what is good, desirable, worthwhile, and so on. For example, through much of American history, Native Americans had something the American government wanted—land. When it did not take it by force, it took it by treaty, by persuading Native Americans to make bad bargains that often the government never intended to keep anyway. The whole process rode on prejudices: Native Americans were savages or children in need of protection by the Great Father in Washington; besides that, they did not "do anything" with the land they had. Because the deceit paid off handsomely for its perpetrators, it went on until there was little land remaining to take.

We would like to tell you that deliberate deceit in argument does not work—that deceivers are exposed and discredited at least, if not punished for what they do. We would like to endorse Abraham Lincoln's famous statement: "You can fool all of the people some of the time, and some of the people all the time, but you can't fool all of the people all of the time." Maybe so—many Native Americans and some independent-thinking white people were not fooled by the false promises of the treaties. But the humorist James Thurber's less famous observation is probably closer to the truth: "You can fool too many of the people too much of the time." This is so because the interest-begotten prejudices of the powerful coincide with or cooperate with the prejudices of a large segment of the audience addressed. That is why Hitler and his propaganda machine was able to create the disastrous Third Reich and why Joseph Stalin, who murdered more Russians than Hitler did, remains a national hero for many Russians even now, after his brutal regime's actions have long been exposed.

So, what can be done about the fallacious arguments of deliberate deceivers, backed as they often are by the power of the state or other potent interests? The most important thing is to examine our own interest-begotten prejudices, because that is what the deceivers use to manipulate us. They will not be able to push our buttons so easily if we know what they are and realize we are being manipulated. Beyond that, we need to recognize the interests of others, who may be in the minority and largely powerless to resist when too many people are fooled too much of the time. We can call attention to the fallacies of deliberate deceivers, exposing their game for others to see. We can make counterarguments, defending enlightened stances with all our skill. There is no guarantee that what should prevail will, but at least we need not lend support to exploiters nor fall into silence when we ought to resist.

SOME COMMON FALLACIES

For reasons that should be clearer now, people often misuse legitimate forms of appeal. We have mentioned two examples already—the misuse of the appeal to authority and the misuse of the appeal to facts. All legitimate appeals can be misused, and because there are too many to discuss them all, we will confine our attention to those most commonly turned into fallacies.

In Chapter 10, "Motivating Action: Arguing to Persuade," we described and illustrated all the forms of appeal (pages 243–244). In sum, we are persuaded by

- *ethos:* the character of the writer as we perceive him or her
- *pathos:* our emotions and attitudes as the argument arouses them
- *style:* how well something is said
- *logos:* our capacity for logic, by the force of reasons and evidence advanced for a thesis

You will encounter people, including many professors, who hold that only logos, rational appeal, *should* persuade. Anything else from their point of view is irrelevant and probably fallacious. We say in response that, regardless of what should be the case, people *are* persuaded by all four kinds of appeal—that we always have been and always will be. It therefore does not help to call appeals to ethos, pathos, and style fallacious. It *can* help to understand how these legitimate forms of appeal can be misused or abused.

The Appeal to Ethos

We do not know many people well whose arguments we encounter in print or in cyberspace. Typically, we do not know them at all. Consequently, we ordinarily rely on their qualifications and reputation as well as our impression of their character from reading what they have written. If ethos is not important or should not matter, we would not find statements about an author's identity and background attached to articles and books they have written. Speakers would not be introduced by someone providing similar information. But ethos does matter; as Aristotle said long ago, it is probably the most potent form of appeal. If we do not trust the person we are hearing or reading, it is highly unlikely we will be persuaded by anything said or written. If we do, we are inclined to assent to all of it. Consequently, appeals to ethos are often misused. Here are some of the common ways.

Personal Attack

There are people we ought never to trust—confidence men who bilk people out of their life savings, pathological liars, and so on. There is nothing wrong with exposing such people, destroying the ethos they often pretend very persuasively to have, thereby rendering their arguments unpersuasive.

But too often good arguments by good people are undermined with unjustified personal attacks. The most common is name-calling. Someone offers an argument opponents cannot see how to refute, so instead of addressing the argument, they call him or her "a liberal," a "neocon," or some other name the audience equates with "bad."

This fallacy is so common in politics that we now refer to it as "negative ads" or "negative campaigning." We ought not to dismiss it because experience and studies show that it often works. It works because once a label is attached to someone it is hard to shake.

Common Opinion

It is hard to find any argument that does not appeal to commonly accepted beliefs, many of which are accurate and reliable. Even scientific argument, which extols the value of skepticism, assumes that some knowledge is established beyond question and that some ways of doing things, like experimental design, are the right ways. When we indicate that we share the common opinions of our readers, thinking and behaving as they do, we establish or increase our ethos.

Used fallaciously, a writer passes off as commonly accepted either a belief that is not held by many informed people or one that is held commonly but is false or highly doubtful. "Of course," the writer says, and then affirms something questionable as if it was beyond question. For example, "Everybody knows that AIDS is spread by promiscuous sexual behavior." Sometimes it is, but one sexual act with one person can transmit the virus, and infection need not be transmitted sexually at all—babies are born with it because their mothers have AIDS, and addicts sharing needles is another common way AIDS is spread. Furthermore, health care workers are at higher risk because they often are exposed to bodily fluids from infected people. The common opinion in this and many other instances is no more than a half-truth at best.

Tradition

Few can see the opening of the musical *Fiddler on the Roof* and not be at least temporarily warmed by the thought of tradition. Tradition preserves our sense of continuity, helps us maintain stability and identity amid the often overwhelming demands of rapid change. No wonder, then, that writers appeal to it frequently to enhance their ethos and often in ways that are not fallacious at all. It was hardly a fallacy after 9/11, for instance, to remind Americans that part of the price we pay for liberty, our supreme traditional value, is greater relative vulnerability to terrorism. A closed, totalitarian society like North Korea can deal with terrorism much more "efficiently" than we can, but at the price of having no liberty.

Many of the abuses of tradition as a source of ethical appeal are so obvious as to need no discussion: politicians wrapping themselves in the flag (or at least red, white, and blue balloons), television preachers oozing piety to get donations. You can easily provide your own examples. Much more difficult to discern is invoking tradition not to dupe the naïve but to justify resisting constructive change. Tradition helped to delay women's right to vote in the United States, for example, and plays a major role in the high illiteracy rate for women in India and many other countries now.

Like all fallacious uses of legitimate appeals, ethical fallacies can be revealed by asking the right questions:

For *personal attack,* ask, "Are we dealing with a person whose views we should reject out of hand?" "Is the personal attack simply a means to dismiss an argument we ought to listen to?"

For *common opinion,* ask, "Is this belief really held by well-informed people?" If it is, ask, "Does the common belief hold only in some instances or in every case?"

For *tradition,* ask, "Have we always really done it that way?" If so, ask, "Have conditions changed enough so that the old way may need to be modified or replaced?"

The Appeal to Pathos

After people understand the indispensable role ethos plays in persuasion, few continue to view it only negatively, as merely a source of fallacies. Pathos is another matter. In Western culture, the heart is opposed to the head, feeling and emotion contrasted with logic and clear thinking. Furthermore, our typical attitudes toward pathos affect ethos as well: Emotional people cannot be trusted. Their arguments betray a disorganized and unbalanced mind.

With cause, we are wary of the power of emotional appeal, especially when passionate orators unleash it in crowds. The result often enough has been public hysteria and sometimes riots, lynchings, and verbal or physical abuse of innocent people. We know its power. Should it, then, be avoided? Are emotional appeals always suspect?

Let's take a brief look at a few of them.

Fear

"The only thing we have to fear is fear itself," Franklin Roosevelt declared, at a time when matters looked fearful indeed. The Great Depression was at its height; fascism was gaining ground in Europe. The new president sought to reduce the fear and despair that gripped the United States and much of the world at the time.

About a year later, in 1933, Hitler came to power, but the authorities in Britain, France, and other countries failed to realize the threat he represented soon enough, despite warnings from Winston Churchill and many others. As a result, the Allied powers in Europe fell to the Nazis, and Britain came to the brink of defeat. Fear can paralyze, as Roosevelt knew, but lack of it can result in complacency when genuine threats loom.

How can we tell the difference? With appeals to fear, as with all appeals to any emotion, this hard-to-answer question is the key: *Does reality justify the emotion a speaker or writer seeks to arouse or allay?* Recently, for instance, it has been easy to play on our fear of terrorists. But the odds of you or me dying in a terrorist plot are very low. The risk of death is greater just driving a car. Far more Americans will die prematurely from sedentary ways than Osama bin Laden and his associates are ever likely to kill. 9/11 has taught us yet again that "eternal vigilance is the price of liberty," but the sometimes nearly hysterical fear of terrorism is not justified.

Pity

Fear has its roots in the body, in the fight-or-flight rush of adrenaline that helps us to survive. Pity, the ability to feel sorry for people suffering unjustly, has social roots. Both are fundamental emotions, part of being human.

Like the appeal to fear, the appeal to pity can be used fallaciously, to mislead us into, for example, contributing to a seemingly worthy cause which is really just a front for con artists. But if pity can be used to manipulate us, we can also fail to respond when pity is warranted. Or we can substitute the emotion for action. The suffering in Darfur in recent years has been acute, but the response of the rest of the world has usually been too little, too late. Like fear, then, we can fail to respond to appeals for pity when they are warranted.

Which is worse? To be conned sometimes or to be indifferent in the face of unjust suffering? Surely the latter. Because fear can lead to hysteria and violence, we should meet appeals to it skeptically. Because unjust suffering is so common, we should meet appeals to pity in a more receptive frame of mind. But with both emotions we require critical thinking. "I just feel what I feel" is not good enough. We have to get past that to distinguish legitimate emotional appeals from fallacious ones.

Ridicule

We mention ridicule because student writers are often advised to avoid it. "Do not ridicule your opponents in an argument" is the standard advice, advice you will find elsewhere in this book. So, is ridicule always fallacious, always a cheap shot, always a way to win points without earning them?

Well, not always. With most positions on most issues, we are dealing with points of view we may not agree with but must respect. But what if a position makes no sense, has little or no evidence to support its contentions, and yet people persist in holding it? What then? Is ridicule justified, at least sometimes?

If it is not, then satire is not justified, for satire holds up for scorn human behavior the satirist considers irrational and destructive. We all enjoy political cartoons, which thrive on ridicule of the absurd and the foolish. How many stand-up comedians would have far less material if ridicule was never justified?

Like pity, ridicule is a social emotion. It tries to bring individuals who have drifted too far away from social norms back into the fold. It allows us to discharge our frustration with stupid or dishonest positions through largely harmless laughter—far better than "let's beat some sense into old So-and-So." Ridicule, then, has its place and its functions.

But it also has its fallacies. Most commonly an intelligent, well-reasoned, and strongly supported position suffers ridicule simply because it is unpopular, because most people have difficulty getting their minds around it. Clearly, the fact that an argument has been dismissed as ridiculous or absurd does not mean that it is, and we must be especially careful when we unthinkingly join in the ridicule.

Like the fallacies related to ethos, pathetic fallacies can be revealed with the right questions:

1. Is the emotion appropriate to the situation, in proportion to what we know about what is going on in the world?

2. What are the consequences of buying into a particular emotional appeal? Where will it take us?

3. Does the emotional appeal *substitute* for reason, for a good argument, or does it reinforce it in justified ways?

4. What is the relation of the appeal to unexamined and possibly unjustified prejudice or bias? Are we being manipulated or led for good reasons to feel something?

The Appeal to Style

Most experienced and educated people are aware of the seductions of ethos and pathos. They know how easy it is to be misled by people they trust or manipulated by emotion into doing something they ordinarily would not and should not do. They have been fooled enough to be wary and therefore critical. However, even experienced and educated people often are not alert to the power of style, to the great impact that something can have *just because it is stated well.* One of the great students of persuasion, the American critic Kenneth Burke, explained the impact of style. He said that when we like the *form* of something said or written, it is a small step to accepting the *content* of it as well. We move very easily from "Well said" to "I agree," or even "It must be true." It is almost as if we cannot distrust at a deep level language that appeals to our sense of rhythm and sound.

Yet fallacies of style are a major industry. It is called advertising. People are paid handsomely to create slogans the public will remember and repeat. From some time ago, for instance, comes this one: "When guns are outlawed, only outlaws will have guns." Has a nice swing to it, doesn't it? The play on words is pleasing, hard to forget, and captures in a powerful formula the fears of the pro-gun lobby. Of course, in reality there has never been a serious movement to outlaw guns in the United States. No one is going to take away your guns, so the slogan is nothing more than scaremongering at best.

Now compare this slogan with another memorable phrase: "Justice too long delayed is justice denied." Martin Luther King used it to characterize the situation of black Americans in 1963 in his classic "Letter from Birmingham Jail." He got the phrase from a Supreme Court justice, but its appeal has less to do with the source of the statement than with its formula-like feeling of truth. It stuck in King's mind so he used it in his situation, and once you read it, you will not forget it either. In other words, it works in much the same way that the fallacious slogan works. But King's use of it is not at all fallacious. As a matter of undisputed fact, black Americans were denied their civil rights legally and illegally for more than a century after the Emancipation Proclamation.

The point, of course, is that the form of a statement says nothing about its truth value or whether it is being used to deceive. If form pushes us toward unthinking assent, then we must exert enough resistance to permit critical thought. Even "justice too long delayed is justice denied" may require some careful thought if it is applied to some other situation. Many people who favor the death penalty, for example, are outraged by the many years it usually takes to move a murderer from conviction to execution. They could well apply the phrase to this state of affairs. How much truth should it contain for someone who has no legal, moral, or religious objections to capital punishment? It is true that often the relatives of a victim must wait a decade or more for justice. It is true that sometimes, for one reason or another, the execution never happens. Is that justice denied? But it is also true that convicted felons on death row have been found innocent and released. Some innocent ones have been executed. Has justice been too long delayed or not? Would it be wise to shorten the process? These are serious questions critical thought must address.

The appeal of style goes well beyond slogans and formulas. We have not offered a list of common stylistic devices and how they may be misused because there are far too many of them. All can be used to express the truth; all can be used to package falsehood in appealing rhythm and sound. Separating ourselves from appeals of language long enough to think about what is being said is the only solution.

The Appeal to Logos

Before we present a short list of common errors in reasoning, the traditional focus of fallacy research, let's review a fundamental point about logic: An argument can be free of errors in reasoning, be logically compelling, and yet be false. Logic can tell us whether an argument makes sense but not whether it is true. For example, consider the following statements:

> Australia began as a penal colony, a place where criminals in England were sent.

> Modern Australians, therefore, are descendents of criminals.

There is nothing wrong with the logical relation of these two statements. But its truth value depends on the *historical accuracy* of the first statement. It depends also on the *actual origins* of all modern Australians. As a matter of fact, Australia was used by the English as a convenient place to send certain people the authorities considered undesirable, but they were not all criminals. Furthermore, native Australians populated the country long before any European knew it existed. And most modern Australians immigrated long after the days of the penal colony. So the truth value of these perfectly logical statements is low. It is true enough for Australians to joke about sometimes, but it is not really true.

Here is a good rule of thumb: *The reality of things reasoned about is far more varied and complex than the best reasoning typically captures.* Sometimes errors in reasoning lead us to false conclusions. But false conclusions result much more often from statements not being adequate to what is known about reality.

With that in mind, let's look at a few fallacies of logical appeal.

False Cause

We have defined *fallacy* as the misuse of a legitimate form of appeal. There is nothing more common or reasonable than identifying the cause of something. We are not likely to repair a car without knowing what is causing that wobble in the steering, or treat a disease effectively, or come up with the right solution to almost any problem without knowing the cause.

The difficulty is that just because "a" follows "b," "b" did not necessarily cause "a." Yet we tend to think so, especially if "a" always follows "b." Hence, the possibility of "false cause," reasoning that misleads by confusing sequence with cause. If we flip a light switch and the light does not go on, we immediately think, "The bulb is burned out." But if we replace the bulb, and it still does not work, we think the problem must be the switch. We may tinker with that for a while before we realize that none of the lights are working: "Oh, the breaker is cut off." By a process of trial and error, we eliminate the false causes to find the real one.

But if we are reasoning about more complex problems, trial and error usually is not an option. For example, a recent newspaper article attributed the decline in the wages of Americans despite increased productivity to the influx of illegal aliens, especially from Mexico. Because they are paid less than most American citizens are, attributing the cause of lower wages to them may seem plausible. But actually some groups of Americans have endured a steady decline for some time, as high-paying industrial jobs were lost and lower-paying service work took their place. Globalization has allowed companies to force wages down and reduce the power of labor unions by taking advantage of people in other countries who will work for much less. It is highly unlikely that depressed wages are caused by illegal aliens alone. But if we do not like them, it is especially tempting to blame them for a more complex problem with which they are only associated. That is called *scapegoating,* and false cause is how the reasoning works that justifies it.

As a rule of thumb, let's assume that complex problems have multiple causes, and let's be especially suspicious when common prejudices may motivate single-cause thinking.

Straw Man

Nothing is more common in argument than stating an opponent's position and then showing what is wrong with it. As long as we state our opponent's position fully and accurately and attack it intelligently, with good reasons and evidence, there is nothing fallacious about such an attack.

The temptation, however, is to seek advantage by attributing to our opponents a weak or indefensible position they do not hold but which resembles their position in some respects. We can then knock it down easily and make our opponents look dumb or silly in the process. That is called "creating a straw man," and it is a common ploy in politics especially. It works because most people are not familiar enough with the position being distorted to realize that it has been misrepresented, and so they accept the straw man as if it was the real argument. Often people whose views have been caricatured fight an uphill battle, first to reestablish their genuine position and then to get it listened to after an audience has accepted the distorted one as genuine. Thus, many fallacies succeed because of ignorance and ill will on the part of both the fallacious reasoner and the audience.

Slippery Slope

Human experience offers many examples of "one thing leading to another." We decide to have a baby, for instance, and one thing follows another from the first diaper change all the way to college graduation, with so much in between and beyond that a parent's life is altered forever and fundamentally. Furthermore, it is always prudent to ask about any decision we face, "If I do *x,* what consequent *y* am I likely to face? And if *y* happens, where will that lead me?"

The slippery-slope fallacy takes advantage of our commonsense notion that actions have consequences, that one thing leads to another. The difference between the truth and the fallacy is that the drastic consequences the arguer envisions could not or are not likely to happen. Those who opposed making the so-called morning-after pill available without a prescription sometimes warned of a wholesale decline in sexual morality, especially among young adults. That has not happened, and in any case, technology is one thing, morality another. What makes sex right or wrong has little to do with the method of contraception.

The slippery-slope fallacy plays on fear, indicating one of the many ways that one kind of appeal—in this case, to logic, or reasoning about consequences— connects with other kinds of appeal—in this case, to emotion. Working in tandem, such appeals can be powerfully persuasive. All the more reason, then, to stand back and analyze any slope an argument depicts critically. Is the predicted slide inevitable or even probable? In many cases, the answer will be no, and we can see through the appeal to what it often is: a scare tactic to head off doing something that makes good sense.

Hasty Generalization

We cannot think and therefore cannot argue without generalizing. Almost any generalization is vulnerable to the charge of being hasty. All that is required for what some logicians label as "hasty generalization" is to find a single exception to an otherwise true assertion. So "SUVs waste gas." But the new hybrid SUVs are relatively gas efficient. "Since 9/11 American Muslims have felt that their loyalty to the United States has been in doubt." Surely we can find individual Muslims who have not felt insecure at all.

The problem with hasty generalization is not exceptions to statements that are by and large true. The problem, rather, is generalization based on what is called a biased (and hence unrepresentative) sample, which results in a generalization that is false. If you visit an institution for the criminally insane, you will probably encounter some schizophrenics. You may conclude, as many people have, that schizophrenics are dangerous. Most of them, however, are not, and the relatively few who are do not pose a threat when they stay on their meds. The common fear of "schizo street people" results from a hasty generalization that can do real harm.

Begging the Question

We end with this because it is especially tricky. Every argument makes assumptions that have not been and in some cases cannot be proven. We simply could not argue at all if we had to prove everything our position assumes. Hence, virtually all arguments can be said to "beg the question," to assume as true that which has not been shown definitively as true. Furthermore, we can never tell when an assumption that almost no one doubts can turn out to be very doubtful as new information emerges. Assumptions we used to make routinely can become hot issues of controversy.

Consequently, we should confine "begging the question" to *taking as settled the very question that is currently at issue*. Someone is charged with a crime, and the press gives it much ink and air time. Inevitably, some people jump to the conclusion that the accused is guilty. This can be such a big problem that it is hard to impanel a jury that has not been hopelessly biased by all the coverage.

We beg the question whenever we assume something that can not be assumed because it is the very thing we must prove. Fallacies of this kind are usually no harder to spot than the juror who thinks the defendant is guilty simply because he or she has been charged with a crime. Pro-lifers, for example, argue in ways that depend on the fetus having the legal status of a person. Of course, if the fetus is a person, there is no controversy. Abortion would be what pro-lifers say it is, murder, and thus prohibited by law. The personhood of the fetus is *the* issue; assuming the fetus is a person is begging the question.

The following exercise does not include what many such exercises offer— fallacies so obvious they would fool no one over the age of ten. You will have to think them through, discuss them at length. In some cases, rather than flatly rejecting or accepting the arguments, you may want to give them "partial credit," a degree of acceptance. That is fine, part of learning to live with shades of gray.

EXERCISE

The following examples come from instances of persuasion that appeared in earlier editions of this book. Some may not be fallacious in any way. Assess them carefully and be prepared to defend the judgment you make.

1. From an ad depicting the VW Beetle: "Hug it? Drive it? Hug it? Drive it?"

2. From a cartoon depicting a man holding a pro-life sign, above which appear two specimen jars, one containing "a dead abortion doctor,"

the other "a dead fetus." The man is pointing at the jar with the dead fetus. The caption reads "We object to this one."

3. From an essay called "The End of Life," James Rachels offers the following interpretation of the Biblical prohibition against taking human life: "The sixth commandment does not say, literally, 'Thou shalt not *kill*'—that is a bad translation. A better translation is, Thou shalt not commit *murder,* which is different, and which does not obviously prohibit mercy killing. Murder is by definition *wrongful killing;* so, if you do not think that a given kind of killing is wrong, you will not call it murder" [author's emphasis].

4. From a panel discussion in *Newsweek* about violence in the media: The moderator asks a representative of the movie industry why the rating NC-17 is not applied to "gratuitously violent movies." The response is "because the definition of 'gratuitous' is shrouded in subjectivity. . . . Creative people can shoot a violent scene a hundred different ways. Sex and language are different, because there are only a few ways [you can depict them on screen]. . . . Violence is far more difficult to pin down."

5. From an essay critical of multiculturalism comes the following quotation from the political scientist Samuel B. Huntington, whose view the essay's author endorses: "Does it take an Osama bin Laden . . . to make us realize that we are Americans? If we do not experience recurrent destructive attacks, will we return to the fragmentation and eroded Americanism before September 11?"

6. From an essay advocating multiculturalism: "The attack on affirmative action isn't really about affirmative action. Essentially it is another tactic in today's war on the gains of the 1960's, a tactic rooted in Anglo resentment and fear. A major source of that fear: the fact that California will almost surely have a majority of people of color in 20 to 30 years at most, with the nation as a whole not far behind."

7. From an essay urging us to move beyond the multiculturalism debate, written by a naturalized American citizen who was born in India: "I take my American citizenship very seriously. I am a voluntary immigrant, and not a seeker of political asylum. I am an American by choice, and not by the simple accident of birth. I have made emotional, social, and political commitments to this country. I have earned the right to think of myself as an American."

8. From an article arguing that militant Islam and Islamic terrorism is like Nazism: "Once again, the world is faced with a transcendent conflict between those who love life and those who love death both for themselves and their enemies. Which is why we tremble."

9. From an article arguing that American foreign policy provokes terrorism and that the root of it all is "our rampant militarism": "Two

of the most influential federal institutions are not in Washington but on the south side of the Potomac River: the Defense Department and the Central Intelligence Agency. Given their influence today, one must conclude that what the government outlined in the Constitution of 1787 no longer bears much relationship to the government that actually rules from Washington. Until that is corrected, we should probably stop talking about 'democracy' and 'human rights.'"

10. From an article that attempts to explain human mating in evolutionary terms: "Feelings and acts of love are not recent products of particular Western views. Love is universal. Thoughts, emotions, and actions of love are experienced by people in all cultures worldwide—from the Zulu in the southern tip of Africa to the Eskimos in the north of Alaska."

For additional examples of fallacies for analysis, see "Stalking the Wild Fallacy" <http://www.fallacyfiles.org/examples.html>.

active voice A statement that has the doer of the action as the subject of the sentence, followed by the verb and the person or thing that receives the action. "The President (subject) criticized (verb) the Congress (receiver of the action) for delaying passage of the legislation. See also **passive voice.** Favor active voice sentences because they are easier to understand and make a stronger impression on readers.

allusion A reference to a person, event, or text the author thinks readers will recognize without explanation. Usually a quick Google search will clarify allusions you do not recognize.

American Psychological Association (APA) style sheet or handbook The guide to research papers used in most natural and social science courses. Most of the information is accessible online. See also **Modern Language Association (MLA) style sheet or handbook.**

annotation Typically a handwritten note in the margins of something we are reading that, for instance, helps us to relocate a major point in a text or raises a question about something the author has said. Form the habit of writing in the margins of print texts and typing in comments for electronic ones, necessary for both critical reading and research.

argument An opinion backed by a reason—for instance, "We should cap tuition (opinion) because too many college students cannot afford the increasing costs" (reason). Arguments are developed into cases by adding more reasons and evidence that supports each reason.

assumptions Principles or values an argument takes for granted and so does not state or defend. "We should cap tuition because too many college students cannot afford the increasing costs" assumes what most Americans take for granted: that extending higher education to as many people as possible is a good thing. When we make arguments, we should examine our assumptions to make sure that they do not need defending. When we assess the arguments of other people, we should expose the assumptions to make sure they should go unchallenged.

audience Also called "readership," designates the particular group of people we hope to reach with an argument. There is no point in trying to convince an audience that already agrees with us, nor an audience unalterably opposed to our opinion. Choose an audience weakly inclined your way, inclined against you but open to reason, or with no position at all. In this middle range of groups, pick the audience you know best and then consciously develop your argument to appeal to their values and interests.

bibliography A list of sources on a particular topic, arranged in alphabetical order according to the last name of the author or, in the case of sources with no author, the first major word in the title. Called "Works Cited" in the Modern Language Association (MLA) handbook used in most English courses.

blog Short for "web log," designates online sites maintained by people who wish to register their opinions on many issues. A vast, democratic expansion of access for popular opinion as compared to print. Increasingly important for the discussion of controversial subjects worldwide.

brief Also called "case structure," an outline of a case, including the claim or thesis you are defending, the reasons that justify or explain your thesis, and the evidence you will offer to develop and support each reason. Useful as a plan for writing a paper. Typically does not include your ideas for beginning and ending the paper and perhaps other details, such as showing why a possible objection to your case does not hold. See also **case strategy** and **refutation.**

case strategy The moves a writer makes to have maximum impact on an audience, including selecting, wording, and ordering reasons and evidence. Audience awareness is the key to case strategy. For instance, if you are arguing for a ban on cell phone use by drivers, you need to propose ways to minimize the loss of freedom and the inconvenience such a ban would cause.

case structure See **brief.**

claim Also called "thesis," the central statement an argument defends, the belief or action you want your audience to accept. A claim is a carefully stated and more specific version of your opinion about something. For example, you may be opposed to the war in Afghanistan (opinion) but your claim might be, "We should withdraw all American troops from Afghanistan within the next year."

climate of opinion The range of existing common viewpoints on any controversial question. As an arguer you need to be acquainted with what people are thinking and what motivates the varying points of view, which usually amounts to the perceived interests of the contending parties.

common knowledge A convention that governs the need for citation of sources. If the information is widely known—say, the kind of information available in a general use encyclopedia or what people who keep up with the news would know—there is no need to provide parenthetical notation or an entry in your Works Cited page. Our advice is to cite anyway if you are in doubt about whether an item qualifies as common knowledge.

connotation What a word or statement implies. For instance, both "famous" and "notorious" mean that someone is well known, but "notorious" implies well known for bad reasons. Because the connotations of words register unconsciously most of time, and therefore are not usually criticized, choosing words carefully for their connotations has a powerful impact on readers. See also **denotation.**

context A word with many meanings, used most commonly in two ways: context of text, which means the place from which a quotation is taken, and context of situation, which means the circumstances in which a writer writes or an interpreter of a text interprets. So, Abraham Lincoln's famous words, "With malice toward none, with charity for all," come near the end of his Second Inaugural, where he is discussing the attitude he would take in victory when the Civil War is over (context of text), a position he argued against those that would punish the South for starting the war (context of situation). See also **rhetorical context.**

conviction An earned opinion achieved through thought, research, and discussion. We often have casual opinions that need to be examined thoroughly to see what they are worth. Many Americans believe, for instance, that Japanese- and German-made vehicles are always better than domestics—are they? What does the best current data show? We should argue (make claims about) only opinions that we have earned.

convincing One of the four aims of argument; to seek assent to a claim not directly tied to taking action. Convincing, or case-making, is especially valued in the academic world, where we are often debating issues or topics about which no action can be taken. "What caused the Great Depression?" for example, is an important question in an American history course, crucial to understanding the past.

critical reading Also called "close reading," a thoughtful examination of a text with the intent of analyzing and evaluating it. Instead of reading a text just to know what it says, we slow down enough to think through what it says and whether or not we should accept what it says as accurate and true.

denotation The dictionary meaning of a word, apart from what it implies. The term "white," for example, in the United States designates anyone whose skin color and facial features allows him or her to pass as white whatever the racial mix in ancestry might be. See also **connotation.**

dialogue Also known as "dialectic," a serious conversation where opinions are both offered and examined critically, often through a process of questioning. If someone says, "We must secure our borders," a legitimate question for exploring the assertion would be, "What do you mean by 'secure'?" What sort of people do you want to prevent entering or leaving our country without documents?

editing As contrasted with revision, or significant rewriting of a paper to improve content, designates attention to such matters as awkward sentences, paragraph coherence, and errors; as such, editing comes after revision and before proofreading. Editing is indispensable to writing well. See also **revision** and **proofreading.**

ethos A word that means "character" in Greek, used to designate how a writer appeals through self-presentation, conforming to what readers admire: being intelligent, well informed, fair, aware of reader fears and desires, and so on. Perhaps the most potent form of appeal because people we do not trust cannot convince or persuade us.

evidence Reasoning, data, and expert opinion advanced to justify or confirm a reason. The amount of evidence needed to support a reason depends on the degree of resistance you estimate your audience will have.

fallacies The misuse of a legitimate form of appeal, sometimes with the intent to deceive. For example, on matters requiring specialized knowledge, we cite expert opinion, as in the case of the law with regard to a particular practice. There is nothing wrong with citing expert opinion, but we must cite a genuine expert and represent his or her opinion accurately to avoid committing a fallacy.

field research Generating your own information through observation, experiment, surveys, and the like rather than using sources. A valuable way to test your opinions and to provide evidence about issues that existing data do not address. If you want to know what students at your college think about living together before marriage, for instance, conducting a survey may be the only way to secure such information.

graphics Visual supplements to a text, including tables, charts, pie graphs, drawings, and the like. Widely used in publications but not exploited nearly enough in academic writing by students.

identification Linking the reader's interest and values with what a writer has said, achieved most commonly and powerfully through shared experiences, such as participation in the same war, the same activity or place, and so on. The writer who advocates preservation of nature by describing a trip as a child to a national park is seeking the identification of readers with the cause.

implied questions All statements we write or read answer (mostly unstated) questions, so that the statement, "The first one hundred days of a new President are not as important as many people think," answers the question, "How well does the first one hundred days predict the success of an administration?" Learning to ask what questions a statement implies can help you with argument in two ways: With your own arguments, you can see better the sequence of questions your sentences are answering, and possibly detect other questions you need to answer and a better sequence for the ones you have answered. With the arguments of others, you can more easily detect different possible answers to the questions the writer's sentences imply.

inquiry One of the four aims of argument, inquiry uses reasoning to analyze and critique existing arguments, as part of the process of arriving at the truth as you see it. Asking and pursuing questions is the key to effective inquiry. See also **conviction.**

issue A controversial question connected to a subject matter or topic. If we are discussing health care, for example, an issue would be, "Should access to health care be considered a right for all U.S. citizens?" See also **stasis.**

logos A Greek word that means "reasoning," used to designate the logical appeal of an argument. Readers respond to well-reasoned cases by saying "This makes sense to me" or "Your logic is compelling," the kind of response logical appeal seeks.

mature reasoning As contrasted with much undisciplined popular reasoning, a mature reasoner is well informed, self-critical, and open to constructive criticism from others; argues with reader needs and concerns in mind; and has a sense of context, the circumstances to which an argument must respond. Mature reasoning is the goal of this book.

mediation One of the four aims of argument, used to find common ground and agreement on a course of action when parties to a dispute are in sharp and seemingly irreconcilable conflict. You will encounter mediating positions on all controversial topics, from which you can learn the valuable skill of bringing people together who, in many cases, have stopped talking to one another.

middle style The kind of style typical of argument, not as passionate and formal as oratory, nor as chatty and familiar as, say, texting a friend. We use middle style when we talk or write to people we do not know well whose opinion of us matters.

Modern Language Association (MLA) style sheet or handbook The guide to research papers used in most liberal arts courses. Most of the information is accessible online. See also **American Psychological Association (APA) style sheet or handbook.**

opinion Most arguments begin with opinions, with something as simple as "I didn't like that movie." When we take an opinion like this and think it through, developing it into a thesis or claim we could defend in a movie review, including good reasons and evidence, we have moved to what we need for arguing well. The same as **position**; contrast with **conviction.**

paraphrase To state what someone else has said or written in your own words, the alternative to quoting someone. You should paraphrase your sources more often than you quote them, reserving quotation for statements from sources where the exact wording matters—for instance, when you want to comment on the wording.

passive voice A sentence where the doer or subject of the verb's action is either left out or moved to a position after the verb. "Congress was criticized by the President for delaying passage of the legislation." Passive voice is harder for readers to understand, and so active voice is preferred. However, passive voice is useful when you do not know who did something or when you do not want to emphasize responsibility for an action. Prefer active voice, but use passive voice when you have a good reason to do so. See also **active voice.**

pathos A Greek word that means "feeling" or "emotion," used to refer to moving readers to act by, for example, showing photographs of people suffering from a natural disaster that has left then destitute. When appropriate emotional appeals are used to supplement sound reasoning, pathos is a legitimate way to persuade others.

persuasion One of the four aims of argument, persuasion moves people to act by combining logical argument with emotional appeals. Advertising is the most common form of persuasion in our culture, but you will find it whenever action is at stake, such as an election, a vaccination campaign, contributions for disaster relief, and so on.

plagiarism The act of presenting someone else's words or ideas as your own, without acknowledging the source. The most common forms of plagiarism result from not supplying parenthetical documentation for information you have paraphrased or paraphrasing in language too close to your source even with documentation. Be careful to supply all documentation and put your source aside when you paraphrase to avoid using the language of your source. See also **paraphrase.**

position An overall, summarizing attitude or judgment about some topic or issue. "I don't like same-sex marriage" is a position that could become an earned opinion and then a thesis or claim in an argument. Positions need to be thought through, researched, discussed, and stated carefully to function well in argumentation. See also **conviction** and **claim.**

prewriting The same as preparing to write, designates everything done prior to the first draft. Good writing results from effort in prewriting and revision, or rewriting. You cannot put too much effort into preparing to write and into revision of first drafts.

proofreading The last phase of writing, coming after revision and editing, the purpose of which is to detect small remaining errors, such as typos and misspellings. A good technique is to read your paper slowly, sentence-by-sentence, beginning with the last paragraph and working back toward the first. This will help you detect errors by breaking up the flow of the prose. See also **revision** and **editing.**

qualifier Acknowledging the strength of one's claim: "Counterinsurgency usually fails when the government of a country lacks popular support." The word "usually" is a qualifier, allowing for exceptions to the claim.

refutation Anticipating objections to your argument a reader is likely to have and showing why they do not hold. Normally appears after you make your case, but if the objections to your case are strongly adhered to by your audience, sometimes the refutation should come first.

revision Literally, "to see again," refers to big changes to improve the quality of a first draft, such as adding content, rearranging the order of presentation, and rewriting to make points clearer and more forceful. See also **editing** and **proofreading**.

rhetoric The art of argument, techniques that convince or persuade. See also **mature reasoning**.

rhetorical context The knowledge of circumstances required to understand a text and therefore to respond to it well: information about the time and place in which it was written, about the author, who published it, and the ongoing debate to which it contributed. Online searches can turn up helpful information quickly and with little effort.

rhetorical prospectus A plan for writing that includes a statement of the thesis, aim of argument or purpose, audience, and organizational plan. See also **brief** and **case strategy**.

sampling A fast and not necessarily sequential reading of a text, such as reading the first sentence in each paragraph, to get a feeling for the territory it covers and as preparation for a more careful reading.

stasis Means "stop" or "stay," and refers to ordering the issues connected with a controversial topic to discover what you should argue. For instance, the proposed sending of astronauts to Mars begins with the question, "Is such a mission worthwhile?" If you say "no," then you stop with this issue and make your case. If you say "yes," then the next issue is technical feasibility. "Can we actually send a human mission to Mars?" If you say "yes," you make your case that it should and can be done. And so on, through other issues connected with the Mars mission. Stasis is a valuable approach to understanding how issues connected with a topic relate to one another. See also **issue**.

thesis See **claim**.

topic A subject matter, such as "American policy in the Middle East." Typically arguments are restricted to some part of a topic, and often to a single issue related to it. Narrowing topics to something that can be handled within the length allowed for an assignment is an important part of prewriting or preparing to write. See also **issue**.

visual rhetoric The use of images, sometimes with sound or other appeals to the senses, to persuade one's audience to act as the image-maker would have them act. Advertising and political cartoons are examples of visual rhetoric.

voice Your voice in writing should be a slightly more formal version of how you speak when you are talking to people you do not know well and whose opinion of you matters. The result is "conversational prose," in general the norm of good writing now. Voice also needs to be adapted to your subject matter, audience, and purpose, so that, for instance, writing about the quality of medical care available to wounded veterans has a high seriousness that, say, a parking problem does not.

CREDITS

Text and Illustration Credits

Noelle Alberto, "Multitasking: A Poor Study Habit." Reprinted by permission.

The American Heritage Dictionary of the English Language, excerpts from definitions of "mature" and "critical." Copyright © 2006 by Houghton Mifflin Company. Reproduced by permission from *The American Heritage Dictionary of the English Language, Fourth Edition.*

Tom Beaudoin, "Consuming Faith: Integrating Who We are With What We Buy," Jul/Aug 2004. © 2004 Tom Beaudoin. Reprinted from TIKKUN: A Bimonthly Interfaith Critique of Politics, Culture, & Society.

Sissela Bok, "Media Literacy" from *Mayhem: Violence as Public Entertainment* by Sissela Bok. Copyright © 1998 by Sissela Bok. Reprinted by permission of Da Capo Press, a member of Perseus Books Group.

Benedict Carey, "Brain Enhancement is Wrong, Right?" From *New York Times,* © March 9, 2008 The New York Times. All Rights Reserved. Used by permission and protected by the Copyright Laws of the United States.

The Chronicle of Higher Education, "This Year's Freshmen at 4-year Colleges: A Statistical Profile" © 2009, The Chronicle of Higher Education. Reprinted with permission.

Ian Fagerstrom, "Comparison of Perspectives on Narcissism" © Ian Fagerstrom. Reprinted by permission.

James Forman, Jr., "Arrested Development: The Conservative Case against Racial Profiling." From *The New Republic,* September 10, 2001. Reprinted by permission of The New Republic. Copyright © 2001 The New Republic, L.L.C.

P. M. Forni, Choosing Civility: The Twenty-five Rules of Considerate Conduct. © 2002 by the author and reprinted by permission of St. Martin's Press, LLC.

David Fryman, "Open Your Ears to Biased Professors," The Justice (Brandeis U.), Sept. 1, 2004, 10. © 2004. David Fryman and The Justice at Brandeis University.

Michael Gerson, "The Rhetoric of the Rant." © May 15, 2009. *The Washington Post.* Reprinted with permission from The Washington Post.

Gerald Graff, "An Argument Worth Having." From The New York Times. © September 5, 2009. The New York Times. All Rights Reserved. Used by permission and protected by the Copyright Laws of the United States.

Duncan Greenberg, "Generation Y and the New Myth of Narcissus." From the Yale Herald. ©

Angi Grellhesl, "Mediating the Speech code Controversy." Reprinted by permission Angi Grellhesl.

David J. Hanson, "Responses to Arguments Against the Minimum Drinking Age," Reprinted with permission of David J. Hanson, Prof. Emeritus.

Natsumi Hazama, "Is Too Much Pressure Healthy?" Reprinted with permission from Natsumi Hazama.

Pat Joseph, "Start by Arming Yourself with Knowledge: Al Gore Breaks Through with His Global-Warming Message," *Sierra,* September/ October 2006. Reprinted with permission from *Sierra,* the magazine of The Sierra Club.

Olivia Judson, "Optimism in Revolution," From The New York Times, © August 13, 2008, The New York Times. Reprinted by permission.

Daniel M. Kammen, "The Rise of Renewable Energy," *Scientific American,* September 2006. Text: Reprinted with permission. Copyright © 2006 by Scientific American, Inc. All rights reserved. Illustrations: Illustration of wind turbines by Kenn Brown/Mondolithic Studios. Reprinted with permission. "Growing Fast, but Still a Sliver" by Jen Christiansen (Sources: *PV News,* BTM Consult, AWEA, EWEA, F. O. Licht and *BP Statistical Review of World Energy 2006),* originally printed in *Scientifi c American;* "Wind Power" (map) by Jen Christiansen (Source: National Renewable Energy Laboratory), originally printed in *Scientific American;* "R&D Is Key" by Jen Christiansen (Source: Reversing the Incredible Shrinking Energy R&D Budget, D. M. Kammen and G. Nemet, in *Issues in Science and Technology,* Fall 2005), originally printed in *Scientific American.* Reprinted by permission of Jen Christiansen.

Roger Kimball, "Institutionalizing Our Demise: America vs. Multiculturalism" from *Lengthened Shadows: America and Its Institutions in the Twenty-First Century,* edited by Roger Kimball and Hilton Kramer. San Francisco: Encounter Books, 2004. First published by Encounter Books. Reprinted by permission of the author.

Martin Luther King, Jr., "Letter from Birmingham Jail." Reprinted by arrangement with The Heirs to the Estate of Martin Luther King Jr., c/o Writers House as agent for the proprietor, New York, NY. Copyright 1963 Dr. Martin Luther King Jr.; Copyright renewed 1991 Coretta Scott King.

Elizabeth Martínez, "Reinventing 'America': Call for a New National Identity" from *De Colores Means All of Us: Latina Views for a Multi-Colored Century* by Elizabeth Martínez. Copyright © 1998 by Elizabeth Martínez. Reprinted by permission of South End Press.

William F. May, "Rising to the Occasion of Our Death." Copyright © 1990 by the *Christian Century.* Reprinted by permission from the July 11–18, 1990, issue of the *Christian Century.*

Richard Moe, "Battling Teardowns, Saving Neighborhoods." Speech given to the Commonwealth Club, San Francisco, California, June 28, 2006. © 2006 National Trust for Historic Preservation. Reprinted with permission.

Bharati Mukherjee, "Beyond Multiculturalism: A Two-Way Transformation," in *Multi-America: Essays on Cultural Wars and Cultural Peace*, ed. Ishmael Reed. Viking, 1997. Copyright © 1997 by Bharati Mukherjee. Reprinted with permission of author.

The Oxford English Dictionary, excerpt from definition of "narcissism." Editing by Simpson & Weiner; reproduced by permission from Oxford Publishing Limited.

T. Boone Pickens, "The Pickens Plan to Free the United States from Dependency on Oil" on http://www.pickensplan.com. Reprinted with permission.

Leonard Pitts, "The Other F Word," *Miami Herald*, February 14, 2008, p. 19A. Copyright 2008 by McClatchy Interactive West. Reproduced with permission of McClatchy Interactive West in the format Textbook via Copyright Clearance Center.

Richard Rhodes, "Hollow Claims about Fantasy Violence." From *New York Times*, September 17, 2000. Copyright © 2000 The New York Times. Reprinted by permission.

Wilbert Rideau, "Why Prisons Don't Work" from Time (March 21, 1994). Copyright © 1994 by Wilbert Rideau. Reprinted with the permission of the author, c/o The Permissions Company, www.permissionscompany.com.

Andy Rudd, "Which 'Character' Should Sport Develop," from Physical Educator 62.4 ©2005 pp. 205–212. By permission of Phi Epsilon Kappa Fraternity.

John F. Schumaker, book chapter, "The Paradox of Narcissism," In Search of Happiness, Praeger, 2007, pp. 167–173 (58%) #35

D. D. Solomon, "How Professors Should Deal with Their Biases," reprinted by permission.

Jean M. Twenge, excerpt from book chapter, "Changes in Narcissism." Reprinted with the permission of The Free Press, a Division of Simon & Schuster, Inc., from

GENERATION ME: Why Today's Young Americans Are More Confident, Assertive, Entitled—and More Miserable Than Ever by Jean M. Twenge, PhD. Copyright © 2006 by Jean M. Twenge, PhD. All rights reserved.

Katharine Weber, op ed article, "The Factories of Lost Children," From The New York Times. © March 25, 2006, The New York Times. All Rights Reserved. Used by permission and protected by the Copyright Laws of the United States.

Kit Yarrow and Jayne O'Donnell, "Gen Y is from Mercury," Gen BuY: How Tweens, Teens, and Twenty-Somethings are Revolutionizing Retail. © 2009. Reproduced with permission of John Wiley & Sons, Inc.

Photo Credits

Preface Photo 1 and 2: © Dave Tyler Photography; 1 p. 5: The J. Paul Getty Museum, Villa Collection, Malibu, California. Interior attributed to Meidias Painter, Attic Red-Figure Kylix, 410 B.C. Terracotta 12.4x13 82.AE.38. © J. Paul Getty Museum; p. 19: © Bill Aron/Photo Edit; p. 69: Courtesy of the Department of Defense; p. 70 (top): © Barbara Alper/Stock Boston; p. 70 (bottom): © Richard Pasley/Stock Boston; p. 72: © Bruce Young/Reuters/Corbis; p. 73 (top): Photo courtesy of the U.S. Department of Defense, photo by Fred W. Baker III; p. 73 (bottom): © Marco Di Lauro/Getty; C1: © Image courtesy of The Advertising Archives; C2: © AP/Wide World Photos/U.S. Postal Service/; C3: © Holzman & Kaplan Worldwide, Bret Wills, photographer; C4: © McGraw-Hill Higher Education, Inc./photographer Lars Niki; C5: © McGraw-Hill Higher Education, Inc./John Flournoy, photographer; C6: © adidas, adidas, the 3-Bars logo and the 3-Striples mark are registered trademarks of the adidas Group; C7: © AP Photo/Seth Wenig; C8: © Frances Fife/AFP/Getty; p. 159, 160 and 164: © Carolyn Channell; p. 173: © John Engstead/Hulton Archive/Getty; p. 184: © John William Waterhouse/The Bridgeman Art Library/Getty; page 220: © 2010 3TIER, Inc.; p. 221: Civic NGV image provided courtesy of American Honda Motor Co., Inc. © 2009 American Honda Motor Co., Inc.; p. 222 (left): © Glen Allison/Getty RF; p. 222 (right): ©moodboard/SuperStock RF

INDEX